新时代人文素养与大学英语育人研究

主　编　迟秀湘
副主编　宗艳红　陈爱明　贾增艳　张燕芳

中国商务出版社
CHINA COMMERCE AND TRADE PRESS

图书在版编目（CIP）数据

新时代人文素养与大学英语育人研究 / 迟秀湘主编
. — 北京：中国商务出版社，2021.9
　ISBN 978-7-5103-3917-2

　Ⅰ. ①新… Ⅱ. ①迟… Ⅲ. ①人文素质教育—教学研究—高等学校②英语—教学研究—高等学校 Ⅳ.
① G40-012② H319.3

中国版本图书馆 CIP 数据核字 (2021) 第 192539 号

新时代人文素养与大学英语育人研究
XINSHIDAI RENWEN SUYANG YU DAXUE YINGYU YUREN YANJIU
主编　迟秀湘

出版发行：中国商务出版社	
地　　址：北京市东城区安定门外大街东后巷 28 号	邮　编：100710
网　　址：http://www.cctpress.com	
责任编辑：汪　沁	
电　　话：010-64212247（总编室）　010-64515163（事业部）	
010-64208388（发行部）　010-64255862（直　销）	
印　　刷：宝蕾元仁浩（天津）印刷有限公司	
开　　本：710 毫米 × 1000 毫米　1/16	
印　　张：30.25	
版　　次：2022 年 7 月第 1 版	印　次：2022 年 7 月第 1 次印刷
字　　数：520 千字	定　价：99.00 元

版权所有　侵权必究　盗版侵权举报可发邮件至 cctp@cctpress.com
购买本社图书如有印装质量问题，请与本社印制部（电话：010-64248236）联系

前　言

　　人文素养是整个人类文化最根本的精神，即对人类生存的意义和价值的关怀。其以追求真、善、美等崇高价值理想为核心，以人的自由和全面发展为终极目的，综合了一个人的思想、情感、信念、意志、个性、能力等丰富内涵，是人完善自身的一种关注和追求。人文素养具体表现为人的文化品位、审美情趣、心理素质、人生态度、道德修养等丰富的精神世界。在大学教育中，培养良好的人文素养是非常重要的教育目标，是促进大学生全面发展和提高综合素养的重要途径。

　　新时代教育要回答的根本问题是"培养什么人、怎样培养人、为谁培养人"，教育的目的就是要贯彻"价值塑造、能力培养、知识传授"三位一体的育人理念。2016年12月，习近平总书记在全国高校思想政治工作会议上指出："各门课都要守好一段渠、种好责任田，使各类课程与思想政治理论课同向同行，形成协同效应"。2019年8月，中共中央办公厅、国务院办公厅印发了《关于深化新时代学校思想政治理论课改革创新的若干意见》，对大学公共基础课程提出以下要求：要重点建设一批提高大学生思想道德修养、人文素质、科学精神、宪法法治意识、国家安全意识和认知能力的课程，注重在潜移默化中坚定学生理想信念，厚植爱国主义情怀，加强品德修养，增长知识见识，培养奋斗精神，提升学生综合素质。这是新时代的要求，也是落实立德树人根本任务的关键举措；这是国之大计，关系到社会主义接班人的培养、民族的复兴、国家的崛起，以及国家的长治久安等重大问题。

　　大学英语作为一门公共基础课程，具有工具性和人文性两大特点。其工具性是指培养学生的语言应用能力；其人文性是指培养学生的人文素养。《大学英语教学指南（征求意见稿）》指出，大学英语课程人文性的核心就是以人为本，弘扬人的价值，注重人的综合素质和全面发展。将人文素养教育融入大学英语教学之中，把知识教育和理想信念教育、道德品格教育有机结合起来。既能丰富英语课程本身的内涵，提高学生的英语应用能力，又能赋予传统的思想政治教育以鲜活的生命力，真正实现大学英语课程所肩负的立德树人这一根本任务的价值；既能够拓展大学英语课程在知识和技能方面的功能，又能够为培养新时代国家建设需要的人才发挥重要作用。

  大学英语课程的教学目标包括显性目标和隐性目标两方面。显性目标与学习外语知识和技能有关；隐性目标与思政育人有关。这两类目标都要通过选择的教学材料和设计的教学活动来实现。显性目标中似乎没有明显的育人元素，但在隐性目标中，教师要有意识地引领学生思考两种哲学理念的主要差异，一方面，希望学生能够学习苏格拉底的打破砂锅问到底的科学精神，以及"修身、齐家、治国、平天下"的家国情怀；另一方面，让学生对谋求社会和谐、家庭和睦、个人幸福的中华文明有更深入的理解，从而获得更坚定的文化自信。在全方位理解育人目标的基础上，教师要深入分析自己教授的内容。思政元素通常内嵌于教学输入的材料中，也可能隐含在练习活动中。教师首先要弄清楚在课堂上教授的显性的外语语言的核心知识和核心技能，还要进一步挖掘其中的育人元素，包括价值导向、情感品格和自我管理等。

  本书立足于《大学体验英语》综合教程第一册、第二册、第三册，共二十个单元，根据该教材各单元的主题，在教学中挖掘提炼出符合社会主义核心价值观和新时代精神的人文素养的闪光元素，在注重提高学生的英语应用能力的同时，重点关注课程的育人目标，即进一步提高学生的人文素养。在教学过程中巧妙地融入有关人文素养的内容。通过结合社会热点事件，融入爱国主义教育内容，提升学生的民族自豪感；充分利用互联网挖掘有教育意义的英语视频和文字材料，在培养学生的英语应用能力的同时，对学生进行精神品格和理想信念教育，提高学生的人文素养。

  本书是集体合作的成果具体分工如下：迟秀湘负责全书的策划，并撰写前言、第一章的第一节、第二节、第三节和第四节；宗艳红撰写第二章的第一节、第六节，以及第三章的第三节、第四节；陈爱明撰写第一章的第六节、第二章的第二节和第三章的第一节、第二节；贾增艳撰写第一章的第五节、第七节，第二章的第三节和第三章的第五节；张燕芳撰写第二章的第四节、第五节、第七节和第三章的第六节；迟秀湘和宗艳红负责全书统稿。本书的编写还得到了同事的大力支持，牛洁珍为本书的编写提出了宝贵的指导意见和建议；计晗、刘国萍、陈周云、张秀清、王思聪、曾华人和崔肖菡均为本书的编写提供了很有价值的素材，在此一并表示感谢！

  由于编者水平有限，难免有疏漏和不当之处，敬请读者批评指正。

编者

2021年9月　北京

目 录

第一章 《大学体验英语》综合教程第一册 …………………………………… 1

    第一单元　肩负重任，珍惜大学教育（Unit 1 College Life）……………… 3

    第二单元　心中有梦想，成功有希望（Unit 2 Song of the Soul）………… 33

    第三单元　社团提升个人素养，平衡生活积极向上（Unit 3 Leisure Activities）

            ………………………………………………………………………… 51

    第四单元　青年人要艰苦奋斗、自立自强（Unit 4 Living on Your Own）…… 73

    第五单元　科学利用信息技术，提升学生核心素养（Unit 5 Sources of Information）

            ………………………………………………………………………… 93

    第六单元　无私奉献的志愿者精神（Unit 6 Volunteering）……………… 128

    第七单元　热爱学习，学会学习（Unit 7 Learning Strategies）………… 152

第二章 《大学体验英语》综合教程第二册 ………………………………… 189

    第一单元　著名大学（Unit 1 Famous Universities）……………………… 191

    第二单元　工作和职业（Unit 2 Jobs and Careers）……………………… 208

    第三单元　关心公益，注重诚信（Unit 3 Advertising）………………… 230

    第四单元　灾难与救援（Unit 4 Calamities and Rescues）……………… 247

    第五单元　成功之路（Unit 5 Ways to Success）………………………… 271

    第六单元　体育与健康（Unit 6 Sports and Health）…………………… 288

    第七单元　家庭关系（Unit 7 Family Ties）……………………………… 309

第三章 《大学体验英语》综合教程第三册 ………………………………… 339

    第一单元　关爱我们的地球（Unit 1 Caring for Our Earth）…………… 341

1

第二单元　诺贝尔奖获得者的科学家精神（Unit 2 Nobel Prize Winner）　360

第三单元　知名企业品牌（Unit 3 Famous Brand Names）……………　387

第四单元　克隆与伦理（Unit 4 Cloning and Ethics）…………………　404

第五单元　关注终身教育，争当终身学习者（Unit 5 Lifelong Education）　425

第六单元　旅行的意义（Unit 6 Travel around the World）……………　452

参考文献 ………………………………………………………………… 474

第一章

《大学体验英语》综合教程第一册

第一单元　肩负重任，珍惜大学教育
(Unit 1 College Life)

1. 思政主题：肩负重任，大学教育的意义

2. 意义

本单元聚焦"新生入学"相关话题，探讨大学教育的意义及父母对子女的期望和嘱托。教师可以从我国的经典古籍和习近平总书记对青年的寄语入手，选取与主题相关的思政素材，鼓励学生思考并理解大学教育的意义，明确学习的目的，树立正确的学习观、人生观和价值观。

青年是国家的希望、民族的未来。作为青年的榜样和朋友，习近平总书记曾多次通过演讲、座谈、回信等方式寄语广大青年，与青年朋友谈学习、谈理想、谈奋斗。在此节选了如下内容。

这场抗击新冠肺炎疫情的严峻斗争，让你们这届高校毕业生经受了磨练、收获了成长，也使你们切身体会到了"志不求易者成，事不避难者进"的道理。前进的道路从不会一帆风顺，实现中华民族伟大复兴的中国梦需要一代一代青年矢志奋斗。同学们生逢其时、肩负重任。希望全国广大高校毕业生志存高远、脚踏实地，不畏艰难险阻，勇担时代使命，把个人的理想追求融入党和国家事业之中，为党、为祖国、为人民多作贡献。

College students who graduate this year have learned a lot from the arduous fight against the COVID-19 epidemic. This also makes you fully aware that those who do not seek easy things will succeed; and those who do not seek refuge will improve. There will be ups and downs along the road ahead, and the great rejuvenation of the Chinese nation can only be achieved through the hard work of generations of youth. I hope college graduates to aim high, be down-to-earth, brave in front of difficulties and obstacles, shoulder the mission of this era, integrate their personal pursuit of ideals into the cause of the Party and the country, and make more contributions to the Party, the country and the people.

——2020年7月7日,给中国石油大学(北京)克拉玛依校区毕业生的回信

在新冠肺炎疫情防控斗争中,你们青年人同在一线英勇奋战的广大疫情防控人员一道,不畏艰险、冲锋在前、舍生忘死,彰显了青春的蓬勃力量,交出了合格答卷。广大青年用行动证明,新时代的中国青年是好样的,是堪当大任的!

Young people and many other front line workers in the fight against the COVID-19 epidemic have spearheaded efforts despite difficulties and threats to their lives, and you have shown the power of youth and handed over qualified answers. You have proved yourselves through actions that the Chinese youth of the new era can be entrusted with great missions.

——2020年3月15日,给北京大学援鄂医疗队全体"90后"党员的回信

我相信,你们一定会以他们为榜样,努力做党和人民信赖的好医生。希望你们珍惜学习时光,练就过硬本领,毕业后到人民最需要的地方去,以仁心仁术造福人民,特别是基层群众。

I believed that you will take the front-line medical workers as examples and strive to be good doctors that Party and people can rely on. I hope that you would cherish your study time and improve your abilities and skills so that you can go where you are most needed by the people and serve them with professional skills and kindheartedness after graduation.

——2020年2月21日,给在首钢医院实习的西藏大学医学院学生的回信

青年在成长和奋斗中,会收获成功和喜悦,也会面临困难和压力。要正确对待一时的成败得失,处优而不养尊,受挫而不短志,使顺境逆境都成为人生的财富而不是人生的包袱。

During one's growth and endeavor, the young may gain success and joy, but may also face difficulties and pressure. One should treat the success and failure at the moment with a positive attitude, not slack in prosperity and not lose faith in adversity. One should consider both the success and failure as wealth in life instead of burdens.

——2017年5月3日,习近平主席到中国政法大学考察并发表重要讲话

希望你们保持对知识的渴望，保持对探索的兴趣，培育科学精神。

I hope you will stay hungry for knowledge, keep your interest in scientific exploration, and foster your scientific spirit.

——2016年12月28日，回信勉励北京市八一学校科普小卫星研制团队学生

价值观的养成就像穿衣服扣扣子一样，如果第一粒扣子扣错了，剩余的扣子都会扣错。人生的扣子从一开始就要扣好。

The cultivation of values is like buttoning up one's jacket. If the jacket is wrongly buttoned at first, the rest will never find their rightful places. Therefore, the buttons of life should be fastened well from the very beginning.

——2014年5月4日，习近平主席在北京大学师生座谈会上的讲话

希望越来越多的青年人以你们为榜样，到基层和人民中去建功立业，让青春之花绽放在祖国最需要的地方，在实现中国梦的伟大实践中书写别样精彩的人生。

I hope that more young people will follow your steps to establish educational careers at the grassroots level, blossom in the places where you are most needed by the mother land, and live a splendid life while turning the Chinese Dream into reality.

——2014年5月3日，给河北保定学院西部支教毕业生群体代表回信

广大青年一定要练就过硬本领。学习是成长进步的阶梯，实践是提高本领的途径。青年的素质和本领直接影响着实现中国梦的进程。

The youth must refine their professional skills. Study is the ladder of progress and practice is the way to improve capability. Quality and capability of the youth is directly linked to the course of realizing the Chinese Dream.

——2013年5月4日，习近平主席在同各界优秀青年代表座谈时的讲话

国家对于青年学生的成长寄予了厚望，青年学生的首要任务就是学习。《劝学》分别从学习的重要性、态度、内容和方法等方面进行了全面而深刻的阐释。教师可安排学生阅读学习《劝学·第一》双语版本，帮助学生明确学习的重要性。

劝学·第一
Encouraging Learning (SECTION 1)

荀子 Hsun Tzu

Translated by Burton Watson

君子曰：学不可以已。

青，取之于蓝，而青于蓝；冰，水为之，而寒于水。……君子博学而日参省乎己，则知明而行无过矣。

The gentleman says: Learning should never cease.

Blue comes from the indigo plant but is bluer than the plant itself. Ice is made of water but is colder than water ever is ... If the gentleman studies widely and each day examines himself, his wisdom will become clear and his conduct be without fault.

故不登高山，不知天之高也；不临深溪，不知地之厚也；不闻先王之遗言，不知学问之大也。干、越、夷、貉之子，生而同声，长而异俗，教使之然也。诗曰："嗟尔君子，无恒安息。靖共尔位，好是正直。神之听之，介尔景福。"神莫大于化道，福莫长于无祸。

If you do not climb a high mountain, you will not comprehend the highness of the heavens; if you do not look down into a deep valley, you will not know the depth of the earth; and if you do not hear the words handed down from the ancient kings, you will not understand the greatness of learning. Children born among the Han or Yüeh people of the south and among the Mo barbarians of the north cry with the same voice at birth, but as they grow older, they follow different customs. Education causes them to differ. The Odes says: Oh, you gentlemen, Do not be constantly at ease and rest! Quietly respectful in your posts. Love those who are correct and upright. And the gods will hearken to you. And aid you with great blessing. There is no greater godliness than to transform yourself with the Way, no greater blessing than to escape misfortune.

吾尝终日而思矣，不如须臾之所学也；吾尝跂而望矣，不如登高之博见也。登高而招，臂非加长也，而见者远；顺风而呼，声非加疾也，而闻者彰。假舆马者，非利足也，而致千里；假舟楫者，非能水也，而绝江河。君子生非异也，善假于物也。

I once tried spending the whole day in thought, but I found it of less value than a moment of study. I once tried standing on tiptoe and gazing into the distance, but I found that I could see much farther by climbing to a high place. If you climb to a high place and wave to someone, it is not as though your arm were any longer than usual, and yet people can see you from much farther away. If you shout down the wind, it is not as though your voice were any stronger than usual, and yet people can hear you much more clearly. Those who make use of carriages or horses may not be any faster walkers than anyone else, and yet they are able to travel a thousand li. Those who make use of boats may not know how to swim, and yet they manage to get across rivers. The gentleman is by birth no different from any other man; it is just that he is good at making use of things.

南方有鸟焉，名曰蒙鸠，以羽为巢，而编之以发，系之苇苕，风至苕折，卵破子死。巢非不完也，所系者然也。西方有木焉，名曰射干，茎长四寸，生于高山之上，而临百仞之渊，木茎非能长也，所立者然也。蓬生麻中，不扶而直；白沙在涅，与之俱黑。兰槐之根是为芷，其渐之滫，君子不近，庶人不服。其质非不美也，所渐者然也。故君子居必择乡，游必就士，所以防邪辟而近中正也。

In the south there is a bird called the meng dove. It makes a nest out of feathers woven together with hair and suspends it from the tips of the reeds. But when the wind comes, the reeds break, the eggs are smashed, and the baby birds killed. It is not that the nest itself is faulty; the fault is in the thing it is attached to. In the west there is a tree called the Yeh-kan. Its trunk is no more than four inches tall and it grows on top of the high mountains, from whence it looks down into a hundred fathoms deep valleys. It is not a long trunk which afford the tree such a view, but simply the place where it stands. If pigweed grows up in the midst of hemp, it will stand up straight without propping. If white sand is mixed with mud, it too will turn black. The root of a certain orchid is the source of the perfume called chih; but if the root were to be soaked in urine, then no gentleman would go near it and no commoner would consent to wear it. It is not that the root itself is of an unpleasant quality; it is the fault of the thing it has been soaked in. Therefore, a gentleman will take care in selecting the community he intends to live in, and will choose men of breeding for his companions. In this way he wards off evil and meanness, and draws close to fairness and right.

物类之起，必有所始。荣辱之来，必象其德。肉腐出虫，鱼枯生蠹。怠慢忘身，祸灾乃作。强自取柱，柔自取束。邪秽在身，怨之所构。施薪若一，火就燥也，平地若一，水就湿也。草木畴生，禽兽群焉，物各从其类也。是故质的张，而弓矢至焉；林木茂，而斧斤至焉；树成荫，而众鸟息焉。醯酸，而蚋聚焉。故言有招祸也，行有招辱也，君子慎其所立乎！

  Every phenomenon that appears must have a cause. The glory or shame that come to a man are no more than the image of his virtue. Meat when it rots breeds worms; fish that is old and dry brings forth maggots. When a man is careless and lazy and forgets himself, that is when disaster occurs. The strong naturally bear up under weight; the weak naturally end up bound. Evil and corruption in oneself invite the anger of others. If you lay sticks of identical shape on a fire, the flames will seek out the driest ones; if you level the ground to an equal smoothness, water will still seek out the dampest spot. Trees of the same species grow together; birds and beasts gather in herds; for all things follow after their own kind. Where a target is hung up, arrows will find their way to it; where the forest trees grow thickest, the axes will enter. When a tree is tall and shady, birds will flock to roost in it; when vinegar turns sour, gnats will collect around it. So, there are words that invite disaster and actions that call down shame. A gentleman must be careful where he takes his stand!

  积土成山，风雨兴焉；积水成渊，蛟龙生焉；积善成德，而神明自得，圣心备焉。故不积跬步，无以至千里；不积小流，无以成江海。骐骥一跃，不能十步；驽马十驾，功在不舍。锲而舍之，朽木不折；锲而不舍，金石可镂。蚓无爪牙之利，筋骨之强，上食埃土，下饮黄泉，用心一也。蟹六跪而二螯，非蛇鳝之穴无可寄托者，用心躁也。是故无冥冥之志者，无昭昭之明；无惛惛之事者，无赫赫之功。行衢道者不至，事两君者不容。目不能两视而明，耳不能两听而聪。螣蛇无足而飞，鼫鼠五技而穷。《诗》曰："尸鸠在桑，其子七兮。淑人君子，其仪一兮。其仪一兮，心如结兮！"故君子结于一也。

  Pile up earth to make a mountain and wind and rain will rise up from it. Pile up water to make a deep pool and dragons will appear. Pile up good deeds to create virtue and godlike understanding will come of itself; there the mind of the sage will find completion. But unless you pile up little steps, you can never journey a thousand li; unless you pile up tiny streams, you can never make a river or a sea. The finest thoroughbred cannot travel ten paces in one leap, but the sorriest nag can go a ten days' journey. Achievement consists of never giving up. If you start carving and then give up, you cannot even cut through a piece of rotten wood; but if you persist without stopping, you can carve and inlay metal or stone. Earthworms have no sharp claws or teeth, no strong muscles or bones, and yet above ground they feast on the mud, and below they drink at the yellow springs. This is because they keep their minds on one thing. Crabs have six legs and two pincers, but unless they can find an empty hole dug by a snake or a water serpent, they have no place to lodge. This is because they allow their minds to go off in all directions. Thus, if there is no dark and dogged will, there will be no shining accomplishment; if there is no dull and determined effort, there will be no brilliant achievement. He who tries to travel two roads at once will arrive nowhere; he who serves two masters will please neither. The wingless dragon has no limbs and yet it can soar; the flying squirrel has many talents but finds itself hard pressed. The odes says: Ringdove in the mulberry, its children are seven. The good man, the gentleman, his forms are one. His forms are one, his heart is as though bound. Thus does the gentleman bind himself to oneness.

昔者瓠巴鼓瑟，而流鱼出听；伯牙鼓琴，而六马仰秣。故声无小而不闻，行无隐而不形。玉在山而草润，渊生珠而崖不枯。为善不积邪？安有不闻者乎？

In ancient times, when Hu Pa played the zither, the fish in the streams came forth to listen; when Po Ya played the lute, the six horses of the emperor's carriage looked up from their feed trough. No sound is too faint to be heard, no action too well concealed to be known. When there are precious stones under the mountain, the grass and trees have a special sheen; where pearls grow in a pool, the banks are never parched. Do good and see if it does not pile up. If it does, how can it fail to be heard of?

（来源：外研社高等英语资讯）

3. 教学设计与思政元素的融入

Passage A

3.1 Warm-up 环节

英文视频：Tips for Freshmen

佐治亚理工学院开学典礼上，大二学长 Nick Selby 结合自身经验向新生提出了10个建议。视频约为7分钟，教师可以在网上搜索该视频，并在 Warm-up 环节请学生观看，并谈谈入学以来从教师、学长、学姐处获得的建议，以及对未来大学生活的规划与期望。

You are probably wondering why I gathered you together today. It is my honor as a representative of the Class of 2016 to welcome the faculty and new students and parents of Georgia Institute of Technology. Congratulations, you are all officially yellow jackets.

When I reflect back upon the many things I have learned during my first year here at Tech. Ten in particular stand out my mind as most important:

1. Call your mother. She will worry about you every day for a while. And it will make her happy if you call her. Just make sure there aren't a bunch of screaming girls, loud music or some guys yelling about obscenities in the background when you call.

2. Unless the professor is truly awful, try to take classes from more difficult professors for your major courses. They tend to make you work the hardest, and you will end up knowing the material better.

3. Do laundry often. I know this sounds obvious. But when you find yourself without neat and clean undies, you will think of this advice and say: man, Nick was right. I bet he has unclean undies right now.

4. Make sure you get out and see new places. Be it through a weekend trip with friends along the east coast or studying abroad. Now it's the best time in our lives to get out and see the world.

5. Join a club, team or extracurricular activity. You are never stagnated, you're either growing and maturing or falling behind.

6. Try to get internships. While difficulties go to a career, giving people your resume is a good practice. And if you get the job, the experiences you gain will help you after college.

7. C style indexing for analyzing the array is 0 to n-1, where as a matlab, it's 1 to n. I don't know if that makes sense to you just yet. But if you're not careful, I will get you eventually.

8. Try to sit up front in classes. Just like Florida was the creature of Hobbit, Georgia Tech students are creatures of habit. Whatever seat you choose on the first day will likely be the seat you get all semester. Set up in the first few rows you will be more likely to pay attention and have the professor remember you.

9. Get sleep. And one of the best ways to ensure that you can get sleep is start working on your homework right when it's assigned and start studying for tests a

week before you take them.

And lastly, No.10. Remember why you are here, to master a body of knowledge. That's the best of my list so far. And I think that last one is the most important. You see, of the many reasons I chose Georgia Tech, one in particular stands out above the rest: I am going to build the ironman suit. That's right. As acute as my application says, "green energy and world peace can wait". I want to fly around the world in an unpuncturable suit of armor, dating Granethe Partural. And really, I like the thing that's why we are all here. As long as I can remember, I wanted to be an inventor. I still carry around a little notebook full of my ideas. And whether you are learning how to enclose a big business deal, or design a major public policy decision, we chose Georgia Tech because we want to do something impossible. And this school equipped with the resources and faculty to help us do just that. And so, in the words of Issac Newton, "if I have seen further, it is by standing on the shoulders of giants." Georgia Tech is proud of its many traditions, but the one I find most exciting is: our tradition of excellence. Our mission as students is not to follow the footsteps of the astronauts, Nobel prize laurels and presidential graduates before us, but to exceeds their footstep, crush the shoulders of giants upon whom we stand, we here are all such innovative people. So, I am telling you, if you want to change the world, you are in Georgia Tech, you can do that; if you want to build an ironman suit, you are in Georgia Tech, you can do that; if you want to play the music during your congregation speech like a badass, we are in Georgia Tech, we can do that, I am doing that!

Congratulations on your acceptance and brace yourself for a hell of a ride on your way of becoming a hell of engineer.

3.2 Discussion 环节

英文文章: Why a College Education Is Important

当前社会对"大学教育是否必要"持有不同的观点。一些人认为人生成功之路上，大学教育不可或缺；另一些人则认为大学教育并非必要。文章作者从大学教育对于人的有形利益与无形利益两个方面论述了为什么大学教育非常重要。文章短小，语言地道且精炼，教师可安排学生阅读，学生可以结合自己的思考阐述观点，或针对两种观点展开辩论。

Defining why a college education is important involves more than just identifying the superficial benefits of more career opportunities. At a deeper level, college is where you will map a path through life that can take you to places you never expected to go.

The beauty of post-secondary education is that college can yield tangible and intangible benefits for you that in turn benefit others — even if school doesn't awaken your sleeping Pablo Picasso, Stephen Hawking, or Bill Gates.

Tangible Benefits of a College Education

It's well established that a college education delivers measurable material benefits. If you were to rattle off the list of reasons you're attending school, these are the first ones you'll mention.

College Education and Wages

A handful of money definitely qualifies as a tangible benefit, and research has matched levels of education to payroll expectations and the ability to find a job.

In 2015, bachelor's degree holders earned 64 percent more than those with a high school diploma.

Bachelor's degree recipients can expect to earn about $1 million more over a lifetime than a person who doesn't go to college.

A posts-secondary education is expected to be required for about two-thirds of available jobs by 2020.

A recent study broke the higher education benefits down even further, finding among other things that a bachelor's degree now means the holder will earn 84 percent more than someone with no post-secondary education. The report went even further, projecting lifetime earnings based on virtually all education levels:

Lifetime wages of a high school dropout —— $ 973,000,

Lifetime wages of a high school graduate —— $ 1.3 million,

Lifetime wages of someone with some college but no degree —— $ 1.5 million,

Lifetime wages of an associate degree holder —— $ 1.7 million,

Lifetime wages of a bachelor's degree holder —— $ 2.3 million,

Lifetime wages of a master's degree holder —— $ 2.7 million,

Lifetime wages of a person with a doctorate —— $ 3.3 million,

Lifetime wages of a professional degree holder —— $ 3.6 million.

Based on U.S. Census Bureau data, the usual median weekly earnings in 2017 for people of varying education levels was:

Doctoral degree holder's median weekly earnings —— $ 1,743,
Professional degree holder's median weekly earnings —— $ 1,836,
Master's degree holder's median weekly earnings —— $ 1,401,
Bachelor's degree holder's median weekly earnings —— $ 1,173,
Associate degree holder's median weekly earnings —— $ 836,
Person with some college (no degree) median weekly earnings —— $ 774,
High school diploma (only) holder's median weekly earnings —— $ 712,
Person without high school diploma median weekly earnings —— $ 520.

The unemployment rates in 2017 for people in those education categories were 1.5 percent for doctoral degree holders, 1.5 percent for professional degree holders, 2.2 percent for master's degree holders, 2.5 percent for bachelor's degree holders, 3.4 percent for associate degree holders, 4 percent for people with some college, 4.6 percent for people with a high school diploma, and 6.5 percent for people without a high school diploma.

Better Jobs Equal Better Benefits, Perks

A college education also usually translates to great benefits and perks as well.

Typical white-collar benefits: health insurance, eyecare insurance, vacation and other paid time off, dental insurance, maternity/paternity leave, pension plan, 401(k).

Potential white-collar perks: transportation and parking reimbursement and/or company car, free food and beverages, flexible schedules and freedom to work from home (or elsewhere), concierge services, golden parachutes (high-dollar severance packages).

For Some, College Is the First Real Adventure

College takes you out of familiar surroundings and presents new challenges. But college doesn't only pave the way for intangible experiences. Adapting to new faces in a fresh place is just the start. The education process can mean internships, overseas travel, exciting research opportunities, and exploration of multiple career paths, all of which can lead to some very tangible results when you start working.

And academic success opens doors to careers where, quite literally in some cases, even the sky and moon aren't the limits. Think aerospace engineering.

Connections that Can Last a Lifetime

The thousands of people you meet, study with, and work alongside in college will range from peers to mentors, along with power players in your chosen field and others. These are connections you will make note of and potentially use to advance yourself and your ideas.

And as far as relationships go, the only romantic label as common as "high school sweetheart" is "college sweetheart".

Intangible Benefits of a College Education

A college education can open doors for your career and your own personal growth. For example, college helps develop many important skills, such as self-awareness, global-mindedness, critical thinking, and more.

People by Nature Desire Knowledge

That is a paraphrase of a premise that the Greek philosopher Aristotle states in his *Metaphysics*. It is affirmed by the connection of head and heart when the study of history helps you forecast the future, when math adds up to real-life solutions, and when the development of skills allows you to produce a masterpiece worthy of the Library of Congress, Metropolitan Museum of Art, or U.S. Patent Office.

In Pursuit of Critical Thinking

Results are in colleges and critical thinking. During one recent study, researchers began with the notion that everyone wants colleges to teach critical-thinking skills and that the challenge routinely is accepted. Here's a key finding: Data show that a student who begins college with critical thinking skills in the 50th percentile can expect to be in the 72nd percentile after four years.

Critical thinking is, according to the Foundation for Critical Thinking, "that mode of thinking — about any subject, content, or problem — in which the thinker improves the quality of his or her thinking by skillfully analyzing, assessing, and reconstructing it." Developing that skill yields endless opportunities to enrich your life both personally and professionally.

College Advances Self-Realization

A college education, if pursued honestly and earnestly, gives you the knowledge and skills needed to pursue a career and your passions. The degree also can bring hard-to-match personal satisfaction. A huge part of ensuring that self-realization process is finding a school that is right for you, where you'll feel safe and comfortable enough to let yourself grow and explore.

（来源：www.ufl.edu）

3.3 Critical thinking 环节

双语视频：上大学的意义是什么

普林斯顿大学 (Princeton University) 校长伊斯格鲁布在2018年毕业典礼上发表演讲。他在演讲中反复强调，上大学是一笔高回报的投资，尤其从长远来看。年轻人应将眼光放远，不该被学历无用的论调欺骗，这种论调会破坏年轻人的前途和国家的未来。普林斯顿大学校长以数据和实例作支撑反驳了一部分社会人士提出的"很多人不用上大学"的观点，阐明了接受大学教育的重要意义。教师可请学生观看视频，思考并讨论：Do you think a university education can change a person's life? In what way and why?

In a few minutes, all of you will march through Fitz Randolph Gate as newly minted graduates of this University. Before you do, it is my privilege to say a few words about the path that lies ahead.

几分钟后，作为这所大学新一批的毕业生，你们都将走出校门。在这之前，我有幸能够对你们说几句，关于未来的话。

It is indeed a privilege, and also a joy, to address you, for all of you who graduate today have accomplished something genuinely important and worth celebrating. You have completed a demanding course of study. It will transform your life in many ways. It will expand the range of vocations you can pursue, increase your knowledge of the world, deepen your capacity to appreciate societies and cultures, and provide a foundation for lifelong learning.

能够在你们面前致辞，这的确是我的殊荣，也是一种喜悦。因为你们完成了一项非常重要且值得庆贺的事，你们完成了学科课程要求。这将在很多方面改变你的生活。它将扩大你的择业范围，增加你对世界的认识，加深你理解社会文化的能力，并为终生学习打好基础。

So we celebrate here on the lawn in front of Nassau Hall, as do other college communities in courtyards, auditoria, arenas, and stadium around the country. Graduates toss caps in the air and professors applaud. Families cheer and holler enthusiastically. Yet, even as we do so, we see a strange trend from columnists, bloggers, think tanks, and politicians. In essays, books, and speeches, some of them suggest that too many students are earning college degrees.

正如我们在拿骚大厅前的草坪上庆祝一样，其他各家学校也都在自己的院落、礼堂、舞台和体育场内举行庆祝活动。毕业生们将帽子抛向空中、教授们在鼓掌、家人们热情欢呼。然而，即使我们是这样做的，我们仍发现社会上有一股奇怪的风气，它来自专栏作家、博主、智库和政治家，他们中的一些人在文章、书籍和演讲中提及，获得大学学位的人太多了。

Too many college graduates: that is a very odd claim, because the economic evidence for the value of a college degree is overwhelming. For example, in 2014, economists Jaison Abel and Richard Deitz of the Federal Reserve Bank of New York estimated the average annual return on investment from a college degree, net of tuition paid and lost earnings, at between 9 percent and 16 percent per year for a lifetime. For the last two decades, the return on investment has hovered at the high end of that range, around 15 percent per year. By comparison, the historical average return on investments in the American stock market is around 7 percent per year.

That is why my friend Morton Shapiro, the president of Northwestern University and a leading educational economist, says that for most people, the decision to invest in a college degree will be "the single best financial decision they make in a lifetime," even if judged purely in terms of financial return on investment.

"大学毕业生太多了"：这是一个非常奇怪的说法。因为已经有经济学数据充分证明了读大学的好处。例如，据2014年纽约联邦储备银行的经济学家Jaison Abel 和 Richard Deitz 的统计，投资一个大学学位的年平均回报率，扣除学费和收入损失后大约在9%到16%之间。尤其是在过去的20年中，投资回报率一直在该范围的高位，约每年15%。相比之下，美国股票市场的平均年投资回报率仅为7%。

这就是为什么我的朋友 Morton shapiro，作为西北大学校长和著名的教育经济学家表示，对于大多数人来说投资大学学位将是"他们一生中做过的最英明的经济抉择"，即使单从经济回报的角度来看。

A degree conveys many other benefits as well.

For example, college graduates report higher levels of happiness and job satisfaction, even after controlling for income. College graduates are healthier than non-graduates. They are more likely to exercise, more likely to vote, and have higher levels of civic engagement. To these pragmatic considerations we should add the joys that come with an increased capacity to appreciate culture, the arts, the world's diversity, and the inherent beauty of extraordinary ideas.

一个大学学位还能带来很多其它好处。

例如，拥有更高的幸福感和工作满意度，即使在收入不多的情况下。大学毕业的人比非大学毕业的人健康，他们有更大概率进行体育锻炼、参与投票并且拥有更高程度的公民参与度。我们还应该加上那些由于对文化、艺术、世界多样性、内在美和卓越观点理解能力的增强而带来的额外乐趣。

The numbers I have quoted are not specific to Princeton. On the contrary, they are averages over all four-year degrees, in all fields, from all colleges in the United States. Think about that for a moment: on average, all degrees in all fields from all colleges generate an annual return between 9 percent and 16 percent, and this return is supplemented by additional benefits to health, happiness, and quality of life. How could anyone think we need fewer college graduates? Some people answer that you can learn a trade without getting a college degree. Welders, they observe, can make more money than many college graduates. That's true. There are, of course, reasons why you might want to get a college degree even if you plan to become a welder. You might worry, for example, about what happens if technology renders your trade obsolete, or arthritis leaves you unable to practice it, or you want to move into management or explore other interests. A college degree equips you to respond to the changes — to yourself, and to the world — that inevitably occur over a lifetime.

我所引用的数据不局限于普林斯顿。相反，它反映了所有接受过美国大学四年制教育后的人会达到的平均水平。想想看，在所有专业领域读完大学的年平均回报率都有9%到16%之间，而这种回报又辅以对健康，幸福和生活质量的额外好处。怎么会有人觉得我们需要更少的大学毕业生？有人会说你可以在不取得大学学位的情况下，学一门手艺。他们发现焊工有时候比毕业生挣的多，这是真的。即使你打算当个焊工，也要先读个大学。比如，你可能会担心自己的手艺会被淘汰，抑或伤病会让你无法胜任这份工作，又或者你想进入管理层，或者是探索其他方面的爱好。大学学历能让你拥有应对更多变化的能力，无论是在你身上还是这个世界发生的变化——这些都是难以避免的。

Still, if pundits and politicians were saying only that America needs better vocational training, I could agree wholeheartedly. It would be terrific if more people could get the training they need to practice a trade. But at the same time, it would also be great if more people, not fewer, could receive the extraordinary benefits that come with a college degree. So I ask again: why would anyone think we need fewer college graduates? I think there is a simple answer. Education requires high-quality teaching. Teaching, in turn, depends upon skilled labor, which is expensive. As a result, the up-front cost for education is real, large, and easy to measure. The returns are equally real and even larger, but they accrue over a lifetime, are hard to measure, and vary from person to person. It is tempting to wish that you could get more certainty at lower cost. The people who call for fewer degrees yield to that temptation. They emphasize the short-term. They focus almost entirely on the price of college and on the salaries students might earn in their first jobs. That is a mistake. A college education is a long-term investment. It enables graduates to develop and adapt, and it pays off spectacularly in the long run. The idea that we would be better off with fewer college graduates is a short-term swindle, a swindle that will cheat America's young people, weaken the nation's economy, and undermine our future.

不过，如果专家和政治家只说美国需要更好的职业规划，我完全赞同。如果更多的人能够在就职前得到培训的机会，那当然很好。但同时，如果更多的人（而不是更少）能够从读大学这件事上有更深远的获益会更好。所以，我再次提问：为什么会有人认为大学生太多了？我认为答案很简单，高等教育意味着高质量的教学，教学反过来又取决于资深的教劳动力，这很昂贵。在教育上预支的费用是切实的，高昂的，能够量化的。回报同样真实，甚至更大。但这种回报难以量化统计，且因人而异。那些想少读书的人会屈服于这种诱惑，他们强调短期内的收益，只关注大学学费和第一份薪水的比较上。这是错误的。大学教育是一种长期投资。它使毕业生不断发展自己和适应世界，从长远来看，这种投资会带来惊人的收益。"减少大学生会让我们更富裕"的短视的想法是一种欺骗美国年轻人的骗局，它会削弱国家经济，并破坏我们的未来。

We need to have the confidence to invest in our young people and to ensure that a college education is accessible and affordable for students from all backgrounds and financial circumstances.

I hope that all of you who graduate today, and who experience the power of education in your own lives, will become advocates for the value of higher education in our society. There is a national conversation taking place right now about the value of higher education, and we need your voice in that conversation. We need you, in other words, to help others to achieve in the future what you achieve today.

How can you help more students earn college degrees? Here are three suggestions. First, become advocates for the importance of completion rates. A college education produces a tremendous return — if you get the degree. Returns are much lower if you start college but do not get the degree. The highest default rates on student loans do not involve college graduates with big debts. They instead involve students with small debts who never finish college and so never get the earnings boost that comes with a degree.

我们要有信心投资我们的年轻人，并确保大学教育对于各种背景和经济状况的学生来说都是可以获得和负担得起的。

我希望，今天的所有毕业生，以及都在自己的生活中体验过教育力量的人，都能成为社会上高等教育的倡导者。关于高等教育的价值有一场全国性的争论，我们需要你的声音；换言之，我们需要你帮助别人在将来实现你今天的成就。

如何帮助更多的人获得大学学位？这里有三个建议。第一，成为学业完成率重要性的倡导者。学生贷款违约率最高的那批人不是负债最高的毕业生，而是没能读完大学的小额债务背负者。由于没有读完大学，他们也未能享受到高校学位带来的收入提升。

A few moments ago, we awarded an honorary degree to President Barbara Gitenstein. Over her nearly two decades leading the College of New Jersey, she raised the College's four-year graduation rate from 58 percent to 75 percent, a number that puts TCNJ's on-time completion rate among the top ten in the nation for public colleges and universities. By raising TCNJ's graduation rate, President Gitenstein has improved the lives of thousands of students who might have left school with debt but no degree. Be an advocate for higher education leaders like Barbara Gitenstein, and for colleges like TCNJ that commit to improving completion rates.

不久之前，我们授予了新泽西学院校长芭芭拉·吉登斯坦荣誉学位。在她领导新泽西学院近20年期间，她将学院四年制毕业率从58%提高到75%。这个数字在全国公立大学排名前5%。通过提高学生的毕业率，吉登斯坦校长改善了成千上万可能已经背负着债务而辍学的学生的生活。支持更多像芭芭拉·吉登斯坦校长这样的高等教育领袖，以及像新泽西学院这样致力于提高毕业率的院校吧。

Second, support America's public institutions of higher education. State subsidies for public colleges and universities have declined precipitously, and state funding represents an increasingly small share of the budget at public research universities. At the University of Michigan, for example, state funding now accounts for only about 9 percent of total revenues. In the 1950s, by contrast, that number was 80 percent. Tuition at state universities has risen not because they have increased their expenditures per student, but because state legislatures have hollowed out their other sources of support.

第二，支持美国的公立高校。各州对公立大学的补助已急剧减少，州政府资助在公立研究型大学的预算占比越来越少。例如在密歇根大学，州政府资助现在只占整个收入的9%。相反，在20世纪50年代，这一数字为8%。公立大学学费的上涨并不是由于他们提高了对学生的花费，而是因为州议会已经掏空了其他支持来源。

America depends on its public colleges and universities. They are engines of social mobility and innovation. Princeton and other private universities make essential contributions to the nation and the world — but there is no way that we could ever replace America's great public institutions. They are a national treasure, and I urge you to support them.

美国依靠其公立大学而强大。他们是社会流动性和发展创新的引擎。普林斯顿大学和其他私立大学为国家和世界做出了重要贡献，但我们无法取代美国人的伟大公立机构。他们是国宝，希望你们支持他们。

Third, stand up for the importance of enabling more students from low-income families to earn college degrees. Princeton's Great Class of 2018 graduates today as the most socioeconomically diverse class in the 272-year history of this University. You will not hold that record for long. Other classes already at Princeton will break your record. Our graduate programs are likewise drawing upon new sources of talent: this spring we admitted the most socioeconomically diverse class of doctoral students in Princeton University's history.

At Princeton we believe in socioeconomic diversity because we know that to achieve excellence as a University and as a nation, we must draw talent from every sector of society. We know, too, that a Princeton degree is a rocket-booster for students seeking socioeconomic mobility. If we want to heal the divisions that inequality has produced in this country, we must ensure that students from low-income backgrounds receive the educations they need to develop their abilities and contribute to our society.

As I look out at our extraordinary class of undergraduate, masters, and doctoral degree recipients, I take pride in your excellence and your diversity, and I am excited about the contributions you will make in the years ahead. The world needs more college degrees, not fewer. We need more celebrations like the one we hold today, with more proud families and happy graduates ready to go out and make a positive difference in the world. All of us on this platform are thrilled to be a part of your celebration. We applaud your achievements. We send our best wishes as you begin the adventures that lie ahead, and we look forward to welcoming you back to this campus on future visits.

To the Great Class of 2018 and all of our graduates, congratulations!

第三，倡导帮助更多低收入家庭学生获得大学学位。普林斯顿2018届的毕业生是本校272年历史上最具社会经济多样性的一级。但你们不会保持这一纪录太久了，普林斯顿大学的其他学生将打破这个纪录。我们的研究生课程同样吸引了各个背景的人才，今年春天，我们录取了本校历史上最具社会经济多样性的博士生。在普林斯顿，我们相信这种多样性的积极意义。因为我们知道，不管是大学还是国家，要想卓越，必须从社会的各个阶层汲取人才。

普林斯顿的学位是学生寻求社会经济流动的助推器。看着我们的本科、硕士和博士毕业时，我真心为你们的优秀和多元化而感到自豪，并为你们在未来几年将做的贡献感到兴奋。世界需要更多的大学生，而不是更少。我们需要更多像今天这样的庆祝活动，需要更多自信和快乐的毕业生，为世界带来积极的变化。在台上的所有人都为能参与到你们的庆祝活动感到振奋，我们为你们取得的成就鼓掌，为你们即将开始的探险，送上最美好的祝福，同时，我们欢迎所有的毕业生将来常来母校看看。

2018届的优秀毕业生，祝福你们，祝贺你们！

（来源：https://www.sohu.com/a/274569265_649537）

3.4 主题拓展资源

英语视频：What Are Universities for?（上大学的意义到底是什么？）

大学生涯关乎个人未来发展、社会立足等重要问题，教师可请学生课后观看该视频，深入思考如何度过有意义的大学生活。

Well, the main thing is to teach people how to make a living. Educating the young to be engineers, biochemists or economists. But there is another strange bigger ambition looking away that somewhere in the background, and it sometimes comes out during commencement addresses or at the lyrical moments of graduation ceremonies. And that's the idea that universities might teach us how to live.

That is that these might be places to go and study in order to work out what really matters. Who we are, where our societies should be headed, and how we can be happier and more fulfilled. Not coincidentally, a great many universities were founded in the mid-nineteenth century. At exactly the time when belief in religion was undergoing a severe, and in the eyes of many, alarming decline. At that time a lot of questions were asked about where people were going to go and find meaning, consultation, wisdom and a sense of community. All the things they once found in a church.

And to certain educationalists there was one answer above all other. What people had once found in churches, they would now be able to discover in things like the dialogues of Plato, the plays of Shakespeare, the novels of Jane Austen, the paintings of Botticelli or Titian. In other words, in a secularizing age, culture would replace scripture. That's a beautiful, moving idea. And it's been responsible for the construction of so many universities, as well as museums, concert halls and libraries.

But there is a problem. Picture up at any actual university, more or less anywhere in the world, and start asking big questions, like, where should I go with my life; where is meaning to be found; how can we change things in this troubled world; And the stunned teaching staff will either call for the police or an insane asylum.

It's just not what you're allowed to ask. The really big questions and inner dramas that people used to take to religion seem strangely out of place in the average university setting. Where the mood is far cooler, more abstract and oddly removed from anything too practical or urgent. Big questions that many students in the humanities have, like, how can I learn about relationships; what should I do with my life; how can I reconcile my demand for money with my requirement for meaning; how does power work out there in the world. Such questions aren't necessarily very well addressed or answered.

Currently, universities have departments named after big academic disciplines, like history, or literature, or philosophy. But such titles really just reflect pretty arcane priorities rather than accurately picking up in issues that actually trouble people in their lives.

In the ideal university of the future, that original dream, that culture could replace scripture would be taking so seriously that departments would be reorganized to reflect the actual priorities of our lives. So, for example, there might be a department for relationships, and another for death, a center for anxiety and an academy for career self-knowledge. You wouldn't study 18th century history or the picaresque novel. You'd study how to be less anxious, or how to be more compassionate. Complaining about how many universities are today isn't a way of giving up on them. It's an attempt to get them to live up to their original promise, which is, in a busy world, where most of us are just scrabbling about full-time trying to make a living, to act as centers which can generate those ideas that we'll truly help us to live and to die well.

（来源：https://www.bilibili.com/video/BV1Dx411271b）

Passage B

3.5 Warm-up 环节

英文文章： Leaving for College: 5 Ways to Prepare to Leave Your Parents

教师可在 Warm-up 环节让学生阅读下面的文章，了解文章中提到的五种离家上大学所做的准备，并且请学生描述自己入学离家之前都做了哪些准备。

College is (finally) just around the corner and you couldn't be more excited. You'll get to stay out however late you want, wake up whenever you want, do whatever you want. Wait. You'll be able to do whatever you want? That's kind of scary. What will you do without the safety net of your parents always at your disposal? How will you even feed yourself? The only thing you've ever made is a peanut butter and jelly sandwich, and it wasn't even very good! How do you possibly mess up a peanut butter and jelly sandwich?!

Breathe easy there, high school grads. Yes, saying goodbye to mom and dad can be pretty overwhelming but with the right prep, the transition can be made way easier. Here, campus talked to college students who have already left the nest and, believe it or not, have lived to tell about it.

DON't think being away from your parents is just another way to say "24/7 party". When Kara, a student at the University of South California, first moved away for college, she let herself get a little carried away. "I had a super strict curfew in high school and suddenly I didn't have any curfew," she explains. "I went out literally every night and it really took a toll on my grades." Instead of partying every single night, use your new curfew-less life for special occasions only. "This past year, I really wanted to see the midnight showing of *The Hunger Games* with some of my friends. I don't normally stay out until the wee hours of the night when I have class the next morning, but I figured this was a special occasion." If it's a one-night event (like a concert or your best friend's birthday), it's totally fun to stay out later than usual, but use your best judgment on a nightly basis. Kara eventually set a curfew for herself. "Unless it's a specific event or I'm up studying, I try to be in bed by 11," she says.

DO figure out who you can call if there is an emergency. Once you tell people where you're going in college, it seems that everyone has a cousin's friend's roommate who you can call if "you ever need anything". You thank them for the referral, but inside you're rolling your eyes. The truth is: it's nice to know who you can call in the event that you do have an emergency. During the spring of her freshman year Katie, a senior at Tufts, found herself in the hospital after having a seizure. It was something far more serious than any of her college friends were able to deal with, and her parents were away in Europe and unreachable when the event happened. "I called my mom's roommate from college, who I've only met a few times, but lives in Boston," says Katie. "I stayed in her house for a week and it was so nice to have an adult that I could call." You never know when an emergency might strike, so keep a list of people in your phone or wallet that you could call. Just remember: "Do you have HBO? I really want to watch *True Blood*" is not an emergency.

DO realize that you'll get homesick. Yes, college is awesome, but leaving your old life and entering a totally new one can be really daunting at times. "No one prepared me for how much I would miss home," says Liz, a sophomore at BU. "Everyone just said 'Oh, it's the best time of your life.' " It's normal to get homesick, but if you feel yourself being homesick all the time and overwhelmed by that feeling, reach out to your school's counseling center. I can assure you that you won't be the first undergrad to walk through their doors saying that you miss your parents. They can help you adjust to college life in a healthy and effective way.

DO figure out a budgeting system. There's no one right way to budget your money. I keep a note on my iPhone and write down every purchase (yes, to the penny) on it. The app from Mint.com is a personal favorite of mine. It syncs with your account on Mint.com (which is equally awesome) and makes it super easy to track spending. Also be sure to download the app for whatever bank you're part of. In that way you never have to deal with wondering whether or not there is enough money in your account to make a purchase. Use this summer before going into college to figure out the system that works for you. Spend the next few months trying out different methods to figure out what works best for you. Even if an app has awesome reviews across the board, it might not make sense for you and your system of budgeting. Be sure to talk to your parents about your budget before you leave, as well. For starters, they can help you come up with a realistic amount to spend each week.

DON't think you can never go home. Kathleen, a rising sophomore at James Madison University, wishes she knew that it's OK to go home if and when you need to. "Sometimes you want to be all on your own and not to rely on your parents, but it is okay to go visit family," she says. If you need to get away for a weekend to breathe, it doesn't mean that you're doing college wrong. Of course, not everyone is just a hop, skip, and a jump from their university, and going home can be crazy expensive for many college students. If you're missing a good conversation with mom but can't afford to go home, set a date every week to have a phone or Skype conversation. That's more than just "Today was great but busy! I love you, too! Bye!" Sunday nights are usually a good time to do this. Also, consider putting some dates down on the calendar now for your parents to visit. Most schools have a Parents Weekend with tons of fun events planned. Consider booking a flight, train, or hotel now before prices skyrocket.

（来源：https://docs.qq.com/doc/DWFNZckZDU2FnRkdE）

3.6 Discussion 环节

英文文章：Tips on How to Spend Your College Life

大一新生刚刚结束了高中生活来到了大学，开启一段新的旅程。多数人对于大学生活还不太了解，兴奋之余，可能会感到迷茫、紧张和焦虑。下面这篇文章是一位大二学生给学弟学妹关于大学的学习的建议。教师可以安排学生阅读下面的文章，并讨论：What are the differences between college and high school?

Welcome to our university. Nice to meet you guys! This university has a long history and is famous for the spirit of being diligent, rigorous, realistic and creative. At the same time last year, I walked into this beautiful campus excitedly but nervously. I was excited because I was admitted by this well-known college. I was nervous because a senior told me that college is more demanding than high school, and my college life would be busy and competitive. Just like the feelings you are having now. But do not worry, I will introduce three essential tips of how to spend your college life to you.

First of all, you should learn to take charge of your time. Generally, a college student without a timetable would be confused and inefficient. A student who does not know when to get up, when to study, when to exercise, even when to eat would find it difficult to live through college. My roommate Hu, whose IQ is above 130, was not a time-conscious man at the beginning of the first semester. He did make a plan for his daily life. There is lots of homework in college and the teaching process is kind of fast, which may be different in your eyes. Not surprisingly, Hu was caught off guard at first. He couldn't finish his homework on time. His mess was mainly due to his carelessness of time. Although he is smart, his average GPA was some kind of low. In the second term, Hu accepted my advice of managing his time. At the end of this semester, Hu thanked me for my advice. He told me that his life was not boring any longer. So, you should take charge of your time and make a plan as soon as possible!

Second of all, you should learn to take note. Note-taking is not only used in classes, but also used in lectures, communications and reading. College is a unique place for studying, mainly because there are many well-known professors, a lot of smart students and different kinds of books. You can acquire knowledge from them. Of course, we can't remember all these things for most of us are not genius, that is to say, you should take a notebook with you. By the way, you'd better go over it in time.

Finally, I will tell you something about how to study a textbook. As is known to us all, textbooks are written by professors who have accumulated much teaching experience. They know how to present knowledge to us students. Definitely, we should make good use of textbooks. Now you may wonder how to take advantage of it. Usually there are three steps: prepare a lesson, take lessons carefully, and review lessons. After almost 15 years of studying, I am sure that you have your own ways to take the three steps.

In a word, a college is more demanding than a high school. It is probably a surprise for you. But you are going to adapt to it gradually. I wish my speech today could help you adapt to the whole new college life. I hope you will have a busy but happy college life! If you have any problems in the near future, you can come and ask me for help. I am glad that I can give you a hand. That's all. Thank you.

（来源：百度文库）

3.7 Critical thinking 环节

英语视频：Steve Jobs 2005 年斯坦福大学毕业演讲

在该视频中，Steve Jobs 提到了关于 "connecting dots" 的观点，教师请学生观看视频并鼓励学生努力创造自己生活中的 "dots"，引导学生思考：Steve Jobs talked about "dots". Can you give an example of your dots?

I am honored to be with you today at your commencement from one of the finest universities in the world. I never graduated from college. Truth be told, this is the closest I've ever gotten to a college graduation. Today I want to tell you three stories from my life. That's it. No big deal. Just three stories.

The first story is about connecting the dots.

I dropped out of Reed College after the first 6 months, but then stayed around as a drop-in for another 18 months or so before I really quit. So why did I drop out?

It started before I was born. My biological mother was a young, unwed college graduate student, and she decided to put me up for adoption. She felt very strongly that I should be adopted by college graduates, so everything was all set for me to be adopted at birth by a lawyer and his wife. Except that when I popped out, they decided at the last minute that they really wanted a girl. So my parents, who were on a waiting list, got a call in the middle of the night asking: "We have an unexpected baby boy, do you want him?" They said, "Of course." My biological mother later found out that my mother had never graduated from college and that my father had never graduated from high school. She refused to sign the final adoption papers. She only relented a few months later when my parents promised that I would someday go to college.

And 17 years later I did go to college. But I naively chose a college that was almost as expensive as Stanford, and all of my working-class parents' savings were being spent on my college tuition. After six months, I couldn't see the value in it. I had no idea what I wanted to do with my life and no idea how college was going to help me figure it out. And here I was spending all of the money my parents had saved their entire life. So I decided to drop out and trust that it would all work out OK. It was pretty scary at the time, but looking back it was one of the best decisions I ever made. The minute I dropped out I could stop taking the required classes that didn't interest me, and begin dropping in on the ones that looked interesting.

It wasn't all romantic. I didn't have a dorm room, so I slept on the floor in friends' rooms, I returned coke bottles for the deposits to buy food with, and I would walk the 7 miles across town every Sunday night to get one good meal a week at the Hare Krishna temple. I loved it. And much of what I stumbled into by following my curiosity and intuition turned out to be priceless later on. Let me give you one example.

Reed College at that time offered perhaps the best calligraphy instruction in the country. Throughout the campus, every poster, every label on every drawer, was beautifully hand-calligraphed. Because I had dropped out and didn't have to take the normal classes, I decided to take a calligraphy class to learn how to do this. I learned about serif and san-serif typefaces, about varying the amount of space between different letter combinations, about what makes great typography great. It was beautiful, historical, artistically subtle in a way that science can't capture, and I found it fascinating.

None of this had even a hope of any practical application in my life. But ten years later, when we were designing the first Macintosh computer, it all came back to me. And we designed it all into the Mac. It was the first computer with beautiful typography. If I had never dropped in on that single course in college, the Mac would have never had multiple typefaces or proportionally spaced fonts. And since Windows just copied the Mac, it's likely that no personal computer would have them. If I had never dropped out, I would have never dropped in on this calligraphy class, and personal computers might not have the wonderful typography that they do. Of course, it was impossible to connect the dots looking forward when I was in college. But it was very, very clear looking backwards ten years later.

Again, you can't connect the dots looking forward; you can only connect them looking backwards. So you have to trust that the dots will somehow connect in your future. You have to trust in something—your gut, destiny, life, karma, whatever. This approach has never let me down, and it has made all the difference in my life.

My second story is about love and loss.

I was lucky—I found what I loved to do early in life. Woz and I started Apple in my parents' garage when I was 20. We worked hard, and in 10 years Apple had grown from just the two of us in a garage into a $2 billion company with over 4000 employees. We had just released our finest creation—the Macintosh—a year earlier, and I had just turned 30. And then I got fired. How can you get fired from a company you started? Well, as Apple grew, we hired someone who I thought was very talented to run the company with me, and for the first year or so things went well. But then our visions of the future began to diverge and eventually we had a falling out. When we did, our Board of Directors sided with him. So at 30 I was out, and very publicly out. What had been the focus of my entire adult life was gone, and it was devastating.

I really didn't know what to do for a few months. I felt that I had let the previous generation of entrepreneurs down—that I had dropped the baton as it was being passed to me. I met with David Packard and Bob Noyce and tried to apologize for screwing up so badly. I was a very public failure, and I even thought about running away from the valley. But something slowly began to dawn on me—I still loved what I did. The turn of events at Apple had not changed that one bit. I had been rejected, but I was still in love. And so I decided to start over.

I didn't see it then, but it turned out that getting fired from Apple was the best thing that could have ever happened to me. The heaviness of being successful was replaced by the lightness of being a beginner again, less sure about everything. It freed me to enter one of the most creative periods of my life.

During the next five years, I started a company named NeXT, another company named Pixar, and fell in love with an amazing woman who would become my wife. Pixar went on to create the world's first computer animated feature film, *Toy Story*, and is now the most successful animation studio in the world. In a remarkable turn of events, Apple bought NeXT, I returned to Apple, and the technology we developed at NeXT is at the heart of Apple's current renaissance. And Laurene and I have a wonderful family together.

I'm pretty sure none of this would have happened if I hadn't been fired from Apple. It was awful tasting medicine, but I guess the patient needed it. Sometimes life hits you in the head with a brick. Don't lose faith. I'm convinced that the only thing that kept me going was that I loved what I did. You've got to find what you love. And that is as true for your work as it is for your lovers. Your work is going to fill a large part of your life, and the only way to be truly satisfied is to do what you believe is great work. And the only way to do great work is to love what you do. If you haven't found it yet, keep looking. Don't settle. As with all matters of the heart, you'll know when you find it. And, like any great relationship, it just gets better and better as the years roll on. So keep looking until you find it. Don't settle.

My third story is about death.

When I was 17, I read a quote that went something like: "If you live each day as if it was your last, someday you'll most certainly be right." It made an impression on me, and since then, for the past 33 years, I have looked in the mirror every morning and asked myself: "If today were the last day of my life, would I want to do what I am about to do today?" And whenever the answer has been "No" for too many days in a row, I know I need to change something.

Remembering that I'll be dead soon is the most important tool I've ever encountered to help me make the big choices in life. Because almost everything—all external expectations, all pride, all fear of embarrassment or failure—these things just fall away in the face of death, leaving only what is truly important. Remembering that you are going to die is the best way I know to avoid the trap of thinking you have something to lose. You are already naked. There is no reason not to follow your heart.

About a year ago, I was diagnosed with cancer. I had a scan at 7:30 in the morning, and it clearly showed a tumor on my pancreas. I didn't even know what a pancreas was. The doctors told me this was almost certainly a type of cancer that is incurable, and that I should expect to live no longer than three to six months. My doctor advised me to go home and get my affairs in order, which is doctor's code for prepare to die. It means to try to tell your kids everything you thought you'd have the next 10 years to tell them in just a few months. It means to make sure everything is buttoned up so that it will be as easy as possible for your family. It means to say your goodbyes.

I lived with that diagnosis all day. Later that evening I had a biopsy, where they stuck an endoscope down my throat, through my stomach and into my intestines, put a needle into my pancreas and got a few cells from the tumor. I was sedated, but my wife, who was there, told me that when they viewed the cells under a microscope the doctors started crying because it turned out to be a very rare form of pancreatic cancer that is curable with surgery. I had the surgery and I'm fine now.

This was the closest I've been to facing death, and I hope its the closest I get for a few more decades. Having lived through it, I can now say this to you with a bit more certainty than when death was a useful but purely intellectual concept.

No one wants to die. Even people who want to go to heaven don't want to die to get there. And yet death is the destination we all share. No one has ever escaped it. And that is as it should be, because death is very likely the single best invention of life. It is life's change agent. It clears out the old to make way for the new. Right now, the new is you, but someday not too long from now, you will gradually become the old and be cleared away. Sorry to be so dramatic, but it is quite true.

Your time is limited, so don't waste it living someone else's life. Don't be trapped by dogma—which is living with the results of other people's thinking. Don't let the noise of other's opinions drown out your own inner voice. And most importantly, have the courage to follow your heart and intuition. They somehow already know what you truly want to become. Everything else is secondary.

When I was young, there was an amazing publication called *The Whole Earth Catalog*, which was one of the bibles of my generation. It was created by a fellow named Stewart Brand not far from here in Menlo Park, and he brought it to life with his poetic touch. This was in the late 1960's, before personal computers and desktop publishing, so it was all made with typewriters, scissors, and polaroid cameras. It was sort of like Google in paperback form, 35 years before Google came along: it was idealistic, and overflowing with neat tools and great notions.

Stewart and his team put out several issues of *The Whole Earth Catalog*, and then when it had run its course, they put out a final issue. It was the mid-1970s, and I was your age. On the back cover of their final issue was a photograph of an early morning country road, the kind you might find yourself hitchhiking on if you were so adventurous. Beneath it were the words: "Stay Hungry. Stay Foolish." It was their farewell message as they signed off. Stay Hungry. Stay Foolish. And I have always wished that for myself. And now, as you graduate to begin anew, I wish that for you.

Stay Hungry. Stay Foolish. Thank you all very much.

（来源：https://www.jianshu.com/p/538c234e5eb4）

3.8 主题拓展资源

英语视频：Why Do We Go to University

Good morning, ladies and gentlemen.

Last month, I asked my 17-year-old brother which university he would like to apply for? He shrugged and answered, "I don't know, it's up to my girlfriend."

Love is blind, huh? His answer was a little immature but should not be under too many reproaches because when I was at his age, I was also aimless about the future. And I went to the university simply because my parents told me to do so for the passport, for a decent job, and a stable life in the future. But now, after two amazing years in the university, I realized that the significance of university is far beyond a degree.

We go to university for self-concept, which embodies the answer to the question "who am I" in terms of academic performance, gender roles as well as racial identity. By attending those career orientation courses, we figure out what we wanna do in the future, and better prepare for tomorrow. We go to university to cultivate our comprehensive abilities. By doing academic research, we acquire ways of assembling and processing information.

By joining students' union, we learn how to cooperate and work with others effectively. And by attending all of those lectures and workshops in different topics, we gain profound knowledge and cultivate our critical thinking. By internalizing all of those comprehensive abilities, we gradually shaped our values and built our characters. We go to university also for higher platform of self-realization. Without the university, I wouldn't have been able to enjoy all of those free learning resources and achieve spiritual enhancement.

Without the university, I wouldn't have been able to represent my city and work for the G20 Summit as well as the World Internet Conference as a volunteer. Without the university, I wouldn't have been able to stand on this stage, expressing my ideas to all of you freely. And that's why we go to university which is designed to be a place of cultivating personal growth and expansion. Some people may argue that what we learn in the university may not be applied to our future career, but remember, ladies and gentlemen, university is not merely for training, but also for education in the understanding of ourselves, others as well as the world we are living in.

Thank you very much!

（来源：https://www.bilibili.com/video/av60220427/）

第二单元　心中有梦想，成功有希望

(Unit 2 Song of the Soul)

1. 思政主题：心中有梦想，成功有希望

2. 意义

本单元聚焦在人的一生当中心怀梦想的重要性。梦想是前行的心灯，是引领成功的风帆。心中有梦，我们才知道要往哪里去，去追求什么。没有梦想，生活就会失去目标方向。一个人不懈追梦，就会不断创造新的人生；一个民族不懈追梦，就会不断创造新美的未来。当梦想成为一个国家、一个民族的坚定信念，就会成为一种神圣的国家意志、民族意志，就会成为不可抗拒的社会变革的伟大力量，并创造出令世界景仰和称颂的人间奇迹，中国梦正是这样一种伟大的精神力量。当代青年人为实现中国梦而奋斗的个体梦想都具有重要意义。

3. 教学设计与思政元素的融入

如今，我们中华民族正在创造和追逐自己的梦想——实现中华民族伟大复兴。"全面建成小康社会""社会主义现代化国家目标""中华民族伟大复兴目标""新三步走战略"为中国经济社会的发展勾勒出了一幅前景无限的美丽画卷，交汇成了一部中国特色社会主义建设的雄壮交响曲。"新三步走战略"的第一步，到建党成立一百周年（2020年）的时候，全面建成小康社会；第二步，到新中国成立一百周年（2049年）的时候，建成富强、民主、文明、和谐的社会主义现代化国家；第三步，在前"两个一百年"奋斗目标的基础上，实现中华民族伟大复兴的中国梦，这是近代以来中华民族最伟大的梦想。其本质内涵是国家富强、民族振兴、人民幸福，因而它有一个与世界上所有国家梦想不同的最大优势，就是能够把最广大民众对国家和民族的憧憬、对自己未来的憧憬汇成一个共同梦想，把国家、民族和个人凝成一个同呼吸、共命运的追梦共同体，造就新的人和新的生活，书写新的中国故事。教师可以让学生阅读下面的文章，引导学生思考个人梦想与中国梦有怎样的联系，如何更好地把个人梦想与民族复兴紧密结合起来。

Potential of the Chinese Dream

Early in November 2012, Chinese leader Xi Jinping articulated a vision for the nation's future that he called the Chinese Dream. The Chinese Dream integrates national and personal aspirations, with the twin goals of reclaiming national pride and achieving personal well-being. It requires sustained economic growth, expanded equality and an infusion of cultural values to balance materialism.

Dreams are powerful. In advancing the Chinese Dream, the government is uniting people around a shared mission and driving change, especially people in lower-tier cities and rural areas, as they experience increased affluence and opportunity.

Externally, the Chinese Dream can improve the image of China as a fast-growing nation striving to improve the welfare of its people and secure its place as a respected leader of the international community. In addition, the Chinese Dream can help elevate the overseas perception of Brand China, the collective reputation of products and services that originates in China.

Like many developments in modern China, awareness of the Chinese Dream happened with a great speed.

Chinese social media is full of postings about the Chinese Dream, in which people express their demand for free education, better air quality and safe food. The government has raised awareness of its view of the Chinese Dream with a poster campaign and other publicity.

When the Chinese people say they support the Chinese Dream, they mean it. They take national pride seriously. According to WPP research from the Futures Company, 67 percent of Chinese say showing national pride is very or extremely important. Only 60 percent of Americans and 48 percent of Britons agree showing national pride is important.

When we asked Chinese what country they feel is most ideal today, they answered the United States. When we asked them what country would be ideal in 10 years, they said China. This optimism may be driven by a phenomenon articulated by the Futures Company, which suggests that personal satisfaction is determined less by one's current status and more by the prospects of improvement in the future. In its Global Monitor 2013, a consumer intelligence tool, the Futures Company found that 58 percent of Chinese say they are very or extremely satisfied with their lives, compared with 48 percent of Americans and only 33 percent of

Britons.

At the same time, Chinese realize that their lives have room for improvement, with an overwhelming 79 percent agreeing that they'd be happier with more possessions. Only 16 percent of Britons and 14 percent of Americans say they need more stuff. Based on Global Monitor research, the Futures Company concludes that once people worldwide satisfy their basic material needs, adding more possessions doesn't usually increase happiness. Chinese aren't there yet. But they are determined to reach this threshold. For the past 30 years, Chinese have been manufacturing and exporting products to meet the materialistic aspirations of consumers in the West. Chinese are now ready to consume what they produce, to realize the materialistic aspect of the Chinese Dream. The only question is whether this acquisition of material goods will unfold as Western-style conspicuous consumption in China or in a more considered way, informed by a Chinese cultural appreciation for keeping life in balance.

Realization of the Chinese Dream is important to Chinese for a practical reason: it will improve the lives of people, particularly in lower-tier cities and rural areas. And it is important for reasons of national identity, to bring a country with a proud history out of the shadows of the troubling last couple of centuries. This commitment to the dream is consistent across all age groups and highest among younger people, ages 30 to 39. These people, who mostly grew up during the period of China's rapid economic growth, tend to be more individualistic and determined to advance either by finding a good job or starting their own business. Two-thirds of the Chinese people surveyed say the Chinese Dream makes them feel more confident about their personal future and 61 percent say the Chinese Dream makes them feel more confident about the future of the country. They also rate the Dream high for strengthening social cohesion, making the country more energetic and influencing positive social change.

（来源：*China Daily*）

Passage A

3.1 Warm-up 环节

英文文章：Chance Favors the Prepared

Les Brown 尽管出身贫寒、资质平平，但从未放弃音乐 DJ 的梦想，凭借对梦想的渴望和坚持，成功化身美国知名的音乐 DJ。这种必胜的信念和为梦想持续努力的精神最终也帮助他成为励志演讲大师和畅销书作家。教师可以请学生阅读下面的文章，思考 Les Brown 是怎样在准备过程中以锲而不舍的信念支撑自己前行，帮助学生深入理解"拥有梦想并为之不懈奋斗"的主题内涵。

  Les Brown and his twin brother were adopted by Mamie Brown, a kitchen worker, shortly after their birth in a poverty-stricken Miami neighborhood.

  Because of his overactive behavior and nonstop talking as a child, Les was placed in special education classes for the learning disabled all the way through high school. Upon graduation, he became a garbage collector. The prospective opportunities for his future looked slim to others, but not to Les. He had a passion, a dream—a big dream that he was ready to work hard for. He was destined to be a disc jockey, also known as a "DJ", one of the radio celebrities mixing music broadcasts for the whole city.

  At night he would take a radio to bed so he could indulge his dream by listening to the local DJs. He created an imaginary radio station in his tiny bedroom. A hairbrush served as his microphone as he energetically practiced speaking his masterpieces to his imaginary listeners.

  He aggravated his friends with his constant practicing. They all told him that he didn't have a chance and he would never be a DJ. They scorned him and said to stop dreaming and focus on the real world. Nonetheless, Les didn't let their negativity stop him. He kept his goals close to his heart and remained wrapped up in his own world, completely absorbed in preparing for his future, preparing to live his dream as a renowned DJ.

  One day Les decided to take the initiative and begin with this enterprise. He boldly went to the local radio station and told the station manager he understood the layout of the station and was ready to be a disc jockey.

  The manager looked dubiously at the untidy young man in overalls and a straw hat and inquired, "Do you have any expertise in broadcasting?"

  Les replied, "No sir, I don't."

  "Well, son, I'm afraid we don't have a job for you then," he responded bluntly. So Les's first chance at success had been a complete bust.

  Les was determined. He adored his adoptive mother, Mamie Brown, and was careful with his money to try and buy her nice things. Despite everyone's discouragement, she believed in him and had taught him to pursue his goals and persist in his dreams no matter what others said.

So, in spite of what the station manager had originally said, Les returned to the station every day for a week. His persistence was very persuasive and the station manager finally gave in and took Les on to do small tasks—at no pay. Les brought coffee and food. He catered to their every need at work and worked overtime whenever necessary. Eventually, his enthusiasm won their confidence and they would send Les in their Cadillac to pick up celebrities, not knowing that he didn't even have a driver's license!

While hanging out with the station's real DJs, Les taught himself their posture and hand movements on the control panel. He stayed around the studio soaking up whatever knowledge he could. He was disciplined; back in his bedroom at night, he faithfully practiced in anticipation of the opportunity he knew would come.

One afternoon at work, the DJ named Rock started to feel very sick while on the air. Les was the only person around, and he realized that Rock was coughing and losing his voice. Les stayed close in case there was some way he might help alleviate his co-worker's distress. He also worried that the illness was sure to doom this broadcast.

Finally, when the phone rang, Les grabbed it. It was the station manager as he knew it would be.

"Les, this is Mr. Klein. I don't think Rock can finish his program."

"Yes," he murmured, "I know."

"Would you call one of the other DJs to come in and take over?"

"Yes sir, I sure will."

But try as he might, none of the regular DJs were available. MC Cormick and DJ Slick were both out of town for the weekend and DJ Neil was also feeling sick. It seemed that the radio station was in big trouble.

Frantic with distress, Les called the general manager. "Mr. Klein, I can't find nobody," Les said.

Mr. Klein then asked, "Young man, do you know how to work the controls in the studio?"

"Yes sir," replied Les, grinning with the sudden opportunity. He didn't even blink before he called his mother and his friends. "You all go out on the front porch and turn up the radio because I'm about to come on the air!" he said.

Les rushed into the booth, hoisted Rock onto a nearby couch, and sat down in his place. He was ready. He flipped on the microphone and eloquently rapped, "Look out! This is me LB, Les Brown! There were none before me and there will be none after me. Therefore, that makes me the one and only. Young and single and love to mingle. Qualified to bring you satisfaction a whole lot of action. Look out baby I'm your lovin' man."

Because of his preparation, Les was ready. He had dazzled the audience and heard applause from his general manager. From that fateful beginning, Les was propelled to become an icon in broadcasting, politics, public speaking and television.

（来源：《新视野大学英语读写教程3》）

3.2 Discussion 环节

英文文章: 11 Ways to Make Living the Dream Life Possible Today

梦想与现实之间往往存在着距离。本文提供了11个让梦想成为现实的具体建议，指导学生树立正确目标、制订可行计划、坦然接受失败，为梦想勇往直前。教师可引导学生结合文章的观点和自身实际，分析成功道路上的困难和挑战，思考和讨论：当我们远离自己的梦想的时候，该如何让自己回归梦想？

How many times have you looked at certain people around you and thought how lucky they are to be living the dream life? How do they get everything they want, and you don't?

Living the dream life is not about luck as much as it's about hope, commitment, and patience. No one just magically gets to "live the dream life". People who are living their dream life have reached that place with consistent effort, hard work, and fearlessness, and you can, too.

Start today by making small changes in your life that are sure to set you up for success. Here are 11 ways you can make living the dream life possible.

1. Know What You Want

Many of us spend more time complaining about our lives rather than figuring out what we actually want.

Firstly, it is okay to not know what you want. While there are people with clear cut goals, there are others who discover theirs with time. What's important is making conscious efforts in discovering what your heart desires.

Give these questions a thought:

What makes you happy?

What are your interests?

What does success mean to you?

What do you want from life?

What are your priorities?

What do you want to change in your life?

Who do you admire?

These are a few questions that will help you figure out your goals better. Write the answers down and keep building on them until you know what you want. After all, the first step in living the dream life is discovering the dream.

If you're not sure how to set your priorities and figure out what you want, check out this article.

2. Have a Concrete Plan

Now that you know what you want, the next step is to devise a plan to make it happen.

One day we are extremely motivated and enthusiastic, and the very next day, we are back to being lazy. Here's why having a plan helps — it reminds you of your dream and keeps you motivated.

Break down your dream to smaller, actionable parts and set achievable goals for yourself. No, not the 5-year plan, but the smaller ones like the 1-year, 6-month, 3-month, and 1-month plans. Setting smaller targets will help you reach a larger goal progressively.

Write your goals down with respect to your personal and professional life, be as precise as possible, and lay out actionable steps for each of them.

3. Take Consistent Action

Consistency is the key to achieving what you want and living the dream life.

However, being consistent is not easy. There will be days when you will begin to lose patience and want to give up, and that's completely understandable.

On such days, take time out and give yourself a break. Once you feel better, get back on track, because everything you do is a building block and will take you closer to your goal.

Whenever you feel disillusioned, revisit your goal and let it motivate you to keep going.

4. Track Your Progress

It's important to track your progress regularly to ensure you are on the right path. You can use journals, calendars, and Apps to keep a record of your progress and assess it.

For the times you feel you didn't achieve your goal, keep a note of what went wrong, and learn from those mistakes. Focus on making progress rather than obsessing over perfection.

Most importantly, remember to celebrate your achievements and give yourself credit for your successes because you wholly deserve it.

5. Be Open to Failure

Life is unpredictable. You can plan all you want, but also know that life won't always go the way you planned it. You are bound to be met with some unforeseen circumstances or failures along the way, so be prepared for them all.

Embrace failure and don't fear it because it's better to try and fail than to never try at all. The key is that do not take failure personally. Instead, use failures as an opportunity to learn and grow.

When you become better at failing, you develop a sense of fearlessness, which helps you get out of your comfort zone, take risks, and reach your goals.

6. Stay Away from Negativity

From your self-depreciating thoughts to people who see the bad in everything, negativity is all around you and won't do anything to help you start living the dream. To not get stressed and bogged down by these thoughts, you need to develop zero tolerance to negativity.

Sometimes, one negative thought or comment can destroy all your efforts. Learn to identify such people or circumstances and set healthy boundaries to maintain your sanity.

Whenever you feel depressed, turn to doing things that distract you or make you happy, like playing a sport, listening to music, or even talking to someone who can make you feel better. Whatever it is, don't harbor negative feelings — the faster you shake them off, the better.

7. Surround Yourself with Positive People

People around you have the power to influence you in many ways. Having the right kind of people around is essential for your growth and development. For instance, someone who is around toxic people is bound to have lower self-esteem and be forever stressed.

What you need is happy, encouraging, and supportive people, those who can guide you, lift your spirits, and help you maintain a positive frame of mind.

8. Believe in Yourself

To live your dream life, you need to first believe in yourself. However "impossible" your dream seems or regardless of what people tell you, don't be afraid to believe in the fact that you will make it happen.

When you are finding it hard to retain your belief, visualize yourself achieving that dream and condition your mind to act as if it has happened. You will be surprised to see how much strength you can derive from this small exercise.

Cut out all the negative self-talk, and don't worry about what others think because the day you move ahead with conviction, nothing can stop you from achieving success and living your dream.

9. Focus on What You Can Control

Sometimes when your mind is going places and leaving you stressed, take a deep breath, stop thinking, and eliminate all the unnecessary thoughts.

Unproductive and unnecessary thoughts do nothing but act as deterrents, leaving you overwhelmed and upset. At such times, just focus on the things that are within your control and forget about the rest.

You need to accept the fact that there are things that are beyond your control, and there is no need to waste your energy obsessing over them.

If you want to learn how to let go of what you can't control, check out this article.

10. Stop Comparing Yourself to Others

Talking about being unproductive, comparing yourself to others is another unproductive thought pattern that has never done anyone any good and can get in the way of living the dream life you've imagined.

In the time of social media, it's difficult not to compare your life to others'. A classmate's LinkedIn update is enough to get you wondering what you are doing with your life. Similarly, reading about a colleague's vacation in some exotic location fills you with envy.

One 2014 study showed that "participants who used Facebook most often had poorer trait self-esteem, and this was mediated by greater exposure to upward social comparisons on social media". So while it may feel good to scroll through and see your best friend's new puppy or your cousin's new house, it is likely that it isn't doing your self-esteem any favors.

Every time you make negative comparisons and feel terrible, consciously stop yourself. Everyone's journey is different, and life is not a race. Compare you to yourself and work towards making progress. That's all that matters.

11. Stop Making Excuses

"I'll start exercising tomorrow" "I'm too old for this" "I'm waiting for the right time" "When XYZ happens, I'll start" — how many times have you found yourself giving such excuses?

These excuses are holding you back and preventing you from getting results. Stop giving yourself excuses, overcome your fears, and act on your plan — that is the only way you will make progress.

The Bottom Line

Life is short, and you certainly must not waste your life living someone else's dream. Years later when you look back at your life, you want to be left smiling rather than be filled with regrets.

To make that happen, start with believing in your dream. Living the dream life does not come to a fortunate few. It comes to all those who diligently work towards turning their dreams into reality.

（来源：https://www.lifehack.org/827403/living-the-dream）

3.3 Critical thinking 环节

双语文章：On Achieving Success 关于获得成功

成功的前提是要有梦想，但还有其它因素。成功不依赖于运气和巧合，确定目标、坚决执行、不懈努力、磨练意志才是成功的必由之路。在文章 On Achieving Success 中，美国作家 Hemingway 针对"如何获得成功"这一话题发表了看法。教师可带领学生阅读文章，请学生思考：一个人从拥有梦想到走向成功，到底需要经历哪些困难以及如何去克服这些障碍？教师可以进一步引导学生树立正确的奋斗观，为实现正确的人生目标而不懈努力。

We cannot travel every path. Success must be won along one line. We must make our business the one life purpose to which every other must be subordinate.

我们不可能把每条路都走一遍。必须执着于一条道路才能获得成功。我们必须有一个终生追求的目标，其他的则从属于这个目标。

I hate a thing done by halves. If it be right, do it boldly. If it be wrong, leave it undone.

我痛恨做事半途而废。如果这件事是对的，就大胆勇敢地去做；如果这件事不对，就不要去做。

The men of history were not perpetually looking into the mirror to make sure of their own size. Absorbed in their work they did it. They did it so well that the wondering world sees them to be great, and labeled them accordingly.

历史长河中的伟人并不是靠终日瞻观镜中的自己来衡量自身形象的。他们的形象来自对事业全身心的投入与追求。他们是如此的卓越超凡，于是芸芸众生觉得他们很伟大，并因此称他们为伟人。

To live with a high ideal is a successful life. It is not what one does, but what one tries to do, that makes a man strong. "Eternal vigilance," it has been said, "is the price of liberty." With equal truth it may be said, "Unceasing effort is the price of success." If we do not work with our might, others will; and they will outstrip us in the race, and pluck the prize from our grasp.

为崇高的理想而活着是一种成功的生活。使人变强大的，不是这个人做了什么，而是他努力尝试去做什么。有人说过，"恒久的警惕是自由的代价"，那同样也可以说，"不懈的努力是成功的代价。"倘若我们不尽全力工作，别人会尽全力，随后他们将在竞争中超越我们，从我们手中夺取胜利的果实。

Success grows less and less dependent on luck and chance. Self-distrust is the cause of most of our failures. The great and indispensable help to success is character.

成功越来越不依赖于运气和巧合。丧失自信是我们失败的主要原因。性格是取得成功不可或缺的重要助力。

Character is a crystallized habit, the result of training and conviction. Every character is influenced by heredity, environment and education. But these apart, if every man were not to be a great extent the architect of his own character, he would be a fatalist, and irresponsible creature of circumstances.

性格是一种固化成形的习惯，是不断培养并坚信于此的结果。每个人的性格都会受到遗传因素、环境和教育的影响。但除此之外，如果人在很大程度上不能成为自己性格的构筑者，那么他就会沦为宿命论者，从而成为环境的失败造物。

Instead of saying that man is a creature of circumstance, it would be nearer the mark to say that man is the architect of circumstance. From the same materials one man builds palaces, another hovel. Bricks and mortar are mortar and bricks, until the architect can make them something else. The true way to gain much is never to desire to gain too much. Wise men don't care for what they can't have.

与其说人是环境的造物，不如说人是环境的建筑师更贴切些。同样的材料，有人能用其建造出宫殿，而有人只能建成简陋的小屋。在建筑师将其变成他物之前，砖泥依然是砖泥。想得到的多就永远不要奢望太多。智者不会在意他们得不到的东西。

3.4 主题拓展资源

英文文章：Les Brown's Biography

Les Brown 出身贫寒，但他追求成功的意志使他成为美国现今著名的励志演说家之一，并获得多项演说奖项。"鼓励人们拥有梦想并为之奋斗，最终超越平庸"是他演讲的主题。教师可组织学生阅读关于他的人物介绍，增进对 Les Brown 人物故事及其所传递的价值观的了解。

Motivational speaker Les Brown made his name encouraging others to overcome any odds that might stand in their way.

Les Brown has a dream, and he is living it. In 1986, broke and sleeping on the cold linoleum floor of his office, he began to pursue a career as a motivational speaker. By the early 1990s, he was one of the highest paid speakers in the nation. His company, Les Brown Unlimited, Inc., earned millions of dollars a year from his speaking tours and the sale of motivational tapes and materials.

Leslie Calvin Brown and his twin brother, Wesley, were born on February 17, 1945, on the floor of an abandoned building in Liberty City, a low-income section of Miami, Florida. Their birth mother, married at the time to a soldier stationed overseas, had become pregnant by another man and went to Miami secretly to give birth to her sons. Three weeks later, she gave them away. At six weeks of age, both boys were adopted by Mamie Brown, a 38-year-old unmarried cafeteria cook and domestic. The importance of her entrance into his life, Brown concludes, was immeasurable. "Everything I am and everything I have I owe to my mother," he told Rachel L. Jones of the *Detroit Free Press*. "Her strength and character are my greatest inspiration, always have been and always will be."

The confidence that Brown's adoptive mother had in him, the belief that he was capable of greatness, was not shared by his teachers. As a child he found excitement in typical boyhood misadventures. He liked to have fun, and he liked attention. Overactive and mischievous, Brown was a poor student because he was unable to concentrate, especially in reading. His restlessness and inattentiveness, coupled with his teachers' insufficient insight into his true capabilities, resulted in his being labeled "educably mentally retarded" in the fifth grade. It was a label he found hard to remove, in large part because he did not try. "They said I was slow so I held to that pace," he recounted in his book.

A major lesson Brown imparts early in Live Your Dreams is that "there comes a time when you have to drop your burdens in order to fight for yourself and your dreams." It was another significant figure in Brown's early life who awakened his listless consciousness and brought about this awareness: LeRoy Washington, a speech and drama instructor at Booker T. Washington High School in Miami. While in high school, Brown "used to fantasize being onstage speaking to thousands of people," he related to Jones, "and I used to write on pieces of paper, I am the world's greatest orator."

But it wasn't until he encountered Washington that he truly learned of the sound and power of eloquent speech to stir and motivate. Brown related in his book that when he once told Washington in class that he couldn't perform a task because he was educably mentally retarded, the instructor responded, "Do not ever say that again! Someone's opinion of you does not have to become your reality." Those words provided Brown's liberation from his debilitating label. "The limitations you have, and the negative things that you internalize are given to you by the world," he wrote of his realization. "The things that empower you — the possibilities — come from within."

Brown read books on public speaking and studied the habits of established speakers. He first spoke to grade school students, then high school students. Clubs and organizations followed. Less than four years later, in 1989, he received the National Speakers Association's highest award—the Council of Peers Award of Excellence—becoming the first African American to receive such an honor. He was known in professional circles as "The Motivator."

"Victories can become obstacles to your development if you unconsciously pause too long to savor them," Brown wrote in his book. "Too many people interpret success as sainthood. Success does not make you a great person; how you deal with it decides that. You must not allow your victories to become ends unto themselves." His goal was not just to win awards, but to inspire people to pursue their own goals.

（来源：http://www.browsebiography.com/bio-les_brown_speaker.html）

Passage B

3.5 Warm-up 环节

英语名言：美国励志演说家 Les Brown 有关梦想、奋斗、成功的论述

以下为 Les Brown 有关梦想和奋斗的观点，也是他对自身成功经验的总结。教师可在导入环节引导学生阅读以下名言，探讨 Les Brown 的动力来源，以及在准备过程中锲而不舍的信念支撑，帮助学生深入理解梦想与奋斗的主题内涵。

- Listen to yourself the voice that's in your heart not your head, it will lead you to your goal.
- Your dream was given to you. If someone else can't see it for you, that's fine, it was given to you and not them. It's your dream. Hold it. Nourish it. Cultivate it!
- Goals help you channel your energy into action.
- Other people's opinion of you does not have to become your reality.
- Just because fate doesn't deal you the right cards, it doesn't mean you should give up. It just means you have to play the cards you get to their maximum potential.
- Be willing to go all out, in pursuit of your dream. Ultimately it will pay off. You are more powerful than you think you are. Go for it.

3.6 Discussion 环节

英文演讲：How Not to Follow Your Dream（5个扼杀梦想的做法）

人人都有梦想，追梦时人们往往关注如何实现目标，但很少思考哪些因素会阻碍目标的实现。巴西作家 Bel Pesce 在演讲中总结了5个扼杀梦想的做法：相信一夜成名、相信别人有你想要的答案、满足一时的成功、怨天尤人、相信只有目标本身才是最重要的。教师可据此启发学生思考追梦过程中需要避免哪些思维误区和错误做法，讨论如何坚持自己的梦想。

I dedicated the past years to understanding how people achieve their dreams. When we think about dreams we have, and the dent we want to leave in the universe, it is striking to see how big of an overlap there is between the dreams we have and projects that never happen. So I'm here to talk to you today about five ways how not to follow your dreams.

One: Believe in overnight success. You know the story, right? The Tech guy built a mobile App and sold it very fast for a lot of money. You know the story may seem real, but I bet it's incomplete. If you go investigate further, the guy has done 30 Apps before and he has done a master's on the topic, a Ph.D. He has been working on a topic for like twenty years. It is really interesting. I, myself have a story in Brazil that people think is an overnight success. I come from a humble family, and two weeks before the deadline to apply for MIT, I started application process. And, voilà! I got in. People may think it's an overnight success, but that only worked because for the seventeen years prior to that, I took life and education seriously. Your overnight success story is always a result of everything you've done in your life through that moment.

Two: Believe someone else has the answers for you. Constantly, people want to help out, right? All sorts of people, your family, your friends or business partners, they all have opinions on which path you should take: "And let me tell you, go through this pipe." But whenever you go inside, there are other ways you have to pick as well. And you need to make those decisions yourself. No one else has the perfect answers for your life. And you need to keep picking those decisions, right? The pipes are infinite and you're going to bump your head, and it's a part of the process.

Three: It's very subtle but very important. Decide to settle when growth is guaranteed. So when your life is going great, you have put together a great team, and you have growing revenue, and everything is set—time to settle. When I launched my first book, I work really, really hard to distribute it everywhere in Brazil. With that, over three million people downloaded it, over fifty thousand people bought physical copies. When I wrote a sequel, some impact was guaranteed. Even if I did little, sales would be okay. but okay is never okay. When you're growing towards a peak, you need to work harder than ever and find yourself another peak. Maybe if I did little, a couple hundred thousand people would read it, and that's great already. But if I work harder than ever, I can bring this number up to millions. That's why I decided, with my new book, to go to every single state of Brazil. And I can already see a higher peak. There's no time to settle down.

Fourth tip, and that's really important: Believe the fault is someone else's. I constantly see people saying, "Yes, I had this great idea, but no investor had the vision to invest." "Oh, I created this great product, but the market is so bad, the sales didn't go well." Or, "I can't find a good talent; my team is so below expectations." If you have dreams, it's your responsibility to make them happen. Yes, it may be hard to find a talent. Yes, the market may be bad. But if no one invested in your idea, if no one bought your product, for sure there is something that is your fault. Definitely. You need to get your dreams and make them happen. And no one achieved their goals alone. But if you didn't make them happen, it's your fault and no one else's. Be responsible for your dreams.

And on last tip, and this one is really important as well: Believe that the only things that matter are the dreams themselves. Once I saw an ad, and it was a lot of friends, they were going up a mountain, it was a very high mountain, and it was a lot of work. You could see that they were sweating and this was tough. And they were going up, and they finally made it to the peak. Of course, they decided to celebrate, right? I'm going to celebrate, so, "Yes! We make it, we're at the top!" Two seconds later, one looks at the other and says, "Okay, let's go down." Life is never about the goals themselves. Life is about the journey. Yes, you should enjoy the goals themselves, but people think that you have dreams, and whenever you get to reaching one of those dreams, it's a magical place where happiness will be all around. But achieving a dream is a momentary sensation, and your life is not. The only way to really achieve all of your dreams is to fully enjoy every step of your journey. That's the best way. And your journey is simple—it's made of steps. Some steps will be right on. Sometimes you will trip. If it's right on, celebrate, because some people wait a lot to celebrate. And if you tripped, turn that into something to learn. If every step becomes something to learn or something to celebrate, you will for sure enjoy the journey.

So, five tips: Believe in overnight success, believe someone else has the answers for you, believe that when growth is guaranteed, you should settle down, believe that fault is someone else's, and believe that only the goals themselves matter. Believe me, if you do that, you will destroy your dreams.

（来源：TED Talks）

3.7 Critical thinking 环节

英语文章：How to Know When It's Time to Give up?

放弃还是坚持？这是个问题。本文分析了5种该适时放弃的情形。教师可安排学生阅读文章，结合课文观点和自身实际经历，思考：是否同意在有些情况下最好放弃而不是坚持？

You might be experiencing a situation that isn't working and wondering whether you should persevere a little longer. You might wonder whether more time will allow you to fix the problem or reach the goal. After all, people always say, "Never give up."

How do you know when it's time to give up? Here are five signs that might help you decide.

Your quest to solve a problem takes over all other aspects of your life.

If you feel that you're not enjoying life to the fullest because you can't stop thinking about your situation, it might be time to reconsider the reasons you continue trying.

I became so overwhelmed by my desire to improve my marriage that I stopped focusing on my friends, family, and career. Don't let this happen to you.

Working toward a worthwhile goal should be elating and exciting. Lack of excitement about achieving what you think you want probably means that you've become used to striving and never arriving. It's "what you do," and this routine doesn't serve you.

Also, you may be justifying a painful situation in the name of psychological comfort. Fear of the unknown or of upsetting other people could be the true driver of your efforts because perceived safety and popularity are comforting.

What would your life be like if you stopped trying? Notice the first feeling that arrives when you ask this question. A feeling of freedom or exhilaration is a sign you are ready to give up.

You aren't able to visualize a positive outcome.

If you continue working to achieve a goal and yet, it seems like an impossible dream to be successful, you'll sabotage your own efforts.

In a quiet place, contemplate the realization of your goal in detail. Can you clearly picture the resolution of your problem? Can you see yourself succeeding and feeling good about your success? If not, it's a good idea to reassess your commitment to the goal.

When I dreamed about a fairytale ending to my marriage issues, my inner voice would often tell me there was a very small chance I would succeed.

However, my rational mind would kick in, and I would find new reasons to keep trying. This process of rationalization would eventually make me feel even worse about the possible outcome.

You start to feel poorly about yourself.

Not being able to achieve your goal might result in self-doubt about your abilities. You might wonder whether there is something wrong with you.

In most cases, a job, relationship, or project that hurts your self-worth isn't worth it.

You're the only person who shows interest in solving the problem or reaching the goal, but the outcome also depends on other people.

This is particularly relevant in relationships.

If you are the only person who initiates contact with a friend or the only one who takes action to improve a relationship, it's unlikely that the relationship will thrive or even survive.

Letting go of relationships in which you're the only person invested will produce temporary pain, but once you've overcome the negative emotions, you'll be able to welcome loving and uplifting people into your life.

When you wake up in the morning, your first thought is to give up.

You're most attuned to your intuition when you first open your eyes after a night of rest, and your intuition always knows what is in your best interest.

The emotional pain I experienced when I chose to silence my inner voice wasn't needed or worth it. Trust that your intuition is guiding you to the places you're meant to go, the career you're meant to have, and the people you're meant to meet.

Making the decision to give up might not be easy, but will open the door to fulfilling and joyful life experiences. Letting go will set you on a path of learning, growth, and expansion!

（来源：https://tinybuddha.com/blog/how-to-know-when-its-time-to- give-up/）

3.8 主题拓展资源

双语视频：年轻人一定要奋斗吗？

视频慷慨激昂、催人奋进，传达了对人类意志韧性十足、无坚不摧的坚定信念，鼓励人们直面恐惧、挫折和失败，坚定梦想，不妥协，不放弃，在坚持中找到前行的方向。视频可作为课文补充资源，深化学生对课文主题的理解。

（来源：http://open.163.com/newview/movie/free?pid=MB3VSRR8I&mid=MB3VVNVF9）

第三单元　社团提升个人素养，平衡生活积极向上
（Unit 3 Leisure Activities）

1. 思政主题：社团提升个人素养，平衡生活积极向上

2. 意义

对大学生来说，学习是第一位的，但是大学生有很多课余时间，如何合理安排好课余时间去参加社会实践，做一些有利于自身成长的事情就显得格外重要。参加学校社团一直是被提倡的社会实践方式。如果大学生能参加自己感兴趣的社团，并且能够平衡好学习和社团活动的关系，那么，参加社团活动的确会有很多益处。

社团活动使青年学生的人生态度更加积极向上。大学生通过参加公益类社团，不断提高思想觉悟，逐步树立科学的世界观和人生观，逐步树立为人民服务的思想意识，将自己个人的理想和追求与时代的发展和人民的需要结合起来。参加"青年志愿者协会"等公益组织的活动，通过走入社区、乡村、福利院、敬老院等地为他人服务，为社会无私奉献，经受社会实践的锻炼，可以使学生树立起无私奉献的价值观和世界观，树立起艰苦奋斗的精神和为人民服务的意识，使大学生的人生态度更加积极向上。

社团活动使青年学生更有集体意识与责任意识。大学生的社团活动集知识性、趣味性于一体，适合青年学生思维活跃、接受信息快、可塑性强的特点，容易被学生所接受，有利于形成向心力、凝聚力，在社团内形成了团结互助、平等友爱、共同前进的人际关系，潜移默化地使大学生的集体主义观念得以增强。社团的荣辱与每位成员休戚相关，人人希望社团发展壮大，人人都关心社团的各项事务，逐步培育了每个成员的责任意识。

社团活动使青年学生创造的潜能得以更大发挥。大学生中蕴含着巨大的创

新潜能，特别是理工科院校的大学生，他们根据自己所学专业以及自身的兴趣爱好，成立了许多科研类社团组织，将具有发明创造潜质的人聚在一起，共同进行研究创造。社团组织真正成为大学生开发潜质、展示自我的舞台。大学校园里学生们的发明创造方兴未艾，如雨后春笋般涌现。

社团活动使大学生提高了素质，陶冶了情操。大学校园里，思想理论类、文学艺术类、体育健身类社团的大量涌现，使更多大学生的理论水平、思想觉悟、文学艺术修养、身体素质等将会有较大提高。通过参加这样的社团活动，不仅使参加者学到了知识，锻炼了才能，掌握了本领，综合素质也在不知不觉中得到了提高，增强了大学生自身的修养，磨练了意志，提升了觉悟。

社团活动提高了大学生适应社会的能力。大学生在假期、周末、课余时间，放下课本，参加社团活动，广泛接触社会，与各种人交往，学到许多在课堂上难以学到的东西，使自己更了解社会、融入社会，改善"书生气十足"、看问题天真幼稚的作风，使自己思想意识接近社会现实。社会实践类社团、志愿者类社团，使学生走出校门，走向社会，深入农村，深入企业，关心社会"弱势群体"，广泛深入地了解社会，与方方面面展开交往，积极进行实习、实践活动，培育了大学生适应社会的能力与素质。

社团活动提高了大学生人际交往的能力。大学生的人际交往中，除同宿舍、同班级外，人际交往比较密切的就是社团里的同伴，而同宿舍都是同性别，同班同学也未必如社团同学这般了解，这般熟悉，这般无拘无束。在共同的爱好、共同的特长、共同的策划、研究与拼搏中，共同享受着成功的乐趣、失败的痛楚。社团同伴间有着共同的喜怒哀乐痛，共同的酸甜苦辣咸，因此，所结下的友谊也非常真挚。社团活动有时要与社会各种各样的人打交道，使青年学生的交际能力大为提高。

社团活动使大学生的个性得以发展。个性是指个人稳定的心理品质，包括个性倾向性和个性心理特征两个方面。个性倾向性包括人的需要、动机、兴趣、信念等，决定着人对现实的态度、趋向和选择；个性心理特征包括人的能力、气质和性格，决定着人的行为方式上的个人特征。每位大学生的需要、动机和兴趣、信念是不同的，所以大学生的个性发展是不同的，应因材施教。因种种条件的限制，大学的课堂教育仅仅解决了大学生的共性培养问题，要做到完全对个性的培养尚存较大差距。社团活动无疑在解决个性培养上发挥着重要作用。

3. 教学设计与思政元素的融入

Passage A

3.1 Warm-up 环节

英文文章：Clubs and Societies in Oxford University

牛津大学共有400多个学生社团，可以满足拥有各种兴趣爱好的学生的需求。下面的文章列出了牛津大学的几个社团。教师可以让学生熟悉牛津大学的社团网页，了解牛津大学都有哪些社团及如何申请，以帮助更好地理解课文内容。

There are over 400 clubs and societies covering a wide variety of interests available for you to join or attend. Below are a few examples of the range of clubs on offer.

Oxford SU (Students' Union)

As a student at Oxford, you automatically become a member of the SU. The SU is a democratic, student led and independent organisation here to represent, support and enhance the lives of Oxford students. Get involved in numerous campaigns run each year, contribute to SU run media channels — Oxide and the Oxford Student — or find out how the SU is representing your interests.

Oxford University Sport

Oxford has 83 University sports clubs, as well as countless college teams and recreational opportunities. Many colleges have their own pitches and facilities, while Oxford University Sport on Iffley Road offers a swimming pool, gym, sports hall, racket sport courts and more. It is also home to the running track on which Roger Bannister broke the four-minute mile.

Clubs and Societies

The University welcomes the contribution made to student life by clubs, societies and other organisations. With more than 150 officially recognised societies listed in the University's Register of Student Clubs, there is something for everybody. However, if you think that there is a gap to be filled, you can set up your own student society.

Common Rooms

The Junior Common Room (JCR) for undergraduates and Middle/Graduate

Common Room (MCR/GCR) for graduates refers to both a physical room and a body, of which students are members. Elected representatives will often run social events and activities as well as providing support and advice services, while providing you with a means of voicing your concerns about college affairs.

Media

Cherwell is the independent student newspaper of Oxford University.

Oxford Student is a weekly newspaper produced by and for members of the University of Oxford; it is sometimes abbreviated to The OxStu.

Isis Magazine—England's longest running independent student magazine was founded at Oxford University in 1892. The magazine runs events, a website and one print issue per term.

University Club (Graduates)

The University Club is located on Mansfield Road and offers graduates a range of sporting facilities including a gym, football and cricket pitches and social spaces such as a bar, cafe and restaurant.

Oxford Newcomers' Club

The Newcomers' Club provides a meeting point for partners of newly arrived graduate students and staff, including coffee mornings, tours of Oxford colleges, visits to museums, and coach trips to places of interest in the surrounding area.

（来源：https://www.ox.ac.uk/students/life/clubs）

3.2 Discussion 环节

英文文章：Why Should You Join a Club?

大学生参加社团的好处有很多，教师可以安排学生先阅读下面两篇英文文章，引导学生思考并讨论大学生参加社团都有哪些益处，以及除了下面的文章里提到了益处，引导学生思考并讨论：参加社团还有哪些益处？

You must have heard of the saying, "All work and no play makes Jack a dull boy".

To demonstrate interests and polish one's aptitude towards personality building clubs are created at the school level.

Some of the motivating reasons are：

Social interaction. Introvert or extrovert are two realms of our persona which define our openness to the outer world. For some, a huge gathering of friends brings fun and frolic and for the others, a novel in hand and silence on the lips frame the entire day. Clubs bring openness to those who face stage fear while creating a sense of belongingness and security in social situations.

Future leaders. Vision and confidence lay the path to a leader in making. Every student holds the potential of being foresighted about his future and extra-curricular in school acts as the base of bringing out the best out of one's human potential which a day-to-day classroom lecture may not provide.

An edge over other applicants when applying for a job after graduation. Dedication towards constructive activities and not just a rote-learner is what employers look for before impressing an individual. With a dash in personality also comes an upgraded resume that throws light upon a wholesome individual.

Stress, O, Stress go away! Not just adults but children face heavy competition while being trapped in the clutches when running in the rat race to outshine others. The increase in the weight of school bags and hustle bustle to attend tuitions post-school creates a sense of an overburdened brain leading to deterioration in performance. Clubs open up a window of exploration where a child enters into the world of vivid imagination and an interest laden staircase to success.

（来源：http://www.jphschool.com/blog/why-should-you-join-a-club-at-school）

英文文章：Benefits of Joining a Club at College

College clubs are normally centered around an interest, goal or an activity. There are clubs focused on career goals, such as a Young Entrepreneurs Club. There are also clubs focused on academic interests, such as a Programming Club or a Chemistry Club. And there are many clubs that are just focused on fun and social activities, such as a Hiking Club, a Film Club, or a Baking Club.

Joining a club at your college or university is a great way to enhance your college experience. Not only will you get to meet lots of new people, but they will all already have a common interest with you. Having that commonality will make it easier to start some real friendships. Many college friendships will last long past graduation, and could in fact last a lifetime. Meeting the right people in college will also provide you with great networking opportunities that will help you immensely in your future career.

（来源：http://www.usastudyguide.com/collegeclubs.htm）

3.3 Critical thinking 环节

英文文章： Smartphone Use Is an Addiction for a Quarter of Youngsters

有很多大学生在课余时间参加社团来提升自己的各种能力，但也有一些大学生不愿意参加社团，他们通过玩手机和电脑来打发闲暇时间。上海某大学大一、大二4000多名学生接受了一项"时间都去哪儿了"的专项调研，结果显示：手机、电脑等网络产品占据大学生大半闲暇时间。数据显示，在空余时间中，82%的学生选择网络休闲；52%的学生参加学习培训；49%的学生参加社团及各类学生组织活动；44%的学生进行运动锻炼；27%的学生选择社会实践；14%的学生兼职实习；另有4%的学生选择其他。

（来源：https://ln.qq.com/a/20140504/014007.htm）

教师可以安排学生阅读下面的英文文章，引导学生思考：大学生应该怎样科学合理地度过闲暇时间，过度使用手机会出现哪些问题？如何合理使用手机？

Experts find one in four youngsters are using the devices in a way that is consistent with behavioural addiction.

A quarter of children and young people are "problematic smartphone" users and are using the devices in a way that is consistent with behavioural addiction, research suggests.

The study, by researchers at King's College London and published in BMC Psychiatry, analysed 41 studies published since 2011 on smartphone usage and mental health involving more than 40,000 under-20s.

It showed that on average 23% of youngsters were showing signs of "problematic smartphone usage" (PSU).

The researchers defined PSU as behaviour linked to smartphone use that has an element of addiction—such as anxiety when the phone is unavailable or causing neglect of other activities.

The study also found that there are links between PSU and mental health issues such as anxiety, stress, poor sleep and depressed moods.

Advertisement

Co-senior author Dr. Nicola Kalk from the Institute of Psychiatry, Psychology and Neuroscience, said: "Smartphones are here to stay and there is a need to understand the prevalence of problematic smartphone usage.

"We don't know whether it is the smartphone itself that can be addictive or the

Apps that people use.

"Nevertheless, there is a need for public awareness around smartphone use in children and young people, and parents should be aware of how much time their children spend on their phones."

The study authors note that 22 of the studies examined were of "poor methodological quality" and that there was wide variation across the research analysed in the definitions of PSU.

Dr. Sam Chamberlain, Wellcome Trust Clinical Fellow, the Honorary Consultant Psychiatrist, University of Cambridge, said: "Research into PSU is important from a public health point of view. The authors report that approximately 10%-30% of young people in the studies included in their meta-analysis met a chosen threshold for having PSU.

"Also, PSU was associated with (by self-report measures) higher levels of depression, anxiety, and worse sleep. These results resonate with previous findings, including those on related topics such as Problematic Usage of the Internet."

He added: "One challenge for the field, in light of this valuable meta-analysis, is that PSU is not consistently defined.

"There are various rating scales, with different cut-offs and criteria, some of which have not been subjected to sufficient clinical (and other) validation."

（来源：https://news.sky.com/story/smartphone-use-is-an-addiction-for-a-quarter-of-youngsters-study-shows-11873083）

3.4 主题拓展资源

双语文章：College Life

教师可以安排学生阅读下面的两篇文章作为拓展资源，有助于学生了解美国大学的非常有特色的宿舍文化和社团情况，以及如何加入社团，如何创办自己的社团，帮助学生开阔视野，了解更多的关于美国大学社团情况。

American college and university students who live away from their families are generally housed in dormitories at least for their first year. Men and women often live in the same building, though they may live on separate floors.

远离家人的美国大学生通常需要在第一年住在学校的宿舍里。男女生常住在同一栋楼的不同楼层。

Some dorms have a theme, like an international house, where students can learn about other cultures. In language houses, students try to avoid speaking their native language. The idea is to learn a different language.

一些宿舍有一个主题，比如国际宿舍，里面的学生可以相互了解其他的文化。在语言宿舍，学生尽可能避免使用母语，其目的是要学习一门不同的语言。

Colleges and universities often have many clubs that students can join. These include political, religious and service clubs, as well as groups for activities like singing, dancing, cooking, even learning how to play magic.

大学里有很多社团供学生参加。其中包括政治、宗教与服务社团，以及唱歌、跳舞、烹饪，甚至学习魔术的活动群。

Schools may also have internal sports clubs. These are for students who do not play for a school team but want organized sports with other students.

学校也有内部运动社团。对那些不想加入校队，但是想与其他同学进行有组织运动的学生很适用。

And schools will often recognize a new club or activity if enough students are interested.

如果一个新的社团和活动吸引了足够多学生的兴趣，便会认可这一社团。

（来源：https://www.bilibili.com/video/BV1Kt411C7QR）

英文文章：Joining a Club in College

Find a club to join. Every college or university will have clubs. A large one may even have hundreds, so finding one that you like should be pretty easy.

At the beginning of the school year, there is usually a fair sponsored by the university that introduces new students to the available clubs. These fairs give you a great opportunity to get to know a lot of clubs very quickly so that you can narrow them down to your favorites. If your school doesn't host a fair, there is very likely going to be a full list of school sponsored clubs on the college's website. The list will include contact information so that you can reach out to the right person to get more information about a club.

Find out as much as you can about a club before you decide to join. Some clubs can be pretty time consuming, so you don't want to over-schedule yourself or commit to more than you can handle. There are also likely to be some expenses associated with a club, so it's best to find that out upfront and determine if it will fit in your budget.

Start your own Club. What can you do if you don't find the right club for you?

Consider starting your own club. If you have a particular interest that isn't currently met by any of the existing clubs, it is possible that there are other students who feel just like you do.

Before starting your club, you need to find out the requirements and regulations for forming a club that is officially sanctioned by the school. Every college or university will have an office that is in charge of setting up and maintaining clubs. You can find the contact for that office on the school's website. There may even be all the information that you need to get started right on the website as well.

Some schools will have an online registration process, but usually there will also be a requirement to have one of the officers of the club (or the person who wants to start the club) come into the office for a face-to-face meeting with a campus official. During this meeting, you will be asked to verify that you are in fact a student currently enrolled at the university. There is likely to be some other requirements as well, so make sure that you find out what those are ahead of time so that you can come fully prepared for your meeting.

Typical requirements for a starting a new college club include the following:

The club will need to have a name and a specified purpose. The university will likely be very interested in the purpose in order to make sure that it is actually different from other existing clubs, and that it also doesn't violate any rules or moral standards of the university.

There is likely to be a minimum membership requirement. This makes sense; what is the point of having a club if there is no interest in the student body for it? It is a good idea to do some research ahead of time to find out if there are other students who are as interested in your club idea as you are. Talking with these students will also help you to better formulate the details of what the club will do and how it will run.

The club will need to have officers who are responsible for running it. At some point you will have to identify who these people are. Officers of the club (just like members of the club) will have to be students who are currently enrolled at the college or university.

Your particular school may have additional specific requirements. But don't be discouraged if this sounds like a lot of work. Starting your own university club will not only be a rewarding social experience, it will look excellent on a resume as a great example of leadership skills.

（来源：http://www.usastudyguide.com/collegeclubs.htm）

Passage B

3.5 Warm-up 环节

英文文章：Tips for a Well Balanced Life

对于大学生来说，平衡好学习与生活是十分重要的。其中，做好时间管理是很关键的。每天写下当天必须要完成的几项任务，分清轻重缓急。保持专注力，提高完成任务的效率。合理利用碎片时间，保持自控力。除此之外，还有安排好时间参加社团活动、社交活动、锻炼身体、健康饮食等。教师可以安排学生阅读下面的第一篇文章，借鉴文章中的建议，引导学生思考"大学生如何平衡学习和生活"以引入课文主题。第二篇文章是关于平衡生活的一些名人名言，教师可以安排学生阅读，引导学生思考并讨论自己最认同的一句名言，并阐述理由，以此引导学生对平衡生活有着更加深入的理解。

The best and safest thing is to keep a balance in your life, acknowledge the great powers around us and in us. If you can do that, and live that way, you are really a wise man.

There are many tips available everywhere about improving your life but these few tips are just simple but can change your life in a better way.

Reflect your life once in a while. There are many errands and work we have to finish each day and sometimes we don't have time to our own selves. One way of achieving balance and equilibrium is to give time also to ourselves. Meditating and reflecting could be a big help most especially in stressful situations.

Be positive. They say, if you think positive thoughts, there is no way for a negative situation because whatever your mind believes and conceive, for sure your body will achieve it. So, let's start to be positive all the time and we should never allow negative emotions and thoughts rule over us because it will just ruin our positive outlook and goals. Researchers said that if you want to be happy, be with happy people because positive vibes are very contagious and so our negative vibes. So, starting being with someone who are positive because they can help you a lot.

Choose foods that you eat, if possible, healthy foods. Eating healthy foods can be so common tip already, but then, it can be a bigger part of our overall health. Eating healthy foods could strongly contribute to our healthy life.

Healthy foods such as: vegetables, fruits, high in antioxidants, wheat, grains, beans, high in protein, milk.

Avoid foods that are: high in sugar, high in salt, have more additives, more preservatives, found in fast foods, high in fat, high in bad cholesterol, canned goods, superficial foods.

Drink a lot of water and fluids. Do not take water for granted because it has a vital role in our health. It is healthier to drink plain water than to drink beverages that are rich in sugar such as sodas and juices.

Detoxify regularly. Detoxification is a process by eating raw foods and pure water in a span of days in order to eliminate toxins and free radicals which are very harmful to our body.

Avoid toxins. Sometimes we are not aware that we have ingested toxic materials already and it is very hazardous for our health. One concrete example is eating junk food and canned foods. We should avoid these foods because it is high in toxins.

Exercise regularly. One way of achieving a healthy body is through exercise. But we should also be aware that it is not done by exercise alone but by some tips as well.

Go natural. Natural in a sense means that you should avoid superficial things in yourself like make-ups. Yes, it can cover blemishes but it will look girls really fake. Just always remember that being bare is natural and less is more.

Love and give worth to yourself. This is the most important tip above all. Love and give yourself a worth, and others will give them to you too. If you want others to love you, you should also show that you love yourself. Nothing is more important than taking care of yourself.

（来源：http://www.tomcorsonknowles.com/blog/tips-for-a-well-balanced-life/）

英文文章：Quotes on Balanced Life

Enjoy these balanced life quotes. We all need balance in our lives.

Be moderate in order to taste the joys of life in abundance.

—Epicurus

Balance. The Ultimate Goal.

—Ricky Lankford

It is better to rise from life as from a banquet — neither thirsty nor drunken.

—Aristotle

I have the feeling that in a balanced life one should die penniless. The trick is dismantling.

—Art Garfunkel

Fortunate, indeed, is the man who takes exactly the right measure of himself and holds a just balance between what he can acquire and what he can use.

—Peter Latham

Be aware of wonder. Live a balanced life—learn some and think some and draw and paint and sing and dance and play and work every day some.

—Robert Fulghum

Happiness is not a matter of intensity but of balance and order and rhythm and harmony.

—Thomas Merton

Balance, peace, and joy are the fruit of a successful life. It starts with recognizing your talents and finding ways to serve others by using them.

—Thomas Kinkade

The best and safest thing is to keep a balance in your life, acknowledge the great powers around us and in us. If you can do that, and live that way, you are really a wise man.

—Euripides

They are sick that surfeit with too much, as they that starve with nothing.

—William Shakespeare

To go beyond is as wrong as to fall short.

—Confucius

We find our energies are actually cramped when we are overanxious to succeed.

—Michel de Montaigne

Work, love and play are the great balance wheels of man's being.

—Orison Swett Marden

Wisdom is your perspective on life, your sense of balance, your understanding of how the various parts and principles apply and relate to each other.

—Steven R. Covey

Problems arise in that one has to find a balance between what people need from you and what you need for yourself.

—Jessye Norman

A well-developed sense of humor is the pole that adds balance to your steps as you walk the tightrope of life.

—William Arthur Ward

We come into this world head first and go out feet first; in between, it is all a matter of balance.

—Paul Boese

We can be sure that the greatest hope for maintaining equilibrium in the face of any situation rests within ourselves.

—Francis J. Braceland

So divinely is the world organized that every one of us, in our place and time, is in balance with everything else.

—Johann Wolfgang von Goethe

I've learned that you can't have everything and do everything at the same time.

—Oprah Winfrey

What I dream of is an art of balance.

—Henri Matisse

The calm and balanced mind is the strong and great mind; the hurried and agitated mind is the weak one.

—Wallace D. Wattles

Next to love, balance is the most important thing.

—John Wooden

（来源：https://www.essentiallifeskills.net/balancedlifequotes.html）

3.6 Discussion 环节

英文文章: How to Succeed in College

大学生活是人生中最为多姿多彩的一段时光，学业和分数不是大学的全部。文章鼓励大学生广泛探索自己的兴趣、专业、走出课堂，通过多样的方式获取资源、探索自己人生的可能性，同时也要注意通过特定方式保持身心健康。教师可以安排学生阅读下面两篇文章，借鉴文章中的建议，引导学生讨论：如何通过不同的方式，平衡好学习和生活的关系，拥抱多彩的大学生活？

It's easy to get tunnel vision when you're working toward a college degree, but you should aspire to more than good grades and graduation. When you finally have that diploma in hand, will you truly feel satisfied? What will you have truly learned and accomplished?

Grades are of course crucial to earning your degree and helping you get into graduate school, but academic success also includes what happens outside your classes. As you take the steps necessary to earn a diploma, look around: College campuses are full of opportunities to experience new activities and meet people who can help you grow.

Explore different subjects

You may arrive at college with a specific career track in mind, or you may not have the slightest idea of what you want to major in. No matter which end of the spectrum you're on, let yourself explore a variety of courses. Take an intro class in a field you know nothing about. Sit it on an unusual seminar. You never know — you may discover something you didn't know you'd love.

Follow your instincts

There will undoubtedly be many people giving you advice about what you should do during — and after — college. Take your time exploring your interests, and once it comes time to make decisions about your future, pick a career and course of study that suits you, not your parents. Pay attention to what excites you and make sure you're happy with your academic plans. Once you've made a choice, feel confident in your decision.

Take advantage of the resources around you

Once you've decided on a major — or even a career — make the most of the time you have left, be it one year or four. Take classes from the best professors in your department. Stop them by during their office hours to get feedback on your performance and ask any questions you couldn't get answered in class. Grab coffee with your favorite professors and talk about what they love about their field.

This concept goes beyond professors, too. If you're struggling with a certain subject or assignment, see if there's a study group or tutoring center that can help you overcome the obstacle. No one expects you to figure out everything on your own.

Find ways to learn outside the classroom

You'll only spend so many hours attending class and doing homework — what are you doing with the remaining hours of your day? How you spend your time outside of the classroom is a critical part of your college experience. Make it a priority to branch out, because you're unlikely to have another time in your life where you can so frequently try new things. In fact, the "real world" is a lot more like what you'll encounter in extracurricular activities than in the classroom, so make time for them.

Join a club or organization that explores your interests and passions. You could even run for a leadership position and develop skills that will serve you later in your career. Consider learning about a different culture by studying abroad. See if you have the opportunity to earn course credit by completing an internship. Attend events put on by clubs you're not a member of. No matter what you do, you'll almost certainly learn something new — even if it's just something new about yourself.

Allow yourself to be happy

College is not just about fulfilling your academic aspirations. You need to enjoy your life at college, too. Make sure to make time in your schedule for the things that keep you healthy, whether it is about going to the gym or attending religious services. Make time to talk to your family, hang out with your friends, eat well, and get enough sleep. In other words: take care of all of yourself, not just your brain.

（来源：https://www.thoughtco.com/how-to-succeed-in-college-793219）

英文文章：5 Tips for Living a Well Balanced Life

A well-balanced life is essential for personal effectiveness, peace of mind and living well. Whether we work, go to school or are retired, we all have responsibilities.

There is always someone, or something, to answer to. There are things we want to do and things we must.

The challenge is to balance what we must do with what we enjoy and choose to do. This is not always easy. If, however, we are unable to reduce stress and manage a well balanced life there can be physical and/or emotional health consequences.

Tips for living a well balanced life:

Take care of and nurture yourself

You cannot accomplish anything if you're unhealthy. Get plenty of rest, exercise and eat properly. Many of us think we can burn the candle at both ends, eat junk food, get very little exercise, and still function adequately. You may be able to get away with this for a while when you're young, however, at some point, this life style catches up with the best of us. Burnout is a real possibility.

Ideally, set aside time each day for an activity that you enjoy, such as walking, working out or listening to music. Or, allow yourself to unwind after a hectic day by reading, meditating or taking a nice hot bath.

Know what your priorities are

Balance does not entail cramming in every activity possible. Examine your values and decide what's important to you; then set your boundaries. You may be in the process of building a career, starting a family or going to school. Depending on what stage you're at in life, your focus and energies will be different.

Avoid becoming overwhelmed by juggling too many big projects in your life at once. Maybe planning a wedding is not a good idea when you're studying for the bar exam. Nor, is starting a family when you are unsure about your career direction, or relationship status.

Not knowing what you want and trying to do everything at once can be a recipe for disaster instead of the road to leading a well-balanced life. As the saying goes, "do not bite off more than you can chew."

Create an efficient mindset

Be organized and plan ahead. Take time at the beginning of each week to assess what needs to be done. Make a to-do list in a planner or calendar for upcoming appointments, impending exams or meetings to attend.

Be sure also to allow for recreation and quality time for yourself and your family. Taking the time to connect with family and friends will recharge your batteries and make you more efficient in a long run.

Expect the unexpected

Rather than get stressed and upset, learn to roll with the punches when something over which you have no control happens. You could get stuck in traffic, your computer could crash, or your child could get sick with the chickenpox. Stuff happens. We've all experienced the unexpected. If you accept that anything can happen at any time, it's less likely it throws you off your stride when it does. Be able to adjust your game plan.

Note also, that there are times when achieving balance may not be possible. For instance, you may have a family or career crisis that needs your immediate and undivided attention. It may require an exceptional amount of your time and resources. When that happens, do whatever it takes and when things go back to normal take time to refresh and rejuvenate yourself.

Maintain a positive mental attitude

Begin each day with the intention of making the best and most of it. It may not always go as planned, but it can go more smoothly if you put it in perspective.

Part of living a well-balanced life is learning how to deal with adversity, unforeseen events and uncertainty. If you practice not letting things get to you, you will not only learn to live a well balanced and less stressful life, you will learn to live in and savor the moment. Once you've done everything you can within your control, let your life unfold. Be prepared for the future, but don't worry about it.

While we can't anticipate and plan for everything in our lives, we can decide how, where and when to concentrate our energies.

This may require some critical thinking and problem solving abilities, but in the end, it will lead to a much less-stressed and a well-balanced life.

（来源：https://www.essentiallifeskills.net/wellbalancedlife.html）

3.7 Critical thinking 环节

英文文章：Having the Time of Your Life at University?

与漫长枯燥的中学生活相比，大学生活使学生拥有更大自主权，更为丰富多彩的大学生活会令人更加向往。大学生们离开父母和家乡，去往更广阔的地方，结识新的朋友，但往往也面临学业压力大、焦虑、自我怀疑、缺乏归属感等问题。文章指出，一项针对伦敦帝国理工学院学生的调查显示，四分之三的学生在大学期间都承受了较大的心理压力。心理咨询专家针对这一现象给出了一些能够减轻大学生压力的建议。教师可基于材料请学生针对以下问题进行思考，以加深对课文主题的理解：What difficulties have you experienced at college campus? What did you do to get through the hard time?

University—the best days of my life! I made lots of friends in my student dorm, went to great parties, joined the debating society... and, well, I did some work too—but I must confess my lecturers were very patient with my tardiness.

It's easy to look back at our university days through rose-tinted spectacles but the truth is that when we first arrived on campus, most of us were out of our comfort zone.

In fact, a survey of students at Imperial College London has revealed that 3 out of 4 students experience high levels of stress, or a mental health condition, during their time at college. The survey, completed by over a thousand students, also found that 70% of those that experience stress do so at least once a week, and 9% of students feel stressed constantly.

Kirsty, a student at Exeter University, didn't enjoy her first days in college. She says: "When I first got to university, I don't think I'd realized that I'd forgotten how to make friends. I'd been with the same school friends for seven years, and so I was trying to balance social success with academic success whilst learning how to look after myself at quite a young age."

Dr. Ruth Caleb of the counselling service at Brunel University in London has some tips that should make life easier for students before they set off for university. She says: "Certain things that I think it would be very helpful for students to have put in place are an ability to do the practical things of life — to do the washing, to do the cleaning and so on — being able to cook. Budgeting is extremely important in university life." And Caleb adds: "You should learn how to spend time on your own comfortably."

I graduated and learnt how to take care of myself the hard way. I hope that new students these days remember to acquire some life skills before they make the big jump.

（来源：http://www.xdf.cn/bbc/yingyu/201511/10375651.html）

3.8 主题拓展资源

英文文章：How Much Time Should I Spend on Studying in College?

对于大学生来说，学习仍然是十分重要的任务，因为大学是学习专业知识的平台，专业知识掌握的好坏直接影响着步入社会后的生存状况。对于想要保研或者考研的学生来说，学习就更加重要了。当然，除了学习，大学生还应该重视提高自己各方面的能力。那么，大学生到底应该花费多少时间在学习上呢？教师可以安排学生阅读下面第一篇文章，进一步了解关于大学生在学习方面的一些看法。第二篇文章是关于大学生交朋友的一些建议，教师可以安排学生进行阅读，帮助他们在学业之余，学会建立健康良好的社交关系。第三篇文章关于保持生活平衡，教师可以安排学生进行阅读，从而对保持平衡生活的重要性以及如何保持平衡生活有了更加深刻的了解。

There's no "right" way to study in college. Even students who have the same majors and take the same classes won't need to spend the same amount of time on coursework because everyone has their own way of learning. That being said, there's a common rule of thumb students and professors use to determine how much time to allocate for studying in college: for each hour you spend in class, you should spend two to three hours studying outside class.

How Should I Study?

Of course, that "outside class" studying can take on different forms: You might take the "traditional" approach to studying by sitting in your room, poring over a textbook or reading assignment. Or perhaps you'll spend time online or in the library further researching topics your professor mentioned in class. Maybe you'll have a lot of lab work to do or a group project that requires meeting other students after class.

The point is studying can take many forms. And, of course, some classes require students to work outside class a lot more time than others. Focus more on what sort of studying will help you complete your necessary coursework and get the most out of your education, rather than trying to meet a specific study-hours quota.

Why Should I Track How Much I Study?

While prioritizing the quality over the quantity of your study time is more likely to help you accomplish your academic goals, it's smart to keep track of how much time you spend doing it. First of all, knowing how much time to spend studying in college can help you gauge if you're spending enough time on your academics. For example, if you're not performing well on exams or assignments — or you get negative feedback from a professor — you can reference the amount of time you've spent studying to determine the best way to proceed: you could try spending more time studying for that class to see if it improves your performance. Conversely, if you've already invested a lot of time in that course, perhaps your poor grades are an indication it's not an area of study that suits you.

Beyond that, tracking how you study can also help you with time management, a skill all college students need to develop. (It's pretty handy in the real world, too.) Ideally, understanding your out-of-class workload can help you avoid cramming for exams or pulling all-nighters to meet an assignment deadline. Those approaches are not only stressful, but they're often not very productive either.

The better you understand how much time it takes you to engage with and comprehend the course material, the more likely you are to reach your academic goals. Think of it this way: you've already invested a lot of time and money going to class, so you might as well figure out how much time you need to do everything necessary for getting that diploma.

（来源：https://www.thoughtco.com/time-to-spend-studying-in-college- 793230）

英文文章：How I Got Past the Small Talk and Made Friends at Uni?

It's been over a year since I moved to Liverpool and started university. One of the things I was most nervous about was getting to know and make friends with my coursemates.

I've never been that good at starting conversations with people, and the fact that I moved to a completely different country where I didn't know anyone really didn't help my nerves.

I was worried about feeling lonely and homesick, so decided to throw myself into things to try to avoid this. Below, you'll find some of my top tips on how to become friends with other students if you're new to uni or feeling lonely.

Join (or create) a group chat

There are usually a bunch of Facebook groups for freshers at your university, and it's a great place to find or socialise with coursemates and potential friends. Join a group chat for your specific course, or start one if there isn't one yet.

If you're not very confident, this can be a really big help, as it gives you the opportunity to get to know people without the awkwardness you might feel in person. This group chat tends to turn into the place where you can complain or discuss uni questions that you might not want to talk to your tutors about.

It's also a great place to make plans with people. Tell them about a cool event you saw going on, or about a restaurant you walked past, and ask if someone wants to go with you. There are probably a lot of people in the same position as you, so if you take the initiative and ask, I guarantee someone is going to take you up on it.

Connect on social media

Looking up and following the people on your course is a great place to get conversation starters from. Their Instagram pictures can give you conversation ideas. For example, if they've uploaded a picture from their summer holiday, ask them what they did during the summer.

Getting away from the standard questions about their name, where they're from and what A-levels they took will help you get a conversation going.

Go to events

Universities usually have a lot of different events going on throughout the year. If you find something that sounds like fun, invite someone from your course to come with you. It might help to get out of the "small talk bubble" if you get away from the lecture hall and do something outside of the classroom.

One of my best memories from freshers' week was when I actually got out of my comfort zone and went to get drinks with some people from my course. Even though I don't drink, just going with them and getting away from the university environment helped ease the expectations of having to get to know someone.

Societies

Universities tend to have a wide range of societies focusing on different interests, so see if there are any you like the look of and join them.

While you might not become best friends with someone straight away, just being in the company of others who share your interests will help stop you from feeling lonely. And better still, you'll be doing something that you enjoy.

As you may have noticed, the biggest thing about getting away from the small talk and really getting to know your coursemates is to try to get away from class and try your best to relax.

University is a place where everyone is in the same position and everyone wants to fit in and make friends. It's the perfect place to meet some amazing and interesting people, but just remember that it doesn't always happen overnight.

（来源：https://www.unitestudents.com/the-common-room/student-living/How-I-got-past-the-small-talk-and-made-friends-at-uni）

英文文章：The Importance of Maintaining Balance

We tend to underestimate how maintaining balance contributes to living life successfully and productively.

As a sports enthusiast, I appreciate how sports are a metaphor for, or a microcosm of life, so you will find me making many comparisons and analogies.

Take the example of an Olympic athlete.

To get optimum results. He/She must train for the event in the most efficient and productive manner because the margin of error in a sporting event is miniscule.

You could win or lose in an Olympic event by a hair or one 1/100th of a second. Not a chance you would want to take.

In training. The athlete must have discipline and maintain a routine that includes the proper balance of sleep, good nutrition and exercise. He/She must also employ psychology to make sure that the necessary mindset or attitude is in place. Attitude and mindset are so important that they could make the difference between winning and losing.

If any one of these components is missing, or out of balance, the athlete will not perform well.

So it is with living life to the fullest. We don't have to adhere to the strict regimen that an Olympic athlete would, but in order to function at our best, we definitely need to balance taking care of ourselves physically, mentally and spiritually. Focusing too much on any one facet catches up with us and leads to health problems in the neglected area.

For instance, if you were to exercise too much (hard to imagine) and not take time to rest and replenish, you would injure yourself. If you read, or do a disproportionate amount of mental work, your body would lack proper circulation and fitness level.

If you spend an enormous amount of time meditating, or relaxing, your brain waves slow down and you lack mental agility.

Whenever you overdo it in any aspect of your life, you lose perspective and balance. As Aristotle said: "Moderation in all things."

How do we maintain balance in our lives?

Know yourself and how much rest, food and exercise you need to function at your best. There are many good books and websites that give great advice on diet and exercise. Decide what works best for you and implement it into your routine.

Keep your mind alert and in shape. As mentioned in the *10 Positive Habits to Develop*, try to learn a new piece of information each day, even if it's in conversation with your spouse and children at the dinner table.

Stay connected with family and friends. At the end of the day share with your spouse and children how the day went for each of you. We lead busy lives, but we should never be too busy to connect with and make at least one phone call to a parent, sibling or friend during the day.

Do something spontaneous. Our lives can be too regimented at times so it's a good idea to do something out of the ordinary every now and then. During your lunch one day go for a pedicure or massage. Take a drive in the countryside one afternoon. On the weekend go to a concert (rock, opera or symphony).

Make time for yourself. Each evening take time to unwind. If that means leaving the dishes overnight, so be it. Take a nice bath, read from the book you started, or listen to some soothing music.

We can all learn from elite athletes who, by knowing how to balance their training routines, are able to function at optimum levels.

（来源：https://www.essentiallifeskills.net/balance.html）

第四单元　青年人要艰苦奋斗、自立自强
（Unit 4 Living on Your Own）

1. 思政主题：青年人要艰苦奋斗、自立自强

2. 意义

为实现中华民族伟大复兴的中国梦而奋斗，是当代中国青年运动的时代主题。青年兴则国家兴，青年强则国家强。党的十八大以来，习近平总书记对青年成长成才问题作出了一系列重要论述。这些重要论述，指明了当代青年成长成才的正确方向，明确了广大青年追逐梦想的历史担当。教育部中国特色社会主义理论体系研究中心韩振峰撰文指出，在实现"两个百年"奋斗目标、贯彻落实"四个全面"战略布局的伟大征程上，广大青年建功立业的舞台空前广阔、梦想成真的前景空前光明。

任何美好的理想，都不会唾手可得，都需要经过不懈努力。在新的历史条件下，继续弘扬中华民族自强不息、艰苦奋斗的精神，既是贯彻落实"四个全面"战略布局的内在要求，也是当代青年成长成才的必由之路。当前，我们国家既面临着重要发展机遇，也面临着前所未有的困难和挑战。实现"两个百年"奋斗目标，实现中华民族伟大复兴的中国梦，需要广大青年锲而不舍、继续奋斗。

"自强不息、艰苦奋斗"不是一句简单的口号，而是必须落实到每个人的行动上。习近平总书记指出，"广大青年要牢记'空谈误国、实干兴邦'，立足本职、埋头苦干，从自身做起，从点滴做起，用勤劳的双手、一流的业绩成就属

于自己的人生精彩""要勇于创业、敢闯敢干,努力在改革开放中闯新路、创新业,不断开辟事业发展新天地"。这是党中央对当代青年提出的殷切希望。

习近平总书记指出,青春由磨砺而出彩,人生因奋斗而升华。面对突如其来的新冠肺炎疫情,全国各族青年积极响应党的号召,踊跃投身疫情防控人民战争、总体战、阻击战,不畏艰险、冲锋在前、真情奉献,展现了当代中国青年的担当精神,赢得了党和人民高度赞誉。我为你们感到骄傲!

因此,在大学英语的教学中,融入青年人要艰苦奋斗,自立自强的思政主题,有助于培养青年大学生自立自强、艰苦奋斗和锲而不舍的精神,为实现中华民族伟大复兴的中国梦而贡献力量。

(来源:新华社、人民网、中国共产党新闻网)

3. 教学设计与思政元素的融入

在过去的20年中,超过500名在北京大学工作的安保人员被录取入读北京大学研究生院或成为大学讲师。他们利用工作之余,广泛阅读文史哲著作,通过撰写日记和抄写故事等方式提高技能,最终成功改变命运。一个人的社会地位是由自己的努力决定的,如果放弃梦想和尝试,将永远不知道是否能有所成就。教师可以请学生阅读文章,培养学生积极向上、追求进步的品质,树立正确的人生观、奋斗观。

"Crouching Tiger, Hidden Dragon": How Security Guards Turned into Educators

More than 500 security guards working at Peking University were admitted to graduate schools or became university instructors in the last 20 years, a recent report revealed.

This figure from one of China's most prestigious post-secondary institutions transforms the stereotype that security guards are under-educated. Their achievements may not seem as glittery as the number of Chinese obtaining degrees overseas, but with a full-time job and family to take care of they have to exert more effort than many on studying.

Netizens have therefore joked that "Peking University security guards are truly 'crouching tigers and hidden dragons'."

Stories of the Peking guards

Wang Guiming, leader of Peking University's security team of 500 guards, said that most of the security personnel have graduated from college; a small number have a bachelor's degree, and 12 made it to graduate schools.

Former NBA all-star Kobe Bryant once asked the reporter in an interview "Do you know what Los Angeles looks like at 4 o'clock in the morning?" after being asked to reveal the secret of his success.

"It is still in the dark at 4 a.m., but I had already gotten up by then and was walking in the dark streets," he said. "More than 10 years passed and the darkness in the streets of Los Angeles was still there at 4 a.m., but I had become a basketball player with strong muscles, excellent physical fitness, strength and a high field goal percentage."

And Kobe wasn't the only one chasing success while deprived of sleep: Napoleon only slept three to four hours a day and got up at 3 a.m. for work; Edison only got four to five hours of sleep a day, and he regarded sleep as a waste of time, "a heritage from our cave days."

These icons are geniuses, but still work so hard to strive for success. What can the Peking University guards do, when they lack such exceptional talents?

Zhang Juncheng, who was the first security guard at Peking campus to attend Gaokao, the national higher education entrance examination, is a vivid example of achieving success through diligence.

Back in 1995, Zhang, who had just graduated from a junior middle school in Changzhi, north China's Shanxi Province, tried different jobs before being hired as a security guard at Peking University.

However, Zhang quickly determined that higher education was the only way to gain esteem and change his life. At Peking University, Zhang embarked on his road of learning by sneaking into lectures, but thanks to help from several professors, he received special permits for some classes, including English, for the importance of knowing a second language.

One professor said he was moved by Zhang's diligence and eagerness for knowledge, and thus encouraged him to read more and "make a plan for his life." Under the guidance of such teachers, Zhang read hundreds of books with themes varying from literature, philosophy, history and English after getting off work. He also wrote diaries and transcribed stories. When the dormitory's lights went out, he continued to read by torchlight.

His efforts were spotted by Cao Yan, an English professor at the school who gave him permits for English class and encouraged him to sit the exam for continuing studies. In the autumn of 1995, Zhang attended the exam and was successfully enrolled in the law department of Peking University.

Zhang, now 41, is currently the principal of a local secondary vocational school in his hometown, and his experience has since inspired many other guards who also wish to change their social status. Zhang said over the past two decades, he has kept doing two things: keeping a diary and getting up early in the morning. Even after rising to be a school headmaster, Zhang gets up at about 6 a.m. every day to go to the school's playground.

Authentic or Fake Positive Energy?

Like Zhang, many former security guards on Peking campus were successfully enrolled into the university, after years of hard work and persistence.

The stories of the Peking University guards illustrate that a person's position in society is not decided by others, but their own efforts. We may not be born rich or good-looking, but we never know whether we can achieve something if we give up dreaming and trying.

Obeying destiny or being the master of our own lives—that may be a question that keeps us thinking with the lessons learned from people like Zhang. Overdoses of "chicken soup for the soul" may bring negative effects, but no intake at all could lead to loss of hope and passion for life.

"There is only one form of heroism in the world, and it consists in seeing the world as it is—and in loving it." So, Romain Rolland wrote in the preface of *The Life of Michael Angelo*. It is way too early to say "I can't do it" before even trying.

（来源：CGTN）

Passage A

3.1 Warm-up 环节

TED 演讲：How College Loans Exploit Students for Profit?

高昂的大学学费让美国学生不得不借助贷款来完成学业，以致学生毕业时都背负着高额贷款。可以请学生课前观看本视频，了解美国的大学教育制度及现状，思考美国大学生选择勤工俭学支付学费的原因，为课文学习增加背景知识，打开思路。

（来源：https://www.bilibili.com/video/BV1pE411f7Zt）

3.2 Discussion 环节

英文文章：Advantages & Disadvantages of Working While Going to School

进入大学后，许多学生选择勤工俭学补贴学费，有人认为这是独立自主的表现，对今后踏入社会也大有裨益，有人则认为这会对学习造成极大的负面影响。教师可请学生阅读以下素材，探讨勤工俭学对于大学生而言究竟是利大于弊还是弊大于利。

本篇文章简要介绍了学生选择勤工俭学的原因，同时从利弊两个方面探究勤工俭学的性质，提供了崭新的角度，教师可请学生阅读文章，结合自身经历开拓思路，谈谈为什么要勤工俭学，进一步思考勤工俭学的意义。

There are many reasons you might want to work part time while you are going to school. Maybe you want to save money for college, assist your family financially or learn useful job skills. On the flip side, your primary job is being a student. Working too many hours could tank your GPA, which would affect your chances of earning a scholarship and getting into your dream college or graduate school.

Percentages of Employed Students

Students with excellent time management skills can balance work and school, but most students are cautious about taking on so much responsibility. As of October 2017, about 23 percent of high school students and 44 percent of full-time college students were employed in the workforce, according to the Bureau of Labor Statistics. More females than males attending high school or college were juggling work and academics.

Reasons for Working While Studying

Money, of course, is a big motivator for students entering the workforce. Which students wouldn't like extra cash? Look at all the places around you where teens are employed — grocery stores, retail, fast food, movie theaters, swimming pools, landscaping businesses and golf courses.

Students who work enjoy the challenge, responsibility and personal satisfaction that comes with being a valued employee. Working from an early age looks great on a resume because it shows employers that you are mature, dependable and goal oriented.

Reasons Against Working While Studying

One of the biggest disadvantages of working while studying is the stress and exhaustion you may experience. Keeping a detailed planner and a list of prioritized tasks can help, but that requires self-discipline and exceptional time management skills.

You may have trouble getting enough sleep. Exercising and self-care can end up low on your priority list. You may neglect your health and end up with mono. Getting sick will cause you to miss school and work, with detrimental consequences.

Advantages of Working While Studying

Working is one of the best ways to sharpen your skills and make a name for yourself. Achieving success on the job can boost your self-confidence. If you're a gifted and talented student, you might want to be a math tutor, guitar instructor, photographer, web designer or landscaper.

You could use your imagination and think really big. Innovative high school students have started multimillion-dollar businesses by incubating and marketing a novel idea. Gaining real-world experience can help you narrow down your list of possible career choices.

Disadvantages of Working While Studying

A part-time job can be less of a benefit and more of a distraction for the typical student. You won't make a lot of money working minimum wage jobs, especially after you factor in transportation costs, meals and work clothes. College recruiters urge students to challenge themselves in high school by tackling difficult subjects, enrolling in honors programs and taking AP classes.

Selective colleges also look at leadership roles students held, community service and level of extracurricular participation. You won't have time for all that if your work shift starts right after school. Why risk your future for a few more dollars each week?

Make the Best Decision for You

Carefully weigh the pros and cons of working before submitting job applications. Consider working summers instead of during the school year, when you could be hanging out with friends at school functions.

Talk to your parents, guidance counselor, teachers and friends about the pros and cons of high school students working part time. You may hear strong opinions. Listen respectfully without arguing. Then, make a written list of the advantages and disadvantages of working while studying.

Keep in mind that some students do thrive when working while in college and in high school. Consider your energy level, your long-range plans and the sacrifices you will have to make if you devote several hours each week to work commitments. You may find it helpful to start out working just a few hours on weekends to see how things go and then slowly increase your hours.

（来源：https://www.theclassroom.com/advantages-disadvantages-of-working-while-going-to-school-12537639.html）

3.3 Critical thinking 环节

双语视频：家长是否该鼓励孩子打工？

勤工俭学有时带来的不只是物质生活质量的提升，更是个人素养上的进步。视频中两个人结合个人经历探讨"家长是否该鼓励孩子打工"这一话题，教师可请学生观看视频，思考：Do you think that part-time jobs may help to build a sense of responsibility, which in turn may enhance students' school performance?

（来源：https://www.bilibili.com/video/BV1NT4y1L7MJ）

英文文章：The Top 7 Life-changing Benefits of Working While Studying

课文 A 主要讲述了一个美国大学生在英国独立工作和生活的经历，并且强调了这种独立生活的好处。本文分享了7条勤工俭学对于人生的益处，教师可请学生阅读，思考并讨论：What are the advantages and disadvantages of part-time employment? 之后，教师可以请学生分享自己对于边上学边工作的思考。

1. Earning income

Well, earning an income is an obvious advantage of having a job.

That's more than likely why you considered having a job in the first place, unless you just love to work for free! But then, that would be called volunteering.

The money you make from working while studying could help to cover the cost for your tuition, school supplies, travel expenses, accommodation, food, and just about anything you'll need.

Even if you are studying with a full scholarship, it wouldn't hurt to earn extra bucks, it's up to you. Who doesn't like to have a few extra bucks, right?

2. Gaining experience in the workplace

In addition to earning money, having a job gives you a full immersion into the world of work.

Whether your job is online or offline, you will get to understand the dynamic within a working environment on a daily basis or however often you work.

You will get to experience the type of teamwork and hierarchical systematic processes that all come together to accomplish one goal in the end.

You will also get a glimpse of how the meritocracy system in the workplace, that is, rewards attributed to hard work which usually manifest in the form of acknowledgement, bonuses, promotions, etc.

This will encourage you to continue to work hard during school as you'll see that hard work truly pays off.

3. Networking

Working in a job that is within your study field or desired career path is ideal, which is a perfect ground for networking. But that won't be the reality for everyone.

So, sometimes we don't necessarily get a job in our study field while we are studying. However, that doesn't mean you shouldn't network.

Once you meet someone that is within your study field, a related field or any field, whom you think could guide you along your career path in some way, don't hesitate to create a solid link.

It could be a co-worker, a company partner, a client/customer or even a brand ambassador.

Networking helps you with building a professional support group or even a potential clientele for future reference.

4. Increase marketability

By the time you are done with studying, you will have a couple of months or years of experience in the workplace that you can add to your professional resume.

No matter where you worked, there is always something that you learn that you can apply in a new work environment.

For many starter jobs that allow you to be working while studying, at least one-year work experience is usually a requirement. So, the more experience you have the better.

5. Improvement of time management skills

In order to always be on time for work and handing in assignments, you will naturally try to create a strict schedule to keep you on track with everything.

You will learn how to prioritize and develop your time management skills when working while studying.

Of course, your working hours will be centered around your school schedule with room for studying if you want to successfully finish your studies.

Having a tight schedule usually forces you to stick to it in order to accomplish your goals.

6. Gaining crucial soft skills

Students learn a plethora of skills when they're exposed to a working environment.

Soft skills such as good communication and decision-making skills usually come in handy when your career kicks off.

To a selected few, such skills come naturally. However, most students acquire these skills when they start working.

In addition, working students also develop a distinct ability to manage their funds and plan their schedules.

Overall, working while studying has both benefits and drawbacks, depending on the number of hours you put in.

7. Providing a sense of independence

Getting a job while still in college allows students to get a unique sense of independence that previously didn't exist.

Most students enjoy their jobs because it offers a certain degree of financial and personal freedom.

The money they get from working while studying is used for a variety of purposes.

Some students use it to settle their rent and utility bills while others create small businesses using the same funds.

Delightfully, money opens a plethora of possibilities. But it's important for working students to learn the crucial art of financial management to avoid wasting their money on unnecessary stuff.

It's easy to get caught up in the world of drugs and alcohol — that's why self-discipline is critical.

（来源：http://suo.im/5Q19fn）

3.4 主题拓展资源

TED 演讲：How to Gain Control of Your Free Time?

时间规划专家 Laura Vanderkam 专门研究工作繁忙的人如何规划生活，并提出了一些策略帮助人们合理利用时间创造想要的生活。教师可以请学生课下观看，学习合理规划时间，思考如何平衡学习与兼职生活。

（来源：https://www.bilibili.com/video/BV1Kt411C7QR）

Passage B

3.5 Warm-up 环节

双语文章：明明你已经成年，他们却还把你当小孩

通过阅读文章，引导青年大学生在培养独立生活能力的同时，正确认识长辈的传统观念，尝试改变某些长辈的不当观念和做法。

有些老人，总是把你当作小孩儿，哪怕你成年自立很久了。一位昵称为 Starpoint 的网友在文章里称"自己 30 岁了还被奶奶当作小孩，十分苦恼"。

I'm 30 years old. I recently moved to the complete opposite coast of the country and have been living on my own successfully.

我已经三十岁了。最近还从西海岸搬到东海岸工作，一个人生活，一切都安排妥当。

When I go home for Christmas, my grandmother treats me like a child. For example, I was baking macaroni and cheese for our Christmas dinner. When it came time to take it out of the oven, she said, "maybe I should take it out". I couldn't believe it. Did she really think that I'm unable to take a dish out of the oven? I'm baking stuff all the time back in my apartment on the other side of the country.

我回家陪家人过圣诞，奶奶还把我当小孩儿对待。比如说，我在那儿做圣诞晚餐，焗芝士通心粉，到了要从烤箱里拿出来的时候，她对我说："要不我来拿吧。"我简直不敢信。她真的觉得我从烤箱里拿个通心粉都不会吗？我在千里之外自己的公寓里可是天天烤东西。

I told her calmly that I could do it, I'm not disabled, and I took it out with no problem whatsoever. Later on, she said that the reason why she said she should take it out was that the oven wasn't normal, or something and that it didn't heat properly (which made no sense to me). She also said it had a tendency to get really hot and that she didn't want her granddaughter to get burned, because she's burned herself before. I lost count of the number of times this kind of things have happened.

我心平气和跟她说："我来吧，我有手有脚的"。然后我把它拿了出来，一点事儿没有。之后，她解释说，自己之所以不让我拿是因为烤箱坏了什么的，加热不正常（这根本说不通）。她还说那个烤箱可能会过热，她自己就被烫到过，不想我也被烫。我已经数不清这种事发生过多少次了。

I have never asked her or any other family members for money (all the money that I have, I earn it from working), I don't break the law, I take care of my cat, I hold down a job, pay rent, my credit card, school loans, and bills on time, trying new things, being independent, traveling on my own without any help, starting therapy to deal with my social anxieties, doing everything that I can possibly do to take responsibility for myself and to be an independent, productive adult.

我从来没跟她或者其他家人要过钱（我现在所有的钱都是自己的劳动所得），我遵纪守法、好好照顾我的猫、踏实地做工作、交房租、还信用卡上的钱、还大学贷款、按时交煤气水电费、尝试新事物、独立自主生活、一个人旅行无须任何帮助、有社会焦虑还会去看心理医生，以及做一切对自己负责的事、做一个独立且高产出的成年人。

I'm by no means perfect, but I'm not relying on family members to dig me out of things and I take care of myself.

当然我绝不完美，但我也没有依赖家里人让他们把我从泥淖里救出来，我能把自己照顾好。

Of course, I appreciate that she's trying to look after me, but it bothers me that despite all I've done, I'm still being treated like I'm unable to do anything. No matter how hard I work to be a productive, responsible adult, she still treats me like I can't do anything.

当然了，我很感谢她这么愿意照顾我。但是我自立这么久，她还这么做，我就有点想不明白了。不论我多么努力工作，尽量成为一个高效又负责的成年人，她还是像我什么都不会一样对待我。

I was treated like that all my life and that's why I generally lacked confidence of growing up. I'm working on building that confidence, and it all goes away when I come back home. Because it seems like my family wants to keep me a little sheltered protected girl forever.

我一直都被这样对待着，这也是为什么我在长大的过程中一直不够自信的原因。我不断在努力建立这种自信，但一回家，就崩盘，因为我的家人看起来还是想把我当成一个需要保护的小女生。

We have a word called gedaiqin (intergenerational love): parents pass their love on to their grandchildren as a way to love their own children.

有个词叫作"隔代亲"（跨越代际的亲密）：祖父母辈会把爱传递给孙辈，以示他们爱自己的孩子。

This is a Chinese tradition I learned from my parents: they helped me care for my two children, and I was brought up by my grandmother. I want to contribute to our children's and grandchildren's lives, and this makes me very happy, very proud and satisfied. This is what a family means.

这是我从我的父母那儿学来的中国传统。他们帮我带我的两个小孩，而我呢，也是由我的奶奶带大的。我想带孙子，给我子女减轻负担，这么做，我也很开心，很骄傲，很满足。这也就是家庭的意义。

（来源：https://mp.weixin.qq.com/s/Fh_SsB7zjpEBmBE5IbQjUA）

3.6 Discussion 环节

双语文章："48岁啃老男宅家7年"引热议

通过让学生阅读这篇文章并讨论关于对"啃老"的看法，鼓励大学生摒弃错误的啃老思想，要争取自立自强。

Q1: There are rumors that parents in the US will "kick the children out" once they turn 18 and stop providing for them financially. Is this true? Will they let you make your own life decisions after you turn 18?

据说美国人满了十八岁，就会被父母赶出家门，让他们靠自己独立生存，这是真的吗？这是不是也意味着父母会彻底放手，让孩子自己做重大的人生决定？

Sort of, but it is probably not like what you imagined. I think there is a big push by American parents for their children to become independent at 18. But it is not like they hate their children or they don't ever want to see them again. It's more likely that they want their children to go out and succeed once they get to college age.

的确有这种说法，但也不全是你们想象的那样。美国家长的确是会督促子女在十八岁时独立，但这并不代表他们从此就不爱子女，或者再也不想见到他们了。他们更多的是盼望小孩能独自出去闯荡，顺利考上大学。

Ideally, we are supposed to move out, rent our own apartment and find a job to support ourselves. If we decide to go to college, we are expected to pay the tuition ourselves, either by doing a part-time job, or getting some financial aids such as scholarships. In theory, after graduating from college, we can find a better job, so that at some point, we can buy our own house, have dogs running in the yard and make all the babies. I think that's how most parents define success. And, if their children don't succeed and aren't able to provide for themselves, that is kind of a failure on the parents' part.

理想情况下，（18岁后）我们应该搬出父母家，租一个公寓，找一份工作养活自己。如果我们决定要读大学，那么就得自己想办法解决学费。要么靠兼职挣钱，要么寻求一些财政帮助，比如申请奖学金。理论上说，大学毕业以后我们就能找到一份好一点的工作，在合适的时候买一套属于自己的房子，在院子里养条狗，生几个小孩。我觉得这是大部分父母对于小孩成功的定义。如果他们的小孩不能独立养活自己，这意味着家庭教育的失败。

But recently, especially in my generation, it's more and more common for people to live at home while they are in college, because it's cheaper, and you don't pay rent at home. And even sometimes to move back in after college because the economy is so bad, kind of everywhere. But that is a new thing. It's more of a relic in our economic situation than it is about America in general.

但是最近几年，尤其是我这一代人，越来越多的人选择上大学后住家里，因为可以省房租，甚至出现了（一些从家里搬出去的大学生）毕业后又搬回去的情况。因为现在每个地方的经济都很糟糕（大学毕业生找不到合适的工作）。但这是一种新的现象，不是美国文化本身是这样，而是社会经济不景气导致的遗留问题。

And about whether they let us make our own decisions or not, yes, most parents, tend to not meddle with children's lives when they are adults. Actually I think we are encouraged to make our own decision even before 18. Parents would rather only give advice. The ability to think independently is a thing we are always encouraged to have, at least after we were able to go to school. This might be a little different from what I have heard in China.

至于父母会不会放手让我们自己做决定，会的。大部分家长在儿女成年后，都倾向于不再干涉他们的生活。事实上，我们从小就被鼓励要自己做决定，父母更愿意以给建议的方式引导。最晚在上学后，父母一直鼓励并培养我们的独立思考能力。这可能和我听到的在中国的情况有一点差别。

For example, my niece, who is only 5, was asked what she wanted to do in the future and she said she wanted to open an ice cream store. Instead of directly making comments about this idea, her parents just helped her figure out what she needs to have or what might happen if she ended up doing that. And they still let her make the decisions. However, I have heard similar stories from my Chinese friends, and it seems like their parents would be more likely to try to tell them yes or no, or what they should do instead. But of course, no matter what methods they use, all parents want the best for their kids.

举个例子，有人问我五岁的侄女以后想做什么，她说她想开个冰激凌店。

她爸妈对此没有发表任何意见，只是帮她想她开店需要什么，或者客观分析开店后可能遇到什么问题，依然让她自己做决定到底要不要开。我也从我的中国朋友那里听到类似的故事，但貌似他们的父母会直接告诉他们这个行或者不行，可能还会告诉他们应该做什么才对。当然天下所有的父母都是为了孩子好，不管他们用的什么方式。

Q2: If children should be independent after 18, before they have a chance to get a real job, how do they pay for college? What about other living expenses?

如果子女18岁以后都应该独立生活了，那么在找到工作之前，他们该怎么负担他们上大学的花销？其他的生活费用呢？

If they go to college, they can get loans for tuition and basic living expenses from the bank, but then they end up owing the bank a lot of money, and it's actually a big problem right now. People try to figure out what to do about that, because the current generation of American college graduates have more debts than any generation has ever had. Some parents do help pay part of tuition or pay the whole thing. So it's not that 100% of Americans don't get any help from their parents.

如果要上大学的话，他们可以从银行贷款，从而解决学费和基本生活费用。所以他们最后会欠银行很多钱，这实际上是我们现在面临的一个问题。人们都在想应该怎么解决这个问题，因为当前这一代的美国大学毕业生，比任何一代欠债都多。但是并不是所有的美国学生都不会得到他们父母的资助，还是有一些父母会根据自己情况，帮忙付全部或者部分的学费。

If they decide to go to graduate school, there will be relatively more financial aid options, especially for Ph.D students. Most of them will have the option of getting hired as a teaching assistant or research associate, so that their tuition fees and basic living expenses are covered by school or grants. There is also financial aid that is available through school and the government. So there are some non-bank ways to get money.

如果决定要读研究生的话，他们能得到更多的资金补助。特别是博士生，会有机会得到学校提供的助研或者助教岗位，如此一来，他们的学费和基本生活费就可以通过学校或科研基金解决。学校和政府还会提供其他的奖助学金来帮助学生。所以除了向银行贷款，还是有一些别的解决办法。

However, if they don't go to college, they can just start working after high school. Those are usually low paid hourly jobs without steady income, since they don't have too many education or experience requirements. People can survive on low wage jobs if they need to, and hopefully move up to be better paid by doing well at their job. Still, it can be pretty tough for working class people. But I think this is true for anywhere in the world.

如果他们不上大学，也可以在高中毕业后直接参加工作，但通常就只能找那种对学历或工作经验没什么要求的工作。这种工作一般来说时薪都比较低、收入不太固定。低收入工作在必要的时候能够让人生存下去，工作做好了，也许能多赚一点。但是他们的生活会很困难，不过我觉得世界上所有地方的工人生活都很艰辛。

About other living expenses, solutions are also all over the place. I worked in a coffee shop to pay for my living while in college, and a lot of people do similar part-time work. The universities usually have part-time positions for students who work in book stores, or as a grader in classes, or work for school organizations. I also know friends who are supported by their parents or siblings. Of course, you can always go to the bank and get yourself more debt.

解决其他生活花销也是各种方法都有。我读大学的时候是在一家咖啡店打工挣生活费，很多人也是这样做类似的兼职，学校也会提供一些兼职岗位，比如说书店营业员、负责帮老师批改作业的助学、学校机构的工作人员。我也认识一些人是靠他们的家人给生活费。当然，你随时都能向银行去借更多钱。

Q3: Are young people in the US expected to care for their parents when they get old? How strong family bonds are after kids come to adulthood?

照顾年迈父母是美国年轻人的义务吗？子女成年后，与原生家庭的关系有多紧密？

In general, I will say that kids are not expected to take care of parents when they get old. I guess that's kind of like a trade-off, parents tend not to care for kids after they are 18 or so, and kids aren't expected to care for parents when they get older.

通常来说，子女没有照顾年迈父母的义务，我觉得这可能算是一种等价交换吧。父母在子女满18岁后就让他们彻底独立生活了，所以当父母年纪大了，子女也没有照顾他们的义务。

Sometimes the kids will be expected to decide on a nursing home, a retirement home, or they might get a nursing assistant to look after them when parents get too old to care for themselves. Generally, it's not the kids who are doing the nursing, it is typically the parents who use their money or the inheritance that they get from their parents to pay for those services. If there is none, then their kids will pay for it. Maybe the government will pay for some amount as well? I am not completely sure because I am not there yet, but I'll catch up with you later.

当父母年纪大了不能照顾自己的时候，有时候会让子女根据他们的身体情况，帮他们做决定是去护理院还是老年公寓，或者雇一个护工来家里照顾他们。但是子女一般不需要亲自照顾父母。父母会用自己的钱或者用从他们的父母那里继承来的遗产来支付这些照顾费用。如果都没钱，子女也会给；或许政府也会给点？我不确定，因为我还没到那一步，到时候再告诉你们。

As for family bonds, it not like parents and children don't like each other, I think it's more likely that we are good friends, once kids become adults. I get along with my parents just fine; I spend time with them a couple of times a year for a week or a long weekend. We have fun together every time that I see them, but it's more of a good friendship than a lot of close-knit family-centered cultures that I have heard of.

子女成年后，并不是就和父母互相看不顺眼了，我觉得我们更像好朋友。我和父母的关系很好，一年见几次，每次待在一起一个星期或者一个长周末，见面的时候都很愉快。跟以家庭为中心的文化里那种很亲近的亲子关系相比，我们和父母的关系更像一种很好的友谊。

Q4: In China, grandparents play a major part in raising grandchildren. Is there a similar phenomenon in the US?

在中国，小朋友一般都是家里老人带大的，美国也有类似现象吗？

Not really. Parents like raising their own children in America. They cherish the experience of taking care of their own babies, and don't want to miss out on any important moments. That's why they have kids, right? I know a few kids who were raised by their grandparents. But that's the exception and not the rule usually.

美国父母喜欢亲自带孩子。他们很珍惜照顾自己孩子的经历，不想错过孩子成长的重要时刻。不然他们为什么要生娃？我只知道很少几个人的孩子是由家里老人带大的，但那都是例外，不是一般的情况。

Grandparents like to be a part of their grandchildren's lives too. They like babysitting them for a day or maybe a weekend. But they also wish to send their grand children home. I think grandparents, because they have already been parents, and have gone through the whole experience of raising children themselves already, once they become grandparents, they really just want to have the fun parts of raising children without having all the hard parts of having them all the time.

爷爷奶奶也想要成为他们孙子生活里的一部分。他们喜欢带孙子们玩一天，或者一个周末，但是他们也希望能够把孙子送还给父母。因为他们在年轻的时候已经做过父母了，完全亲历过抚养小孩长大的一整套过程。当他们升级成爷爷奶奶的时候，他们只想偶尔享受天伦之乐，不想要那些琐碎磨人的部分。

So they like being around to see them grow up, see them turn into awesome people. But they just want to be able to play with them and spoil them with gifts on holidays, instead of having to deal with all of the diaper changing, crying, and other unpleasant parts of raising children. I have heard that some Chinese grandparents will come live with their children for years, in order to babysit the new born for them, which is less likely to happen here. Some grandparents, at most, are willing to come by and help for the first month, or hire a nanny to help.

所以他们喜欢在孙子的附近住着，看着他们渐渐长大。但他们也只是想能和孙子们玩耍、宠他们、过节买一堆礼物送给他们，而不想一直应付像换尿布、哭闹之类的不太愉快的部分。我听说有些中国的老人为了帮子女照顾新生儿，会来和他们住很长一段时间。这种情况在美国比较少。顶多会有一些老人愿意在最初的一个月来帮忙，或者出钱请个保姆。

If the new parents both have to work, they'll probably send their kids to day care or hire a nanny. But I also know a handful of friends, whose parents, living nearby, are willing to help take care of their babies when they are at work. That's more likely to be a big favor rather than an obligation, and they still have a part-time nanny at the same time so they can change shifts. Babies seldom live with anyone except their parents.

如果新手爸妈都要上班，他们会把小孩送托儿所，或者请保姆。但我也认识少数几个朋友的爹妈，就住在他们附近，愿意在他们上班的时候帮忙看小孩。但这只是帮忙，不是义务，而且他们也雇有兼职保姆来换班。小孩几乎不会和除了父母以外的任何人一起生活。

Unlike in some family-centered cultures, in which grandkids are the center of the whole group, kids here are just part of their grandparents' life. After retiring, people finally have free time to do the things they enjoy, such as traveling, learning art and hanging out with old friends. They still love their offsprings, but they are not the whole world to them.

不同于一些文化中，小孩是一个大家庭的中心，这里的小孩只是他们爷爷奶奶生活里的一部分。人们退休后，终于有自由支配的时间来做自己想做的事情，比如旅游、学艺术、和老朋友聚会。他们仍然爱他们的子孙，但是那不是生活的全部。

（来源：https://mp.weixin.qq.com/s/_kcbIpvGV_eOYawqqLnRBg）

3.7 Critical thinking 环节

双语文章：白金汉宫宣布，哈里与梅根将不再使用王室头衔

英国王位第六顺位继承人哈里王子与美国演员梅根于2018年5月在英国成婚，育有一子阿奇。两人1月初发表声明，表示不想继续担任王室高级成员职务，希望能逐步寻求经济独立，在英国和北美生活。通过让学生阅读这篇文章，引导学生就此问题思考：Your opinions on Prince Harry and Meghan's pursuit of living on their own.（你是如何看待哈里与梅根追求更加独立生活的？）

白金汉宫的声明说，根据新安排，哈里夫妇将不再使用王室头衔，不再代表王室出席活动，也不再获得用于支持王室职务的公共资金。

Prince Harry and Meghan will no longer use their HRH titles and will not receive public funds for royal duties, Buckingham Palace has announced.（HRH：His/Her Royal Highness，殿下，对王室部分成员的尊称）The couple will also no longer formally represent the Queen.

这一安排将于2020年春季正式生效。

The new arrangement comes into effect in spring this year, the Palace said.

根据声明，王室允许哈里保留目前他们一家三口在英国的住宅。哈里夫妇表示有意偿还当初为翻修这栋住宅而花掉的240万英镑的纳税人的钱。但声明没有提及哈里夫妇未来的安保安排和费用。

The Duke and Duchess of Sussex intend to repay £2.4m of taxpayer money for the refurbishment of Frogmore Cottage, which will remain their UK family home, the statement added.

英国女王伊丽莎白二世1月18日发表声明说："哈里、梅根和阿奇永远是我家庭中深受喜爱的成员。我认识到他们在过去两年里因受到过度关注而经历了诸多挑战，我支持他们追求更加独立生活的愿望。"

Queen Elizabeth said in a statement on January 18th: "Harry, Meghan and Archie will always be much loved members of my family. I recognise the challenges they have experienced as a result of intense scrutiny over the last two years and support their wish for a more independent life."

（来源：中国日报双语新闻）

3.8 主题拓展资源

习近平总书记在纪念五四运动100周年大会上的重要讲话

纪念五四运动100周年大会（a ceremony to mark the centenary of the May

Fourth Movement)在人民大会堂举行。中共中央总书记、国家主席、中央军委主席习近平出席大会并发表重要讲话。

五四运动的意义

习近平指出，五四运动是中国近现代史上具有划时代意义的一个重大事件，是中国旧民主主义革命走向新民主主义革命的转折点，在近代以来中华民族追求民族独立和发展进步的历史进程中具有里程碑意义。

五四运动是一场以先进青年知识分子为先锋、广大人民群众参加的彻底反帝反封建的伟大爱国革命运动。

The May Fourth Movement was a great patriotic and revolutionary campaign pioneered by advanced young intellectuals and participated by the people from all walks of life to resolutely fight imperialism and feudalism.

五四运动是一场中国人民为拯救民族危亡、捍卫民族尊严、凝聚民族力量而掀起的伟大社会革命运动。

The May Fourth Movement was a great social revolutionary movement launched by the Chinese people to save the nation from subjugation, safeguard national dignity and pool national strength together.

五四运动是一场传播新思想新文化新知识的伟大思想启蒙运动和新文化运动。

The May Fourth Movement was a great enlightenment and new cultural movement of disseminating new thought, new culture and new knowledge.

五四运动以全民族的力量高举起爱国主义的伟大旗帜。

The May Fourth Movement is a grand flag of patriotism raised with the power of the whole nation.

五四运动以全民族的行动激发了追求真理、追求进步的伟大觉醒。

The May Fourth Movement is a grand enlightenment for the entire nation to pursue truth and progress.

五四运动以全民族的搏击培育了永久奋斗的伟大传统。

The May Fourth Movement has cultivated a great tradition of permanent endeavor.

对新时代中国青年提出要求

新时代中国青年要树立对马克思主义的信仰、对中国特色社会主义的信念、对中华民族伟大复兴中国梦的信心。

Young Chinese of the new era should establish belief in Marxism, faith in socialism with Chinese characteristics, as well as confidence in the Chinese dream of national rejuvenation.

新时代中国青年要热爱伟大祖国。爱国主义的本质就是坚持爱国和爱党、爱社会主义高度统一。

Chinese youth of the new era should love their country ardently, the essence of patriotism is having unified love for the country, the Communist Party of China, and socialism.

新时代中国青年要听党话、跟党走，胸怀忧国忧民之心、爱国爱民之情。

Young Chinese of the new era should follow the instructions and guidance of the Party, and remain dedicated to the country and the people.

新时代中国青年要有感恩之心，感恩党和国家，感恩社会和人民。

Chinese youth of the new era should be grateful to the Party, the country, the society and the people.

新时代中国青年，要有家国情怀，也要有人类关怀。

Young people should not only care about their family and country, but also have concerns for humanity.

新时代中国青年要自觉树立和践行社会主义核心价值观，自觉抵制拜金主义、享乐主义、极端个人主义、历史虚无主义等错误思想。

Young people should nurture and practice core socialist values, and guard against wrong ideas such as money worship, hedonism, extreme individualism and historical nihilism.

新时代中国青年要努力学习马克思主义立场观点方法，努力掌握科学文化知识和专业技能，努力提高人文素养。

Young people should work hard in learning the Marxist stance, viewpoints and methods, mastering scientific and cultural knowledge and professional skills, and improving their humanistic quality.

（来源：中国日报双语新闻）

第五单元　科学利用信息技术，提升学生核心素养

(Unit 5 Sources of Information)

1. 思政主题：科学利用信息技术，提升学生核心素养

2. 意义

本单元的主题是信息来源。教师可帮助学生了解各种信息来源的利弊，引导学生科学利用现代信息技术，学会审慎思考，提高学生的批判性思维能力，提升学生的核心素养。

3. 教学设计与思政元素的融入

Passage A

3.1 Warm-up 环节

英文视频：四岁小孩打911电话求教数学问题

在视频中，一个四岁的美国小男孩遇到了一个自己没法解决的数学难题，于是打911电话求助。该视频内容跟课文 A 中的故事类似，教师可在讲解课文之前播放该视频，激发学生的学习兴趣。

以下为电话录音内容：

Operator: 911 emergencies.

Boy: Yeah. I need some help.

Operator: What's the matter?

Boy: With my math.

Operator: With your mouth?

Boy: No. With my math. I have to do it. Will you help me?

Operator: Sure. What kind of math do you have that you need help with?

Boy: I have. I have taken away.

Operator: Oh. You have to do the take-aways.

Boy: Yeah.

Operator: Alright. What's the problem?

Boy: Um. You have to help me with my math.

Operator: Okay. Tell me what the math is?

Boy: Okay. 16 take away 8 is what?

Operator: You tell me. How much do you think it is?

Boy: I don't know. One?

Operator: How old are you?

Boy: I'm only 4.

Operator: Four?

Boy: Yeah.

Operator: What's another problem? That was a tough one.

Boy: Um, oh here's one.5 take away 5.

Operator: 5 take away 5 and how much do you think that is?

Boy: Five.

Woman: Johnny, what do you think you are doing?!

Boy: The policeman is helping me with my math.

Woman: What did I tell you about going on the phone?

Operator: It's the mother.

Boy: You said if I need some help, to call somebody.

Woman: I didn't mean the police.

（来源：https://www.iqiyi.com/w_19rrrkktl5.html）

3.2 Discussion 环节

英语文章：Benefits of China's Education Technology Sector amid COVID–19

现代信息技术在教育中起着越来越重要的作用，尤其是新冠肺炎疫情暴发后，但因为有现代信息技术的辅助，各学校可以开展在线教学，保证教学进度与教学质量。教师可引导学生阅读本文章，感受疫情期间现代信息技术为教育带来的积极作用，并进一步讨论现代信息技术的重要性。

(Haider Rifaat is a writer for the *South China Morning Post*, *Arabian Moda* magazine, *Good Times* magazine and *OK! Pakistan*. The article reflects the author's opinions and not necessarily the views of CGTN.)

Education-technology is anything but a new phenomenon. Ed-tech firms have been operating across the world for decades, but we have realized their due importance during a COVID-19 pandemic. Almost all schools and universities have opted for online education during the novel coronavirus outbreak, and the ed-tech business has since blossomed, particularly in China.

These companies are responsible for merging innovative technological tools like web-based software platforms and artificial intelligence with education to foster advanced learning among students. This strategy helps learners of all ages perform better in their academics.

China remains second to none in the ed-tech business. Chinese education-technology companies have outdone themselves during the global crisis. Two of the leading Beijing-based ed-tech firms, Zuoyebang and Yuanfudao, earned profits worth 750 million and 1 billion U.S. dollars, respectively this year. Research has also found that online education will surge over 58 billion dollars in 2020 against 38 billion amassed last year.

The global economy continues to suffer at an exponential rate, and the aftermath of the pandemic will only worsen the overall economic performance. Recovering from this loss will be a huge challenge for almost every country. However, the ed-tech market appears to have accelerated its growth in China in the last few months, which is an indication that the country's education sector is in safe hands.

Students at home can now access e-learning platforms and virtual classes to extract the best knowledge without interruptions. Parents and their children can collaborate during online sessions and achieve daily targets with ease. Creative learning enables students to think outside the box and posit solutions to challenging problems. This results in better learning outcomes.

Communication is made easier with zero infrastructure costs involved. More importantly, curriculum tailored to the needs of each student can help them learn at their own pace. College and university students can also earn their degrees through distance learning without feeling left out.

Hu Xiaoqian, a teacher at Tsinghua University, uses an online educational system to teach a baseball class in Beijing, China, February 17, 2020.

Advanced technology and internet usage have allowed ed-tech firms to thrive in China. Without these tools, education technology would not be the successful phenomenon it is today. E-learning is a sustainable alternative to education in the long-term if we take COVID-19 out of the equation. Students can access these platforms effortlessly, barring a few segments of the population that are deprived of online facilities and other important channels.

Distance learning requires no transportation or physical effort. Subject-based knowledge is readily available to students, and learning is immersive, enjoyable and collaborative. Technology-based education also makes administrative tasks easier to handle. Enrollment, progress reports and monitoring of other miscellaneous duties are made more efficient in an online system. No paperwork is involved. Everything is digitally accessible.

Countries with emerging technologies should take a page from China and implement similar success models to make a difference in their education sector. It is high time the ed-tech market took charge of the education sector. Allowing schools and universities to register with ed-tech companies can benefit both parties and help achieve a synergized effect.

Education technology firms should take on an expansive approach that engages all students, including those who lack basic facilities to learn from home. Education is an investment in our children's future, and turning a blind eye to it serves no purpose to quality education.

In an ever-evolving world of technology, registering more schools with ed-tech startups not only benefits the economy but fast tracks the growth of education. In the age of COVID-19, China is doing what it does the best: getting things in order and incentivizing parents and their children to get good education at home.

（来源：https://news.cgtn.com/news/2020-08-23/Benefits-of-China-s-education-technology-sector-amid-COVID-19-TbIanyVDzO/index.html）

3.3 Critical thinking 环节

英文视频：TED 演讲 Beware Online "Filter Bubbles"

你在享受网络信息的便利时，是否知道很多网络公司会根据我们的个人喜好"定制"他们的服务（包括新闻和搜索结果）？这带来的后果：我们被困在一个"过滤泡沫"（filter bubble）中。Eli Pariser 以 facebook 和 google 为例，讲述了这些"过滤泡沫"的存在。教师可引导学生观看该视频，并思考：如何看待网络技术进步？怎样对各种网络信息进行批判性分析？

Mark Zuckerberg, a journalist was asking him a question about the news feed. And the journalist was asking him, "Why is this so important?" And Zuckerberg said, "A squirrel dying in your front yard may be more relevant to your interests right now than people dying in Africa." And I want to talk about what a Web based on that idea of relevance might look like.

So when I was growing up in a really rural area in Maine, the Internet meant something very different to me. It meant a connection to the world. It meant something that would connect us all together. And I was sure that it was going to be great for democracy and for our society. But there's this shift in how information is flowing online, and it's invisible. And if we don't pay attention to it, it could be a real problem. So I first noticed this in a place I spend a lot of time — my Facebook page. I'm progressive, politically — big surprise — but I've always gone out of my way to meet conservatives. I like hearing what they're thinking about; I like seeing what they link to; I like learning a thing or two. And so I was surprised when I noticed one day that the conservatives had disappeared from my Facebook feed. And what it turned out was going on was that Facebook was looking at which links I clicked on, and it was noticing that, actually, I was clicking more on my liberal friends' links than on my conservative friends' links. And without consulting me about it, it had edited them out. They disappeared.

So Facebook isn't the only place that's doing this kind of invisible, algorithmic editing of the Web. Google's doing it too. If I search for something, and you search for something, even right now at the very same time, we may get very different search results. Even if you're logged out, one engineer told me, there are 57 signals that Google looks at — everything from what kind of computer you're on to what kind of browser you're using to where you're located — that it uses to personally tailor your query results. Think about it for a second: there is no standard Google anymore. And you know, the funny thing about this is that it's hard to see. You can't see how different your search results are from anyone else's.

But a couple of weeks ago, I asked a bunch of friends to Google "Egypt" and to send me screen shots of what they got. So here's my friend Scott's screen shot. And here's my friend Daniel's screen shot. When you put them side-by-side, you don't even have to read the links to see how different these two pages are. But when you do read the links, it's really quite remarkable. Daniel didn't get anything about the protests in Egypt at all in his first page of Google results. Scott's results were full of them. And this was the big story of the day at that time. That's how different these results are becoming.

So it's not just Google and Facebook either. This is something that's sweeping the Web. There are a whole host of companies that are doing this kind of personalization. Yahoo News, the biggest news site on the Internet, is now personalized — different people get different things. *Huffington Post, the Washington*

Post, the New York Times — all flirting with personalization in various ways. And this moves us very quickly toward a world in which the Internet is showing us what it thinks we want to see, but not necessarily what we need to see. As Eric Schmidt said, "It will be very hard for people to watch or consume something that has not in some sense been tailored for them."

So I do think this is a problem. And I think, if you take all of these filters together, you take all these algorithms, you get what I call a filter bubble. And your filter bubble is your own personal, unique universe of information that you live in online. And what's in your filter bubble depends on who you are, and it depends on what you do. But the thing is that you don't decide what gets in. And more importantly, you don't actually see what gets edited out. So one of the problems with the filter bubble was discovered by some researchers at Netflix. And they were looking at the Netflix queues, and they noticed something kind of funny that a lot of us probably have noticed, which is there are some movies that just sort of zip right up and out to our houses. They enter the queue, they just zip right out. So "Iron Man" zips right out, and "Waiting for Superman" can wait for a really long time.

What they discovered was that in our Netflix queues there's this epic struggle going on between our future aspirational selves and our more impulsive present selves. You know we all want to be someone who has watched "Rashomon," but right now we want to watch "Ace Ventura" for the fourth time. So the best editing gives us a bit of both. It gives us a little bit of Justin Bieber and a little bit of Afghanistan. It gives us some information vegetables; it gives us some information dessert. And the challenge with these kinds of algorithmic filters, these personalized filters, is that, because they're mainly looking at what you click on first, it can throw off that balance. And instead of a balanced information diet, you can end up surrounded by information junk food.

What this suggests is actually that we may have the story about the Internet wrong. In a broadcast society — this is how the founding mythology goes — in a broadcast society, there were these gatekeepers, the editors, and they controlled the flows of information. And along came the Internet and it swept them out of the way, and it allowed all of us to connect together, and it was awesome. But that's not actually what's happening right now. What we're seeing is more of a passing of the torch from human gatekeepers to algorithmic ones. And the thing is that the algorithms don't yet have the kind of embedded ethics that the editors did. So if algorithms are going to curate the world for us, if they're going to decide what we get to see and what we don't get to see, then we need to make sure that they're not just keyed to relevance. We need to make sure that they also show us things that are uncomfortable or challenging or important — this is what TED does — other points of view.

And the thing is, we've actually been here before as a society. In 1915, it's not like newspapers were sweating a lot about their civic responsibilities. Then people noticed that they were doing something really important. That, in fact, you couldn't have a functioning democracy if citizens didn't get a good flow of information, that the newspapers were critical because they were acting as the filter, and then journalistic ethics developed. It wasn't perfect, but it got us through the last century. And so now, we're kind of back in 1915 on the Web. And we need the new gatekeepers to encode that kind of responsibility into the code that they're writing.

I know that there are a lot of people here from Facebook and from Google — Larry and Sergey — people who have helped build the Web as it is, and I'm grateful for that. But we really need you to make sure that these algorithms have encoded in them a sense of the public life, a sense of civic responsibility. We need you to make sure that they're transparent enough that we can see what the rules are that determine what gets through our filters. And we need you to give us some control so that we can decide what gets through and what doesn't. Because I think we really need the Internet to be that thing that we all dreamed of it being. We need it to connect us all together. We need it to introduce us to new ideas and new people and different perspectives. And it's not going to do that if it leaves us all isolated in a Web of one.

Thank you.

（来源：https://www.ted.com/talks/eli_pariser_beware_online_filter_bubbles）

3.4 主题拓展资源

A. 英语视频：TED 演讲 Connected, but alone

该视频是一个 TED 演讲，演讲人是 Sherry Turkle。她讲述了人们在各种情境下因为使用手机而忽略了实际对话的情况。手机让我们能够互相"联系"的同时，是不是也让我们感觉更孤独了？你怎么看？教师可引导学生观看该视频，并思考：手机给我们的生活带来了什么？

Just a moment ago, my daughter Rebecca texted me for good luck. Her text said, "Mom, you will rock." I love this. Getting that text was like getting a hug. And so there you have it. I embody the central paradox. I'm a woman who loves getting texts who's going to tell you that too many of them can be a problem.

Actually that reminder of my daughter brings me to the beginning of my story. 1996, when I gave my first TED Talk, Rebecca was five years old and she was sitting right there in the front row. I had just written a book that celebrated our life on the Internet and I was about to be on the cover of *Wired* magazine. In those heady days, we were experimenting with chat rooms and online virtual communities. We were exploring different aspects of ourselves. And then we unplugged. I was excited. And, as a psychologist, what excited me most was the idea that we would use what we learned in the virtual world about ourselves, about our identity, to live better lives in the real world.

Now fast-forward to 2012. I'm back here on the TED stage again. My daughter's 20. She's a college student. She sleeps with her cellphone, so do I. And I've just written a new book, but this time it's not one that will get me on the cover of *Wired* magazine. So what happened? I'm still excited by technology, but I believe, and I'm here to make the case, that we're letting it take us places that we don't want to go.

Over the past 15 years, I've studied technologies of mobile communication and I've interviewed hundreds and hundreds of people, young and old, about their plugged in lives. And what I've found is that our little devices, those little devices in our pockets, are so psychologically powerful that they don't only change what we do, they change who we are. Some of the things we do now with our devices are things that, only a few years ago, we would have found odd or disturbing, but they've quickly come to seem familiar, just how we do things.

So just to take some quick examples: People text or do email during corporate board meetings. They text and shop and go on Facebook during classes, during presentations, actually during all meetings. People talk to me about the important new skill of making eye contact while you're texting. People explain to me that it's hard, but that it can be done. Parents text and do email at breakfast and at dinner while their children complain about not having their parents' full attention. But then these same children deny each other their full attention. This is a recent shot of my daughter and her friends being together while not being together. And we even text at funerals. I study this. We remove ourselves from our grief or from our revery and we go into our phones.

Why does this matter? It matters to me because I think we're setting ourselves up for trouble — trouble certainly in how we relate to each other, but also trouble in how we relate to ourselves and our capacity for self-reflection. We're getting used to a new way of being alone together. People want to be with each other, but also elsewhere — connected to all the different places they want to be. People want to customize their lives. They want to go in and out of all the places they are because the thing that matters most to them is control over where they put their attention. So you want to go to that board meeting, but you only want to pay attention to the bits that interest you. And some people think that's a good thing. But you can end up hiding from each other, even as we're all constantly connected to each other.

A 50-year-old business man lamented to me that he feels he doesn't have colleagues anymore at work. When he goes to work, he doesn't stop by to talk to anybody, he doesn't call. And he says he doesn't want to interrupt his colleagues because, he says, "They're too busy on their email." But then he stops himself and he says, "You know, I'm not telling you the truth. I'm the one who doesn't want to be interrupted. I think I should want to, but actually I'd rather just do things on my Blackberry."

Across the generations, I see that people can't get enough of each other, if and only if they can have each other at a distance, in amounts they can control. I call it the Goldilocks effect: not too close, not too far, just right. But what might feel just right for that middle-aged executive can be a problem for an adolescent who needs to develop face-to-face relationships. An 18-year-old boy who uses texting for almost everything says to me wistfully, "Someday, someday, but certainly not now, I'd like to learn how to have a conversation."

When I ask people, "What's wrong with having a conversation?" People say, "I'll tell you what's wrong with having a conversation. It takes place in real time and you can't control what you're going to say." So that's the bottom line. Texting, email, posting, all of these things let us present the self as we want to be. We get to edit, and that means we get to delete, and that means we get to retouch, the face, the voice, the flesh, the body — not too little, not too much, just right.

Human relationships are rich and they're messy and they're demanding. And we clean them up with technology. And when we do, one of the things that can happen is that we sacrifice conversation for mere connection. We short-change ourselves. And over time, we seem to forget this, or we seem to stop caring.

I was caught off guard when Stephen Colbert asked me a profound question, a profound question. He said, "Don't all those little tweets, don't all those little sips of online communication, add up to one big gulp of real conversation?" My answer was "no, they don't add up". Connecting in sips may work for gathering discrete bits of information, they may work for saying, "I'm thinking about you," or even for saying, "I love you,"—I mean, look at how I felt when I got that text from my daughter—but they don't really work for learning about each other, for really coming to know and understand each other. And we use conversations with each other to learn how to have conversations with ourselves. So a flight from conversation can really matter because it can compromise our capacity for self-reflection. For kids growing up, that skill is the bedrock of development.

Over and over I hear, "I would rather text than talk." And what I'm seeing is that people get so used to being short-changed out of real conversation, so used to getting by with less, that they've become almost willing to dispense with people altogether. So for example, many people share with me this wish, that some day a more advanced version of Siri, the digital assistant on Apple's iPhone, will be more like a best friend, someone who will listen when others won't. I believe this wish reflects a painful truth that I've learned in the past 15 years. That feeling that no one is listening to me is very important in our relationships with technology. That's why it's so appealing to have a Facebook page or a Twitter feed—so many automatic listeners. And the feeling that no one is listening to me make us want to spend time with machines that seem to care about us.

We're developing robots, they call them sociable robots, that are specifically designed to be companions—to the elderly, to our children, to us. Have we so lost confidence that we will be there for each other? During my research I worked in nursing homes, and I brought in these sociable robots that were designed to give the elderly the feeling that they were understood. And one day I came in and a woman who had lost a child was talking to a robot in the shape of a baby seal. It seemed to be looking in her eyes. It seemed to be following the conversation. It comforted her. And many people found this amazing.

But that woman was trying to make sense of her life with a machine that had no experience of the arc of a human life. That robot put on a great show. And we're vulnerable. People experience pretend empathy as though it were the real thing.

So during that moment when that woman was experiencing that pretend empathy, I was thinking, "That robot can't empathize. It doesn't face death. It doesn't know life."

And as that woman took comfort in her robot companion, I didn't find it amazing; I found it one of the most wrenching, complicated moments in my 15 years of work. But when I stepped back, I felt myself at the cold, hard center of a perfect storm. We expect more from technology and less from each other. And I ask myself, "Why have things come to this?"

And I believe it's because technology appeals to us most where we are most vulnerable. And we are vulnerable. We're lonely, but we're afraid of intimacy. And so from social networks to sociable robots, we're designing technologies that will give us the illusion of companionship without the demands of friendship. We turn to technology to help us feel connected in ways we can comfortably control. But we're not so comfortable. We are not so much in control.

These days, those phones in our pockets are changing our minds and hearts because they offer us three gratifying fantasies. One, that we can put our attention wherever we want it to be; two, that we will always be heard; and three, that we will never have to be alone. And that third idea, that we will never have to be alone, is central to changing our psyches. Because the moment that people are alone, even for a few seconds, they become anxious, they panic, they fidget, they reach for a device. Just think of people at a checkout line or at a red light. Being alone feels like a problem that needs to be solved. And so people try to solve it by connecting. But here, connection is more like a symptom than a cure. It expresses, but it doesn't solve, an underlying problem. But more than a symptom, constant connection is changing the way people think of themselves. It's shaping a new way of being.

The best way to describe it is "I share therefore I am". We use technology to define ourselves by sharing our thoughts and feelings even as we're having them. So before it was: I have a feeling, I want to make a call. Now it's: I want to have a feeling, I need to send a text. The problem with this new regime of "I share therefore I am" is that, if we don't have connection, we don't feel like ourselves. We almost don't feel ourselves. So what do we do? We connect more and more. But in the process, we set ourselves up to be isolated.

How do you get from connection to isolation? You end up isolated if you don't cultivate the capacity for solitude, the ability to be separate, to gather yourself.

Solitude is where you find yourself so that you can reach out to other people and form real attachments. When we don't have the capacity for solitude, we turn to other people in order to feel less anxious or in order to feel alive. When this happens, we're not able to appreciate who they are. It's as though we're using them as spare parts to support our fragile sense of self. We slip into thinking that always being connected is going to make us feel less alone. But we're at risk, because actually it's the opposite that's true. If we're not able to be alone, we're going to be more lonely. And if we don't teach our children to be alone, they're only going to know how to be lonely.

When I spoke at TED in 1996, reporting on my studies of the early virtual communities, I said, "Those who make the most of their lives on the screen come to it in a spirit of self-reflection." And that's what I'm calling for here, now: reflection and, more than that, a conversation about where our current use of technology may be taking us, what it might be costing us. We're smitten with technology. And we're afraid, like young lovers, that too much talking might spoil the romance. But it's time to talk. We grew up with digital technology and so we see it as all grown up. But it's not, it's early days. There's plenty of time for us to reconsider how we use it, how we build it. I'm not suggesting that we turn away from our devices, just that we develop a more self-aware relationship with them, with each other and with ourselves.

I see some first steps. Start thinking of solitude as a good thing. Make room for it. Find ways to demonstrate this as a value to your children. Create sacred spaces at home — the kitchen, the dining room — and reclaim them for conversation. Do the same thing at work. At work, we're so busy communicating that we often don't have time to think, we don't have time to talk, about the things that really matter. Change that. Most important, we all really need to listen to each other, including to the boring bits. Because it's when we stumble or hesitate or lose our words that we reveal ourselves to each other.

Technology is making a bid to redefine human connection — how we care for each other, how we care for ourselves — but it's also giving us the opportunity to affirm our values and our direction. I'm optimistic. We have everything we need to start. We have each other. And we have the greatest chance of success if we recognize our vulnerability that we listen when technology says it will take something complicated and promises something simpler.

So in my work, I hear that life is hard, relationships are filled with risk. And then there's technology — simpler, hopeful, optimistic, ever-young. It's like calling in the cavalry. An ad campaign promises that online and with avatars, you can, "Finally, love your friends love your body, love your life, online and with avatars." We're drawn to virtual romance, to computer games that seem like worlds, to the idea that robots, robots, will someday be our true companions. We spend an evening on the social network instead of going to the pub with friends.

But our fantasies of substitution have cost us. Now we all need to focus on the many, many ways technology can lead us back to our real lives, our own bodies, our own communities, our own politics, our own planet. They need us. Let's talk about how we can use digital technology, the technology of our dreams, to make this life, the life we can love.

Thank you.

（来源：https://www.ted.com/talks/sherry_turkle_connected_but_alone）

B. 双语文章：Are Digital Devices Killing Conversation?

本文展示了 Sherry Turkle 和 Alexandra Samuel 关于数字设备是否会破坏对话能力的不同观点。Sherry Turkle 认为技术对年轻人的交流产生了不好的影响。Alexandra Samuel 认为数字设备也可用于深入交流。你怎么看？可组织学生课下讨论：Are digital devices ruining our ability to have deep and meaningful conversations, emphasizing desperate and superficial connections instead? How can we sustain healthy relationships?

What's the Latest Development?

MIT psychologist Sherry Turkle says that digital devices are transforming our communication habits for the worse, making the kinds of conversation that humans depend on for social support, and self-reflection, rarer than ever. Not only do we immerse ourselves in our devices but we turn to them, rather than people, when we feel lonely. Turkle says that younger generations have all but lost the capacity to feel self-assured when they are away from their social group, preferring to connect all the time which, says Turkle, means conversing none of the time.

What's the Big Idea?

Alexandra Samuel, professor of social media at Emily Carr University in Vancouver, rebuts Turkle's arguments. Samuel says that looking at the communication tendencies of one generation versus another is to miss the obvious point that new technology affects everyone, not just whippersnappers. Chat windows, blogs and affinity groups are all vehicles for real conservation, not just desperate and superficial connections. "We are making that digital shift together—old and young, geeky and trepidatious—and we are only as alone as we choose to be."

（来源：https://bigthink.com/ideafeed/are-digital-devices-killing-conversation）

Passage B

3.5 Warm-up 环节

英语新闻： Digitalization Sweeps Catering Industry

新冠肺炎疫情期间，中国的餐饮业通过自主在线订购方式，进一步开启了餐饮企业的数字发展想象力，促进了其加速向在线迁移，帮助餐饮业渡过了疫情"寒冬"。教师可引导学生阅读本新闻，并启发学生思考网络给我们的生活带来的便利，以及在新冠肺炎疫情期间的积极作用。

Digital technologies are reshaping China's traditional catering industry, as large catering enterprises are increasingly investing in digitalization, and small and medium-sized companies ramp up efforts in digital transformation, a recent report said.

The report, issued by Beijing-based research consultancy Acewill, said digitalization is the current main trend in China's catering industry.

Kong Lingbo, founder of Acewill, said: "No matter which type of business mode, or what kind of cuisine, the propelling engine for the rapid growth of catering chain stores is digital transformation."

"The ambition of every entrepreneur is different. However, the route of digital transformation is the same. The digitalization trend in the catering industry is gaining momentum, and is indeed necessary for catering entrepreneurs to spend more time to ponder on it."

Data from the National Bureau of Statistics showed that in 2020, despite challenges brought by COVID-19, China's catering industry totaled nearly 4 trillion yuan ($616.8 billion) in business, and digital catering took up an increasing share.

In recent years, a great number of catering chain stores have been embracing digitalization.

Hotpot chain Haidilao launched a smart restaurant in Shanghai in April. Apart from dish-serving robots, robotic arms are equipped in warehouses to arrange raw materials.

The restaurant also adopts a system, namely Insight Knowledge Management System, to conduct real-time monitoring, management and maintenance of the entire unmanned back-stage operations.

From ordering to serving, the dishes are produced automatically. Haidilao said the system can save nearly 37 percent of back kitchen labor costs.

Heytea Go, an ordering app developed by China's leading milk tea chains Heytea, acquired 6 million registered users in seven months after it was launched, and raised the repurchase rate of milk tea by 300 percent.

A report issued by on-demand service platform Meituan said China's digital catering industry experienced rapid growth despite the challenges of COVID-19. Last year, online food orders surged 107.9 percent on a yearly basis.

"China's 14th Five-Year Plan (2021-25) clearly points out that digital transformation of the service industry will be further promoted. At present, the online and offline integrated development of the catering industry has become a general trend, and the trend has reshaped both the supply and demand sides," said the report.

The report added that although COVID-19 struck China's catering industry in 2020, online ordering in the catering industry quickly recovered to 2019 levels, and experienced explosive growth in the next seven months. In December, online orders surged 107.9 percent year-on-year.

"Online ordering methods such as takeaway platforms, WeChat mini programs, catering platforms and brand's self-built online ordering platforms have further opened up the digital development imagination of catering enterprises, and promoted their accelerated migration to online," the Meituan report said.

"For catering enterprises, how to embrace the online and offline integrated scenario, make services no longer limited to physical restaurants, offer services to numerous customers online and extend the service range from within 100 meters to over 10 kilometers, is a new proposition," the report added.

Wang Donghao, an independent expert of digital catering, said: "The digital transformation is an inevitable trend of the catering industry. Digital marketing helps enterprises capture consumer demand and collect user data. It also enables enterprises to deal with and satisfy consumer needs in a quicker manner, which is increasingly important in a fast-paced society."

Tang Xingtong, an independent expert in digital transformation, said: "To realize digitalization, catering enterprises should collect user data, form a real-time response mechanism and have artificial intelligence-empowered automatic services. Their ability to manage data will be their core competitiveness."

（来源：https://www.chinadaily.com.cn/a/202108/13/WS6115cb32a310efa1bd6688f4.html）

3.6 Discussion 环节

英语文章：What Is Internet Addiction Disorder?

随着科技的发展，网络上的丰富信息吸引着极具好奇心的青年群体，但也有些人因此染上"网瘾"。教师引导学生阅读本文章，并启发学生讨论：网络给我们的生活带来便利的同时，也随之产生了哪些负面影响？我们该怎样做？比如，如何避免"网瘾"，如何保证信息安全？

Internet addiction disorder (IAD) is also referred to as Problematic Internet Use (PIU), Compulsive Internet Use, (CIU), Internet overuse, problematic computer use, pathological computer use, or I-Disorder. IAD is excessive computer use which interferes with daily life.

Habits such as reading email, playing computer games, or binge viewing every *Twilight* movie or entire seasons of *Breaking Bad* are troubling only to the extent that these activities interfere with normal life. IAD is often separated by the activity involved in the compulsive actions, such as video or online gaming, online social networking, blogging, online stock trading, online gambling, inappropriate Internet pornography use, reading email, or Internet shopping.

Cyber-Relationship Addiction has been described as the addiction to accessing and using social networking platforms such as Facebook, Vine, or online dating services such as Match.com and creating fictitious relationships with others through the Internet. Along with many other meet-up platforms, such as Tinder or Siren, which are mobile phone apps using a GPS that create a way to meet new people, finding online friends has been made very easy. Yet very dangerous because there is no way to check the backgrounds of these fictitious friends. These virtual online friends start to gain more importance to the addict, eventually becoming more important than family and real-life friends.

Most, if not all "Internet addicts", already fall under existing diagnostic labels.

For many individuals, overuse or inappropriate use of the Internet is a manifestation of their depression, anxiety, impulse control disorders, or pathological gambling. According to the Center for Internet Addiction Recovery's director Kimberly S. Young, "Internet addicts suffer from emotional problems such as depression and anxiety-related disorders and often use the fantasy world of the Internet to psychologically escape unpleasant feelings or stressful situations." More than half are also addicted to alcohol, drugs, tobacco, pornography or sex.

What kind of treatment is available?

Corrective strategies to thwart an Internet addiction include using software that will control or block the unwanted content, such as porn or gaming sites from an individual's computer, addiction counselling, and cognitive behavioral therapy. One might consider placing time limits on smart phone or computer use, such as no smart phone use during homework time or no computer use after 9pm. The major reasons that the Internet is so addicting is the lack of limits and the absence of accountability by parents, teachers, and health professionals. Professionals generally agree that, for Internet addiction, controlled use is a more practical goal than total abstinence.

Families in the People's Republic of China and South Korea have turned to unlicensed training camps that offer to "wean" their children, often in their teens, from overuse of the Internet. An internet addiction treatment center was started in Delhi, the capital city of India by a nonprofit organization, the Uday Foundation. In 2009, ReSTART, a residential treatment center for "pathological computer use", opened near Seattle, Washington. The Ranch, a treatment center in Nunnelly, TN, that focuses on behavioral addictions has an internet addiction program. Dr Kimberly Young directs a treatment program called the Internet Addiction Program as part of the Behavioral Health Services Dual Diagnosis Unit at Bradford Regional Medical Center in Bradford, PA. Dr. Maressa Orzack, has treated addictive behaviors at the Computer Addiction Services unit at the McLean Hospital, in Belmont and Newton Center, Massachusetts. The Illinois Institute for addiction recovery has an Internet addictions treatment track with locations in Peoria, Normal, Harvey and Springfield Illinois. New Beginnings offers treatment for Internet addiction with facilities in many states.

For those that are not exactly sure they need treatment for an Internet addiction, there is Online Gamers Anonymous, (OLGA, and OLG-Anon). Founded in 2002, by Elizabeth (Liz) Woolley after her son, Shawn Woolley, committed suicide while logged into EverQuest. OLGA is a twelve-step, self-help, support and recovery organization for gamers (OLGA) and their loved ones (OLG-Anon) who are suffering from the adverse effects of addictive computer gaming. It offers resources such as discussion forums, online chat meetings, Skype meetings and links to other resources.

（来源：https://www.linkedin.com/pulse/what-internet-addiction-disorder-melissa-killeen）

3.7 Critical thinking 环节

英文视频：TED 演讲 How to Separate Fact and Fiction Online?

怎样辨别网络上的信息是真是假？教师可让学生观看本视频（主讲人 Markham Nolan），并引导学生展开批判性思考：Is information explosion a blessing or a curse?

I've been a journalist now since I was about 17, and it's an interesting industry to be in at the moment, because as you all know, there's a huge amount of upheaval going on in media, and most of you probably know this from the business angle, which is that the business model is pretty screwed, and as my grandfather would say, the profits have all been gobbled up by Google.

So it's a really interesting time to be a journalist, but the upheaval that I'm interested in is not on the output side. It's on the input side. It's concerned with how we get information and how we gather the news. And that's changed, because we've had a huge shift in the balance of power from the news organizations to the audience. And the audience for such a long time was in a position where they didn't have any way of affecting news or making any change. They couldn't really connect. And that's changed irrevocably.

My first connection with the news media was in 1984, the BBC had a one-day strike. I wasn't happy. I was angry. I couldn't see my cartoons. So I wrote a letter. And it's a very effective way of ending your hate mail: "Love Markham, Aged 4." Still works. I'm not sure if I had any impact on the one-day strike, but what I do know is that it took them three weeks to get back to me. And that was the round journey. It took that long for anyone to have any impact and get some feedback. And that's changed now because, as journalists, we interact in real time. We're not in a position where the audience is reacting to news. We're reacting to the audience, and we're actually relying on them. They're helping us find the news. They're helping us figure out what is the best angle to take and what is the stuff that they want to hear. So it's a real-time thing. It's much quicker. It's happening on a constant basis, and the journalist is always playing catch up.

To give an example of how we rely on the audience, on the 5th of September in Costa Rica, an earthquake hit. It was a 7.6 magnitude. It was fairly big. And 60 seconds is the amount of time it took for it to travel 250 kilometers to Managua. So the ground shook in Managua 60 seconds after it hit the epicenter. Thirty seconds later, the first message went onto Twitter, and this was someone saying "temblor," which means earthquake. So 60 seconds was how long it took for the physical earthquake to travel. Thirty seconds later news of that earthquake had traveled all around the world, instantly. Everyone in the world, hypothetically, had the potential to know that an earthquake was happening in Managua. And that happened because this one person had a documentary instinct, which was to post a status update, which is what we all do now, so if something happens, we put our status update, or we post a photo, we post a video, and it all goes up into the cloud in a constant stream.

And what that means is just constant, huge volumes of data going up. It's actually staggering. When you look at the numbers, every minute there are 72 more hours of video on YouTube. So that's, every second, more than an hour of video gets uploaded. And in photos, Instagram, 58 photos are uploaded to Instagram a second. More than three and a half thousand photos go up onto Facebook. So by the time I'm finished talking here, there'll be 864 more hours of video on YouTube than there were when I started, and two and a half million more photos on Facebook and Instagram than when I started.

So it's an interesting position to be in as a journalist, because we should have access to everything. Any event that happens anywhere in the world, I should be able to know about it pretty much instantaneously, as it happens, for free. And that goes for every single person in this room.

The only problem is, when you have that much information, you have to find the good stuff, and that can be incredibly difficult when you're dealing with those volumes. And nowhere was this brought home more than during hurricane Sandy. So what you had in hurricane Sandy was a superstorm, the likes of which we hadn't seen for a long time, hitting the iPhone capital of the universe—and you got volumes of media like we'd never seen before. And that meant that journalists had to deal with fakes, so we had to deal with old photos that were being reposted. We had to deal with composite images that were merging photos from previous storms. We had to deal with images from films like *The Day After Tomorrow.* And we had to deal with images that were so realistic it was nearly difficult to tell if they were real at all.

But joking aside, there were images like this one from Instagram which was subjected to a grilling by journalists. They weren't really sure. It was filtered in Instagram. The lighting was questioned. Everything was questioned about it. And it turned out to be true. It was from Avenue C in downtown Manhattan, which was flooded. And the reason that they could tell that it was real was because they could get to the source, and in this case, these guys were New York food bloggers. They were well respected. They were known. So this one wasn't a debunk, it was actually something that they could prove. And that was the job of the journalist. It was filtering all this stuff. And you were, instead of going and finding the information and bringing it back to the reader, you were holding back the stuff that was potentially damaging.

And finding the source becomes more and more important — finding the good source — and Twitter is where most journalists now go. It's like the de facto real-time newswire, if you know how to use it, because there is so much on Twitter.

And a good example of how useful it can be but also how difficult was the Egyptian revolution in 2011. As a non-Arabic speaker, as someone who was looking from the outside, from Dublin, Twitter lists, and lists of good sources, people we could establish were credible, were really important. And how do you build a list like that from scratch? Well, it can be quite difficult, but you have to know what to look for. This visualization was done by an Italian academic. He's called André Pannison, and he basically took the Twitter conversation in Tahrir Square on the day that Hosni Mubarak would eventually resign, and the dots you can see are retweets, so when someone retweets a message, a connection is made between two dots, and the more times that message is retweeted by other people, the more you get to see these nodes, these connections being made. And it's an amazing way of visualizing the conversation, but what you get is hints at who is more interesting and who is worth investigating. And as the conversation grew and grew, it became more and more lively, and eventually you were left with this huge, big, rhythmic pointer of this conversation. You could find the nodes, though, and then you went, and you go, "Right, I've got to investigate these people. These are the ones that are obviously making sense. Let's see who they are."

Now in the deluge of information, this is where the real-time web gets really interesting for a journalist like myself, because we have more tools than ever to do that kind of investigation. And when you start digging into the sources, you can go further and further than you ever could before.

Sometimes you come across a piece of content that is so compelling, you want to use it, you're dying to use it, but you're not 100 percent sure if you can because you don't know if the source is credible. You don't know if it's a scrape. You don't know if it's a re-upload. And you have to do that investigative work. And this video, which I'm going to let run through, was one we discovered a couple of weeks ago.

Video: Getting real windy in just a second.

Markham Nolan: Okay, so now if you're a news producer, this is something you'd love to run with, because obviously, this is gold. You know? This is a fantastic reaction from someone, very genuine video that they've shot in their back garden. But how do you find if this person, if it's true, if it's faked, or if it's something that's old and that's been reposted?

So we set about going to work on this video, and the only thing that we had to go on was the username on the YouTube account. There was only one video posted to that account, and the username was Rita Krill. And we didn't know if Rita existed or if it was a fake name. But we started looking, and we used free Internet tools to do so. The first one was called Spokeo, which allowed us to look for Rita Krills. So we looked all over the U.S. We found them in New York, we found them in Pennsylvania, Nevada and Florida. So we went and we looked for a second free Internet tool called Wolfram Alpha, and we checked the weather reports for the day in which this video had been uploaded, and when we went through all those various cities, we found that in Florida, there were thunderstorms and rain on the day. So we went to the white pages, and we found, we looked through the Rita Krills in the phonebook, and we looked through a couple of different addresses, and that took us to Google Maps, where we found a house. And we found a house with a swimming pool that looked remarkably like Rita's. So we went back to the video, and we had to look for clues that we could cross-reference. So if you look in the video, there's the big umbrella, there's a white lilo in the pool, there are some unusually rounded edges in the swimming pool, and there's two trees in the background. And we went back to Google Maps, and we looked a little bit closer, and sure enough, there's the white lilo, there are the two trees, there's the umbrella. It's actually folded in this photo. Little bit of trickery. And there are the rounded edges on the swimming pool. So we were able to call Rita, clear the video, make sure that it had been shot, and then our clients were delighted because they were able to run it without being worried.

Sometimes the search for truth, though, is a little bit less flippant, and it has much greater consequences. Syria has been really interesting for us, because obviously a lot of the time you're trying to debunk stuff that can be potentially war crime evidence, so this is where YouTube actually becomes the most important repository of information about what's going on in the world.

So this video, I'm not going to show you the whole thing, because it's quite gruesome, but you'll hear some of the sounds. This is from Hama.

Video: (Shouting)

And what this video shows, when you watch the whole thing through, is bloody bodies being taken out of a pickup truck and thrown off a bridge. The allegations were that these guys were Muslim Brotherhood and they were throwing Syrian Army officers' bodies off the bridge, and they were cursing and using blasphemous language, and there were lots of counterclaims about who they were, and whether or not they were what the video said it was.

So we talked to some sources in Hama who we had been back and forth with on Twitter, and we asked them about this, and the bridge was interesting to us because it was something we could identify. Three different sources said three different things about the bridge. They said, one, the bridge doesn't exist. Another one said the bridge does exist, but it's not in Hama. It's somewhere else. And the third one said, "I think the bridge does exist, but the dam upstream of the bridge was closed, so the river should actually have been dry, so this doesn't make sense." So that was the only one that gave us a clue. We looked through the video for other clues. We saw the distinctive railings, which we could use. We looked at the curbs. The curbs were throwing shadows south, so we could tell the bridge was running east-west across the river. It had black-and-white curbs. As we looked at the river itself, you could see there's a concrete stone on the west side. There's a cloud of blood. That's blood in the river. So the river is flowing south to north. That's what that tells me. And also, as you look away from the bridge, there's a divot on the left-hand side of the bank, and the river narrows.

So onto Google Maps we go, and we start looking through literally every single bridge. We go to the dam that we talked about, we start just literally going through every time that road crosses the river, crossing off the bridges that don't match. We're looking for one that crosses east-west. And we get to Hama. We get all the way from the dam to Hama and there's no bridge. So we go a bit further. We switch to the satellite view, and we find another bridge, and everything starts to line up. The bridge looks like it's crossing the river east to west. So this could be our bridge. And we zoom right in. We start to see that it's got a median, so it's a two-lane bridge. And it's got the black-and-white curbs that we saw in the video, and as we click through it, you can see someone's uploaded photos to go with the map, which is very handy, so we click into the photos. And the photos start showing us more detail that we can cross-reference with the video. The first thing that we see is we see black-and-white curbing, which is handy because we've seen that before. We see the distinctive railing that we saw the guys throwing the bodies over. And we keep going through it until we're certain that this is our bridge.

So what does that tell me? I've got to go back now to my three sources and look at what they told me: the one who said the bridge didn't exist, the one who said the bridge wasn't in Hama, and the one guy who said, "Yes, the bridge does exist, but I'm not sure about the water levels." Number three is looking like the most truthful all of a sudden, and we've been able to find that out using some free Internet tools sitting in a cubicle in an office in Dublin in the space of 20 minutes. And that's part of the joy of this. Although the web is running like a torrent, there's so much information there that it's incredibly hard to sift and getting harder every day, if you use them intelligently, you can find out incredible information. Given a couple of clues, I could probably find out a lot of things about most of you in the audience that you might not like me finding out.

But what it tells me is that, at a time when there's more—there's a greater abundance of information than there ever has been, it's harder to filter, we have greater tools. We have free Internet tools that allow us, help us do this kind of investigation. We have algorithms that are smarter than ever before, and computers that are quicker than ever before.

But here's the thing. Algorithms are rules. They're binary. They're yes or no, they're black or white. Truth is never binary. Truth is a value. Truth is emotional, it's fluid, and above all, it's human. No matter how quick we get with computers, no matter how much information we have, you'll never be able to remove the human from the truth-seeking exercise, because in the end, it is a uniquely human trait. Thanks very much. (Applause)

（来源：https://www.ted.com/talks/markham_nolan_how_to_separate_fact_and_fiction_online）

3.8 主题拓展资源

A. 英语视频：TED 演讲 How Can You Help Transform the Internet into a Place of Trust?

No matter who you are or where you live, I'm guessing that you have at least one relative that likes to forward those Emails. You know the ones I'm talking about — the ones with dubious claims or conspiracy videos. And you've probably already muted them on Facebook for sharing social posts like this one.

It's an image of a banana with a strange red cross running through the center. And the text around it is warning people not to eat fruits that look like this, suggesting they've been injected with blood contaminated with the HIV virus. And the social share message above it simply says, "Please forward to save lives." Now, fact-checkers have been debunking this one for years, but it's one of those rumors that just won't die. A zombie rumor. And, of course, it's entirely false.

It might be tempting to laugh at an example like this, to say, "Well, who would believe this, anyway?" But the reason it's a zombie rumor is because it taps into people's deepest fears about their own safety and that of the people they love. And if you spend as enough time as I have looking at misinformation, you know that this is just one example of many that taps into people's deepest fears and vulnerabilities.

Every day, across the world, we see scores of new memes on Instagram encouraging parents not to vaccinate their children. We see new videos on YouTube explaining that climate change is a hoax. And across all platforms, we see endless posts designed to demonize others on the basis of their race, religion or sexuality.

Welcome to one of the central challenges of our time. How can we maintain an internet with freedom of expression at the core, while also ensuring that the content that's being disseminated doesn't cause irreparable harms to our democracies, our communities and to our physical and mental well-being? Because we live in the information age, yet the central currency upon which we all depend — information — is no longer deemed entirely trustworthy and, at times, can appear downright dangerous. This is thanks in part to the runaway growth of social sharing platforms that allow us to scroll through, where lies and facts sit side by side, but with none of the traditional signals of trustworthiness.

And goodness — our language around this is horribly muddled. People are still obsessed with the phrase "fake news," despite the fact that it's extraordinarily unhelpful and used to describe a number of things that are actually very different: lies, rumors, hoaxes, conspiracies, propaganda. And I really wish we could stop using a phrase that's been co-opted by politicians right around the world, from the left and the right, used as a weapon to attack a free and independent press.

Because we need our professional news media now more than ever, and besides, most of this content doesn't even masquerade as news. It's memes, videos, social posts. And most of it is not fake; it's misleading. We tend to fixate on what's true or false. But the biggest concern is actually the weaponization of context, because the most effective disinformation has always been that which has a kernel of truth to it.

Let's take this example from London, from March 2017, a tweet that circulated widely in the aftermath of a terrorist incident on Westminster Bridge. This is a genuine image, not fake. The woman who appears in the photograph was interviewed afterwards, and she explained that she was utterly traumatized. She was on the phone to a loved one, and she wasn't looking at the victim out of respect. But it still was circulated widely with this Islamophobic framing, with multiple hashtags, including: #BanIslam. Now, if you worked at Twitter, what would you do? Would you take that down, or would you leave it up? My gut reaction, my emotional reaction, is to take this down. I hate the framing of this image. But freedom of expression is a human right, and if we start taking down speech that makes us feel uncomfortable, we're in trouble.

And this might look like a clear-cut case, but, actually, most speech isn't. These lines are incredibly difficult to draw. What's a well-meaning decision by one person is outright censorship to the next. What we now know is that this account, Texas Lone Star, was part of a wider Russian disinformation campaign, one that has since been taken down. Would that change your view? It would mine, because now it's a case of a coordinated campaign to sow discord. And for those of you who would like to think that artificial intelligence will solve all of our problems, I think we can agree that we're a long way away from AI that's able to make sense of posts like this.

So I'd like to explain three interlocking issues that make this so complex and then think about some ways we can consider these challenges. First, we just don't have a rational relationship to information, we have an emotional one. It's just not true that more facts will make everything OK, because the algorithms that determine what content we see, well, they're designed to reward our emotional responses. And when we're fearful, oversimplified narratives, conspiratorial explanations and language that demonizes others is far more effective. And besides, many of these companies, their business model is attached to attention, which means these algorithms will always be skewed towards emotion.

Second, most of the speech I'm talking about here is legal. It would be a different matter if I was talking about child sexual abuse imagery or content that incites violence. It can be perfectly legal to post an outright lie. But people keep talking about taking down "problematic" or "harmful" content, but with no clear definition of what they mean by that, including Mark Zuckerberg, who recently called for global regulation to moderate speech. And my concern is that we're seeing governments right around the world rolling out hasty policy decisions that might actually trigger much more serious consequences when it comes to our speech. And even if we could decide which speech to take up or take down, we've never had so much speech. Every second, millions of pieces of content are uploaded by people right around the world in different languages, drawing on thousands of different cultural contexts. We've simply never had effective mechanisms to moderate speech at this scale, whether powered by humans or by technology.

And third, these companies — Google, Twitter, Facebook, WhatsApp — they're part of a wider information ecosystem. We like to lay all the blame at their feet, but the truth is, the mass media and elected officials can also play an equal role in amplifying rumors and conspiracies when they want to. As can we, when we mindlessly forward divisive or misleading content without trying. We're adding to the pollution.

I know we're all looking for an easy fix. But there just isn't one. Any solution will have to be rolled out at a massive scale, internet scale, and yes, the platforms, they're used to operating at that level. But can and should we allow them to fix these problems? They're certainly trying. But most of us would agree that, actually, we don't want global corporations to be the guardians of truth and fairness online. And I also think the platforms would agree with that. And at the moment, they're marking their own homework. They like to tell us that the interventions they're rolling out are working, but because they write their own transparency reports, there's no way for us to independently verify what's actually happening.

And let's also be clear that most of the changes we see only happen after journalists undertake an investigation and find evidence of bias or content that breaks their community guidelines. So yes, these companies have to play a really important role in this process, but they can't control it.

So what about governments? Many people believe that global regulation is our last hope in terms of cleaning up our information ecosystem. But what I see are lawmakers who are struggling to keep up to date with the rapid changes in technology. And worse, they're working in the dark, because they don't have access to data to understand what's happening on these platforms. And anyway, which governments would we trust to do this? We need a global response, not a national one.

So the missing link is us. It's those people who use these technologies every day. Can we design a new infrastructure to support quality information? Well, I believe we can, and I've got a few ideas about what we might be able to actually do. So firstly, if we're serious about bringing the public into this, can we take some inspiration from Wikipedia? They've shown us what's possible. Yes, it's not perfect, but they've demonstrated that with the right structures, with a global outlook and lots and lots of transparency, you can build something that will earn the trust of most people, because we have to find a way to tap into the collective wisdom and experience of all users. This is particularly the case for women, people of color and underrepresented groups. Because guess what? They are experts when it comes to hate and disinformation, because they have been the targets of these campaigns for so long. And over the years, they've been raising flags, and they haven't been listened to. This has got to change. So could we build a Wikipedia for trust? Could we find a way that users can actually provide insights? They could offer insights around difficult content-moderation decisions. They could provide feedback when platforms decide they want to roll out new changes.

Second, people's experiences with the information is personalized. My Facebook news feed is very different from yours. Your YouTube recommendations are very different from mine. That makes it impossible for us to actually examine what information people are seeing. So could we imagine developing some kind of centralized open repository for anonymized data, with privacy and ethical concerns built in? Because imagine what we would learn if we built out a global network of concerned citizens who wanted to donate their social data to science; because we actually know very little about the long-term consequences of hate and disinformation on people's attitudes and behaviors. And what we do know, most of that has been carried out in the US, despite the fact that this is a global problem. We need to work on that, too.

And third, can we find a way to connect the dots? No one sector, let alone nonprofit, start-up or government, is going to solve this. But there are very smart people right around the world working on these challenges, from newsrooms, civil society, academia, activist groups. And you can see some of them here. Some are building out indicators of content credibility. Others are fact-checking, so that false claims, videos and images can be down-ranked by the platforms.

A nonprofit I helped to found, First Draft, is working with normally competitive newsrooms around the world to help them build out investigative, collaborative programs. And Danny Hillis, a software architect, is designing a new system called The Underlay, which will be a record of all public statements of fact connected to their sources, so that people and algorithms can better judge what is credible. And educators around the world are testing different techniques for finding ways to make people critical of the content they consume. All of these efforts are wonderful, but they're working in silos, and many of them are woefully underfunded.

There are also hundreds of very smart people working inside these companies, but again, these efforts can feel disjointed, because they're actually developing different solutions to the same problems.

How can we find a way to bring people together in one physical location for days or weeks at a time, so they can actually tackle these problems together but from their different perspectives? So can we do this? Can we build out a coordinated, ambitious response, one that matches the scale and the complexity of the problem? I really think we can. Together, let's rebuild our information commons.

Thank you.

（来源：https://www.ted.com/talks/claire_wardle_how_you_can_help_transform_the_internet_into_a_place_of_trust）

B. 英语视频：TED 演讲 The Next 5,000 Days of Web

The Internet, the web as we know it, the kind of web — the things we're all talking about — is already less than 5,000 days old. So all of the things that we've seen come about, starting, say, with satellite images of the whole Earth, which we couldn't even imagine happening before, all these things rolling into our lives, just this abundance of things that are right before us, sitting in front of our laptop, or our desktop. This kind of cornucopia of stuff just coming and never ending is amazing, and we're not amazed. It's really amazing that all this stuff is here. It's in 5,000 days, all this stuff has come. And I know that 10 years ago, if I had told you that this was all coming, you would have said that that's impossible. There's simply no economic model that that would be possible. And if I told you it was all coming for free, you would say, this is simply — you're dreaming. You're a Californian utopian. You're a wild-eyed optimist. And yet it's here.

The other thing that we know about it was that 10 years ago, as I looked at what even *Wired* was talking about, we thought it was going to be TV, but better. That was the model. That was what everybody was suggesting was going to be coming. And it turns out that that's not what it was. First of all, it was impossible, and it's not what it was. And so one of the things that I think we're learning — if you think about, like, Wikipedia, it's something that was simply impossible. It's impossible in theory, but possible in practice. And if you take all these things that are impossible, I think one of the things that we're learning from this era, from this last decade, is that we have to get good at believing in the impossible, because we're unprepared for it.

So, I'm curious about what's going to happen in the next 5,000 days. But if that's happened in the last 5,000 days, what's going to happen in the next 5,000 days? So, I have a kind of a simple story, and it suggests that what we want to think about is this thing that we're making, this thing that has happened in 5,000 days—that's all these computers, all these handhelds, all these cell phones, all these laptops, all these servers—basically what we're getting out of all these connections is we're getting one machine. If there is only one machine, and our little handhelds and devices are actually just little windows into those machines, but that we're basically constructing a single, global machine.

And so I began to think about that. And it turned out that this machine happens to be the most reliable machine that we've ever made. It has not crashed; it's running uninterrupted. And there's almost no other machine that we've ever made that runs the number of hours, the number of days. 5,000 days without interruption—that's just unbelievable. And of course, the Internet is longer than just 5,000 days; the web is only 5,000 days. So, I was trying to basically make measurements. What are the dimensions of this machine? And I started off by calculating how many billions of clicks there are all around the globe on all the computers. And there is a 100 billion clicks per day. And there's 55 trillion links between all the Web pages of the world.

And so I began thinking more about other kinds of dimensions, and I made a quick list. Was it Chris Jordan, the photographer, talking about numbers being so large that they're meaningless? Well, here's a list of them. They're hard to tell, but there's one billion PC chips on the Internet, if you count all the chips in all the computers on the Internet. There's two million emails per second. So it's a very big number. It's just a huge machine, and it uses five percent of the global electricity on the planet. So here's the specifications, just as if you were to make up a spec sheet for it: 170 quadrillion transistors, 55 trillion links, emails running at two megahertz itself, 31 kilohertz text messaging, 246 exabyte storage. That's a big disk. That's a lot of storage, memory. Nine exabyte RAM. And the total traffic on this is running at seven terabytes per second. Brewster was saying the Library of Congress is about twenty terabytes. So every second, half of the Library of Congress is swooshing around in this machine. It's a big machine.

So I did something else. I figured out 100 billion clicks per day, 55 trillion links is almost the same as the number of synapses in your brain. A quadrillion transistors is almost the same as the number of neurons in your brain. So to a first approximation, we have these things—twenty petahertz synapse firings. Of course, the memory is really huge. But to a first approximation, the size of this machine is the size—and its complexity, kind of—to your brain, because in fact, that's how your brain works — in kind of the same way that the web works. However, your brain isn't doubling every two years. So if we say this machine right now that we've made is about one HB, one human brain, if we look at the rate that this is increasing, 30 years from now, there'll be six billion HBs. So by the year 2040, the total processing of this machine will exceed a total processing power of humanity,

In raw bits and stuff. And this is, I think, where Ray Kurzweil and others get this little chart saying that we're going to cross. So, what about that? Well, here's a couple of things. I have three kind of general things I would like to say, three consequences of this. First, that basically what this machine is doing is embodying. We're giving it a body. And that's what we're going to do in the next 5,000 days — we're going to give this machine a body. And the second thing is, we're going to restructure its architecture. And thirdly, we're going to become completely codependent upon it.

So let me go through those three things. First of all, we have all these things in our hands. We think they're all separate devices, but in fact, every screen in the world is looking into the one machine. These are all basically portals into that one machine. The second thing is that — some people call this the cloud, and you're kind of touching the cloud with this. And so in some ways, all you really need is a cloudbook. And the cloudbook doesn't have any storage. It's wireless. It's always connected. There's many things about it. It becomes very simple, and basically what you're doing is you're just touching the machine, you're touching the cloud and you're going to compute that way. So the machine is computing.

And in some ways, it's sort of back to the kind of old idea of centralized computing. But everything, all the cameras, and the microphones, and the sensors in cars and everything is connected to this machine. And everything will go through the web. And we're seeing that already with, say, phones. Right now, phones don't go through the web, but they are beginning to, and they will. And if you imagine what, say, just as an example, what Google Labs has in terms of experiments with Google Docs, Google Spreadsheets, blah, blah, blah — all these things are going to become web based. They're going through the machine. And I am suggesting that every bit will be owned by the web. Right now, it's not. If you do spreadsheets and things at work, a word document, they aren't on the web, but they are going to be. They're going to be part of this machine. They're going to speak the web language. They're going to talk to the machine. The web, in some sense, is kind of like a black hole that's sucking up everything into it. And so every thing will be part of the web. So every item, every artifact that we make, will have embedded in it some little sliver of web-ness and connection, and it will be part of this machine, so that our environment — kind of in that ubiquitous computing sense — our environment becomes the web. Everything is connected.

Now, with RFIDs and other things — whatever technology it is, it doesn't really matter. The point is that everything will have embedded in it some sensor connecting it to the machine, and so we have, basically, an Internet of things. So you begin to think of a shoe as a chip with heels, and a car as a chip with wheels, because basically most of the cost of manufacturing cars is the embedded intelligence and electronics in it, and not the materials. A lot of people think about the new economy as something that was going to be a disembodied, alternative, virtual existence, and that we would have the old economy of atoms. But in fact, what the new economy really is, is the marriage of those two, where we embed the information, and the digital nature of things into the material world. That's what we're looking forward to. That is where we're going — this union, this convergence of the atomic and the digital.

And so one of the consequences of that, I believe, is that where we have this sort of spectrum of media right now — TV, film, video — that basically becomes one media platform. And while there's many differences in some senses, they will share more and more in common with each other. So that the laws of media, such as the fact that copies have no value, the value's in the uncopiable things, the immediacy, the authentication, the personalization. The media wants to be liquid. The reason why things are free is so that you can manipulate them, not so that they are "free" as in "beer," but "free" as in "freedom." And the network effects rule, meaning that the more you have, the more you get. The first fax machine — the person who bought the first fax machine was an idiot, because there was nobody to fax to. But here she became an evangelist, recruiting others to get the fax machines because it made their purchase more valuable. Those are the effects that we're going to see. Attention is the currency.

So those laws are going to kind of spread throughout all media. And the other thing about this embodiment is that there's kind of what I call the McLuhan reversal. McLuhan was saying, "Machines are the extensions of the human senses." And I'm saying, "Humans are now going to be the extended senses of the machine," in a certain sense. So we have a trillion eyes, and ears, and touches, through all our digital photographs and cameras. And we see that in things like Flickr, or Photosynth, this program from Microsoft that will allow you to assemble a view of a touristy place from the thousands of tourist snapshots of it. In a certain sense, the machine is seeing through the pixels of individual cameras.

Now, the second thing that I want to talk about was this idea of restructuring, that what the web is doing is restructuring. And I have to warn you, that what we'll talk about is — I'm going to give my explanation of a term you're hearing, which is a "semantic web".

So first of all, the first stage that we've seen of the Internet was that it was going to link computers. And that's what we called the net; that was the Internet of nets. And we saw that, where you have all the computers of the world. And if you remember, it was a kind of green screen with cursors, and there was really not much to do, and if you wanted to connect it, you connected it from one computer to another computer. And what you had to do was — if you wanted to participate in this, you had to share packets of information. So you were forwarding on. You didn't have control. It wasn't like a telephone system where you had control of a line: you had to share packets.

The second stage that we're in now is the idea of linking pages. So in the old one, if I wanted to go on to an airline web page, I went from my computer, to an FTP site, to another airline computer. Now we have pages — the unit has been resolved into pages, so one page links to another page. And if I want to go in to book a flight, I go into the airline's flight page, the website of the airline, and I'm linking to that page. And what we're sharing were links, so you had to be kind of open with links. You couldn't deny — if someone wanted to link to you, you couldn't stop them. You had to participate in this idea of opening up your pages to be linked by anybody. So that's what we were doing.

We're now entering to the third stage, which is what I'm talking about, and that is where we link the data. So, I don't know what the name of this thing is. I'm calling it the one machine. But we're linking data. So we're going from machine to machine, from page to page, and now data to data. So the difference, is that rather than linking from page to page, we're actually going to link from one idea on a page to another idea, rather than to the other page. So every idea is basically being supported — or every item, or every noun — is being supported by the entire Web. It's being resolved at the level of items, or ideas, or words, if you want. So besides physically coming out again into this idea that it's not just virtual, it's actually going out to things. So something will resolve down to the information about a particular person, so every person will have a unique ID. Every person, every item will have something that will be very specific, and will link to a specific representation of that idea or item. So now, in this new one, when I link to it, I would link to my particular flight, my particular seat. And so, giving an example of this thing, I live in Pacifica, rather than — right now Pacifica is just sort of a name on the web somewhere. The web doesn't know that that is actually a town, and that it's a specific town that I live in, but that's what we're going to be talking about. It's going to link directly to — it will know, the web will be able to read itself and know that that actually is a place, and that whenever it sees that word, "Pacifica", it knows that it actually has a place, latitude, longitude, a certain population.

So here are some of the technical terms, all three-letter things, that you'll see a lot more of. All these things are about enabling this idea of linking to the data. So I'll give you one kind of an example. There's like a billion social sites on the web. Each time you go into there, you have to tell it again who you are and all your friends are. Why should you be doing that? You should just do that once, and it should know who all your friends are. So that's what you want, is all, your friends are identified, and you should just carry these relationships around. All this data about you should just be conveyed, and you should do it once and that's all that should happen. And you should have all the networks of all the relationships between those pieces of data. That's what we're moving into — where it sort of knows these things down to that level. A semantic web, web 3.0, giant global graph — we're kind of trying out what we want to call this thing. But what's it's doing is sharing data. So you have to be open to having your data shared, which is a much bigger step than just sharing your web page, or your computer. And all these things that are going to be on this are not just pages, they are things. Everything we've described, every artifact or place, will be a specific representation, will have a specific character that can be linked to directly. So we have this database of things. And so there's actually a fourth thing that we have not get to, that we won't see in the next 10 years, or 5,000 days, but I think that's where we're going to. And as the Internet of things — where I'm linking directly to the particular things of my seat on the plane — that that physical thing becomes part of the web. And so we are in the middle of this thing that's completely linked, down to every object in the little sliver of a connection that it has.

So, the last thing I want to talk about is this idea that we're going to be codependent. It's always going to be there, and the closer it is, the better. If you allow Google to, it will tell you your search history. And I found out by looking at it that I search most at 11 o'clock in the morning. So I am open, and being transparent to that. And I think total personalization in this new world will require total transparency. That is going to be the price. If you want to have total personalization, you have to be totally transparent. Google. I can't remember my phone number; I'll just ask Google. We're so dependent on this that I have now gotten to the point where I don't even try to remember things — I'll just Google it. It's easier to do that. And we kind of object at first, saying, "Oh, that's awful." But if we think about the dependency that we have on this other technology, called the alphabet, and writing, we're totally dependent on it, and it's transformed culture. We cannot imagine ourselves without the alphabet and writing. And so in the same way, we're going to not imagine ourselves without this other machine being there. And what is happening with this is some kind of AI, but it's not the AI in conscious AI, as being an expert, Larry Page told me that that's what they're trying to do, and that's what they're trying to do. But when six billion humans are Googling, who's searching who? It goes both ways. So we are the Web, that's what this thing is. We are going to be the machine. So the next 5,000 days, it's not going to be the web and only better. Just like it wasn't TV and only better. The next 5,000 days, it's not just going to be the web but only better — it's going to be something different. And I think it's going to be smarter. It'll have an intelligence in there, that's not, again, conscious. But it'll anticipate what we're doing, in a good sense. Secondly, it's become much more personalized. It will know us, and that's good. And again, the price of that will be transparency. And thirdly, it's going to become more ubiquitous in terms of filling your entire environment, and we will be in the middle of it. And all these devices will be portals into that.

So the single idea that I wanted to leave with you is that we have to begin to think about this as not just "the web, only better", but a new kind of stage in this development. It looks more global. If you take this whole thing, it is a very big machine, very reliable machine, more reliable than its parts. But we can also think about it as kind of a large organism. So we might respond to it more as if this was a whole system, more as if this wasn't a large organism that we are going to be interacting with. It's a "one". And I don't know what else to call it, than the one. We'll have a better word for it. But there's a unity of some sort that's starting to emerge. And again, I don't want to talk about consciousness, I want to talk about it just as if it was a little bacteria, or a volvox, which is what that organism is.

So, to do, action, take-away. So, here's what I would say: there's only one machine, and the web is its OS. All screens look into the one. No bits will live outside the web. To share is to gain. Let the one read it. It's going to be machine-readable. You want to make something that the machine can read. And the one is us. We are in the one. I appreciate your time.

（来源：https://www.ted.com/talks/kevin_kelly_the_next_5_000_days_of_the_web）

第六单元　无私奉献的志愿者精神
（Unit 6 Volunteering）

1. 思政主题

志愿者精神是指一种互助、不求回报的精神，它提倡"互相帮助、助人自助、无私奉献、不求回报"。志愿者凭借自己的双手、头脑、知识、爱心开展各种志愿服务活动，无偿帮助那些需要帮助的人们。志愿服务者以"互助"精神唤醒了许多人内心的仁爱和慈善，帮助人们走出困境，自强自立，重返生活舞台。

2. 意义

本单元聚焦"志愿服务"相关话题，探讨志愿服务的类型、意义以及志愿者精神。教师可以从武汉抗击疫情、志愿者无私奉献入手，选取与主题相关的思政素材，鼓励学生思考志愿服务的意义，志愿服务的好处，树立互相帮助、无私奉献、不求回报的志愿者精神。

疫情期间，最美逆行者无私奉献，忘我付出，帮助武汉抗击疫情，还有各行各业的众多普通人也默默做出了自己的贡献，是战"疫"成功不可或缺的无名英雄，教师可以通过视频或文字让学生感受无数志愿者和无名英雄的奉献精神和人间大爱，培养感恩之情。

作为大学生，或多或少都会加入一些志愿者协会，利用课余时间为社会奉献自己的力量。让学生思考为什么要这样做？志愿活动能够为他们带来什么好处？如此生活的意义是什么？生活的意义可能并不像电影或者哲学书中探讨的那样复杂，帮助他人、勇于付出与通过自己的努力去改变他人的生活都是生活的意义所在。

志愿服务的意义与价值是传递爱心，传播文明。志愿者在把关怀带给社会的同时，也传递了爱心，传播了文明，这种"爱心"和"文明"从一个人身上到另一个人身上，最终会汇聚成一股强大的社会暖流。

志愿服务有助于建立和谐社会。志愿工作，提供了社交和互相帮助的机会，加强了人与人之间的交往及关怀，减低彼此间的疏远感，促进社会和谐。

志愿服务可以促进社会进步。社会的进步需要全社会的共同参与和努力。志愿工作正是鼓励越来越多的人参与到服务社会的行列中来，对促进社会进步有一定的积极作用。

志愿服务可以奉献社会。志愿者通过参与志愿工作，为社会出力，尽一份公民责任和义务，丰富生活体验。志愿者利用闲暇时间，参与一些有意义的工作和活动，既可扩大自己的生活圈子，又可亲身体验社会的人和事，加深对社会的认识，这对志愿者自身的成长和提高是十分有益的。

志愿服务可以提供学习的机会。志愿者在参与志愿工作过程中，除了可以帮助他人以外，更可培养自己的组织及领导能力。学习新知识、增强自信心及学会与人相处等。

3. 教学设计与思政元素的融入

Passage A

3.1 Warm-up 环节

英文视频：No One Lives on an Isolated Island（没有人是一座孤岛）

2020年4月15日，武汉大学在读研究生王琇琨作为中方唯一青年代表参加了联合国秘书长青年特使办公室、世界卫生组织等联合举办的"共同应对新冠病毒网络研讨会"，分享她组织"与逆行者同行，为奉献者奉献"志愿服务，并通过为一线医务人员的孩子提供在线家教和心理疏导的方式参与战疫斗争的经历和故事。

王琇琨的坦诚分享与精彩评述为全球青年参与抗疫拓宽了思路，使来自中国的故事和声音被更多人知晓，在国际舞台上传递了来自中国青年的正能量。

Eleven days ago, China held a nationwide mourning event for over 3,000 Chinese people who lost their lives in the COVID-19 pandemic. A large part of these are from the city where my university is located, Wuhan. After 76 days of lockdown, the city is reopened on April 8th and the life of people in Wuhan has gradually returned to normal.

11天之前，中国为3000多名在新冠肺炎疫情中逝世的同胞举行了全国哀悼活动。他们中的大多数来自我的大学所在地——武汉。在武汉封城76天后，这座城市在4月8日又重新开放了，人们在武汉的生活逐渐恢复了正常。

With timely and effective measures taken by various levels, with the devotion of medical staff and responders in many areas, and also with the voluntary sacrifice of normal life like me, and of the billion people, my country is recovering rapidly.

由于采取了及时和有效的措施，医务工作者和不同领域的人们贡献出了自己的力量，以及十几亿同胞，包括我，自愿放弃了正常的生活，我的国家很快便可以恢复常态。

In the early days, I felt anxious and worried like many others in Wuhan. I worried about the safety of my family and friends. Staying at home every day with my parents also led to some misunderstanding and quarrels between us. And I felt reluctant to do anything when I stayed alone. But when I saw the news that many people were helping by delivering medical supplies, raising funds or serving in communities. I realized that I could also help by joining them.

刚开始的时候，我同很多在武汉的人一样感到焦虑和担心，我很担心家人和朋友的安危。每天我都与父母待在家里，也导致我们之间会出现一些误会和争吵。我独处的时候，做任何事都提不起兴趣，但是当我从新闻中得知有很多人通过提供医疗用品、募集资金或者做社区服务来共同抗击疫情时，我意识到我也可以加入他们。

I notice that many front-line medical staff are tirelessly treating patients that they cannot take care of their children at home. Therefore, I organized a live volunteer service team with my schoolmates to provide online tutoring, mental assistance, and companionship for these children. Now we have 1500 volunteers serving 641 children aged from 5 to 18 years old, and I was greatly inspired and cheered up in this process.

我发现许多一线医务工作者不知疲倦地救治病人，他们自己的孩子疏于照顾。因此，我和学校的同学们一起组织了在线义工服务团队，去提供一些教学、心理援助和陪伴。现在我们有1500名志愿者为641名5至18岁的孩子提供帮助。在这个过程中，我备受鼓舞并且十分感动。

So out of my own experiences, things that worked for my mental health that I want to share with you is trying to keep yourself engaged in daily life. Since we can only stay at home, I made a routine list of what I should do every day. I used this time to learn something new and also developed some good habits like exercising and reading. And besides, I communicated more with my parents and told them my feelings. This really helped me release my pressure and made our relationship more intimate.

所以，根据我自己的经历，在疫情期间，我想分享给你们保持心理健康的建议是让自己生活得更充实。因为只能待在家里，我为自己每日的日常生活列了一张清单，我利用这段时间学习了新的知识并养成了一些好的习惯，比如锻炼和阅读。除此之外，我和我的父母有了更多的沟通，和他们交流我的感受，这真的帮助我缓解了压力，并让我们更加亲密无间。

In addition to volunteer services, I am offering now really encouraged me a lot. So, I'd like to suggest you do something meaningful and positive to help others.

除去我的志愿服务经历，我现在所做的分享也让我深受激励。所以我会建议大家做一些有意义的、积极的事情来帮助别人。

When I hear the word "self-care", I want to share with you two key words. One is confidence. The difficulties we are going through are temporary. And the belief we will overcome it can keep us stay calm and strong. Another one is cooperation. No one lives on an isolated island. So human unity and international cooperation, like us, are vital for the fight against the pandemic. As young people, we need to give our hands, stand together and fight shoulder to shoulder.

当我听到"自顾"这个词的时候，我想和你们分享两个词。第一个是"信心"，我们现在所面临的困境是暂时的，只要心怀信念，我们就能保持冷静和坚强。另外一个词是"合作"。没有人是一座孤岛，人与人团结和国与国合作，就像我们现在所做的一样，是抗击疫情的关键。作为年轻人，我们需要携手同行，并肩作战。

（来源：外研社高等英语资讯）

3.2 Discussion 环节

英文文章： Volunteering and Its Surprising Benefits

不少大学生都会加入一些志愿者协会，利用课余时间为社会奉献自己的力量。我们为什么要这样做？志愿活动能够为我们带来什么好处？本篇文章能够启发学生：在志愿活动中，我们不仅能收获友情和技能，还能让自己更加健康向上地生活。

Volunteering can help you make friends, learn new skills, advance your career, and even feel happier and healthier. Learn how to find the right volunteer opportunity for you.

Why volunteer?

With busy lives, it can be hard to find time to volunteer. However, the benefits of volunteering can be enormous. Volunteering offers vital help to people in need, worthwhile causes, and the community, but the benefits can be even greater for you, the volunteer. The right match can help you to find friends, connect with the community, learn new skills, and even advance your career.

Giving to others can also help protect your mental and physical health. It can reduce stress, combat depression, keep you mentally stimulated, and provide a sense of purpose. While it's true that the more you volunteer, the more benefits you'll experience, volunteering doesn't have to involve a long-term commitment or take a huge amount of time out of your busy day. Giving in even simple ways can help those in need and improve your health and happiness.

Benefits of volunteering: 4 ways to feel healthier and happier

1. Volunteering connects you to others.

2. Volunteering is good for your mind and body.

3. Volunteering can advance your career.

4. Volunteering brings fun and fulfillment to your life.

Benefit 1: Volunteering connects you to others

One of the more well-known benefits of volunteering is the impact on the community. Volunteering allows you to connect to your community and make it a better place. Even helping out with the smallest tasks can make a real difference to the lives of people, animals, and organizations in need. And volunteering is a two-way street: It can benefit you and your family as much as the cause you choose to help. Dedicating your time as a volunteer helps you make new friends, expand your network, and boost your social skills.

Make new friends and contacts

One of the best ways to make new friends and strengthen existing relationships is to commit to a shared activity together. Volunteering is a great way to meet new people, especially if you are new to an area. It strengthens your ties to the community and broadens your support network, exposing you to people with common interests, neighborhood resources, and fun and fulfilling activities.

Increase your social and relationship skills

While some people are naturally outgoing, others are shy and have a hard time meeting new people. Volunteering gives you the opportunity to practice and develop your social skills, since you are meeting regularly with a group of people with common interests. Once you have momentum, it's easier to branch out and make more friends and contacts.

Volunteering as a family

Children watch everything you do. By giving back to the community, you'll show them firsthand how volunteering makes a difference and how good it feels to help other people and animals and enact change. It's also a valuable way for you to get to know organizations in the community and find resources and activities for your children and family.

Benefit 2: Volunteering is good for your mind and body

Volunteering provides many benefits to both mental and physical health.

Volunteering helps counteract the effects of stress, anger, and anxiety. The social contact aspect of helping and working with others can have a profound effect on your overall psychological well-being. Nothing relieves stress better than a meaningful connection to another person. Working with pets and other animals has also been shown to improve mood and reduce stress and anxiety.

Volunteering combats depression. Volunteering keeps you in regular contact with others and helps you develop a solid support system, which in turn protects you against depression.

Volunteering makes you happy. By measuring hormones and brain activity, researchers have discovered that being helpful to others delivers immense pleasure. Human beings are hard-wired to give to others. The more we give, the happier we feel.

Volunteering increases self-confidence. You are doing good for others and the community, which provides a natural sense of accomplishment. Your role as a volunteer can also give you a sense of pride and identity. And the better you feel about yourself, the more likely you are to have a positive view of your life and future goals.

Volunteering provides a sense of purpose. Older adults, especially those who have retired or lost a spouse, can find new meaning and direction in their lives by helping others. Whatever your age or life situation, volunteering can help take your mind off your own worries, keep you mentally stimulated, and add more zest to your life.

Volunteering helps you stay physically healthy. Studies have found that those who volunteer have a lower mortality rate than those who do not. Older volunteers tend to walk more, find it easier to cope with everyday tasks, are less likely to develop high blood pressure, and have better thinking skills. Volunteering can also lessen symptoms of chronic pain and reduce the risk of heart disease.

I have limited mobility—can I still volunteer?

People with disabilities or chronic health conditions can still benefit greatly from volunteering. In fact, research has shown that adults with disabilities or health conditions ranging from hearing and vision loss to heart disease, diabetes or digestive disorders all show improvement after volunteering.

Whether due to a disability, a lack of transportation, or time constraints, many people choose to volunteer their time via phone or computer. In today's digital age, many organizations need help with writing, graphic design, email, and other web-based tasks. Some organizations may require you to attend an initial training session or periodical meetings while others can be conducted completely remotely. In any volunteer situation, make sure that you are getting enough social contact, and that the organization is available to support you should you have questions.

Benefit 3: Volunteering can advance your career

If you're considering a new career, volunteering can help you get experience in your area of interest and meet people in the field. Even if you're not planning on changing careers, volunteering gives you the opportunity to practice important skills used in the workplace, such as teamwork, communication, problem solving, project planning, task management, and organization. You might feel more comfortable stretching your wings at work once you've honed these skills in a volunteer position first.

Teaching you valuable job skills

Just because volunteer work is unpaid does not mean the skills you learn are basic. Many volunteering opportunities provide extensive training. For example, you could become an experienced crisis counselor while volunteering for a women's shelter or a knowledgeable art historian while donating your time as a museum docent.

Volunteering can also help you build upon skills you already have and use them to benefit the greater community. For instance, if you hold a successful sales position, you can raise awareness for your favorite cause as a volunteer advocate, while further developing and improving your public speaking, communication, and marketing skills.

Gaining career experience

Volunteering offers you the chance to try out a new career without making a long-term commitment. It is also a great way to gain experience in a new field. In some fields, you can volunteer directly at an organization that does the kind of work you're interested in. For example, if you're interested in nursing, you could volunteer at a hospital or a nursing home.

Your volunteer work might also expose you to professional organizations or internships that could benefit your career.

When it comes to volunteering, passion and positivity are the only requirements

While learning new skills can be beneficial to many, it's not a requirement for a fulfilling volunteer experience. Bear in mind that the most valuable assets you can bring to any volunteer effort are compassion, an open mind, a willingness to pitch in wherever needed, and a positive attitude.

Benefit 4: Volunteering brings fun and fulfillment to your life

Volunteering is a fun and easy way to explore your interests and passions. Doing volunteer work you find meaningful and interesting can be a relaxing, energizing escape from your day-to-day routine of work, school, or family commitments. Volunteering also provides you with renewed creativity, motivation, and vision that can carry over into your personal and professional life.

Many people volunteer in order to make time for hobbies outside of work as well. For instance, if you have a desk job and long to spend time outdoors, you might consider volunteering to help plant a community garden, walk dogs for an animal shelter, or help out at a children's camp.

How to find the right volunteer opportunity?

There are numerous volunteer opportunities available. The key is to find a position that you would enjoy and are capable of doing. It's also important to make sure that your commitment matches the organization's needs. Ask yourself the following:

· Would you like to work with adults, children, animals, or remotely from home?

· Do you prefer to work alone or as part of a team?

· Are you better behind the scenes or do you prefer to take a more visible role?

· How much time are you willing to commit?

· What skills can you bring to a volunteer job?

· What causes are important to you?

Consider your goals and interests

You will have a richer and more enjoyable volunteering experience if you first take some time to identify your goals and interests. Think about why you want to volunteer. What would you enjoy doing? The opportunities that match both your goals and your interests are most likely to be fun and fulfilling.

What are your volunteering goals?

To find a volunteer position that's right for you, look for something that matches your personality, skills, and interests. Ask yourself if there is something specific you want to do or achieve as a volunteer.

For example, you might want to:

· Improve your neighborhood.

· Meet new people with different outlooks or experiences.

· Try something new.

· Do something rewarding with your spare time.

· See new places or experience a different way of living.

· Try a new type of work that you might want to pursue as a full-time job.

· Expand on your interests and hobbies.

Consider several volunteer possibilities

Don't limit yourself to just one organization or one specific type of job. Sometimes an opportunity looks great on paper, but the reality is quite different. Try to visit different organizations and get a feel for what they are like and if you click with other staff and volunteers.

Where to find volunteer opportunities?

· Community theaters, museums, and monuments.

· Libraries or senior centers.

· Service organizations such as Lions Clubs or Rotary Clubs.

- Local animal shelters, rescue organizations, or wildlife centers.
- Youth organizations, sports teams, and after-school programs.
- Historical restorations, national parks, and conservation organizations.
- Places of worship such as churches or synagogues.
- Online directories and other resources.

How much time should you volunteer?

Volunteering doesn't have to take over your life to be beneficial. In fact, research shows that just two to three hours per week, or about 100 hours a year, can confer the most benefits—to both you and your chosen cause. The important thing is to volunteer only the amount of time that feels comfortable to you. Volunteering should feel like a fun and rewarding hobby, not another chore on your to-do list.

Getting the most out of volunteering

You're donating your valuable time, so it's important that you enjoy and benefit from your volunteering. To make sure that your volunteer position is a good fit:

Ask questions. You want to make sure that the experience is right for your skills, your goals, and the time you want to spend. Sample questions for your volunteer coordinator might address your time commitment, if there's any training involved, who you will be working with, and what to do if you have questions during your experience.

Make sure you know what's expected. You should be comfortable with the organization and understand the time commitment. Consider starting small so that you don't over commit yourself at first. Give yourself some flexibility to change your focus if needed.

Don't be afraid to make a change. Don't force yourself into a bad fit or feel compelled to stick with a volunteer role you dislike. Talk to the organization about changing your focus or look for a different organization that's a better fit.

If volunteering overseas, choose carefully. Some volunteer programs abroad can cause more harm than good if they take much-needed paying jobs away from local workers. Look for volunteer opportunities with reputable organizations.

Enjoy yourself. The best volunteer experiences benefit both the volunteer and the organization. If you're not enjoying yourself, ask yourself why. Is it the tasks you're performing? The people you're working with? Or are you uncomfortable simply because the situation is new and unfamiliar? Pinpointing what's bothering you can help you decide how to proceed.

（来源：https://www.helpguide.org/articles/healthy-living/volunteering-and-its-surprising-benefits.htm#）

3.3 Critical thinking 环节

TED 演讲：来自消防员的一课：不要等待成为英雄

视频时长约4分钟，志愿消防员 Mark Bezos 讲述了自己第一次参与救火的经历——幻想着大展身手却只为屋主太太"救"下了一双鞋，看似"失败"的志愿者英雄故事却给他上了重要一课：慷慨的善行与微小的勇气同等重要，每个人随时都可以成为英雄。

Back in New York, I am the head of development for a non-profit called Robin Hood. When I'm not fighting poverty, I'm fighting fires as the assistant captain of a volunteer fire company. Now in our town, where the volunteers supplement a highly skilled career staff, you have to get to the fire scene pretty early to get in on any action.

I remember my first fire. I was the second volunteer on the scene, so there was a pretty good chance I was going to get in. But still it was a real footrace against the other volunteers to get to the captain in charge to find out what our assignments would be. When I found the captain, he was having a very engaging conversation with the homeowner, who was surely having one of the worst days of her life. Here it was, the middle of the night, she was standing outside in the pouring rain, under an umbrella, in her pajamas, barefoot, while her house was in flames.

The other volunteer who had arrived just before me—let's call him Lex Luther—got to the captain first and was asked to go inside and save the homeowner's dog. The dog! I was stunned with jealousy. Here was some lawyer or money manager who, for the rest of his life, gets to tell people that he went into a burning building to save a living creature, just because he beat me by five seconds. Well, I was next. The captain waved me over. He said, "Bezos, I need you to go into the house. I need you to go upstairs, past the fire, and I need you to get this woman a pair of shoes." I swear. So, not exactly what I was hoping for, but off I went—up the stairs, down the hall, past the "real" firefighters, who were pretty much done putting out the fire at this point, into the master bedroom to get a pair of shoes.

Now I know what you're thinking, but I'm no hero. I carried my payload back downstairs where I met my nemesis and the precious dog by the front door. We took our treasures outside to the homeowner, where, not surprisingly, his received much more attention than did mine. A few weeks later, the department received a letter from the homeowner thanking us for the valiant effort displayed in saving her home. The act of kindness she noted above all others: someone had even gotten her a pair of shoes.

In both my vocation at Robin Hood and my avocation as a volunteer firefighter, I am witness to acts of generosity and kindness on a monumental scale, but I'm also witness to acts of grace and courage on an individual basis. And you know what I've learned? They all matter. So as I look around this room at people who either have achieved, or are on their way to achieving, remarkable levels of success, I would offer this reminder: don't wait. Don't wait until you make your first million to make a difference in somebody's life. If you have something to give, give it now. Serve food at a soup kitchen. Clean up a neighborhood park. Be a mentor.

Not every day is going to offer us a chance to save somebody's life, but every day offers us an opportunity to affect one. So get in the game. Save the shoes.

Thank you.

（来源：https://www.bilibili.com/video/BV1Z7411V7H9/?spm_id_from=333.788.videocard.6）

3.4 主题拓展环节

双语文章：北京冬奥会志愿者全球招募

According to the Beijing Organizing Committee for the 2022 Olympic and Paralympic Winter Games (BOCOG), 27,000 Games volunteers will be needed for the Olympic Winter Games and 12,000 for the Paralympic Winter Games.

北京冬奥组委计划招募2.7万名冬奥会赛会志愿者、1.2万名冬残奥会赛会志愿者。

Successful candidates will be trained to assist organizers in 12 service categories before and during the Games, including international liaison, competition organization, media operations and venue services, in three zones: downtown Beijing, the capital's northwest Yanqing district and Zhangjiakou, according to Beijing 2022 organizers.

北京冬奥组委表示，成功入选的志愿者经过培训后将分布于北京、延庆、张家口三个赛区，参与国际联络、竞赛组织、媒体运营、场馆运行等12类志愿服务。

As a highly significant branding and visual element of the Olympic and Paralympic Winter Games Beijing 2022, the volunteer logo is designed to fully arouse the enthusiasm of the volunteers; carry forward and foster the volunteering spirit; and build a culture dedicated to embodying the volunteering spirit.

北京2022年冬奥会和冬残奥会志愿者标识是冬奥会和冬残奥会重要的形象景观元素，是着眼于充分调动志愿者的积极性，弘扬和培育志愿服务精神，打造志愿者文化所作的原创性设计。

The red and yellow colour in the logo symbolizes passion and hospitality. The motif of the universally-acknowledged sign language for "I love you" manifests global, trending and youthful ideas. The elegant and dynamic "ribbon" represents the rhythm of a heartbeat and showcase the vision for a "Joyful rendezvous upon pure ice and snow".

标识颜色由红色、黄色组成，代表热情和欢迎。图形采用国际通用手势"我爱你"，体现国际化、时尚化、年轻化。通过飘逸、动感的飘带形式，表达"心动"的感觉，体现"纯洁的冰雪，激情的约会"愿景。

The upper part of the logo resembles a triple "V", signifying a winning streak and the aspirations of volunteers to participate in the Winter Games. The smiling face on the bottom half of the logo aims to inspire dedication, friendship and happiness. A volunteer's smile will light up the Beijing 2022 Games. It is both the legacy of the Beijing 2008 Games and the embodiment of the volunteering spirit of dedication, friendship, mutual assistance and progress.

标识上半部图形由寓意连胜的"VVV"组成，象征志愿者"手拉手"参与冬奥服务冬奥的热情；图形下半部分"笑脸"表达了"奉献、爱与微笑"的主题。志愿者的微笑是北京最好的名片，既是对2008年北京奥运会的传承，也是对志愿精神"奉献、友爱、互助、进步"的体现。

（来源：https://language.chinadaily.com.cn/a/201912/06/WS5de9c6e1a310cf3e3557c6ed.html）

英语文章：Volunteer Spirit — Legacy of 2008 Beijing Summer Olympic Games

Dubbed "Granny Chang," Beijing native Chang Zhifu worked as a volunteer for 90 days at the 2008 Olympic Games.

"I never thought I was too old to join at that time," said Chang, who was then a robust 66. "I just wanted to do my part for the Beijing Olympics which was a rare opportunity."

She recalled facing a reporter from a Chinese news media and saying she thought it was not necessary to discuss whether the middle-aged and the aged were suitable for volunteering.

"I am the best example," she said, "Once Olympic and Paralympic volunteer projects started, I signed up immediately and became a volunteer."

Chang, now 76, learned the rudiments of first aid, English, sign language and Olympic history as a novice, and also read books and magazines about the Olympics and later made reading notes for information collection.

She said many foreigners would come to Beijing for the Olympics which required her learning a few English words about rituals and tourist attractions.

"I took free English courses in the city, wrote down the pronunciations in Chinese, and recited them."

Another Games volunteer was Althea Liu, a 19-year-old undergraduate at the Communication University of China at the time. She worked as a press operations volunteer with the Beijing Organizing Committee.

Liu told CGTN after training from the end of June 2008, her almost-one-month job was assisting with baseball game reports as well as offering a correspondent service.

Based on Chinese official data in 2008, over 74,000 volunteers from 98 countries and regions were enrolled at the Beijing Olympics. Some 98 percent were from the Chinese mainland, about 500 from China's special administrative regions–Hong Kong and Macao, and Chinese Taiwan, along with more than 900 foreigners.

August 8, 2018, marks the 10th anniversary of the start of the Beijing Olympic Games. Volunteers at the Games impressed the world with their efficiency, goodwill and hospitality.

During the decade since, Granny Chang has been dedicated to volunteering, whether in sports events like the Beijing Marathon or at public places such as subway stations.

Her greatest dream is to become a volunteer at the Beijing Winter Olympic Games in 2022 when she will be 80.

（来源：https://news.cgtn.com/news/3d3d674d77557a4d79457a6333566d54/index.html）

Passage B

3.5 Warm-up 环节

英语视频： International Volunteer Day — The Spirit of Giving

12月5日是国际志愿者日。在 CGTN 的"走到一起"系列的这一集中，特里·克罗斯曼来自美国，是后海莲花巷的志愿者，在北京住了24年，已经退休了，他从事志愿者工作已经有段时间了，帮助游客在北京西城区这个美丽的城区指路。克罗斯曼在中国提供帮助，还有许多中国志愿者正在世界其他地区发挥作用。詹尉珍出生于中国杭州，但现在在黎巴嫩与叙利亚难民一起工作，主要关注儿童和妇女。教师可以让学生观看视频，看看志愿活动如何帮助世界各地的人们分享爱和关怀。

Editor's note: December 5 marks International Volunteer Day. In this episode of CGTN's "Come Together" series, we look at how volunteering helps people around the world share love and care.

"I'm a volunteer here in Lotus Lane in Houhai. I've lived in Beijing for 24 years and I'm from the United States. I'm 64 years old and I'm retired," said Terry Crossman. "I spend some of my time volunteering, helping tourists find their way around this beautiful area of Xicheng District in Beijing."

Crossman gives directions to tourists in fluent Chinese, but things were not easy for him when he started volunteering in March 2017, since he was unfamiliar with the surroundings.

Being a fluent Mandarin speaker and the only man in a volunteer group called "Aunties from Xicheng District," Crossman has gone viral online. Many tourists visit the lake Houhai just to have a photo taken with him.

"The spirit of volunteering is you get more than what you give in a way," Crossman told CGTN. "I love volunteering because I love doing things for people. I like to make people happy. I think by making people happy they make other people happy. It's like throwing a stone into the river and it has little waves and your happiness can be given to other people."

Volunteering is a sign of an advanced and civilized society. China's first regulation on volunteer services took effect in December 2017, clarifying the principles and establishing administrative institutions in this regard. According to the 2018 Statistical Report on the Development of Civil Affairs Undertakings in

China, there are 129,000 voluntary community organizations nationwide and 10.72 million volunteers like Crossman have volunteered for 23.88 million hours.

Volunteers are serving the world beyond borders. Crossman helps out on the streets of China, and plenty of Chinese volunteers are making a difference in other parts of the world.

Zhan Weizhen was born in east China's Hangzhou but is now in Lebanon working with Syrian refugees.

Since 2011, the outbreak of the civil war has left millions of Syrians homeless, seeking refuge abroad. Among them, children have suffered the worst. The project, which Zhan has joined, was launched by the Peaceland Foundation and the Common Future Foundation in 2016. It aims to support Chinese youth volunteers who venture to the Middle East to lend a helping hand to Syrian refugees, especially teenagers and children.

Zhan is working on helping Hassan, a 24-year-old Syrian in Lebanon who wants to be a comedian. "He is working on that dream. At the moment, we teach him Chinese and English. And hopefully if he can really get to learn the two languages, he will gain more skills and become more competitive on the job market," said Zhan.

In recent years, with the increasing number of major international competitions and conferences held in China, volunteers are playing a vital part in facilitating events such as the 2008 Beijing Olympic Games, the 2010 Shanghai World Expo, the G20 Hangzhou Summit in 2016 and the 7th Military World Games in 2019.

"Nowadays, the Chinese government is also paying attention to the volunteer service," said Zhan. "The Belt and Road Initiative mentions people-to-people exchanges, which encourage volunteer work."

（来源：https://news.cgtn.com/news/2019-12-05/International-Volunteer-Day-The-Spirit-of-Giving-MaT8ZDKYOk/index.html）

3.6 Discussion 环节

双语文章：国家志愿者在全球各地的角色给人留下深刻印象

教师可安排学生阅读，引导学生思考：青年人参与志愿服务，具有什么样的重要意义？如果有机会，你愿意参加中国青年志愿者海外服务项目吗？

志愿服务是社会文明程度的重要标志，是培养时代新人、弘扬时代新风的重要途径。党和国家高度重视志愿服务，习近平总书记给中国志愿服务联合会的贺信指出，志愿者"走进社区、走进基层，为他人送温暖、为社会作贡献，充分彰显了理想信念、爱心善意、责任担当，成为人民有信仰、国家有力量、民族有希望的生动体现"[1]。党的十八大以来，习近平总书记多次给大学生志愿者群体回信，鼓励大学生弘扬奉献、友爱、互助、进步的志愿精神，坚持与祖国同行、为人民奉献，以青春梦想、用实际行动为实现中国梦作出新的更大贡献。

党的十九届四中全会提出"健全志愿服务体系"[2]，其中包括最活跃、最有创造力的青年志愿服务体系。青年志愿服务在"育人"方面具有非常突出的价值和非常重要的意义。一方面，青年人正处于人生观、价值观、世界观的形成时期，参加志愿服务有利于认识社会、形成信念、坚定意志、提高素质；另一方面，青年人处于对"同龄人"影响大、受"朋辈"吸引，以及形成各种见解的时期，参加志愿组织就能够结交有爱心、有进取心、有创造力、有互助精神的同龄朋友，在积极心态的影响下，不断增强正能量，逐渐成为爱国、爱党、爱社会主义、乐于为人民美好生活奋斗的新一代[3]。

实践表明，青年参与志愿服务，不仅为推动社会主义现代化建设起到了积极作用，而且对促进其思想发展和人格成长，具有特别重要的意义。志愿服务为大学生锻炼自我、提高自我，增强社会责任感搭建了有效平台，已成为大学生参与社会建设和关爱他人、弘扬社会主义核心价值观的重要途径。

青年志愿者除了在本国参与志愿服务外，还可以积极参加海外志愿服务项目。向国外派遣志愿者是国际上的一个通行做法，被派往海外的志愿者通过借助本国本土资源和现有的技术，对受助国进行经济和技术援助。中国青年志愿者海外服务项目涉及汉语教学、体育教学、计算机培训、中医诊治、农业技术、国际救援等多个领域。

中国的海外志愿服务经过了十几年的探索与实践，初步形成了对外援助与合作交流并重的基本框架，在对外传播进程中发挥着重要影响，其作用主要表现为：以对外援助为主要内容，塑造积极国家形象，提升了中国的文化软实力；以合作交流为发展趋势，创新对外传播手段，开辟了文化"走出去"的路径；以青年群体为实施主体，拓展民间交往空间，提供了青年外交的新平台；以志愿精神为组织愿景，顺应国际社会理念，消弭了国家地区间的差异；以个

---

[1] 习近平. 习近平致中国志愿服务联合会第二届会员代表大会的贺信 [EB/OL]., 2019-07-24, http://www.xinhuanet.com//politics/2019-07/24/c_1124792815.htm.

[2] 中共中央关于坚持和完善中国特色社会主义制度 推进国家治理体系和治理能力现代化若干重大问题的决定 [N]. 人民日报, 2019-11-06.

[3] 谭建光. 论青年志愿服务的"双功能"：助人与育人 [J]. 中国青年社会科学, 2020(2):84-85.

体实践为具体形式，赋予传播情感向度，实现了影响力的深度扩散[①]。

中国青年志愿者海外服务计划不仅促进了受援国经济社会发展，而且有效地服务了国家外交大局，树立了中国负责任大国的国际形象。同时，增进了中外青年和人民的友谊，为国家培养了一批既有国际视野又有社会责任感的优秀青年人才，受到了党中央、国务院的高度重视和充分肯定，也得到国际社会的广泛赞誉和高度认可。

"国之交在于民相亲，民相亲在于心相通"。目前中国国力大增，提升中国的国际形象意义重大，海外志愿者展现着近距离的中国形象，对于海外了解中华文化发挥了积极作用，也为推进中国同世界各国人文交流、促进多元多彩的世界文明发展做出了重要贡献[②]。中国青年志愿者海外服务计划在各相关部门的共同的协作下，积极发挥着公共外交作用，一定会有更广阔的发展前景和空间。

Nation's Volunteers Impress In Roles Around the Globe
Young workers act as goodwill ambassadors to promote friendly exchanges

When Xu Yujun arrived in the Seychelles after an 18-hour flight from Guangzhou, capital of Guangdong province, in January 2018, the first sight that greeted her was the poorly equipped airport, which was smaller than a typical railway station in China.

For the next year, she worked as an engineer and Chinese youth volunteer for a government-owned company in Victoria, the tiny capital of the Indian Ocean archipelago, where she was responsible for operating and maintaining a computer server.

Although she had trained for the work and was fully prepared to fulfill her duties, Xu faced challenges.

The first problem was daily commuting. "Buses in the Seychelles are similar to those that became obsolete in China in the 1980s, so you often have to wait a long time for one to arrive. This prompted me to walk 30 minutes to work every day as the best form of commuting," she said.

But the biggest challenge she encountered in the first three months was difficulty in communicating.

On her first working day, Xu was invited to attend a regular department

---

① 徐媛媛. 中国海外志愿服务参与对外传播的分析与思考 [J]. 对外传播，2021:44-46.
② 朱勇. 海外志愿者跨文化交际影响因素与对策 [C]. 中华文化海外传播研究. 2018(01), 107-109.

meeting.

"However, I found it hard to understand what people were saying during the two-hour meeting, due to their accents. I had a general idea about the working process, but I knew nothing about the details of my department's work."

"The meeting almost destroyed my confidence, and I was worried whether I could do my job and complete my volunteer service."

Xu then met a group of sympathetic colleagues. "My supervisor explained the work to me patiently and encouraged me to express my thoughts," she said.

The encouragement and support she received from her colleagues meant a lot, Xu said, and after three months of adapting to her new surroundings, she overcame the communication difficulties and became more efficient at work.

She said voluntary service gave her the courage to adapt to a new environment, embrace challenges, strengthen her determination to improve her skills, and offer a helping hand to more people.

China began providing assistance to the Seychelles in 1977. In addition to helping with construction of hospitals and schools, by the end of 2018, the nation had sent 106 of its young people to the Seychelles to work voluntarily, according to the Ministry of Commerce.

The Seychelles is among 23 developing countries in Africa, Asia and Latin America to which China has sent hundreds of young volunteers to offer assistance in various fields. These include Mandarin tuition, physical education, medical treatment, information technology and agricultural techniques.

China's international voluntary service began in 2002 with the government-sponsored China Youth Volunteers Overseas Service Program launched by the Chinese Young Volunteers Association.

In 2005, the program was formally incorporated in the government's foreign aid policy. From 2006 to 2009, the program sent 300 young volunteers to help in African countries, fulfilling a goal set at the third Forum on China-Africa Cooperation in 2006.

Yang Yegong, head of the overseas service program, said China sends volunteers based on the needs of recipient countries.

The program was launched in line with the country's "going out" strategy, Yang said, adding that young Chinese volunteers act as goodwill ambassadors to promote friendly exchanges with other countries and interaction between China and the world.

He said the nation's young volunteers have the passion to help those in need, act with good intentions and have a strong desire to engage in meaningful humanitarian affairs.

Conscientious Chinese volunteers have made positive contributions to promoting economic and social development in recipient countries, he added.

Technical help

In the Seychelles, China's assistance is aimed at helping that country resolve the problem of a lack of talent, Xu said, adding that volunteers have gone there to share advanced technology and experience.

Xu stressed that volunteers should focus more on doing their best to complete their work and should not exaggerate their roles.

"I believe that over time, a little help from us will bring some changes," she said.

Her views strike a chord with Sun Wei, a volunteer from Shanghai who worked as a basketball coach in Laos for seven months in 2017, sharing his expertise in training and tactics with teams in the Southeast Asian nation.

Sun's outstanding work teaching the Vientiane provincial team and the Laotian national youth team secured him a leading role in coaching the country's national men's squad.

After becoming chief coach of the men's team, he overcame a series of difficulties, including limited training facilities and also medical problems, helping the team defeat Myanmar at the 2017 Southeast Asian Games in Malaysia.

It was the first time in 20 years that the Laotian men's basketball team had returned to regional competition — achieving its first victory and also improving its ranking with the International Basketball Federation, Sun said. "Such a result was beyond my expectations," he added.

People-to-people bonds

A shortage of drinking water was one of the problems faced during training, which Sun said was hard to imagine in any professional national team. He often bought water for the players, invited them out for meals to boost their nutritional intake, and also donated basketballs to the men's team.

At the 2017 Southeast Asian Games, he helped treat an injured player, massaging the athlete's knees for an hour.

"The players said no coach they worked with had done anything like this before. I was very moved, and they treated me like their big brother," Sun said, adding that the players helped him foster friendship, along with trust and happiness.

As a national team coach in Laos, Sun refused a salary from the country's basketball association, and before returning to China, he received a "No. 1" jersey from the national team as a gift.

"Volunteer service asks for nothing in return—something that cannot be measured by money," he said.

Sun's voluntary service was cited as an example of active people-to-people exchanges between China and Laos in a signed article written by President Xi Jinping during his visit to Laos in November 2017.

Sun said a sport such as basketball is a way of communication that crosses cultures and languages, adding that it helps bring people closer.

Yang, the overseas program head, said friendship between different people is key to sound state-to-state relations. The young Chinese volunteers are also individuals with free and open minds, and their daily contact with locals helps shape these people's positive views about China, he said.

Overseas service offers volunteers more opportunities to take part in international exchanges, Yang added.

"International voluntary work also helps cultivate high-quality talent with a sense of social responsibility and international competitiveness", he said.

Multilateral stage

To encourage more young Chinese to take part in international affairs, the Chinese Young Volunteers Association and United Nations Volunteers Programme, or UNV, jointly launched a program in 2019 to send such workers from the country to UN agencies worldwide.

UNV Programme and Partnership Specialist in China, Zhang Nan, said that in 2019 and this year, 30 volunteers were sent to 15 UN agencies to serve in areas such as poverty reduction, gender equality, quality education, environmental protection, climate action and youth development.

"We believe that voluntary service has great potential to promote inclusive development and contribute to a better world," Zhang said.

She added that she hopes the program will offer a platform for ambitious and responsible young Chinese to improve their global vision, take look at themselves, and contribute to society.

"We are committed to bringing more outstanding young Chinese volunteers to serve in UN agencies and professional fields to contribute their wisdom, experience and expertise in realizing sustainable development goals," Zhang said.

"We also aim to create opportunities for young Chinese to take part in volunteer activities in a multilateral environment, tap their potential to promote world peace and development and to become leaders in advancing international development cooperation."

Zhou Shiyue, a volunteer worker from Jinan, Shandong province, at the UN Development Programme office in Ulaanbaatar, the Mongolian capital, said such work has no borders, adding that she hopes to serve in a multicultural capacity.

One of her tasks is to research comparisons between the cashmere industry in Mongolia and China, and explain China's experience and policies in developing this industry.

"I don't know if my work will make a vast difference to the country's development, but my strengths and the Chinese perspective I offer are all new to the UN agency in Mongolia," she said, adding that if her service benefits the department, she will be happy.

Guo Shuo, 28, from Shijiazhuang, capital of Hebei province, has been a volunteer at the Office of the UN Secretary-General's Envoy on Youth in New York since January 2020. Her job involves producing content and maintaining and updating the office's social media accounts, which include Twitter, Facebook, Instagram and TikTok.

"Being a volunteer at the UN allows me to experience and explore a bigger world, which has broadened my perspective and increased my determination to work for the public good and social development," she said.

Guo said her role is to convey UN action on global youth development to young people around the world including in China while bringing their stories to the international arena.

Last year, when the pandemic was raging worldwide, she was responsible for updating the envoy's blog every week to highlight the work of young people fighting COVID-19 in their communities.

She gathered information and published the stories of nine young Chinese. They included a volunteer providing mental help and online tutoring for children of frontline medical workers, a deliveryman offering a vital lifeline to countless people forced to remain at home, and a girl who cooked for medical workers.

"I'm happy and proud that the stories of these exemplary young Chinese can be viewed around the world, as the details have been posted on Western-dominated social media platforms," Guo said.

She added that if more young Chinese joined the international body in contributing to global governance, this would give China a stronger voice.

Ma Zhenhua, from Qingdao, Shandong, a volunteer with the International Organization for Migration in Uzbekistan, said China is closely connected with other countries through various cooperation channels, especially the Belt and Road Initiative.

In addition to focusing on domestic development, Ma said young Chinese volunteers with the spirit of internationalism need to communicate with other countries to show them that China's rise is not a threat.

"I hope I can show that as a young Chinese, I can accept diverse cultures and am willing to sincerely help the country I serve in better understand China and view its young people objectively," she said.

Ma added that her office is looking for opportunities to work with China as part of the Belt and Road Initiative. She is studying a program to better protect the interests and safety of Chinese workers in Uzbekistan, and will apply this experience to protecting all migrants in that country.

"I hope I can make a small contribution, not only in the interests of Chinese compatriots, but also to improving migration governance and migrant protection at a higher level," she said.

All things and people, even if they are far apart, are interconnected to a certain degree, Ma said, adding that she is committed to lending a helping hand and working for a harmonious and sustainable world.

（来源：https://global.chinadaily.com.cn/a/202112/31/WS61ce407aa310cdd39bc7e6bc_1.html）

3.7 Critical thinking 环节

英文视频：最美志愿教师："95后"女孩筑梦山区艺术教育

文章讲述了一位女大学生毕业后选择回到家乡，成为一名公益组织艺术老师的故事。虽然工作在偏远小镇，没有丰厚的薪水，但冯玉琼认为自己在完成一件很有意义的事情。教师可安排学生阅读，引导学生思考职业选择与人生意义的关联。

School of Art and Craft is a non-profit organization founded by Chinese artist Xin Wangjun. It is designed to help left-behind children in China's remote areas embrace their artistic spirits.

In 2016, Xin established the first School of Art and Craft in frontier Lianghe county, southwest China's Yunnan Province. Lianghe county is an agricultural area lying dozens of kilometers from the Sino-Myanmar border area.

A lot of young Chinese people move to big cities, leaving the elderly and children at home. Feng Yuqiong, 22, is different. She is an art teacher at the School of Art and Craft. "School of Art and Craft is a place fulfilling my childhood dream," she said.

In September 2017, Feng went to the mountains by motorcycle to teach art to 60 students at Qingping primary school in Mangdong town, Lianghe county of Dehong Prefecture in Yunnan Province.

Only seven teachers taught lessons in the school. None specialized in art or music. If she weren't there teaching, the art classroom would have been locked up.

Feng prepared many songs for students to sing at her first class. To her delight and surprise, all the children joined her in singing *Flying Worm*.

She wants the children to feel happy, free, and love nature, while opening their imaginations. By teaching the children to paint by rubbing and printing leaves on paper, she wants them to learn that getting in touch with nature is something to be proud of.

She sang the song *You Are My Sunshine* to all the children because they light up her days, giving her the courage and will to keep teaching in the mountains. "Their smiling faces are the best sugar I have ever eaten," said Feng.

In the future, she hopes to invite local high school students to clean up the School of Art and Craft and enhance the sense of community among youngsters.

Feng drew a door of time travel on the wall, and hopes to lead the children through it. She is determined to continue working at the School of Art and Craft because only by doing so can she make a difference to the education of the locals.

（来源：https://mp.weixin.qq.com/s/kBjrfwwo4UtuZivZ0O1HFw）

3.8 主题拓展资源

英文视频：A Salute to Wuhan's Unsung Heroes

武汉是中国对抗新冠肺炎病毒的主要战场之一，疫情期间来自各行各业的众多普通人志愿者默默做出了自己的贡献，是战"疫"成功不可或缺的无名英雄。时长约3分钟，教师可安排学生观看，感受无名志愿者们的无私奉献精神，思考志愿者行为背后的高尚品质。

（来源：https://news.cgtn.com/news/2020-04-08/A-salute-to-Wuhan-s-unsung-heroes-PwTF85Hw3e/index.html）

第七单元　热爱学习，学会学习
（Unit 7 Learning Strategies）

1. 思政主题：热爱学习，学会学习

2. 意义

本单元的主题是 Learning Strategies。教师可帮助学生理解学习的意义，以及独立思考批判性思维在学习中的重要作用。

3. 教学设计与思政元素的融入

Passage A

3.1 Warm-up 环节

英文视频：奥巴马演讲——我们为什么要上学

在讨论学习策略之前，我们是否要先思考：我们为什么要上学？教师引导学生观看本视频，启发学生思考大学的意义。

Hello, everybody! Thank you. Thank you. Thank you, everybody. All right, everybody goes ahead and have a seat. How is everybody doing today? How about Tim Spicer? I am here with students at Wakefield High School in Arlington,

Virginia. And we've got students tuning in from all across America, from kindergarten through 12th grade. And I am just so glad that all could join us today. And I want to thank Wakefield for being such an outstanding host. Give yourselves a big round of applause.

I know that for many of you, today is the first day of school. And for those of you in kindergarten, or starting middle or high school, it's your first day in a new school, so it's understandable if you're a little nervous. I imagine there are some seniors out there who are feeling pretty good right now — with just one more year to go. And no matter what grade you're in, some of you are probably wishing it were still summer and you could've stayed in bed just a little bit longer this morning.

I know that feeling. When I was young, my family lived overseas. I lived in Indonesia for a few years. And my mother, she didn't have the money to send me where all the American kids went to school, but she thought it was important for me to keep up with an American education. So she decided to teach me extra lessons herself, Monday through Friday. But because she had to go to work, the only time she could do it was at 4:30 in the morning.

Now, as you might imagine, I wasn't too happy about getting up that early. And a lot of times, I'd fall asleep right there at the kitchen table. But whenever I'd complain, my mother would just give me one of those looks and she'd say, "This is no picnic for me either, buster."

So I know that some of you are still adjusting to being back at school. But I'm here today because I have something important to discuss with you. I'm here because I want to talk with you about your education and what's expected of all of you in this new school year.

Now, I've given a lot of speeches about education. And I've talked about responsibility a lot.

I've talked about teachers' responsibility for inspiring students and pushing you to learn.

I've talked about your parents' responsibility for making sure you stay on track, and you get your homework done, and don't spend every waking hour in front of the TV or with the Xbox.

I've talked a lot about your government's responsibility for setting high standards, and supporting teachers and principals, and turning around schools that aren't working, where students aren't getting the opportunities that they deserve.

But at the end of the day, we can have the most dedicated teachers, the most supportive parents, the best schools in the world — and none of it will make a difference, none of it will matter unless all of you fulfill your responsibilities, unless you show up to those schools, unless you pay attention to those teachers, unless you listen to your parents and grandparents and other adults and put in the hard work it takes to succeed. That's what I want to focus on today: the responsibility each of you has for your education.

I want to start with the responsibility you have to yourself. Every single one of you has something that you're good at. Every single one of you has something to offer. And you have a responsibility to yourself to discover what that is. That's the opportunity an education can provide.

Maybe you could be a great writer — maybe even good enough to write a book or articles in a newspaper — but you might not know it until you write that English paper — that English class paper that's assigned to you. Maybe you could be an innovator or an inventor — maybe even good enough to come up with the next iPhone or the new medicine or vaccine — but you might not know it until you do your project for your science class. Maybe you could be a mayor or a senator or a Supreme Court justice — but you might not know that until you join student government or the debate team.

And no matter what you want to do with your life, I guarantee that you'll need an education to do it. You want to be a doctor, or a teacher, or a police officer? You want to be a nurse or an architect, a lawyer or a member of our military? You're going to need a good education for every single one of those careers. You cannot drop out of school and just drop into a good job. You've got to train for it and work for it and learn for it.

And this isn't just important for your own life and your own future. What you make of your education will decide nothing less than the future of this country. The future of America depends on you. What you're learning in school today will determine whether we as a nation can meet our greatest challenges in the future.

You'll need the knowledge and problem-solving skills you learn in science and math to cure diseases like cancer and AIDS, and to develop new energy technologies and protect our environment. You'll need the insights and critical-thinking skills you gain in history and social studies to fight poverty and homelessness, crime and discrimination, and make our nation more fair and more free. You'll need the creativity and ingenuity you develop in all your classes to build new companies that will create new jobs and boost our economy.

We need every single one of you to develop your talents and your skills and your intellect so you can help us old folks solve our most difficult problems. If you don't do that — if you quit on school — you're not just quitting on yourself, you're quitting on your country.

Now, I know it's not always easy to do well in school. I know a lot of you have challenges in your lives right now that can make it hard to focus on your schoolwork.

I get it. I know what it's like. My father left my family when I was two years old, and I was raised by a single mom who had to work and who struggled at times to pay the bills and wasn't always able to give us the things that other kids had. There were times when I missed having a father in my life. There were times when I was lonely and I felt like I didn't fit in.

So I wasn't always as focused as I should have been on school, and I did some things I'm not proud of, and I got in more trouble than I should have. And my life could have easily taken a turn for the worse.

But I was — I was lucky. I got a lot of second chances, and I had the opportunity to go to college and law school and follow my dreams. My wife, our First Lady Michelle Obama, she has a similar story. Neither of her parents had gone to college, and they didn't have a lot of money. But they worked hard, and she worked hard, so that she could go to the best schools in this country.

Some of you might not have those advantages. Maybe you don't have adults in your life who give you the support that you need. Maybe someone in your family has lost their job and there's not enough money to go around. Maybe you live in a neighborhood where you don't feel safe, or have friends who are pressuring you to do things you know aren't right.

But at the end of the day, the circumstances of your life — what you look like, where you come from, how much money you have, what you've got going on at home — none of that is an excuse for neglecting your homework or having a bad attitude in school. That's no excuse for talking back to your teacher, or cutting class, or dropping out of school. There is no excuse for not trying.

Where you are right now doesn't have to determine where you'll end up. No one's written your destiny for you, because here in America, you write your own destiny. You make your own future.

That's what young people like you are doing every day, all across America.

Young people like Jazmin Perez, from Roma, Texas. Jazmin didn't speak English when she first started school. Neither of her parents had gone to college. But she worked hard, earned good grades, and got a scholarship to Brown University — is now in graduate school, studying public health, on her way to becoming Dr. Jazmin Perez.

I'm thinking about Andoni Schultz, from Los Altos, California, who's fought brain cancer since he was three. He's had to endure all sorts of treatments and surgeries, one of which affected his memory, so it took him much longer — hundreds of extra hours — to do his schoolwork. But he never fell behind. He's headed to college this fall.

And then there's Shantell Steve, from my hometown of Chicago, Illinois. Even when bouncing from foster home to foster home in the toughest neighborhoods in the city, she managed to get a job at a local health care center, start a program to keep young people out of gangs, and she's on track to graduate high school with honors and go on to college.

And Jazmin, Andoni, and Shantell aren't any different from any of you. They face challenges in their lives just like you do. In some cases they've got it a lot worse off than many of you. But they refused to give up. They chose to take responsibility for their lives, for their education, and set goals for themselves. And I expect all of you to do the same.

That's why today I'm calling on each of you to set your own goals for your education — and do everything you can to meet them. Your goal can be something as simple as doing all your homework, paying attention in class, or spending some time each day reading a book. Maybe you'll decide to get involved in an extracurricular activity, or volunteer in your community.

Maybe you'll decide to stand up for kids who are being teased or bullied because of who they are or how they look, because you believe, like I do, that all young people deserve a safe environment to study and learn. Maybe you'll decide to take better care of yourself so you can be more ready to learn. And along those lines, by the way, I hope all of you are washing your hands a lot, and that you stay home from school when you don't feel well, so we can keep people from getting the flu this fall and winter.

But whatever you resolve to do, I want you to commit to it. I want you to really work at it.

I know that sometimes you get that sense from TV that you can be rich and successful without any hard work — that your ticket to success is through rapping or basketball or being a reality TV star. Chances are you're not going to be any of those things.

The truth is, being successful is hard. You won't love every subject that you study. You won't click with every teacher that you have. Not every homework assignment will seem completely relevant to your life right at this minute. And you won't necessarily succeed at everything the first time you try.

That's okay. Some of the most successful people in the world are the ones who've had the most failures. J.K. Rowling's — who wrote *Harry Potter* — her first *Harry Potter* book was rejected 12 times before it was finally published. Michael Jordan was cut from his high school basketball team. He lost hundreds of games and missed thousands of shots during his career. But he once said, "I have failed over and over and over again in my life. And that's why I succeed."

These people succeeded because they understood that you can't let your failures define you — you have to let your failures teach you. You have to let them show you what to do differently the next time. So if you get into trouble, that doesn't mean you're a troublemaker, it means you need to try harder to act right. If you get a bad grade, that doesn't mean you're stupid, it just means you need to spend more time studying.

No one's born being good at all things. You become good at things through hard work. You're not a varsity athlete the first time you play a new sport. You don't hit every note the first time you sing a song. You've got to practice. The same principle applies to your schoolwork. You might have to do a math problem a few times before you get it right. You might have to read something a few times before you understand it. You definitely have to do a few drafts of a paper before it's good enough to hand in.

Don't be afraid to ask questions. Don't be afraid to ask for help when you need it. I do that every day. Asking for help isn't a sign of weakness, it's a sign of strength because it shows you have the courage to admit when you don't know something, and that then allows you to learn something new. So find an adult that you trust — a parent, a grandparent or teacher, a coach or a counselor — and ask them to help you stay on track to meet your goals.

And even when you're struggling, even when you're discouraged, and you feel like other people have given up on you, don't ever give up on yourself, because when you give up on yourself, you give up on your country.

The story of America isn't about people who quit when things got tough. It's about people who kept going, who tried harder, who loved their country too much to do anything less than their best.

It's the story of students who sat where you sit 250 years ago, and went on to wage a revolution and they founded this nation. Young people. Students who sat where you sit 75 years ago who overcame a Depression and won a World War; who fought for civil rights and put a man on the moon. Students who sat where you sit 20 years ago who founded Google and Twitter and Facebook and changed the way we communicate with each other.

So today, I want to ask all of you, what's your contribution going to be? What problems are you going to solve? What discoveries will you make? What will a President who comes here in 20 or 50 or 100 years say about what all of you did for this country?

Now, your families, your teachers, and I are doing everything we can to make sure you have the education you need to answer these questions. I'm working hard to fix up your classrooms and get you the books and the equipment and the computers you need to learn. But you've got to do your part, too. So I expect all of you to get serious this year. I expect you to put your best effort into everything you do. I expect great things from each of you. So don't let us down. Don't let your family down or your country down. Most of all, don't let yourself down. Make us all proud.

Thank you very much, everybody. God bless you. God bless America. Thank you.

（来源：https://www.iqiyi.com/w_19rui8euvp.html）

3.2 Discussion 环节

子曰："学而不思则罔，思而不学则殆。"

Confucius: Learning without thinking is labor lost; thinking without learning is dangerous.

教师可引导学生重温孔子的这句名言，启发学生讨论并论证学习过程中积极思考、审慎思考的重要性，提倡反思性学习。

3.3 Critical thinking 环节

21世纪以来，国际间人口流动加速，文化也在不断突破国界，人类面临前所未有的挑战和机遇[①]，这对当下的人才培养提出了更高的要求。传统意义上的知识传输已不足够，独立思考和批判性思维能力的提高才能帮助学生分析、评价、转换、运用知识，甚至创造新知，以应对各种要求和挑战。因此，越来越多的中国学者意识到批判性思维在教育中的重要性，比如董毓[②]、谷振诣[③]、谢小庆[④]等。董毓认为"批判性思维是素质、通识教育的心脏部件，是实现中国复兴梦的必备条件"[⑤]。

2016年，《中国学生发展核心素养》出台并实施，中国教育进入了"核心素养时代"。批判性思维的相关内容已经融入我国学生发展核心素养的总框架之中，"要求学生具有问题意识，能独立思考、独立判断、思维缜密，能多角度、辨证地分析问题，做出选择和决定"[⑥]。对批判性思维的培养已经有了顶层设计。

英文视频：What Is Critical Thinking?

学生阅读文章并进一步思考批判性思维的意义，以及如何将批判性思维用于大学英语的学习当中。

Critical thinking is the ability to apply reasoning and logic to new or unfamiliar ideas, opinions, and situations. Thinking critically involves seeing things in an open-minded way and examining an idea or concept from as many angles as possible. This important skill allows people to look past their own views of the world and to better understand the opinions of others. It is often used in debates, to form more cogent and well-rounded arguments, and in science.

Open-Minded Approach

Overcoming a fear of heights through rational thinking is one way critical thinking can be applied. The ability to think critically is essential, as it creates new possibilities in problem solving. Being "open-minded" is a large part of critical

---

[①] Teo, Peter. Teaching for the 21st Century: A Case for Dialogic Pedagogy[J]. Learning, Culture and Social Interaction, 2019, (21): 170-178.
[②] 董毓. 批判性思维原理和方法——走向新的认知和实践[M]. 北京：高等教育出版社，2010:5-14.
[③] 谷振诣. 批判性思维教学：理论与实践[J]. 工业和信息化教育，2014(3):43-53.
[④] 谢小庆. 应将思维品质的考核列为高考重要目标[J]. 湖北招生考试，2019（25）：1.
[⑤] 董毓. 我们应该教什么样的批判性思维课程[J]. 工业和信息化教育，2014（3）：36-42.
[⑥] 林崇德. 中国学生核心素养研究[J]. 心理与行为研究，2017,15（2）:145-154.

thinking, allowing a person to not only seek out all possible answers to a problem, but to also accept an answer that is different from what was originally expected. Open-minded thinking requires that a person does not assume that his or her way of approaching a situation is always best, or even right. A scientist, for example, must be open to the idea that the results of an experiment will not be what is expected; such results, though challenging, often lead to tremendous and meaningful discoveries.

Rational Considerations

Another aspect of critical thinking is the ability to approach a problem or situation rationally. Rationality requires analyzing all known information, and making judgments or analyses based on fact or evidence, rather than opinion or emotion. An honest approach to reasoning requires a thinker to acknowledge personal goals, motives, and emotions that might color his or her opinions or thought processes. Rational thought involves identifying and eliminating prejudices, so that someone can have a fresh and objective approach to a problem.

Empathy

The ability to think critically creates new possibilities in problem solving. Critical thinking often relies on the ability to view the world in a way that does not focus on the self. Empathizing with a person usually involves a thinker trying to put himself or herself in the place of someone else. This is often done by students of history, for example, in an attempt to see the world as someone would have while living in an ancient civilization or during a violent conflict. Communication skills, teamwork, and cooperation are typically improved through empathy, which makes it valuable in many professional fields.

How to Apply It

Elements of critical thinking can be taught starting in elementary school. Effective critical thinking often begins with a thinker analyzing what he or she knows about a subject, with extra effort made to recognize what he or she does not know about it. This forms an initial knowledge base for consideration. The thinker can then look at what research has been done on the subject, and identify what he or she can learn simply by looking over such work. This approach is often used in science, as it allows a scientist to determine what people do not yet know or understand, and then look for ways to discover this information through experimentation.

When someone applies this approach to his or her own life, he or she often places more emphasis on finding prejudices and preconceived notions he or she holds. This lets the thinker strive to eliminate or avoid these opinions, to come to a more honest or objective view of an issue. Someone struggling with a fear of heights, for example, might strive to determine the cause of this fear in a rational way. By doing so, he or she might be better able to deal with the root cause directly and avoid emotional responses that could prevent self-improvement.

（来源：https://www.infobloom.com/what-is-critical-thinking.htm）

英语视频： This Tool Will Help Improve Your Critical Thinking

学生观看视频并思考：什么样的问题是好问题？如何进行合理质疑、有效提问？

Socrates, one of the founding fathers of Western philosophical thought, was on trial. Many Athenians believed he was a dangerous enemy of the state, accusing the philosopher of corrupting the youth and refusing to recognize their gods. However, Socrates wasn't feared for claiming to have all the answers, but rather, for asking too many questions.

While he loathed formal lectures, the philosopher frequently engaged friends and strangers in lengthy conversations about morality and society. These discussions weren't debates, nor would Socrates offer explicit advice. In fact, the philosopher often claimed to know nothing at all, responding to his partner's answers only with further questions. But through this process, Socrates probed their logic, revealing its flaws and helping both parties reach a more robust understanding. These insightful questions made Socrates beloved by his followers. Two of his students, Plato and Xenophon, were so inspired that they replicated their mentor's process in fictional dialogues. These invented exchanges provide perfect examples of what would come to be known as the Socratic Method. In one of these fabricated dialogues, Socrates is conversing with a young man named Euthydemus, who is confident that he understands the nature of justice and injustice. Socrates probes the student's values by asking him to label actions such as lying and theft as just or unjust. Euthydemus confidently categorizes them as injustices, but this only prompts another question: is it just for a general to deceive or pillage a hostile army? Euthydemus revises his assertion. He claims that these actions are just when done to enemies, and unjust when done to friends. But Socrates isn't finished. He asks the young man to consider a commander lying to his troops to boost their morale. Before long, Euthydemus is despondent. It seems that every answer leads to further problems, and perhaps he's not quite sure what constitutes justice after all.

In employing this question-oriented approach, Socrates described himself as a midwife, whose inquiries assist others in giving birth to their ideas. His method of questioning draws out an individual's unexamined assumptions, and then challenges those biases. It doesn't always provide definitive answers, but the method helps clarify the questions and eliminate contradictory or circular logic. And by following a line of inquiry where it logically leads, both the question asker and answerer can end up in unexpected places.

This technique isn't limited by the conversation's content, making it incredibly useful in numerous fields. During the Renaissance, the method was used to teach clinical medicine. Students proposed their rationale for different diagnoses, while a doctor questioned their assumptions and moderated discussion. In this model, the method could even produce conclusive results. This same approach was later used in other sciences, such as astronomy, botany, and mathematics. Following the Protestant Reformation, it was adapted to tackle abstract questions of faith. In the 19th century, the method became an essential part of American legal education. Professors explored students' understanding of judicial reasoning by challenging them with unforeseen hypothetical situations. This approach is still used today by the Supreme Court to imagine the unintended impacts of passing a law.

The Socratic Method can be adapted to teach almost any topic that relies on critical reasoning, but its success depends on the teacher employing it. An effective Socratic educator must be well versed in their subject. Rather than bullying their students or showing off their superior intellect, they should be modest, genuinely curious, and affirming of every contribution.

In this regard, Socrates himself may not have been the most subtle Socratic teacher. Historians believe he was deeply critical of Athens' particular brand of democracy, and known to pass those concerns onto his followers. These subversive beliefs were distorted in public forums and thought to have inspired two of his pupils to treasonous ends. It was likely for these ideas Socrates was brought to trial, and eventually, sentenced to death. But even on his deathbed, artists depict a serene philosopher— ever curious to explore the ultimate question.

（来源：https://www.ted.com/talks/erick_wilberding_this_tool_will_help_improve_

your_critical_thinking）

3.4 主题拓展资源

英语视频：耶鲁大学校长开学典礼演讲——勇于提问，培养好奇心

Good morning! To all Eli Whitney students, transfer students, visiting international students, and first-year Yale College students: Welcome to Yale! On behalf of my colleagues here on stage, I extend a warm greeting to the families here today and thank you for joining us. Please enjoy these first moments of your loved one's college career.

早上好！向所有Eli Whitney项目的学生，所有的交换生，国际访问学生以及我们新一届的耶鲁新生致敬，欢迎你们来到耶鲁！我代表台上所有的同事，向你们的家人表示问候和感谢！请与你们挚爱的孩子一起享受这大学生活的最初时刻！

Usually in an opening address, university presidents tell undergraduates that they are amazing individuals, selected from among the most talented high school students in the world today.

通常来说，在开学演讲中，校长都会告诉学生：你们是从世界上万千的精英高中生里选拔出来的，都是能独挡一面的个体。

That is, of course, true, but it is not the point I want to make. Instead, I want to encourage you to approach college unimpressed by how impressive you are; have more questions than answers; admit to being puzzled or confused; be willing to say, "I don't know...but I want to find out." And, most important, have the courage to say, "Perhaps I am wrong, and others are right."

当然，这是事实，不过这并非我今天想要表达的观点。相比之下，我更想鼓励你们：不要因为自己的独特而怡然自得；学生们应当多接触我们的校园；相比答案，能更多地提出自己的问题；能承认自己处于迷茫或困惑的状态；愿意表达"虽然我不太了解……但我会去寻找答案"。并且，最重要的是，我们的学生要勇于承认"或许我错了，其他人的观点是正确的"。

That is how you will learn the most from your teachers and classmates. And that is why we have all come to this place. We are here to ask questions — questions about one another and about the world around us. We are at Yale to nurture a culture of curiosity.

这是新生们从老师与同学处最能学到的东西。并且，这也是我们聚集于此的原因。我们来耶鲁大学是为了提出问题，提出关于彼此；关于我们所处世界的问题。在耶鲁大学，我们注重对好奇文化的培养。

This summer I read a story about Isidor Isaac Rabi, one of this country's most extraordinary scientists. He remembered an important question his mother asked him. Brought to this country as an infant, Rabi conducted research into particle beams that led to the development of the MRI and many other scientific advances. He won the Nobel Prize for Physics in 1944.

在刚刚度过的夏天里，我阅读了一个有关于伊西多·艾萨克·拉比的故事，拉比是美国最杰出的科学家之一。拉比记得母亲曾问过他一个重要的问题。拉比还是个婴儿的时候被带到了美国。长大后，他开始注重对粒子束的研究，他的相关研究让核磁共振以及诸多学科获得了提升。1944年，拉比还因为自身的成就获得了诺贝尔物理学奖。

Rabi's parents ran a small grocery store in Brooklyn. His mother had no formal education. The other moms, he remembered, asked their children every afternoon if they had learned anything in school. "Not my mother," he recalled. "She always asked me a different question. 'Izzy', she would say, 'did you ask a good question today?'" He believed her reminder to ask good questions helped set him on a path to becoming a distinguished scientist.

拉比的父母在布鲁克林经营着一家小杂货店。他的母亲没有受过正规教育。普通的家长，每天下午都会向孩子提问："你今天在学校里学到了什么？"拉比表示，自己的母亲与其他家长不同。"她只会问我一件事——你今天有提出一个优质问题吗？"拉比认为，正是母亲的这一举动，让他养成了不断提出优秀问题的习惯，为迈向杰出科学家的道路埋下了伏笔。

So, to all the families here today, when you call your Yale student—when you ask them about their classes and their roommates and the food—remember also to ask about their questions.

所以，我建议在场的所有家长，当你们给孩子打电话的时候，在关注他们的同学、室友与就餐情况之外，请记得问问孩子，看看他们近期提出过什么问题。

Imagine all the great discoveries that have come from asking a question — from Newton's theory of gravity to the astonishing breakthroughs in quantum science — some of which are happening at Yale. When a musician experiments with a new melody, or a sociologist observes a social interaction, they ask "why" and "what would happen if...?" Their curiosity lights up our world and points us in new directions. Self-discoveries come from asking questions, too. What do you learn when you ask yourself, "Why do I believe that?" or "Why did I do that?"

从牛顿的万有引力到量子科学的重大突破,这些或来自耶鲁大学或来自其他顶尖高校的伟大发现,其实都是基于提问产生的。当音乐家开始采用一段新的旋律;社会学家开始观察一段社交行为时,他们都会问"为什么?""如果这样/那样的话,会发生什么事情呢?"正是他们的好奇心,点燃了人们心中的火苗,并且引领世界朝着全新的方向前进。对自我的发掘与提升,同样来自于提问。比如,当我们质疑一件事并表示"为什么我要相信它?""为什么我要这么做?"的时候,我们其实已经学会了反思,并获得了成长。

I think of these lines from the poet Billy Collins: "the trouble with poetry is that it encourages the writing of more poetry."

我想起了诗人比利·柯林斯的一句诗:"诗歌存在的问题,就是在鼓励更多诗歌的出现。"

I would say the same of asking questions. One leads to another, which opens doors to still another. Sometimes our questions lead to a dead-end. We realize the question we asked wasn't quite right, and a door closes. But along the way we have learned something. Perhaps in the future we will ask better questions.

我认为这句诗同样适用于提问。诗歌和提问,都是通过一个点,去点亮另一个点;通过一扇门,去打开更多的门。有些时候,我们的问题会把自己引向一条死胡同。这个问题或许并不能带来正确的解答,一扇知识的大门也因此无法打开。但请你们牢记:沿途中的那些收获,能帮助我们在将来提出更优秀的问题。

In a well-known scene in the movie *The Pink Panther*, Inspector Clouseau checks into a hotel in Germany. He sees a dachshund in the lobby and asks the hotel owner, "Does your dog bite?" The owner replies, "No." When Clouseau goes to pet the dog, it bites his hand-hard! Shocked, he tells the hotel owner, "I thought you said your dog doesn't bite!" The owner responds, "That is not my dog." Inspector Clouseau simply hadn't asked the right question.

电影《粉红豹》中有一个著名的场景:"乌龙探长"克鲁索在一家德国酒店检查,他在酒店大堂看到了一只腊肠犬,所以向酒店老板询问:"你的狗咬人么?""我的狗不会咬人,先生。"得到答复的克鲁索便放开戒备逗狗,没想到自己的手却被狠狠地咬了一口。他开始与老板对峙:"我记得你告诉过我,你的小狗不咬人。""那只腊肠犬并不是我的狗,先生。"显然,克鲁索没有提出正确的问题。

Years ago, I taught an undergraduate seminar. One of the questions on the application to the course was, "What is the most important thing you've changed your mind about?" We were surprised that quite a few students had not changed their minds about anything at all! We decided to accept to the class only students who had changed their minds about something important.

很多年前，我曾参与组织了一场本科研讨会。这个课程讨论的其中一个问题是——你曾为哪一件重要的事情改变过自己的想法？令我感到惊奇的是，有少部分学生从来没有为任何一件事而改变自身最初的想法！最终，我们决定，这门课只接收那些改变过想法的学生。

So, be willing to change your mind. Ask questions and embrace Yale's culture of curiosity. Be open to different viewpoints and experiences, and see them as opportunities to learn—even if sometimes you get your hand bit.

所以，我们的学生应当乐于转变自身的观念；勇于提问并且拥抱耶鲁大学的"好奇文化"；对不同的观点与经验持开放的态度，并将其视为一种学习的契机，即使有时会因此受到一些伤害。

I am a social psychologist. As a graduate student at Yale, my curiosity was sparked by the study of emotions, and by a question my undergraduate advisor first asked me: "Peter, why do you think humans even have emotions? What do they do for us?" One of my major areas of research almost ever since then has been emotional intelligence.

我是一名社会心理学家。作为耶鲁大学曾经的研究生，我的好奇心是在对情绪的相关研究中迸发的。当然，我的好奇心也受到了我的本科导师的启发，他曾问过我："彼得，你觉得人类为什么会有情感？情感对我们产生了怎样的作用？"从那时起，我与团队的课题之一，就是情商研究。

In our earliest work, we described emotional intelligence as a set of skills that one could learn that would help a person extract the information—the "data"—contained in emotions, either one's own or those of another person. After a few years of research, it was obvious to me and my collaborators that we weren't asking exactly the right questions. We needed to be able to show that emotional intelligence predicted outcomes in life—the ability to form friendships, succeed in school, work as part of a team, and the like.

在早期的工作中，我们将情商视为一种技能——通过系统性的学习，人们可以掌握情商这项能力，并借此解析人们情感中所包含的那些"数据"。多年的相关研究后，我和我的同事们意识到：我们并没有提出那个正确的问题。我们需要确保情商能在日常生活中展现出来——能组建朋友圈、能在学业上取得成功、能融入团队工作，诸如此类的能力。

  Trouble was, how do you measure the skills of emotional intelligence? We asked ourselves a series of questions starting with, "How are personal characteristics typically measured by psychologists? The answer is by asking people to rate themselves — these are called "self-reports". But this led to approaches that disappointed us: How would someone know if they were the kind of person who was especially good at identifying, understanding, managing, and using emotions? Perhaps thinking that you had spectacular emotional intelligence was a sign of not having much of it at all!

  但是问题来了：我们如何进行情商能力的评级？就此，团队进行了内部提问："通常而言，心理学家如何进行个人特征的测量？"答案是他们经常让人们给自己打分，即一份称之为"自我评估"的报告。然而，这一答案使得我们更为沮丧：人们怎么样才能知道自己是一个善于识别、理解、管理并且运用情绪的人呢？我们有没有想过，或许自己以为的高情感张力，对他人而言是情商缺乏的表现呢？

  So that door closed, and we asked ourselves another question: If we wanted to know if someone possessed the skills of a great baseball player-hitting, throwing, and catching a ball; running bases effectively-how confident would we be of self-report? Not very: All ball players think they are the next A-Rod! As a child, I thought I would be the next Carl Yastrzemski when playing in the backyard with my brother, but, in fact, I barely got out of Little League with my pride intact.

  我们的错误提问使得真理之门无法打开。为此，团队提出了一个新的问题：如果我们想要了解一个人是否具备优秀的棒球运动员的能力（比如：击球、投掷、接球、高效地跑垒等），那么，此时的"自我评估"有多少的可信度呢？显然，可信度不高，因为所有的球员都认为自己是下一位阿莱克斯·罗德里格兹。小时候，我和哥哥在家中后院玩耍时，还自认为是下一位卡尔·雅泽姆斯基。但还好，我从未因为自己的这种骄傲而被排挤。

  Why would emotional intelligence be any different than baseball? If we wanted to know whether someone had high E.I., we needed to assess these skills as abilities. And what would an ability measure of emotional intelligence even look like? Asking ourselves these questions led to an answer that made sense, and our ability-based measure of emotional intelligence has now been used in hundreds of studies. Knowing that we didn't have all the answers and taking an inquisitive, curious attitude allowed us the opportunity to create something new.

为什么情商的评级与棒球不同呢?如果我们想要知道某人是否具备高情商,我们就需要将这些技能视为能力。那怎样的标准可以用来衡量情商能力呢?扪心自问一下上述问题将有助于我们更接近正确答案(目前,基于能力的情商测试已经被运用于上百个研究中)。承认我们并非无所不知,并抱有一种好学、好奇的态度,有助于我们去创造或发现全新的事物。

So, what questions will you ask? What will spark your curiosity?

所以,身为学生的你们将会提出什么样的问题呢?你们将来的好奇心又会因何而启发呢?

Not long ago, I received an email from a very proud Yale College parent. He told me about his son, who heard seventy-seven different speakers during his first year at Yale. Seventy-seven! He had learned from thinkers and leaders across the political spectrum and attended events organized by a wide range of campus organizations. What a way to spend your first year! Could you do this and not change your mind about something important?

不久前,我收到了一封来自一位耶鲁大学家长的邮件。这位家长在信中十分骄傲的与我分享:自己的儿子在耶鲁大学的第一年,就已经听完了77位不同演讲者的讲座。77位!他从这些政治领域的思想家和领导者那里学到了很多,并且还参加了由各种社团举行的活动。这是度过第一学年多么优秀的方法!在场的诸位,你们能这样坚持一年,并且初心不改吗?

And it turns out this student is also very good at asking questions: he is doing a project where in the past year, he has interviewed dozens of people — scholars and activists, journalists and entrepreneurs from many different sectors. Like so many students, faculty, and staff, he is nurturing a culture of curiosity at Yale.

事实证明,这位学生还十分擅于提问。他在过去的一年中采访了数十人,这其中,有来自不同领域的学者、活动家、记者以及企业家。在耶鲁大学,这位同学就像许多学生与教职工一样,培养自身的一种好奇文化。

Indeed, the Yalies who have come before you have asked a dazzling array of questions. I think of the pioneers of coeducation. Fifty years ago, in 1969, 588 women came to study in Yale College. They entered what had long been an all-male institution, and they asked questions that hadn't been asked before. We will commemorate this milestone — along with the 150th anniversary of women entering at Yale in the School of Art — throughout this year.

实际上,往届的耶鲁大学人已经提出了许多的问题。比如,那些提出男女同校的先驱们。50年前,在1969年,588名妇女来到耶鲁大学学习。她们进入了一个长期以来都是男性的机构，并且提出了长期从未被提及的问题。在女性入读耶鲁艺术学院150周年之际，我们也将纪念这一具有里程碑意义的事件。

I think of Margaret Warner, Class of 1971. An award-winning journalist, she knows how to ask brilliant questions. She has reported from warzones for decades, witnessing history firsthand and trying to understand our world.

我还想起1971届的玛格丽特·华纳，她是一位屡获殊荣的记者，知道如何提出那些精彩的问题。她从事战区报道数十年，见证了历史并试图借此了解我们世界的真实模样。

I think, too, of Alice Young, Class of 1971. She looked around this campus and asked why there weren't more students from public schools, so she became an ambassador for Yale back in her home state of Hawaii. She was also one of the founders of the Asian American Students Alliance, which also celebrates its 50th anniversary this year.

我也想起1971届的爱丽丝·杨，她曾环顾整个校园，并疑惑为什么没有更多来自公立学校的学生入学。后来，她成为了耶鲁大学的大使并回到家乡夏威夷州进行宣传。她还是亚裔美国学生联盟的创始人之一，今年是该联盟成立的50周年。

And we remember other important anniversaries and the curious students who were part of these changes. In 1969, thanks to student efforts, the Afro-American Cultural Center, known as "The House", opened, and what is now the Department of African American Studies was created. And that same year, students established the Yale chapter of Movimiento Estudiantil Chicano de Aztlán, also known as MEChA. I believe we owe a debt of gratitude to all the courageous pioneers, throughout our history, who have made Yale what it is today.

我们还记得其他重要的纪念日，以及参与这些变化的那些好奇的学生。1969年，在学生们的努力，被称为"The House"的非裔美国文化中心成立，现在这一中心正在创建非裔美国人研究院。同年，学生们建立了MEChA的耶鲁大学分会。我相信，我们应该感谢所有勇敢的开拓者。纵观耶鲁大学的历史，是他们成就了今天的耶鲁大学。

What questions will you ask? And how will your questions transform Yale and improve our world?

你将会提出什么样的问题呢？你的问题又会如何改变耶鲁大学及我们的世界呢？

Your time at Yale is an unparalleled opportunity to engage with a wide range of people, ideas, and experiences. More than at any other point in your life, you will have the means and the opportunity to hear from — and converse with — world-renowned experts in many fields. You will have the chance to create knowledge through rigorous research, and attend arts, literary, and athletics events that challenge and inspire you. You will spend time with peers whose lives have been wildly different from your own.

你们在耶鲁大学度过的这些时光，是与众人、众多思想以及众多经验进行互动的最佳时光。在这里，你能与诸多领域中世界知名的专家进行交谈。你们将有机会通过严谨的研究去创造知识，并且参加那些能挑战自我、激发灵感的艺术、文学或体育活动。在耶鲁大学，你们将会度过一段与同龄人完全不同的生活！

What if you nurtured your own curiosity by pushing yourself beyond the familiar and the comfortable? What would that look like for you?

勇敢走出舒适与安全区，并借此培养自己的好奇心，那样的你们将会是何等耀眼！

It might mean attending a talk on a topic you don't know much about or by someone who doesn't share your beliefs. Or conducting research in a Yale laboratory or collaborating on an exhibit at one of our amazing museums. Or perhaps your curiosity will be sparked having coffee with a classmate who comes from a different part of the world or a different place on the political spectrum.

它可能意味着你去与别人讨论一个你不是很了解或者与你观点不同的问题。它可能意味着你能在耶鲁大学实验室或某一展览中进行研究；意味着你能接触到来自世界不同地区，不同政治领域的同学。

And when you do these things, when you take advantage of the opportunities Yale makes possible, what questions will you ask?

当你做这些事情时，当你利用这些耶鲁大学带来的机会时，你会提出怎样的问题呢？

There is so much we do not know. Let us embrace, together, our humility — our willingness to admit what we have yet to discover. After all, if you knew all the answers, you would not need Yale. And if humanity knew all the answers, the world would not need Yale.

世界上存在着太多的未知。因此，我们需要为自身的谦逊而庆贺——我们愿意承认目前存在许多自己尚未能发现的事物。毕竟，如果你知道所有的答案，你就不需要耶鲁大学；如果人类知道所有的答案，世界就不需要耶鲁大学。

So, what questions will you ask today? Tomorrow? The next day? And in the days, months, and years after I have shaken your hand at Commencement, let me know what questions you've asked that have changed your life.

所以，今天我们的学生会提出什么样的问题呢？但明天呢？后天呢？我希望在毕业典礼我与你握手之后的几天、几个月、或者几年之内，你能告诉我，那些你所提出来的、切实地改变了你生活的问题。

Good luck, Class of 2023!

2023届的耶鲁大学新生们，祝你们好运！

（视频来源：https://v.qq.com/x/page/o05435zdg8t.html）

（文本来源：https://www.360kuai.com/pc/9bcb57af3d656f6ed?cota=4&kuai_so=1&tj_url=so_rec&sign=360_57c3bbd1&refer_scene=so_1）

Passage B

3.5 Warm-up 环节

英语视频：Creativity at Core of Competitiveness in China's Youth

有人说中国的年轻一代在创造力方面远远落后于西方国家，这是事实吗？听一听外国学者怎么说。引导学生观看本视频，并思考：如何进一步提高中国年轻人的创造力，进而提高他们在世界舞台上的竞争力。

As a lawyer, policy adviser, filmmaker and social enterprise pioneer, Laurence Brahm is not only a keen observer but an active participant in China's reform and opening-up. "*Laurence Brahm's Diary on China in Change*" is a special series dissecting the colossal changes Brahm has witnessed in his 37-year stay in China. In the fifth episode, Brahm shares his views with CGTN on China's young people.

CGTN: What has reform and opening-up brought young Chinese people?

Brahm: China's reform and opening-up has brought opportunity for change and personal growth to Chinese teenagers. They are totally interconnected with everything that's happening anywhere in the world in terms of trends, art, music, lifestyle... There are no barriers in terms of their access.

It's given them a material foundation to go beyond the material; it's given them an opportunity to be able to be part of the rest of the world; and it's given them the opportunity in the next generation to even be leaders in an integrated, dynamic, and synergistic planet.

Because all of this stuff going on right now in the United States with nationalism, with populism, with de-globalization and anger, all this stuff is polarizing the planet. But I do believe at the core of Asian values is a belief in harmony, synergy. Black and white are not opposites. They are part of an integrated whole.

And I think that young people from China, from India, from Southeast Asia, South Asia, have this at the core of their value system. It's in their DNA. And if we can combine that with the technologies, I think we could have a very different planet in the future and get away from some of these antagonistic zero-sum game — only one country is No.1, views which are only going to drag us backward.

CGTN: How do you compare the Chinese educational system with that of the West?

Brahm: I would probably say that the Chinese educational system, from elementary school through high school, is better than the Western educational systems — more solid in terms of math, sciences, even humanities. But the higher level of education, I think that there are still some very big gaps. And I think that people are aware of that. Chinese [students] want to go overseas, they want to get the best of education, particularly Master's degree, Ph.D., that level of research.

And from that perspective, I think that those students who are coming back, they will be a very powerful force for the change of China and the future. It's not only a global economic power but is one that has a new soft power.

CGTN: Many argue that Chinese teenagers, who have grown up under the one-child policy, lag behind their foreign counterparts in creativity and self-care. What's your take on this?

Brahm: In many ways, China is on the cutting edge of innovation and creativeness. The fundamental shifts in the past 40 years do not come in a society that doesn't have creativity and innovation. The government at the top is responding to popular demands and all kinds of infiltration of information and changes in ideas that are coming up from all directions. It is responding more than it is necessarily commanding and leading. And in this respect, I think we have to see that Chinese society has a lot of creativity and innovation.

CGTN: How can the competitiveness of young people in China be improved?

Brahm: China is a fascinating country, because it integrates; it is the melting pot; it takes ideas. What you have in China is you have a nation and people who are constantly reinventing themselves. I think that is where this incredible creativity comes in and again I turn to the young generation because I see them more prepared to reinvent themselves here than anywhere else in the world. And it's already happening.

I think the more that young people can be working together, can be integrating, can be communicating, can be exchanging ideas and can be realizing that at the end of the day humanity, they don't care whether you're in China, you're in America, you're in Europe, you're in Southeast Asia, Africa, we all have much more in common with each other than we have differences, and I think that the younger generation will be better positioned to realize that and to make the most of it.

（来源：https://news.cgtn.com/news/3d3d774e774d7a4d31457a6333566d54/index.html）

3.6 Discussion 环节

英文新闻: Learning Apps Boom During Pandemic Lockdown

新冠肺炎疫情期间，远程学习成为必需，很多学习的 Apps 应势而生。教师引导学生阅读本新闻，并组织学生讨论：大家都使用过哪些应用程序？它们各有什么优点和缺点？

As the COVID-19 pandemic forces schools to close and anyone who can to work from home, one sector is benefitting: learning apps.

Once the domain of travelers looking to pick up a few handy phrases before they hit the beaches, these apps have positioned themselves as mainstream teaching aids. And that's now putting them in a position to give an outlet to those stuck at home and become the new classroom for language students.

"Depending on when isolation measures are put in place... we see these really big spikes [in new users]," said Cindy Blanco, of Duolingo.

One of those firms, Berlin-based Babbel, announced on Wednesday it would make its services free for all U.S. school and college students whose institution is closed by the pandemic.

"Babbel is offering those affected three months' access for free to its app and platform, in any and all of its 14 languages offered," the company said in a statement.

"As students are being forced to stay at home, Babbel is in a position to help right now and that is exactly what we want to do," added CEO Julie Hansen.

Other apps have already experienced massive upticks in user numbers, as well as changing trends around the time of day learners are logging on.

Blanco, a learning scientist at Duolingo, told CGTN Europe the company has "seen a real spike in usage during the day... people are completing more lessons while they're at home. And because they're [now] home all times of the day, that's really reflected [in Duolingo data]."

（来源：https://newseu.cgtn.com/news/2020-03-26/Learning-apps-boom-during-pandemic-lockdown-P9X6re5Bq8/index.html）

3.7 Critical thinking 环节

英文视频：How to Escape Education's Death Valley

教师引导学生观看该视频并思考：学校只有尊重了每个学生的个性特点，才能激发学生的创造力。你同意这个观点吗？为什么？

I moved to America 12 years ago with my wife Terry and our two kids. Actually, truthfully, we moved to Los Angeles — thinking we were moving to America, but anyway — it's a short plane ride from Los Angeles to America.

I got here 12 years ago, and when I got here, I was told various things, like, "Americans don't get irony".

Have you come across this idea? It's not true. I've traveled the whole length and breadth of this country. I have found no evidence that Americans don't get irony. It's one of those cultural myths, like, "The British are reserved".

I don't know why people think this. We've invaded every country we've encountered.

But it's not true Americans don't get irony, but I just want you to know that that's what people are saying about you behind your back. You know, so when you leave living rooms in Europe, people say, thankfully, nobody was ironic in your presence.

But I knew that Americans get irony when I came across that legislation, "No Child Left Behind."

Because whoever thought of that title gets irony.

Don't they?

Because it's leaving millions of children behind. Now I can see that's not a very attractive name for legislation: "Millions of Children Left Behind." I can see that. What's the plan? We propose to leave millions of children behind, and here's how it's going to work.

And it's working beautifully.

In some parts of the country, 60 percent of kids drop out of high school. In the Native American communities, it's 80 percent of kids. If we halved that number, one estimate is it would create a net gain to the U.S. economy over 10 years, of nearly a trillion dollars. From an economic point of view, this is good math, isn't it, that we should do this? It actually costs an enormous amount to mop up the damage from the dropout crisis.

But the dropout crisis is just the tip of an iceberg. What it doesn't count are all the kids who are in school but being disengaged from it, who don't enjoy it, who don't get any real benefit from it.

And the reason is not that we're not spending enough money. America spends more money on education than most other countries. Class sizes are smaller than in many countries. And there are hundreds of initiatives every year to try and improve education. The trouble is, it's all going in the wrong direction. There are three principles on which human life flourishes, and they are contradicted by the culture of education under which most teachers have to labor and most students have to endure.

The first is this, that human beings are naturally different and diverse. Can I ask you, how many of you have got children of your own? Okay. Or grandchildren. How about two children or more? Right. And the rest of you have seen such children.

Small people wandering about.

I will make you a bet, and I am confident that I will win the bet. If you've got two children or more, I bet you they are completely different from each other. Aren't they?

You would never confuse them, would you? Like, "Which one are you? Remind me." "Your mother and I need some color-coding system so we don't get confused."

Education under "No Child Left Behind" is based on not diversity but conformity. What schools are encouraged to do is to find out what kids can do across a very narrow spectrum of achievement. One of the effects of "No Child Left Behind" has been to narrow the focus onto the so-called STEM disciplines. They're very important. I'm not here to argue against science and math. On the contrary, they're necessary but they're not sufficient. A real education has to give equal weight to the arts, the humanities, to physical education. An awful lot of kids, sorry, thank you.

One estimate in America currently is that something like 10 percent of kids, getting on that way, are being diagnosed with various conditions under the broad title of attention deficit disorder, ADHD. I'm not saying there's no such thing. I just don't believe it's an epidemic like this. If you sit kids down, hour after hour, doing low-grade clerical work, don't be surprised if they start to fidget, you know?

Children are not, for the most part, suffering from a psychological condition. They're suffering from childhood.

And I know this because I spent my early life as a child. I went through the whole thing. Kids prosper best with a broad curriculum that celebrates their various talents, not just a small range of them. And by the way, the arts aren't just important because they improve math scores. They're important because they speak to parts of children's being which are otherwise untouched.

The second principle that drives human life flourishing is curiosity. If you can light the spark of curiosity in a child, they will learn without any further assistance, very often. Children are natural learners. It's a real achievement to put that particular ability out, or to stifle it. Curiosity is the engine of achievement. Now the reason I say this is because one of the effects of the current culture here, if I can say so, has been to de-professionalize teachers. There is no system in the world or any school in the country that is better than its teachers. Teachers are the lifeblood of the success of schools. But teaching is a creative profession. Teaching, properly conceived, is not a delivery system. You know, you're not there just to pass on received information. Great teachers do that, but what great teachers also do is mentor, stimulate, provoke, engage. You see, in the end, education is about learning. If there's no learning going on, there's no education going on. And people can spend an awful lot of time discussing education without ever discussing learning. The whole point of education is to get people to learn.

An old friend of mine — actually very old, he's dead.

That's as old as it gets, I'm afraid.

But a wonderful guy he was, wonderful philosopher. He used to talk about the difference between the task and achievement senses of verbs. You can be engaged in the activity of something, but not really be achieving it, like dieting.

It's a very good example. There he is. He's dieting. Is he losing any weight? Not really.

Teaching is a word like that. You can say, "There's Deborah, she's in room 34, she's teaching." But if nobody's learning anything, she may be engaged in the task of teaching but not actually fulfilling it.

The role of a teacher is to facilitate learning. That's it. And part of the problem is, I think, that the dominant culture of education has come to focus on not teaching and learning, but testing. Now, testing is important. Standardized tests have a place. But they should not be the dominant culture of education. They should be diagnostic. They should help.

If I go for a medical examination, I want some standardized tests. I do. I want to know what my cholesterol level is compared to everybody else's on a standard scale. I don't want to be told on some scale my doctor invented in the car.

"Your cholesterol is what I call Level Orange."

"Really?"

"Is that good?"

"We don't know."

But all that should support learning. It shouldn't obstruct it, which of course it often does. So in place of curiosity, what we have is a culture of compliance. Our children and teachers are encouraged to follow routine algorithms rather than to excite that power of imagination and curiosity.

And the third principle is this: that human life is inherently creative. It's why we all have different résumés. We create our lives, and we can recreate them as we go through them. It's the common currency of being a human being. It's why human culture is so interesting and diverse and dynamic. I mean, other animals may well have imaginations and creativity, but it's not so much in evidence, is it, as ours? I mean, you may have a dog. And your dog may get depressed. You know, but it doesn't listen to Radiohead, does it?

And sit staring out the window with a bottle of Jack Daniels.

"Would you like to come for a walk?"

"No, I'm fine."

"You go. I'll wait. But take pictures."

We all create our own lives through this restless process of imagining alternatives and possibilities, and one of the roles of education is to awaken and develop these powers of creativity. Instead, what we have is a culture of standardization.

Now, it doesn't have to be that way. It really doesn't.

Finland regularly comes out on top in math, science and reading. Now, we only know that's what they do well at, because that's all that's being tested. That's one of the problems of the test. They don't look for other things that matter just as much. The thing about work in Finland is this: they don't obsess about those disciplines. They have a very broad approach to education, which includes humanities, physical education, the arts.

Second, there is no standardized testing in Finland. I mean, there's a bit, but it's not what gets people up in the morning, what keeps them at their desks.

The third thing—and I was at a meeting recently with some people from Finland, actual Finnish people, and somebody from the American system was saying to the people in Finland, "What do you do about the drop-out rate in Finland?"

And they all looked a bit bemused, and said, "Well, we don't have one. Why would you drop out? If people are in trouble, we get to them quite quickly and we help and support them."

Now people always say, "Well, you know, you can't compare Finland to America." No. I think there's a population of around five million in Finland. But you can compare it to a state in America. Many states in America have fewer people in them than that. I mean, I've been to some states in America and I was the only person there.

Really. Really. I was asked to lock up when I left.

But what all the high-performing systems in the world do is currently what is not evident, sadly, across the systems in America—I mean, as a whole. One is this: they individualize teaching and learning. They recognize that it's students who are learning and the system has to engage them, their curiosity, their individuality, and their creativity. That's how you get them to learn.

The second is that they attribute a very high status to the teaching profession. They recognize that you can't improve education if you don't pick great people to teach and keep giving them constant support and professional development. Investing in professional development is not a cost. It's an investment, and every other country that's succeeding well knows that, whether it's Australia, Canada, South Korea or Singapore. They know that to be the case.

And the third is, they devolve responsibility to the school level for getting the job done. You see, there's a big difference here between going into a mode of command and control in education — that's what happens in some systems. Central or state governments decide, they know best and they're going to tell you what to do. The trouble is that education doesn't go on in the committee rooms of our legislative buildings. It happens in classrooms and schools, and the people who do it are the teachers and the students, and if you remove their discretion, it stops working. You have to put it back to the people.

There is wonderful work happening in this country. But I have to say it's happening in spite of the dominant culture of education, not because of it. It's like people are sailing into a headwind all the time. And the reason I think is this: that many of the current policies are based on mechanistic conceptions of education. It's like education is an industrial process that can be improved just by having better data, and somewhere in the back of the mind of some policy makers is this idea that if we fine-tune it well enough, if we just get it right, it will all hum along perfectly into the future. It won't, and it never did.

The point is that education is not a mechanical system. It's a human system. It's about people, people who either do want to learn or don't want to learn. Every student who drops out of school has a reason for it which is rooted in their own biography. They may find it boring. They may find it irrelevant. They may find that it's at odds with the life they're living outside of school. There are trends, but the stories are always unique. I was at a meeting recently in Los Angeles of — they're called alternative education programs. These are programs designed to get kids back into education. They have certain common features. They're very personalized. They have strong support for the teachers, close links with the community and a broad and diverse curriculum, and often programs which involve students outside school as well as inside school. And they work. What's interesting to me is, these are called "alternative education".

You know? And all the evidence from around the world is, if we all did that, there'd be no need for the alternative.

So I think we have to embrace a different metaphor. We have to recognize that it's a human system, and there are conditions under which people thrive, and conditions under which they don't. We are after all organic creatures, and the culture of the school is absolutely essential. Culture is an organic term, isn't it?

Not far from where I live is a place called Death Valley. Death Valley is the hottest, driest place in America, and nothing grows there. Nothing grows there because it doesn't rain. Hence, Death Valley. In the winter of 2004, it rained in Death Valley. Seven inches of rain fell over a very short period. And in the spring of 2005, there was a phenomenon. The whole floor of Death Valley was carpeted in flowers for a while. What it proved is this: that Death Valley isn't dead. It's dormant. Right beneath the surface are these seeds of possibility waiting for the right conditions to come about, and with organic systems, if the conditions are right, life is inevitable. It happens all the time. You take an area, a school, a district, you change the conditions, give people a different sense of possibility, a different set of expectations, a broader range of opportunities, you cherish and value the relationships between teachers and learners, you offer people the discretion to be creative and to innovate in what they do, and schools that were once bereft spring to life.

Great leaders know that. The real role of leadership in education — and I think it's true at the national level, the state level, at the school level — is not and should not be command and control. The real role of leadership is climate control, creating a climate of possibility. And if you do that, people will rise to it and achieve things that you completely did not anticipate and couldn't have expected.

There's a wonderful quote from Benjamin Franklin. "There are three sorts of people in the world: Those who are immovable, people who don't get it, or don't want to do anything about it; there are people who are movable, people who see the need for change and are prepared to listen to it; and there are people who move, people who make things happen." And if we can encourage more people, that will be a movement. And if the movement is strong enough, that's, in the best sense of the word, a revolution. And that's what we need.

Thank you very much.

（来源：https://www.ted.com/talks/sir_ken_robinson_how_to_escape_education_s_death_valley?referrer=playlist-how_can_we_fix_the_learning_crisis&language=en）

3.8 主题拓展资源

A: 双语文章: How to Succeed in College

大学生活丰富多彩。文章鼓励大学生广泛探索自己的兴趣，深入研究自己的专业，走出教室，通过多样化的方式探索资源，挖掘自己的潜力，同时也要注意保持身心健康。教师可引导学生阅读文章，并借鉴文章中有道理的建议，拥抱更加精彩的大学生活。

A successful college experience is about much more than your grades.

It's easy to get tunnel vision when you're working toward a college degree, but you should aspire to more than good grades and graduation. When you finally have that diploma in hand, will you truly feel satisfied? What will you have truly learned and accomplished?

Grades are of course crucial to earning your degree and helping you get into graduate school, but academic success also includes what happens outside your classes. As you take the steps necessary to earn a diploma, look around: College campuses are full of opportunities to experience new activities and meet people who can help you grow.

Explore Different Subjects

You may arrive at college with a specific career track in mind, or you may not have the slightest idea of what you want to major in. No matter which end of the spectrum you're on, let yourself explore a variety of courses. Take an intro class in a field you know nothing about. Sit it on an unusual seminar. You never know — you may discover something you didn't know you'd love.

Follow Your Instincts

There will undoubtedly be many people giving you advice about what you should do during — and after — college. Take your time exploring your interests, and once it comes time to make decisions about your future, pick a career and course of study that suits you, not your parents. Pay attention to what excites you and make sure you're happy with your academic plans. Once you've made a choice, feel confident in your decision.

Take Advantage of the Resources Around You

Once you've decided on a major — or even a career — make the most of the time you have left, be it one year or four. Take classes from the best professors in your department. Stop by during their office hours to get feedback on your performance and ask any questions you couldn't get answered in class. Grab coffee with your favorite professors and talk about what they love about their field.

This concept goes beyond professors, too. If you're struggling with a certain subject or assignment, see if there's a study group or tutoring center that can help you overcome the obstacle. No one expects you to figure out everything on your own.

Find Ways to Learn Outside the Classroom

You'll only spend so many hours attending class and doing homework — what are you doing with the remaining hours of your day? How you spend your time outside of the classroom is a critical part of your college experience. Make it a priority to branch out, because you're unlikely to have another time in your life where you can so frequently try new things. In fact, the "real world" is a lot more like what you'll encounter in extracurricular activities than in the classroom, so make time for them.

Join a club or organization that explores your interests and passions. You could even run for a leadership position and develop skills that will serve you later in your career. Consider learning about a different culture by studying abroad. See if you have the opportunity to earn course credit by completing an internship. Attend events put on by clubs you're not a member of. No matter what you do, you'll almost certainly learn something new — even if it's just something new about yourself.

Allow Yourself to Be Happy

College is not just about fulfilling your academic aspirations. You need to enjoy your life at college, too. Make sure to make time in your schedule for the things that keep you healthy, whether it be going to the gym or attending religious services. Make time to talk to your family, hang out with your friends, eat well, and get enough sleep. In other words: take care of all of yourself, not just your brain.

（来源：https://www.thoughtco.com/how-to-succeed-in-college-793219）

B. 英文视频：Let's Teach for Mastery — not Test Scores

教师可让学生观看本视频，并引导学生展开批判性思考：能力和分数，哪个更重要？

I'm here today to talk about the two ideas that, at least based on my observations at Khan Academy, are kind of the core, or the key leverage points for learning. And it's the idea of mastery and the idea of mindset.

I saw this in the early days working with my cousins. A lot of them were having trouble with math at first, because they had all of these gaps accumulated in their learning. And because of that, at some point they got to an algebra class and they might have been a little bit shaky on some of the pre-algebra, and because of that, they thought they didn't have the math gene. Or they'd get to a calculus class, and they'd be a little bit shaky on the algebra. I saw it in the early days when I was uploading some of those videos on YouTube, and I realized that people who were not my cousins were watching.

And at first, those comments were just simple thank-yous. I thought that was a pretty big deal. I don't know how much time you all spend on YouTube. Most of the comments are not "Thank you".

They're a little edgier than that. But then the comments got a little more intense, student after student saying that they had grown up not liking math. It was getting difficult as they got into more advanced math topics. By the time they got to algebra, they had so many gaps in their knowledge they couldn't engage with it. They thought they didn't have the math gene. But when they were a bit older, they took a little agency and decided to engage. They found resources like Khan Academy and they were able to fill in those gaps and master those concepts, and that reinforced their mindset that it wasn't fixed; that they actually were capable of learning mathematics.

And in a lot of ways, this is how you would master a lot of things in life. It's the way you would learn a martial art. In a martial art, you would practice the white belt skills as long as necessary, and only when you've mastered it you would move on to become a yellow belt. It's the way you learn a musical instrument: you practice the basic piece over and over again, and only when you've mastered it, you go on to the more advanced one.

But what we point out — this is not the way a traditional academic model is structured, the type of academic model that most of us grew up in. In a traditional academic model, we group students together, usually by age, and around middle school, by age and perceived ability, and we shepherd them all together at the same pace. And what typically happens, let's say we're in a middle school pre-algebra class, and the current unit is on exponents, the teacher will give a lecture on exponents, then we'll go home, do some homework. The next morning, we'll review the homework, then another lecture, homework, lecture, homework. That will continue for about two or three weeks, and then we get a test. On that test, maybe I get a 75 percent, maybe you get a 90 percent, maybe you get a 95 percent. And even though the test identified gaps in our knowledge, I didn't know 25 percent of the material. Even the A student, what was the five percent they didn't know?

Even though we've identified the gaps, the whole class will then move on to the next subject, probably a more advanced subject that's going to build on those gaps. It might be logarithms or negative exponents. And that process continues, and you immediately start to realize how strange this is. I didn't know 25 percent of the more foundational thing, and now I'm being pushed to the more advanced thing. And this will continue for months, years, all the way until at some point, I might be in an algebra class or trigonometry class and I hit a wall. And it's not because algebra is fundamentally difficult or because the student isn't bright. It's because I'm seeing an equation and they're dealing with exponents and that 30 percent that I didn't know is showing up. And then I start to disengage.

To appreciate how absurd that is, imagine if we did other things in our life that way. Say, home-building.

So we bring in the contractor and say, "We were told we have two weeks to build a foundation. Do what you can."

So they do what they can. Maybe it rains. Maybe some of the supplies don't show up. And two weeks later, the inspector comes, looks around, says, "OK, the concrete is still wet right over there, that part's not quite up to code ... I'll give it an 80 percent."

You say, "Great! That's a C. Let's build the first floor."

Same thing. We have two weeks, do what you can, inspector shows up, it's a 75 percent. Great, that's a D-plus. Second floor, third floor, and all of a sudden, while you're building the third floor, the whole structure collapses. And if your reaction is the reaction you typically have in education, or that a lot of folks have, you might say, maybe we had a bad contractor, or maybe we needed better inspection or more frequent inspection. But what was really broken was the process. We were artificially constraining how long we had to something, pretty much ensuring a variable outcome, and we took the trouble of inspecting and identifying those gaps, but then we built right on top of it.

So the idea of mastery learning is to do the exact opposite. Instead of artificially constraining, fixing when and how long you work on something, pretty much ensuring that variable outcome, the A, B, C, D, F—do it the other way around. What's variable is when and how long a student actually has to work on something, and what's fixed is that they actually master the material.

And it's important to realize that not only will this make the student learn their exponents better, but it'll reinforce the right mindset muscles. It makes them realize that if you got 20 percent wrong on something, it doesn't mean that you have a C branded in your DNA somehow. It means that you should just keep working on it. You should have grit; you should have perseverance; you should take agency over your learning.

Now, a lot of skeptics might say, well, hey, this is all great, philosophically, this whole idea of mastery-based learning and its connection to mindset, students taking agency over their learning. It makes a lot of sense, but it seems impractical. To actually do it, every student would be on their own track. It would have to be personalized, you'd have to have private tutors and worksheets for every student. And these aren't new ideas — there were experiments in Winnetka, Illinois, 100 years ago, where they did mastery-based learning and saw great results, but they said it wouldn't scale because it was logistically difficult. The teacher had to give different worksheets to every student, give on-demand assessments.

But now today, it's no longer impractical. We have the tools to do it. Students see an explanation at their own time and pace? There's on-demand video for that. They need practice? They need feedback? There's adaptive exercises readily available for students.

And when that happens, all sorts of neat things happen. One, the students can actually master the concepts, but they're also building their growth mindset, they're building grit, perseverance, they're taking agency over their learning. And all sorts of beautiful things can start to happen in the actual classroom. Instead of it being focused on the lecture, students can interact with each other. They can get deeper mastery over the material. They can go into simulations, Socratic dialogue.

To appreciate what we're talking about and the tragedy of lost potential here, I'd like to give a little bit of a thought experiment. If we were to go 400 years into the past to Western Europe, which even then, was one of the more literate parts of the planet, you would see that about 15 percent of the population knew how to read. And I suspect that if you asked someone who did know how to read, say a member of the clergy, "What percentage of the population do you think is even capable of reading?" They might say, "Well, with a great education system, maybe 20 or 30 percent." But if you fast forward to today, we know that that prediction would have been wildly pessimistic, that pretty close to 100 percent of the population is capable of reading. But if I were to ask you a similar question: "What percentage of the population do you think is capable of truly mastering calculus, or understanding organic chemistry, or being able to contribute to cancer research?" A lot of you might say, "Well, with a great education system, maybe 20, 30 percent."

But what if that estimate is just based on your own experience in a non-mastery framework, your own experience with yourself or observing your peers, where you're being pushed at this set pace through classes, accumulating all these gaps? Even when you got that 95 percent, what was that five percent you missed? And it keeps accumulating—you get to an advanced class, all of a sudden you hit a wall and say, "I'm not meant to be a cancer researcher; not meant to be a physicist; not meant to be a mathematician." I suspect that that actually is the case, but if you were allowed to be operating in a mastery framework, if you were allowed to really take agency over your learning, and when you get something wrong, embrace it — view that failure as a moment of learning — that number, the percent that could really master calculus or understand organic chemistry, is actually a lot closer to 100 percent.

And this isn't even just a "nice to have." I think it's a social imperative. We're exiting what you could call the industrial age and we're going into this information revolution. And it's clear that some things are happening. In the industrial age, society was a pyramid. At the base of the pyramid, you needed human labor. In the middle of the pyramid, you had an information processing, a bureaucracy class, and at the top of the pyramid, you had your owners of capital and your entrepreneurs and your creative class. But we know what's happening already, as we go into this information revolution. The bottom of that pyramid, automation, is going to take over. Even that middle tier, information processing, that's what computers are good at.

So as a society, we have a question: All this new productivity is happening because of this technology, but who participates in it? Is it just going to be that very top of the pyramid, in which case, what does everyone else do? How do they operate? Or do we do something that's more aspirational? Do we actually attempt to invert the pyramid, where you have a large creative class, where almost everyone can participate as an entrepreneur, an artist, as a researcher?

And I don't think that this is utopian. I really think that this is all based on the idea that if we let people tap into their potential by mastering concepts, by being able to exercise agency over their learning, that they can get there. And when you think of it as just a citizen of the world, it's pretty exciting. I mean, think about the type of equity we can we have, and the rate at which civilization could even progress. And so, I'm pretty optimistic about it. I think it's going to be a pretty exciting time to be alive. Thank you.

（来源：https://www.ted.com/talks/sal_khan_let_s_teach_for_mastery_not_test_scores?referrer=playlist-how_can_we_fix_the_learning_crisis&language=en）

第二章

《大学体验英语》综合教程第二册

2

第一单元　著名大学
（Unit1 Famous Universities）

1. 思政主题：大学教育，新时代青年的使命担当

2. 意 义

本单元聚焦"著名大学"相关话题探讨大学教育的意义。教学中教师需要引导学生理解上大学的意义，引导学生做好大学生涯规划，志存高远、脚踏实地，不畏艰难险阻，勇担时代使命，把个人的理想追求融入党和国家事业之中，为党、为祖国、为人民多作贡献。党的十八大以来，习近平总书记多次发表关于青年成长成才的重要讲话，对于做好新时代青年工作具有重大的指导意义。党的十九大报告指出，青年一代有理想、有本领、有担当，国家就有前途，民族就有希望。

少年兴则国兴，少年强则国强。习近平总书记曾多次通过演讲、座谈会、回信等方式与青年朋友谈理想信念、人生价值、奋斗成长。本材料整理了习总书记给全国各族青年的回信，帮助学生体会国家对于新时代青年的殷切期望，激励青年树立远大理想，担当时代责任，投身强国伟业。

新时代中国青年要努力学习马克思主义立场观点方法，努力掌握科学文化知识和专业技能，努力提高人文素养。

Young people should work hard in learning the Marxist stance, viewpoints and methods, mastering scientific and cultural knowledge and professional skills, and improving their humanistic quality.

——2019年4月30日，在纪念五四运动100周年大会上发表的重要讲话

希望你们珍惜身穿戎装的机会，把热血挥洒在实现强军梦的伟大实践之中。

I hope that you would cherish the opportunity to serve in the army and commit yourselves to the country's goal of building a strong army.

————2017年9月23日，给南开大学8名新入伍大学生的回信

祖国的青年一代有理想、有追求、有担当，实现中华民族伟大复兴就有源源不断的青春力量。

As long as the younger generation of the country has ideals, pursuits and shoulders, there will be an endless power of youth supporting the Chinese nation's rejuvenation.

————2017年8月15日，回信勉励第三届中国"互联网＋"大学生创新创业大赛"青年红色筑梦之旅"的大学生

希望你和所有大学生村官热爱基层、扎根基层、增长见识、增长才干，促进农村发展。

I hope that other college graduates will find enthusiasm for their work, as you have done, settling in grassroots positions and dedicating themselves to the development of villages.

————2014年1月28日，给山东大学生基层干部张广秀复信

希望广大海外学子秉持崇高理想，在中国人民实现中国梦的伟大奋斗中实现自身价值，努力书写无愧于时代的华彩篇章。

I hope all Chinese who study overseas will uphold lofty ideals, fulfill their own goals by participating in the Chinese people's endeavor for realizing the Chinese dream, and write excellent chapters that will live up to the times.

————2014年1月16日，给全体在德留学人员回信

只有把人生理想融入国家和民族的事业中，才能最终成就一番事业。希望你们珍惜韶华、奋发有为，为实现中国梦奉献智慧和力量。

Only by integrating individual dreams to the national cause can one finally make great achievement. I hope that you will cherish the glorious youth, strive with pioneer spirit and contribute your wisdom and energy to the realization of the Chinese dream.

————2013年5月2日，给北京大学考古文博学院2009级本科团支部全体同学回信

3. 教学设计与思政元素的融入

Passage A

3.1 Warm-up 环节

英语视频：My College Life

视频中，一位大一新生讲述了自己在新生适应期的困惑、迷茫和孤独，以及如何通过认识新朋友、发展兴趣爱好等方式调整心态，重新找回自我和生活重心的故事，可作为课文导入材料，引发学生对大学适应期问题的关注和探讨。

（来源：https://v.qq.com/x/page/c0954na9q02.html）

3.2 Discussion 环节

双语文章：生逢其时，勇敢担当；泥泞喂养，前路芬芳

2020年，面对疫情考验，新一代中国青年用自己的方式为抗疫贡献力量。他们积极思考、勇于承担，彰显中国青年的家国情怀与责任担当。3月31日，在以"抗击新冠肺炎疫情，全球命运与共"为主题的线上"新时代大讲堂"上，清华大学武汉籍学生张睿茹讲述了武汉封城后，自己及家人的亲身经历，分享了疫情期间的思考与感悟。从恐惧慌乱到冷静应对、自立自强，疫情让张睿茹第一次深刻认识到自己对父母和家庭的爱，第一次亲身体会医护人员的艰辛与不易，第一次与无数陌生人建立情感共鸣，第一次读懂国歌中中华民族"万众一心"的含义。张睿茹希望借助自己的故事，传达积极乐观的心态，鼓励全国人民团结一致，携手并进，共同期待一个更加美好的春天。

Chinese have always demonstrated a strong sense of unity in the face of challenges. I'm a real Generation Z girl who was born in 2000. At the age of three, I could sing the national anthem and first encountered the word "Wan Zhong Yi Xin", which in at least one translation is rendered as "millions of hearts with one mind".

中国人民面对挑战，总能团结起来。我是"00后"，2000年出生。三岁时我就会唱国歌，第一次听到了"万众一心"。有的语言里会翻译成"无数人同一颗心"。

At the age of 8, I first learned the meaning of "Yi Fang You Nan, Ba Fang Zhi Yuan", referring to helps from all directions, when I saw people tried their best to save others' lives in Wenchuan Earthquake.

8岁时，我第一次知道了"一方有难，八方支援"，就是"大家一起援助"的意思。那时全国上下齐心协力，支援地震后的汶川。

It's only now, at the age of 20, that I fully appreciate what those words mean. Chinese people have all stood up as one to fight COVID-19. Medical workers from all over the country descended on Wuhan to save others' lives. Resources including food are sent to the city from all over China. And, most importantly, hundreds of millions of people stayed at home to prevent the virus from spreading.

但直到现在，我20岁了，才真正理解了这些词的含义。中国人民齐心协力对抗疫情，全国各地的医护人员纷纷驰援武汉。各个城市也都支援物资、食品。最重要的是，几亿人居家，避免病毒扩散。

I am so proud that people in my country have all joined in this collective effort. It's natural to fear illness, death, and uncertainty, and it's also natural to feel compassion when we see others suffering.

祖国人民齐心协力，我非常骄傲。面对疾病、死亡和未知，我们都会恐惧；看到他人受苦，我们也会心生同情。

It is the love towards the others that turns the most timid of souls into strongest warriors, ready to bear the toughest responsibilities and even at risk to their lives to save others. In this fight against COVID-19, I saw this love shining in medical people, volunteers, restaurant owners, bus drivers, and countless others.

正是对他人的爱，让最胆小的人也能成为最勇敢的战士，承担最重大的责任，甚至舍己救人。在对抗新冠肺炎疫情的战斗中，我在医护人员、志愿者、饭店老板、公交司机以及无数人身上看到了这份爱。

What we are living through now is undoubtedly horrible, with a pandemic the likes of which hasn't been seen in more than 100 years. But I still choose to be optimistic. Because I see "Wan Zhong Yi Xin" around the world that people are working together to try to help others, and with them I think we can look forward to the day that COVID-19 is finally defeated.

我们现在的经历固然很可怕。面对这场百年一遇的疫情，我依然选择乐观。因为我看到全世界人民万众一心，一起帮助他人。正是因为有了这些人，我才相信我们终有一天会战胜疫情。

（来源：外研社高等教育资讯）

3.3 Critical thinking 环节

英语文章： Stanford University: Why Do the Humanities Matter? Insights

Into Everything

了解斯坦福大学针对"人文学科的重要性"这一话题的观点评论，可作为辩论活动等的参考素材。

Through exploration of the humanities we learn how to think creatively and critically, to reason, and to ask questions. Because these skills allow us to gain new insights into everything from poetry and paintings to business models and politics, humanistic subjects have been at the heart of a liberal arts education since the ancient Greeks first used them to educate their citizens.

Understanding Our World

Research into the human experience adds to our knowledge about our world. Through the work of humanities scholars, we learn about the values of different cultures, about what goes into making a work of art, about how history is made. Their efforts preserve the great accomplishments of the past, help us understand the world we live in, and give us tools to imagine the future.

Bringing Clarity to the Future

Today, humanistic knowledge continues to provide the ideal foundation for exploring and understanding the human experience. Investigating a branch of philosophy might get you thinking about ethical questions. Learning another language might help you gain an appreciation for the similarities in different cultures. Contemplating a sculpture might make you think about how an artist's life affected her creative decisions. Reading a book from another region of the world, might help you think about the meaning of democracy. Listening to a history course might help you better understand the past, while at the same time offer you a clearer picture of the future.

3.4 主题拓展资源

数据资料：《2019年中国大学生就业报告》发布

第三方社会调查机构麦可思研究院在北京发布的《2019年中国大学生就业报告》（"就业蓝皮书"）显示，2018届大学毕业生就业率为91.5%，其中2018与2017两届高职高专毕业生就业率高于同届本科。

本科毕业生就业率连续四年下降

麦可思研究院副院长马妍介绍，2018届本科毕业生就业率为91.0%，与过去四届相比略有下降；2018届高职高专毕业生就业率为92.0%，与过去四届相比稳中有升。

根据报告显示，2018届本科毕业生待就业比例为4.2%，高职高专毕业生待就业比例为7.5%，与2014届相比均有下降。"由于深造的分流，毕业生待就业压力没有明显增加，"马妍说。

从就业去向来看，民营企业、地级城市及以下地区等依然是主要就业去向，2014至2018届本科毕业生在民营企业就业的比例从50.0%上升到54.0%，2014至2018届高职高专毕业生在民营企业就业的比例从65.0%上升到68.0%。

从就业职业、行业来看，2018届本科毕业生从事最多的职业类是"中小学教育"，就业比例为19.3%，就业比例增长最多的行业是"中小学及教辅机构"，就业比例为12.7%；2018届高职高专毕业生从事最多的职业类是"销售"，就业比例为8.9%，就业比例增长最多的行业是"学前、小学及教辅机构"，就业比例为6.6%。

2018届大学毕业生的月收入

2018届大学毕业生的月收入为4624元，比2017届的4317元增长了307元，比2016届的3988元增长了636元。其中，2018届本科毕业生的月收入5135元比2017届的4774元增长了361元，比2016届的4376元增长了759元；2018届高职高专毕业生的月收入4112元，比2017届的3860元增长了252元，比2016届的3599元增长了513元。

从以上三届的趋势可以看出，应届大学毕业生月收入呈上升趋势。2018届大学毕业月收入高于3271元的城镇居民2018年月均可支配收入。

软件工程等专业就业率排名靠前

高考结束后，考生将进入填报志愿阶段，考生如何选择大学专业？这份针对大学生求职就业的调查报告，提供了相关参考。

调查显示，2018届本科毕业生就业率排前三位的专业是软件工程（96.8%）、能源与动力工程（96.8%）、工程管理（95.8%）。

数据分析，从学科门类来看，2018届本科毕业生就业率最高的学科门类是工学（93.1%），其次是管理学（92.7%），哲学学科门类因为样本较少，没有包括在内。

对于高职高专就业率而言，数据显示，2018届高职高专毕业生就业率排前三位的专业是高压输配电线路施工运行与维护（97.1%）、电气化铁道技术（95.9%）、电力系统自动化技术（95.5%）。

报告显示，从2016—2018届的就业率变化趋势可以看出，本科学科门类中的艺术学、经济学、理学毕业生就业率下降较多。高职高专专业大类中的资源开发与测绘大类、医药卫生大类、土建大类毕业生就业率上升较多。

历史学、音乐表演、法学连续三届被亮红牌

专业就业率往往对大学毕业生找工作的情况产生重要影响。那么，从数据来看，哪些专业被亮起了红牌？

报告解释，红牌专业指失业量较大，就业率、薪资和就业满意度综合较低的专业。2019年本科就业红牌专业包括绘画、历史学、应用心理学、音乐表演、化学、法学。其中，历史学、音乐表演、法学连续三届被亮红牌。

此外，报告也列举了就业率保持良好的绿牌专业。所谓绿牌专业，指失业量较小，就业率、薪资和就业满意度综合较高的专业，为需求增长型专业。

2019年本科就业绿牌专业包括信息安全、软件工程、网络工程、物联网工程、数字媒体技术、通信工程、数字媒体艺术。其中，信息安全、软件工程、网络工程、通信工程、数字媒体艺术连续三届绿牌。

（来源：http://hn.cnr.cn/hngbxwzx/20190612/t20190612_524647162.shtml）

2019年美国就业率最高的十个专业

可用于佐证课文中"学生倾向于选择专业技能类专业"这一现状，且这一情况不只发生在课文背景中的美国，同样发生在中国。

The 10 Highest-paying College Majors of 2019, According to PayScale

College students arriving on campuses across the U.S. this fall may think that choosing a school was the biggest decision they'd have to make for a while.

But now, they'll need to choose a major. "Research shows that in many ways it doesn't really matter where you go to college," Jon Marcus, higher education editor at *The Hechinger Report*, tells CNBC Make It. "What major you pick has a greater influence on your future postgraduate earnings and career success."

As part of its annual College Salary Report, released today, PayScale analyzed data from graduates of more than 2,500 schools in order to spotlight how much graduates typically make early and mid-way through their careers. The site also identified the highest-paying college majors, and polled workers about whether or not they felt their work makes the world a better place.

Here are the 10 highest-paying college majors, according to PayScale:

10. Aeronautics & Astronautics

Median salary for alumni with 0-5 years of experience: $73,100

Median salary for alumni with 10+ years of experience: $131,600

Percent who say their work makes the world a better place: 59%

9. Pharmacy

Median salary for alumni with 0-5 years of experience: $79,600

Median salary for alumni with 10+ years of experience: $132,500

Percent who say their work makes the world a better place: 77%

8. Business Analysis

Median salary for alumni with 0-5 years of experience: $57,200

Median salary for alumni with 10+ years of experience: $133,200

Percent who say their work makes the world a better place: 50%

7. Electrical Power Engineering

Median salary for alumni with 0-5 years of experience: $72,400

Median salary for alumni with 10+ years of experience: $134,700

Percent who say their work makes the world a better place: 63%

6. Actuarial Mathematics

Median salary for alumni with 0-5 years of experience: $63,300

Median salary for alumni with 10+ years of experience: $135,100

Percent who say their work makes the world a better place: 46%

5. Political Economy

Median salary for alumni with 0-5 years of experience: $57,600

Median salary for alumni with 10+ years of experience: $136,200

Percent who say their work makes the world a better place: 38%

4. Operations Research

Median salary for alumni with 0-5 years of experience: $77,900

Median salary for alumni with 10+ years of experience: $137,100

Percent who say their work makes the world a better place: 48%

3. Applied Economics and Management

Median salary for alumni with 0-5 years of experience: $58,900

Median salary for alumni with 10+ years of experience: $140,000

Percent who say their work makes the world a better place: 69%

2. Electrical Engineering & Computer Science

Median salary for alumni with 0-5 years of experience: $88,000

Median salary for alumni with 10+ years of experience: $142,200

Percent who say their work makes the world a better place: 44%

1. Petroleum Engineering

Median salary for alumni with 0-5 years of experience: $94,500

Median salary for alumni with 10+ years of experience: $176,900

Percent who say their work makes the world a better place: 72%

（来源：https://www.cnbc.com/2019/08/20/the-10-highest-paying-college-majors-of-2019.html）

Passage B

3.5 Warm-up 环节

双语视频：Don't Let Anyone Rush You with Their Time Lines

在愈加快节奏的社会里，人生似乎一眼就望得到尽头，好好学习、找个好工作……遵循着既定的模板。我们的人生就该如此吗？励志演说家Jay Shetty告诉我们：不是的。人生有很多可能，人生的意义是做有意义、有目标、有价值感的事。过有意义的生活最重要，创造属于自己的充满意义的人生，学会用这些去影响点亮他人的生活。视频约4分钟，教师可请学生思考并讨论What do you think are essential to a good life? 分享自己对于人生意义的思考。

Today's assembly is about the start of a journey, the start of the rest of your lives. 今天的集会是关于一段新的开始，它将开启你们的余生。

In 2 years time all of you will be finishing your A Levels. 再过两年，你们就会完成高中的学业。

In 3 yeas time you'll be studying across the world, studying at the university of your choice. 再过三年，你们就会去到自己想去的国家，上自己想上的大学。

In 5 years time you'll have started your careers. 再过五年，你们就会开启自己的职业生涯。

Many of you will be in this room working for the top institutions across the globe. 你们在座的很多同学会进入世界顶尖公司工作。

You will then get married, you then may buy a house. 然后你们会结婚，买房。

In 10 years time your life will be set for you. 十年之后，你的人生就会安定下来。

In 10 years you'll be 30 and from then on your path, your life will be set. 再过10年，你就30岁了，你的人生轨迹就会定型。

另一位老师：

I'm sorry, Mr. Headmaster, let me tell you why that approach may fail you. 抱

歉，校长，我想告诉你为什么你的这些话是错的。

I know people who graduated at 21 and didn't get a job until they were 27. 有的人21岁毕业，到27岁才找到工作。

I know people who graduated late at 25 and they found work immediately. 有的人25岁才毕业，但马上就找到了工作。

I know people who never went to university, but found what they love at 18. 有的人没上过大学，却在18岁就找到了热爱的事。

I know people who found a job straight out of college making decent money, but hate what they do. 有的人毕业就找到好工作，赚很多钱，却过得不开心。

I know people who took gap years and found their purpose. 有的人选择间隔年，去寻找自我。

I know people who were so sure about what they were going to do at 16, they change their mind at 26. 有的人在16岁就清楚知道自己要什么，但在26岁时改变了想法。

I know people who have children but are single, and I know people who are married but had to wait 8 to 10 years to have children. 有的人有了孩子，却还是单身。有的人结了婚，却等了10年才生孩子。

I know people in relationships who love someone else. 有的人身处一段感情，爱的却是别人。

I know people who love each other but are not together. 有的人明明彼此相爱，却没有在一起。

So my point is everything in life happens according to our time, our clock. 我想说的是，人生中的每一件事都取决于我们自己的时间。

You may look at some of your friends and think that they're ahead of you, maybe some of them you feel are behind, but everything happens at their own pace. 你身边有些朋友也许遥遥领先于你。有些朋友也许落后于你，但凡事都有它自己的节奏。

They have their own time and clock and so do you. 他们有他们的节奏，你有你自己的。

Be patient. 耐心一点。

At age 25, Mark Cuban was a bartender in Dallas. 库班25岁时还在酒吧做酒保。

It took till 32 for J.K. Rowling to be published for *Harry Potter* after being rejected by 12 publishers. 在被拒12次后，J.K.罗琳到32岁才出版了《哈利·波特》。

Ortega launched Zara when he was 39. Ortega 到39岁才创办了 Zara。

Jack Ma started Alibaba when was 35. 马云35岁才建立了阿里巴巴。

Steve Carell only got his break after 40 years old. Steve Carell 40岁才出名。

Virgin was started by Richard Branson at 34. Richard Branson 34岁才创办维珍航空。

Getting your degree after 25 is still an achievement. 25岁后才拿到文凭，依然值得骄傲。

Not being married at 30 but still happy is beautiful. 30岁没结婚，但过得快乐也是一种成功。

Starting a family after 35 is still possible and buying a house after 40 is still great. 35岁之后成家也完全可以，40岁买房也没什么丢脸的。

Don't let anyone rush you with their timelines. 不要让任何人打乱你的时间表。

Because as Einstein said, "Not everything that counts can be counted, and not everything that's counted truly counts." 因为爱因斯坦曾说过："并不是每一件算得出来的事，都有意义；也不是每一件有意义的事，都能够被算出来。"

And this is the most important thing, I want you to be able to create meaningful purposeful fulfilling lives for yourselves and learn how to use that to make an impact and a difference in the lives of others. 这才是最重要的事，我希望你们可以创造属于自己的充满意义的人生，学会用这些去影响点亮他人的生活。

That will be true success. 这才是真正的成功。

（来源：https://www.bilibili.com/video/BV1Cs411K7LK）

3.6 Discussion 环节

双语视频：The Bucket List

视频节选自高分电影《遗愿清单》，讲述两位身患癌症的病人，机缘巧合之下相识结为好友，并决定在余下的日子一起完成他们的遗愿清单，互相扶持奋力追寻人生意义的故事。教师可安排学生观看片段，列出自己的"梦想清单"，讨论追寻梦想与人生意义之间的联系。

（来源：https://v.qq.com/x/page/l09628gptxv.html）

3.7 Critical thinking 环节

本单元聚焦"著名大学"相关话题探讨大学教育的价值以及新时代青年的理想。理想指引人生方向，信念决定事业成败，没有坚定的理想信念，就会导致精神上"缺钙"[1]。在中国特色社会主义新时代,青年一代有坚定的理想信念,实现中华民族伟大复兴中国梦才会有不竭的动力和胜利的希望[2]。作为肩负民族复兴大任的新时代大学生,能否坚定理想信念,事关党和国家各项事业的兴衰成败[3]。

党的十八大以来,习近平总书记多次发表关于青年成长成才的重要讲话,对于做好新时代青年工作具有重大的指导意义。习近平在寄语青年时,一以贯之的主题就是理想信念。他强调新时代的中国青年要树立远大理想、热爱伟大祖国、担当时代责任、勇于砥砺奋斗、练就过硬本领、锤炼品德修为。[4]习近平总书记对青年的寄语,鲜明地阐释了对大学生加强理想信念教育的重要意义。教师在教学中可以从习总书记对青年的寄语入手,选取与主题相关的思政素材,引导学生充分认识和理解上大学的意义;引导学生做好大学生涯规划,志存高远、脚踏实地,不畏艰难险阻,勇担时代使命,把个人的理想追求融入党和国家事业之中,为党、为祖国、为人民多作贡献;引导学生思考人生信念与追求,树立正确的人生价值观念,拓宽单元主题内涵,体现外语课程思政育人价值。通过培养更多大学生成为有大爱大德大情怀的人,进而为实现中华民族伟大复兴的中国梦提供强大精神力量和有力道德支撑。[5]

本篇阅读材料指出大学第一学年是学生形成成熟的自我认知、寻找真正自我的黄金时期。文章鼓励学生积极尝试新鲜事物、培养独立人格,拒绝盲目融入,对度过新生迷茫期有一定的指导意义。教师可安排学生阅读此文章,组织学生讨论如何在学习生活中有意识地培养独立自主性,加深自我了解。

Self-identity Is Key to College Success

The first week of school is always the most tedious. You have to memorize your schedule, buy the proper supplies, and figure out the cheapest way to get books. Entering my second year of college as a sophomore, I'm pretty accustomed to the university and the people in it.

However, my perspective of college has changed since I completed my freshman year. Every incoming student has a vision of how they will live their college experience. Often times they see themselves making new friends, getting involved or going to parties. But that vision may be modified with the more you

---

[1] 王利国. 不忘初心使命 加强新时代大学生理想信念教育[J]. 税务与经济, 2022(1):3-4.
[2] 侯莲梅. 新时代大学生理想信念教育状况及对策研究[J]. 岭南师范学院学报, 2020(12):18-25.
[3] 朱艳红, 张立. 高校大学生理想信念教育的时代价值与模式构建[J]. 教书育人, 2021(11):54-56.
[4] 习近平. 在纪念五四运动100周年大会上的讲话[N]. 人民日报, 2019-05-01(2).
[5] 衣凤先. 加强高校大学生理想信念教育的有效路径探析[J]. 现代交际, 2021(1):156-158.

experience.

The number one modification of my college vision is my lack of desire to fit in. Being away from home gave me the opportunity to learn more about myself as an individual. Not having parental supervision and learning to make important decisions on my own has impacted my character both as a student and as an adult. I appreciate the friends I already have, but I've learned that the real ones come when you are ready; not when it's forced.

One of the best things to establish during your college years, in my opinion, is independence. Being able to rely on myself and make decisions on my own has helped in my transition to adulthood. Over the years I have gained and lost many friends. It even got to the point where I blamed myself. But in reality, the reason is because I didn't know what to look for in a friend.

Throughout high school and even in my freshman year of college, all I wanted to do was fit in. I wanted people to like me, and so I did everything in my power to be "likeable" to certain people. The friendships that I did make didn't last because I wasn't able to relate to them on a personal level. The reason is because I didn't even know who I was as a person. I was so focused on being liked that I never took the time to get to know myself.

Being in college has really given me the opportunity to stay in tune with my inner-self. I left home to come to a completely new place and I found my way without guidance from my parents. It was like starting from scratch. Now, entering my sophomore year, I'm very comfortable with who I am which means I don't need to look for acceptance from anyone else. If I make friends now, it's because me and those people have something in common.

All of this goes to say that it's okay to be independent. My advice to all of the incoming freshman is to know yourself before trying to get to know others. Find out your interests. Join clubs with people who like the same things as you. Don't be afraid to be different and try new things. I'm not saying you shouldn't have friends, but make sure your friendships are based off of the right things. It's cooler to stand out than to fit in, and it's even better to be completely comfortable with who you are as an individual.

（来源：https://docs.qq.com/doc/DVklpU0lXaWhVaENW）

3.8 主题拓展资源

英语文章：How to Make Friends at University During a Pandemic

本文的作者是一位大学生，作者在文中讲到，受到疫情的影响，自己入学的第一个月完全是一个人孤单度过的。随着时间推移，情况逐渐好转，但作者非常强烈地表示，如果能在搬进学生公寓后尽快和同住一所公寓的学生熟悉起来，日子会好过很多。作者在文中为大学新生提出了一些在疫情特殊情况下结交新朋友的建议。疫情期间，不少大学新生都面临着文中类似的问题，教师可请学生讨论特殊的现实情况对于他们在新环境中建立归属感有哪些影响，他们是通过何种方式逐渐融入新环境的。

I spent my first month at university living in a flat with four other students. At the time, my days consisted of trying to avoid going back to the flat and trying every single meal deal that you can imagine.

This was mainly because I didn't know anything about my flatmates and was too scared to actually try to get to know them.

As time went on, everything started to get easier, but I definitely think getting to know my flatmates and coursemates before or quickly after moving in would have helped a lot.

So, the first thing I'd advise you to do is to join any group chats with your flatmates and your coursemates. They're a great way to just get the first few awkward interactions out of the way and sometimes help things flow better when you're getting together in person.

When you're in a group chat with your coursemates, making friends tends to feel a little easier. Not only can you start getting to know each other, but you can also help each other with your studies.

The great thing about this is that you can quickly begin to have regular contact with people on your course. And even if it's a quick chat about a certain essay, having and building that connection with others can really make you feel good.

Break free from small talk

I've previously written another article about how hard it can be to actually start a conversation and get past the small talk stage with new people. One of my main tips to get to know someone better is to get out of the university environment, rather than just finding out what they did for their A-Levels.

Try to invite someone for a drink or a walk (as long as local COVID-19 guidance allows you to do so). You could also think about other activities to do that might be relevant to your course or interests.

One of my closest friends and I bonded over our love for pancakes. We made it a mission to find the best pancakes in Liverpool (my favourite is at Potts Coffee). Fancy doing the same? Just remember to check local restrictions where you are, follow social distancing guidance and don't forget your face coverings.

Or if you don't want to venture out into the city, try doing something with your flatmates at home. Make a roast dinner together, decorate your flat, or try one of these fun ideas.

Embrace online events

This academic year is going to be different, especially if you're starting university for the first time. But that's no reason to not try to make it as good and memorable as you can. This year, I actually think making friends at university will, in one way, be easier than ever. It's just going to be different.

Even if it's online, your university will most likely have several events where you'll get to meet other students. No matter how lame they might sound at first, they are great places to find new people to talk to.

You could also look up any societies that you might be interested in. Although these may also have to be online for the time being, it's a lot easier getting to know people with similar interests to you than it is getting to know people from your Zoom lectures.

Just like your university, your students' union is there to help you during your studies. It was created to always be there when you need it and to make your time at university as enjoyable as possible. It's more than likely that your union will come up with things to help you get settled and make friends.

Make the most of other opportunities

One way to get to know people while also enhancing your CV would be to actually get involved with your students' union. You could join a society, become a course representitive, or even work your way up to become a student officer. The possibilities are endless and pretty much always lead to new friendships.

You could also look out for other volunteering opportunities outside of your university. A lot of students tend to volunteer in their free time to enhance their CV while also doing something they're interested in.

Physical placements may be limited right now, but there are actually a lot of remote volunteering opportunities available. This means you can volunteer from the comfort of your own home, making a difference, meeting new people and enhancing your CV.

I know this is such a cliché to say, but try to remember that everyone is in the same position as you and are probably just as nervous. It's really not as scary as it sounds when you actually start talking to someone. Just be yourself and you might find everything else falls into place.

（来源：https://www.unitestudents.com/the-common-room/student-living/how-to-make-friends-at-university-during-a-pandemic）

B. 英语文章：Is College Preparing You for Real Life?

本文针对大学生如何使自己在就业市场具有优势，更有准备地走入职场提出了实用的建议。

Many of today's students report that their undergraduate experience had not prepared them adequately for life after college. Rightly expecting to use their degrees to find jobs in their chosen career path, they are too often dissatisfied with their employment outcomes upon graduation.

According to a survey by McGraw-Hill Education, only 40% of college seniors feel prepared to pursue a career after they receive their degree.

In contrast to the lacking resources and experiences that are most often offered at schools around the nation, McGraw-Hill's research shows that the majority of students across majors recognize the need for internships and other experiential learning, the opportunity to take advantage of career services and training for the job market, and professional networking opportunities while in college. In fact, 71% of students in their survey view the kind of career planning that is commonly overlooked as an "extremely important" aspect of their college education. They reported a need for greater assistance in identifying transferable skills from their majors and promoting themselves to potential employers.

Importance of internships

When we consider the needs of students who are preparing for new careers, internships have the most noticeable benefit.

Internships (as well as cooperative education, or co-ops) may have been around for decades, but they weren't ever high priorities for many academic institutions that otherwise focused their resources on classroom learning.

Internship programs take students off campus, giving them real-life experience in their chosen career field to contrast their more stagnant lectures within the classroom. To gain temporary, highly useful job experience, students apply for internships at private companies or nonprofit organizations to do part-time work as they continue to take classes. Or, by working in co-ops, students can take a full semester off to work on a full-time basis. Regardless of program, students who participate get practical training and guidance from professional, hands-on mentors.

Interns not only receive practical work experience, but they also gain opportunities to learn more about their intended profession while networking with others who may even be their future employers. As a result of their experiences and new connections, many students can leverage their internships and co-ops into full-time careers.

As the job market tightens up, employers don't want to take chances with untested college graduates. Having at least one internship or co-op experience while in college can dramatically improve a student's chances of getting hired. In fact, as reported by the National Association of Colleges and Employers (NACE) in 2015, 56% of students who had an internship or co-op received job offers upon graduation in contrast to 36% of students without internships.

The type of education matters

There's little question that internships are critical to improve students' chances in the job market. However, graduates' ongoing success also depends on their ability to adapt to changing professions as well as to function within an increasingly global and technological society.

In 2015, the Roosevelt Institute in New York published "Creative Schools for a Thriving Economy," a document in which it is argued that schools should teach creativity instead of "routine cognitive skills".

This research reinforces my own belief that we need to change the fundamental nature of higher education itself. By pursuing an education that incorporates such high-impact practices as writing-intensive classes, research, and capstone projects that incorporate the entirety of a student's academic career, college students can learn how to synthesize a variety of different information. They interact with people from different cultures through service-learning and study abroad, teaching them to consider and appreciate diverse perspectives. And through collaborative courses, first-year experiences, and learning communities, they learn how to work with others in a creative effort to solve problems with an interdisciplinary approach.

How can college students become better prepared?

It's no longer enough to attend classes and get good grades. Instead, college students should consider what kinds of extracurricular, interactive, and hands-on experiences their universities offer, taking advantage of programs that promote truly interactive learning. Education beyond the classroom is key, and prospective college students should choose schools with a consideration not just of the campus culture, but also of the out-of-the-box opportunities they provide.

For all college students, it's imperative to communicate effectively and work collaboratively. All should take advantage of communities and initiatives that challenge them to be intellectually and socially successful.

By encouraging students to be active participants in their degrees, as by reimagining college education itself, we can better prepare our students for the demanding world that awaits them beyond their undergraduate careers.

（来源：https://collegesofdistinction.com/advice/is-college-preparing-you-for-real-life/）

第二单元　工作和职业

（Unit 2 Jobs and Careers）

1. 思政主题：爱岗敬业、无私奉献、开拓创新、持续专注、精益求精等职业精神和工匠精神

2. 意义

2017年10月，党的十九大报告中明确提出，要"建设知识型、技能型、创新型劳动者大军，弘扬劳模精神和'工匠精神'，营造劳动光荣的社会风尚和精益求精的敬业风气……要全面贯彻党的教育方针，落实立德树人根本任务，发展素质教育，推进教育公平，培养德智体美全面发展的社会主义建设者和接班人"。2021年4月，全国职业教育大会召开，习近平总书记做出的重要指示中强调，要"弘扬工匠精神，提高技术技能人才社会地位，为全面建设社会主义现代化国家、实现中华民族伟大复兴的中国梦提供有力人才和技能支撑"。

职业精神既是一个人内在的认识思维系统，是对职业的理性认知及其崇尚景

仰的心理状态，表现为一个人在从业过程中的热爱、严谨、细致、负责、高效的行为及风貌。职业精神最基本的表现就是爱岗敬业，以工作任务为重，以服务他人和社会为荣，以自我价值的实现为目标。

现代职业精神由多种要素构成。思想意识方面包括职业团队的归属意识、职业岗位的热爱意识、职业理想的实践意识、职业协作的和谐意识、公平合理的竞争意识和精益求精的责任意识。风范品格方面包括实现职业憧憬的执着态度、发奋图强的进取精神、艰苦奋斗的创业作风、开拓创新的求异品格、服务社会的人文情怀和诚实守信的仁义品质。实践动力方面包括持续不断工作热情、坚持不懈的信念追求、敢于竞争的不屈斗志等。这些要素分别从特定方面反映着新时期社会主义职业需求的特定本质和基础，同时又相互配合，形成严谨完整的职业精神形态。

职业精神与个人的职业生活相结合，具有较强的稳定性和连续性。形成具有导向性的职业心理和职业习惯，在很大程度上改善着从业者在学校和家庭生活中所形成的品行，影响主体的精神风貌。行业群体的职业精神水平制约着国家经济、政治、文化、教育水平的发展。由于社会分工的细化，行业群体在社会中的作用越来越大，而且彼此之间的联系越来越紧密，社会对行业产品的质量、服务水平、员工个体职业精神等各方面的要求也越来越高。行业的职业精神水平决定了产品的质量、服务的水平等。每个公民都应该具备并恪守自己的职业精神。

新时代的中国也呼唤工匠精神，工匠精神主要包括以下内涵：一是技艺精湛、追求卓越。在自己所从事的生产、工艺、管理等工作中执著钻研、精益求精，其精湛的技艺达到了行业、领域、国内乃至国际一流水平。为了做得更好，工匠会不断学习、不懈追求，依靠创新实现一次又一次的超越。二是爱岗敬业、高度负责。爱岗敬业是成长为工匠人才的必要条件，只有全心投入，才会有所建树，才能实现超越。爱岗敬业反映出从业者对待自己职业的一种态度，它体现的是从业者热爱自己的工作岗位、对工作极端负责、敬重自己所从事的职业的道德操守，是从业者对自己工作的敬畏之心，以及视职业为生命的精神境界。三是淡泊名利、一生坚守。因为热爱己所从事的职业，所以能够耐得住寂寞，守得住清贫，受得了委屈。在艰难困苦之时，在攻坚克难之际，不计较个人得失，勇于担当，不怕牺牲。对于真正的工匠而言，物质、荣誉只是身外之物，内心的需要、个人的志向和自我价值的实现才是最根本的动力。四是道技合一、革新创造。"道"是指一种对人生境界的领悟和渗透；"技"是指工匠所掌握的手艺技巧。"道"的内涵非常丰富，革新创造之道是其中最典型的代表。在革新创造之道的引领下，工匠们打破僵化、突破常规、解放思想、锐意创新，一次次攻坚克难，将常人眼中的各种不可能变为可能，又将可能变为现实。

工匠精神对国家发展的有很重要的意义，正是因为有了工匠精神，我们才能架起中国桥，铺设中国路，驶动中国车，建造中国港，搭建中国网等方式，将"中国梦"这张大美画卷一帧帧变为现实，大美的"中国梦"画卷正在徐徐展开。中国桥梁、中国卫星、中国高铁、中国超算……中国制造正在进一步转型成为"中国智造"，从大众产品到国防军工，从引进技术到输出技术，从自主创新到制定标准，鼓舞人心的"中国制造"频频刷屏，一张张有底气的大国名片背后，无一不是一个个奋斗的大国工匠。

大国工匠代表性人物，继承发展了传统的民族工匠精神，以舍我其谁的信念，从我做起，脚踏实地，追求完美，不仅将生命化作绝技，而且打破传统观念，不把技能当资本，而把绝活儿当作国家、民族的财富，千方百计开辟传承发展之路，成为一颗颗大国工匠的种子，倡导、实践"国家兴亡，匹夫有责"的责任担当精神。他们善于与时俱进，在平凡的工作中，创造了属于时代的伟大，干一行、爱一行、钻一行，把握规律，追求卓越，心无旁骛，默默奉献，培育了不甘落后、开拓创新的精神，用行动诠释了"创新是一个民族的灵魂，一个国家兴旺发达的不竭动力"。

让工匠精神成为一种文化，要从青年一代开始抓起，不能仅仅是一句口号，应是实实在在的行动。这既需要职业教育的培养、制度机制的保障、政府部门的引导，更需要全社会参与其中。这样我们才会对工匠精神多一份敬重敬畏、多一份纯粹、多一份脚踏实地、多一份专注持久，才能让我们从坐论工匠精神到自觉践行工匠精神，才能让工匠精神支撑"中国制造"转型升级"中国智造"，才能让工匠精神内化为我们的民族气质和精神气质。

President Xi Encourages Young People to Pursue Excellence in Craftsmanship

Chinese President Xi Jinping on Monday encouraged young people to pursue excellence in craftsmanship, stating that a good grasp of technical skills would make them competent professionals to better serve the country.

President Xi Jinping made the remarks in a written instruction to congratulate Chinese contestants on their good results at the 45th World Skills Competition held in Kazan, Russia, last month.

The quality of workers is crucial to the development of a nation, Xi Jinping said, adding that skilled workers are an important foundation to support "Made in China" and "Created in China," and play an important role in promoting high-quality economic development.

It is necessary to improve the training, use, evaluation, and incentive systems for skilled personnel, develop technical education, conduct vocational skills training, and accelerate the training of a large number of high-quality workers and technical personnel, Xi Jinping noted.

Xi Jinping also stressed the need to carry forward the spirit of craftsmanship in the whole society and inspire young people to serve the country by grasping technical skills.

The 46th World Skills Competition will be held in east China's Shanghai Municipality in 2021. Calling for sound preparation and organization, Xi Jinping said we should strengthen exchanges and mutual learning with other countries in the field of skills, demonstrate the achievements and levels of vocational skills training in China, and strive to host a new world-class skills competition with new ideas and influence.

Chinese Premier Li Keqiang said skilled workers are precious resources for China and important support for industry upgrade and high-quality development.

Premier Li urged more attention to the training of skilled workers and called for international cooperation in this field.

World Skills Competition is held every two years. China finished this year's competition with 16 gold medals, 14 silver and 5 medals, putting China at the top of the medal rankings.

（来源：CGTN）

3. 教学设计与思政元素的融入

Passage A

3.1 Warm-up 环节

英语文章：中国外卖小哥登《时代周刊》封面，"非凡的使命感"令外媒耳目一新

文章介绍了自从新冠肺炎疫情以来，外卖骑手的工作方式发生了很大变化。《时代周刊》还专门对北京、武汉两位外卖小哥为代表的骑手做了报道。一位是在病毒肆虐中国时仍坚守岗位的外卖骑手，还有一名外卖骑手步行12小时从老家返回武汉工作。学生可以看完文章后讨论两位外卖小哥为什么这么做，他们的行为反映了什么品质？

It features six different covers, each with a portrait of individuals directly impacted by the virus, ranging from the tragically hard-hit Life Care Center in Kirkland, Wash., to the balconies of Tehran and the streets of China. Together, they offer a sense of how COVID-19 is forcing regular people around the world to adapt to a new reality.

Beijing. Gao Zhixiao, 32, a delivery driver who has continued working as the virus spread across China.

Ever since the COVID-19 outbreak erupted in China, the delivery driver has to take a health test each morning and spend 20 minutes disinfecting his motorcycle and clothes to avoid spreading germs during his route.

Meituan has experienced a 400% spike in online grocery sales in some cities. Online retailer JD.com has also seen orders of kitchenware, baking products and home fitness equipment soar.

Without these drivers putting themselves at risk, families would go hungry and the sick wouldn't get vital supplies.

Reducing human contact doesn't lessen drivers' sense of humanity.

"After I gave her medicine, I stayed to talk to her," he says. "Because I am also from a single-parent family, I understand what it means to be old and living alone. She said that she hadn't eaten yet, because it was difficult to find food during the epidemic. So I made her instant noodles and two poached eggs, then took the trash out when I left."

He sympathized with how bored the patient would be without entertainment, he says.

Li Fengjie took things a few steps further. As a Meituan rider in the Hubei province capital of Wuhan, where the COVID-19 epidemic first erupted in late December, he knew that his services would be essential after the city of 11 million was locked down on Jan 23. Li walked 30 miles to get to work after all public transport was halted.

"I felt a sense of responsibility because I manage a team of other riders, and some were still working in Wuhan, so I had to help them," he says. "All the doctors and nurses are coming to Wuhan to help, so we, the riders, should also fight with them on the frontline."

"The majority of people are staying home, but we don't have that luxury," he says. "Every day, we have to choose between being safe and making a living."

It's the first revision to the list since 2015 and should mean better training, working conditions, job opportunities and career development for riders in the future.

（来源：https://language.chinadaily.com.cn/a/202003/29/WS5e7ff310a310 128217282c09.html）

3.2 Discussion 环节

英文文章：Benefits of Working

文章介绍了工作的好处，学生在阅读完文章后讨论：What are the benefits of working?

From the day man decided to stop wandering and settle down in colonies or settlements, he has been going out to work to ensure that his family and dependents had enough food to eat. In these modern days, working is no longer limited to men and no longer do people work just for food. Whether working for a multinational or owning and managing it, work is no longer just a means for meeting basic needs of hunger, shelter, and clothing. Let's look at some of the major benefits of working.

1. Means to fulfilling requirements

In addition to fulfilling basic needs of hunger, clothing, and shelter, work today is necessary to earn the money required for meeting all other requirements, whether essential or luxurious. The work a person does and the salary he earns, decides the quality of his life, and the future of his children. From educating children to providing healthcare to old parents, meeting essentials and maintaining luxuries, work is what decides the ability of a man to take care of all these requirements.

2. Outlet for creativity

Everyone has different skills, talents, knowledge, and attributes. Work is the outlet where people can use and exhibit their talents and skills productively. Using varied skills and talents enables the generation of more ideas and better solutions, which further leads to growth and development.

3. Satisfaction

An idle mind is a devil's workshop. A job is not only a means of creative outlet for man, but also ensures that their intelligence and talents are used productively and positively for common good. Working also gives a satisfaction for men that cannot be attained only be achieving basic human needs. It helps man grow beyond the basic and prove his superiority in nature.

4. Social networking

Even the most intelligent and most talented individual cannot do all the tasks by himself. To build an organization, to build society, man needs to work as a team. Thus work brings about social interaction and networking, which further strengthens human bonding and positive growth of society.

5. Promotes continued development

If people worked in isolation or work was a single man's interest or task, we would not have been able to accomplish the development and advancement in these many years. Work has been more of an organization or entity-based concept, and this has enabled generations to continue from where their forefathers left off. Otherwise, man would still be discovering making fire through each generation. Thus working as a concept promotes development and advancement through the generations.

6. Enhances individual responsibility

Although, today people go to work as more of routine-driven, success-driven, or satisfaction-driven task, going to work in itself entails discipline and responsibility. Further, working in an organization requires accepting responsibilities, sharing responsibilities, and fulfilling responsibilities. Thus work makes individuals more responsible for their actions even in their social setup.

7. Promotes team-spirit

An organization is filled with people from different social, cultural, and educational backgrounds. Further, the people in an organization work at different levels and share different responsibilities. Thus, it is only by team work that an organization can accomplish their goals. This team work ensures positive attitude among workers, ensuring a positive social and cultural bonding that also permeates into the society. Thus working is not just about making money, or getting job satisfaction, it also has greater benefits to the individual as well as to the society as a whole.

（来源：http://benefitof.net/benefits-of-working/）

3.3 Critical thinking 环节

英文视频：Should I Quit My Job and Start a Business?

在你决定创业之前，首先要考虑五个方面：生活费用、创业内容、成本、存款与时间。教师可安排学生观看，结合自身实际思考。

（来源：https://v.qq.com/x/page/o3077c6l8cy.html）

英语文章：Quitting Your Job to Start a Business

You are probably in a full-time job, and at the end of the month, you have always been assured of getting a salary. The benefit perks associated with your position are also lucrative. Recently, you have been feeling this burning desire to start and manage your own business. After all, would it not be a source of pride and achievement running a successful enterprise that is self-sustaining and also generates a lot of profit at the end of the month? This burning desire is fueled by the fact that you have seen some of your old time friends quitting their jobs to start their own businesses. They have made a lot of cash that they would not have realized supposing they had decided to remain in full-time employment.

Quitting your job to start a business

Moreover, you have also heard of stories of overnight success by those who quit their full-time jobs to run their own businesses, and this has made you feel like a weakling because you are still relying on employment to help you settle your bills. So the big question that keeps on lingering in your mind is, "should I quit my job now and start my own business or should I let things take its course?"

Before you quit your job, you should first have a very clear plan that dictates your next move. Yes, your next move is starting your own business, but have you determined whether you have enough cash to establish the same? Is your emergency reserve fund loaded enough to see you through the "rainy" days? Are you sure this is the right thing for you to do? Do you have what it takes to endure more than three consecutive months of making losses? Will you be able to settle all your bills on time? These are just a few of the basic questions you need to ask yourself before you quit your current job.

"I want to quit my job"... Slow down

Perhaps, the most suitable strategy that will help you to transition smoothly from full-time employment to running your own enterprise would be to start your own job while you are still in employment. This will help you monitor the first crucial stages of a business while still under the security of a salary from a full-time job. Additionally, you need to ensure that the interests of your business are not in conflict with those of your employer. Avoid burning bridges as it could ruin your reputation. Leaving your job in good faith should be a priority.

The starting phase of a business is the toughest stage, because during this time, the business is still trying to recover the cost of setting it up. The business is also trying to attract customers since it is still new and therefore not known to the prospective customers. That is why a large number of new businesses fail at this stage. For those companies that are lucky to grow past this juncture, more significant percentage of them also fail because they fail to respond to the dynamics of the business environment. So, you should not be in a hurry to call it quits before considering how you are going to sustain your business successfully. Rather than facing these tough phases of starting your own business in a jobless state, it will be better that you start your own business while still in employment. That way, it will be easier for you to know when the time to quit your job comes.

Fear of quitting a job

Sometimes, you find out that you are afraid to quit your job the main reason being that when things do not go your way, you will feel like an idiot when you ask yourself why did I quit my job in the first place? But in your mind, you have heard from successful business people that they had to face the fact that in entrepreneurship, there is no sure way to success. Not all bunch of challenges that face the entrepreneurs are the same. Some are unique. Therefore, you should not be afraid of taking that leap of faith.

One of the key determinants that will help set you apart when you decide to set your own business is establishing a business based on a unique idea. Of course, this unique idea gives you a competitive edge among your business competitors. It is interesting to note that some of the most successful unique business ideas were born out of individuals who found themselves bored and uninspired by the daily work routine. As a matter of fact, a time will come in your career when you feel like calling it a day because of the boredom encountered. It is best for this time to find you when your business is already up and running so that you can find a valid reason to quit your daily job and move on into a challenging task of managing your own business enterprise.

Before you quit, think about your reasons for quitting a job

So before you leave your full-time job for self-employment, you will first need to have a well-articulated plan. For the risk averse individuals, it will be necessary that you make it a point to start your business while still in employment so that you can cushion yourself against the risks associated with the early stages of the business. Another thing, ensure that you have a loaded emergency fund to see you through the first few months when your business will be picking itself up.

Do not expect to start making huge profits overnight. What your friends and those who claim to have enjoyed overnight success don't tell you is, that they had to endure sleepless nights and even go without food during some days. As a matter of fact, some of those overnight success stories are false. So do not despair when your business is four or five months old, and there is nothing for you to be proud of. Remember that a baby doesn't even start walking immediately after it is born.

（来源：https://www.laowaicareer.com/blog/quit-job-start-business/）

3.4 主题拓展环节

TED 演讲：Grit: The Power of Passion and Perseverance

Angela Lee Duckworth 辞去企业管理咨询行业的一份前途无量的工作，到纽约的一所公立学校教七年级学生数学。她很快意识到 IQ 并不是将成功的学生和失败的学生区分开的唯一标准。她解释了自己的理论——成功的重要因素是"毅力"。教师可以让学生观看视频，了解坚韧不拔的毅力和持续专注的精神对于事业成功的重要性。

When I was 27 years old, I left a very demanding job in management consulting for a job that was even more demanding: teaching. I went to teach seventh graders math in the New York City public schools. And like any teacher, I made quizzes and tests. I gave out homework assignments. When the work came back, I calculated grades.

What struck me was that IQ was not the only difference between my best and my worst students. Some of my strongest performers did not have stratospheric IQ scores. Some of my smartest kids weren't doing so well. And that got me thinking. The kinds of things you need to learn in seventh grade math, sure, they're hard: ratios, decimals, the area of a parallelogram. But these concepts are not impossible, and I was firmly convinced that every one of my students could learn the material if they worked hard and long enough.

After several more years of teaching, I came to the conclusion that what we need in education is a much better understanding of students and learning from a motivational perspective, from a psychological perspective. In education, the one thing we know how to measure best is IQ. But what if doing well in school and in life depends on much more than your ability to learn quickly and easily?

So I left the classroom, and I went to graduate school to become a psychologist. I started studying kids and adults in all kinds of super challenging settings, and in every study my question was, who is successful here and why? My research team and I went to West Point Military Academy. We tried to predict which cadets would stay in military training and which would drop out. We went to the National Spelling Bee and tried to predict which children would advance farthest in competition. We studied rookie teachers working in really tough neighborhoods, asking which teachers are still going to be here in teaching by the end of the school year, and of those, who will be the most effective at improving learning outcomes for their students? We partnered with private companies, asking, which of these salespeople is going to keep their jobs? And who's going to earn the most money? In all those very different contexts, one characteristic emerged as a significant predictor of success. And it wasn't social intelligence. It wasn't good looks, physical health, and it wasn't IQ. It was grit.

Grit is passion and perseverance for very long-term goals. Grit is having stamina. Grit is sticking with your future, day in, day out, not just for the week, not just for the month, but for years, and working really hard to make that future a reality. Grit is living life like it's a marathon, not a sprint.

A few years ago, I started studying grit in the Chicago public schools. I asked thousands of high school juniors to take grit questionnaires, and then waited around more than a year to see who would graduate. Turns out that grittier kids were significantly more likely to graduate, even when I matched them on every characteristic I could measure, things like family income, standardized achievement test scores, even how safe kids felt when they were at school. So it's not just at West Point or the National Spelling Bee that grit matters. It's also in school, especially for kids at risk for dropping out.

To me, the most shocking thing about grit is how little we know, how little science knows, about building it. Every day, parents and teachers ask me, "How do I build grit in kids? What do I do to teach kids a solid work ethic? How do I keep them motivated for the long run?" The honest answer is, I don't know.

What I do know is that talent doesn't make you gritty. Our data show very clearly that there are many talented individuals who simply do not follow through on their commitments. In fact, in our data, grit is usually unrelated or even inversely related to measures of talent.

So far, the best idea I've heard about building grit in kids is something called "growth mindset". This is an idea developed at Stanford University by Carol

Dweck, and it is the belief that the ability to learn is not fixed, that it can change with your effort. Dr. Dweck has shown that when kids read and learn about the brain and how it changes and grows in response to challenge, they're much more likely to persevere when they fail, because they don't believe that failure is a permanent condition.

So growth mindset is a great idea for building grit. But we need more. And that's where I'm going to end my remarks, because that's where we are. That's the work that stands before us. We need to take our best ideas, our strongest intuitions, and we need to test them. We need to measure whether we've been successful, and we have to be willing to fail, to be wrong, to start over again with lessons learned.

In other words, we need to be gritty about getting our kids grittier.

Thank you.

（来源：https://www.ted.com/talks/angela_lee_duckworth_grit_the_power_of_passion_and_perseverance/transcript?referrer=shawn_achor_work_happier）

Passage B

3.5 Warm-up 环节

英语视频: Craftsman of the Nation: One-handed Expert in Welding

视频时长3.5分钟，讲述了中国兵器首席技师——"独臂焊侠"卢仁峰的故事。能在关键岗位成为技术能手一直是卢仁峰的梦想，为此他勤学苦练，不断精进技艺，享受攻克技术难题的乐趣。教师可组织学生观看视频，启发学生思考什么是大国工匠精神，工作自豪感是什么、从何而来等问题。

Many were impressed with a new generation of tanks and Armored Fighting Vehicles during China's massive parade commemorating the 70th anniversary of the end of World War Two on September 3rd, but few people know some of the vehicles that required special welding technology were made by a one-handed welding craftsman.

52-year-old Lu Renfeng is the Chief Mechanic of the Inner Mongolia First Machinery Group Corporation. He has worked in the company, which produces many Chinese Armored Fighting Vehicles, for over three decades.

Since the first day he came to the workshop, he has worked hard to practice his skills to become a top mechanic in refining and welding.

However, in 1986, an accident cost him the left hand — which was a huge blow to a welder. After surgery, he could not even hold up a cup of water with his left hand.

Lu didn't give up. Instead, he read all the books about welding during hospital and even practiced to hold heavy steel materials with his mouth. With unremitting efforts, Lu restored his welding skills and even excelled at dealing with many of the demanding tasks.

For example, difficulties came when developing a new type of tanks that required the use of special kind of hard steel. It was almost impossible to complete the welding work on this material since cracks always appeared during the welding.

Many gave up but Lu didn't. He conducted 133 experiments over several years and finally succeeded — the new welding can even survive a gunshot.

Lu told CCTV that the job requires perfect technique, accurate skills and carefulness, since usually there're hundreds of welding lines on the entire body of a vehicle.

"We have to weld every line carefully because this is an amphibious vehicle. It is going to go in water, sometimes into the sea. You have to guarantee the lives of our soldiers," Lu said.

（来源：https://mp.weixin.qq.com/s/c-rskHGBJob9vcWQlI7XXA）

3.6 Discussion 环节

英语文章： How to Take Pride in Your Work

本文详细介绍了3种培养工作自豪感的方法：调整心态，拒绝抱怨，赋予工作更多意义和价值感；采取主动，追求卓越，关注真正重要的部分；合理评估自己的工作表现，积极回应他人的肯定。文章案例生动，可供学生阅读，学习如何从日常工作学习获得更多意义和自我价值感。

You can have pride in your work without bragging or being arrogant — there's a difference between being pleased with what you've accomplished and thinking you're better than other people. Try to approach your work with a positive attitude and work hard to do the best job you can, so you can rest assured that you're giving your all. Take it one day at a time, and before you know it, you'll be feeling better about your daily accomplishments.

Adopting the Right Mindset

1. Start your day with positive affirmations to get you in the right mindset. Rather than getting up and dreading the day, remind yourself that you're fortunate to have a job and to get to work, even if you don't love what you're doing. Try to

remember that if you aren't happy where you are, your situation doesn't have to be permanent. Commit to doing a good job in the space where you currently are.

Choosing to be an active participant in your job rather than a reluctant one can make a huge difference in your attitude and productivity, which in turn can really help make you more proud of the work you do.

2. Remember the "why" behind your work. Of course, most people work because they need to make a living. Beyond that, though, are you working to help take care of a family, to provide a life for yourself, to help out your community, to learn a new trade, to meet new people, or to offer your skills to others? Try to remember that there is more to your work than just getting a paycheck.

· Keeping the right motivation in mind will help you take more pride in your work, and it'll keep you in the right mindset during times when you might feel unsatisfied or bored.

3. Take ownership of your work rather than letting others dictate your success. If you are working on a project either by yourself or in a group, decide that you personally are going to do the best job that you can. It could be easy to blame a coworker or partner for your work being subpar, but in reality, your work efforts are up to you.

· If you are working with someone who isn't doing their part, talk to them about it directly. If that doesn't work, bring the situation up to your supervisor or boss. Avoid criticizing the person or complaining about them. Instead, say something simple, like, "Hi Renee, I wanted to let you know that Joe has been coming in late to work the past few weeks. It's affecting our ability to get the store opened up in time. I wanted to make you aware of the issue."

4. Avoid complaining about your job, boss, or coworkers. If you focus on the negative or annoying things, you'll feel less motivated to do a good job. When you feel tempted to complain, instead think of something positive to say.

· For example, if you are annoyed by how often you're asked to cover for a coworkers task, instead try thinking about how you feel proud that your boss can rely on you to help pick up the slack.

Creating Something You Can Be Proud of

1. Take time to prepare for your day rather than winging it. It'll be easier for you to stay focused and motivated if you start your tasks with a clear head, so take 10 to 20 minutes at the beginning of each day to write a To-Do list, review your

calendar, and respond to a few emails. Giving yourself a little mental breathing space before jumping into things will help make you a better worker.

· Make it a goal to get to the office 10 to 20 minutes early each day for one week and see how it changes your attitude throughout the day.

2. Focus on the quality of your work, even if no one will ever see it. You'll feel better about your work and about yourself if you commit to doing the best job you can do in any situation. Instead of trying to rush through a task or project simply to get it done, ask yourself, "Is this something I can be proud of?"

Tip: There are definitely times where you may have a time constraint for a project. If that's the case, do the best job you can in the time allotted. Think about ways you can streamline your work to really focus, like turning off your phone, not browsing the internet, and taking minimal breaks.

3. Take the initiative to go above and beyond the minimum expectations. Proofread your work, do tasks that you notice need to be done, even if they aren't technically your responsibility, answer questions that might come up down the road, and think outside of your job description. Think about ways you can make your work even more dynamic, and try to implement those ideas when you can.

· For example, if your job is to write a report about sales from the previous month, you could also include information about holidays, employees calling off work, power outages, and other factors that may have affected the results.

· Taking initiative and being responsible doesn't mean you have all the answers. If you're unsure of how to do something, don't be afraid to ask questions.

4. Set up accountability if you need help doing your best work. Sometimes people do need a little reinforcement to help them stay on track, and that's perfectly fine. If you need this, arrange with a supervisor or a coworker to check in at a specific time every week for a "mini-deadline" to help you get your work done in time.

· For example, if you're working on a big presentation that is due in a month, arrange to send your supervisor a copy of what you've worked on every Friday at noon. That way, you know you have several deadlines to work toward and need to show something new every week rather than procrastinating until the last day to get things done.

Responding to Praise

1. Accept compliments with a smile and a "thank you." When someone praises your work, accept the recognition rather than brushing it away. You don't need to

elaborate on how much work you did, but there is nothing wrong with graciously letting others recognize your work. Try saying something like this the next time someone compliments your work:

· "I appreciate your noticing my work; thanks for telling me."

· "I'm really pleased everything went well with the project."

· "Thank you. It was hard work, but I'm glad I was able to do it."

2. Avoid downplaying your work or being self-deprecating. When people pay attention to your work, you may be tempted to say that it was nothing, it wasn't hard work, or someone else could have done it better. If you feel tempted to say things like this, simply say "thank you", and smile.

· It takes practice to accept compliments and to not feel uncomfortable from the attention. Remember, you did good work and there is nothing wrong with admitting you worked hard!

3. Give recognition to people who helped you. While it's important to graciously accept praise, it's just as important to recognize and name the people who were instrumental in your success. Maybe you worked on a team or got a lot of helpful information from a senior coworker. Try saying something like:

· "Thank you. It was definitely a team effort and my coworkers and I worked hard on the project."

· "Thanks so much. Robert from the underwriting department really helped me understand the processes so much better."

· "Mary definitely helped encourage me to keep going when I got stuck."

4. Ask a question to keep the conversation moving. After you've accepted a compliment, move the conversation along so that it doesn't seem like you just want to talk more about yourself. For example, you could say something like, "Thank you so much, Mark. It was a hard project but it feels good to have done it. By the way, I heard you were working on a new proposal. How is that going?"

Tip: If people have questions about your work or want more information, then it's totally okay to keep the focus on you. Just try to take cues from the other person to know when it's time to move on.

5. Remember that you can take pride in your work even if no one sees it. Depending on the kind of work you do, you may not ever have someone give you a lot of praise for it. You can definitely still feel proud of your work, and you can even mention that you're proud when telling other people about what you do.

For example, if someone asks you how work is going, you could say something like, "It's going well. I actually just completed a month-long research project and feel really good about what I did."

（来源：https://www.wikihow.com/Take-Pride-in-Your-Work）

3.7 Critical thinking 环节

英语文章：10 Reasons Why Following Your Passion Is More Important Than Money

薪水对于工作来说固然重要，但一份能使人充满热情的工作更能带来个人满足感与成就感。文章列举了10个应选择使人充满热情的工作的原因，教师可结合文章，组织学生在课上开展相关话题的讨论。

Elite Daily have got some great points as to why you should chase down your dream job, regardless of how much the wage is. If you're feeling unfulfilled in your career, maybe it's because you're on a path that doesn't connect with your passion? Maybe it's time to steer right off that road and take a different route.

Money is a very powerful thing, it builds empires and breaks down kingdoms, it allows for dreams to come true and it takes others away, it makes some people happy and others completely miserable. Today the pursuit of money is almost directly linked to the pursuit of happiness, many will argue that money = happiness.

However, this is inherently problematic as this mindset leads many people to stray down a path that doesn't best suit them. When people choose their careers, they are sometimes blinded by money and so choose to follow the paper trail. Although money is great and can buy us all the things that will temporarily make us happy, no amount of money can buy time. Time is our most valuable asset and it is something, that while on this earth, we should spend most wisely. You shouldn't feel like you're mindlessly wasting your life away.

This generation is particularly in trouble because jobs are scarce and many of us will be stuck doing jobs we hate just because we need money. Although this may be the right move for our careers now, this shouldn't be something we do for the rest of our lives. it is best we search for something we are passionate about. Here are the 10 reasons why you should follow your passion and not the money.

1. Working for money may seem like good enough motivation for one to keep at their career.

Every morning Monday through Friday, you go to work 9 to 5 sitting their punching away the hours stressing about the work at hand. This is not a way to enjoy your life. Working for 8 hours a day 5 times a week at something that makes you miserable is not the way you live life to the fullest.

Many people who choose careers that don't make them happy will tell you that they would all do it differently if they had the chance. You only have one life, so don't waste it working somewhere you hate just because of the money.

2. You're more passionate about the work you are doing.

There is nothing worse than having to wake up every morning during the week to mindlessly go to work that you don't even care about. However, this is never really an issue when you are passionate about the work you do. If you are not forced to work somewhere because of monetary constraint, you truly enjoy what you do and you never really work a day in your life.

3. You can relate more to the work and come up with better ideas.

Being forced to do work is one of the most draining experiences. While there are times at every job where you may feel the work may be draining and dull, you have to realize that not every day is going to be an enjoyable one. There are highs and lows, but when you are passionate about the work you look past the dull days. Your creative process is also different. You are more inclined to come up with creative ideas when you like what you do.

4. Work doesn't feel like it's forced upon you.

When you value money over your overall health and your passion, you will find yourself in an endless cycle of misery. Work no longer becomes a career or a journey, but more of a taxing nuisance on your mind and body that has to get done.

Every day that you go to work with this mindset you begin to hate your job more and more. While many people feel that they must work hard to retire and have money to enjoy themselves, what's the point of enjoying yourself in your later years when you spent your life being miserable?

5. No matter how much money you make, nothing will help you overcome the feeling of doing something you hate.

Many accountants come into corporate America, put in reckless hours during the week and make a great paycheck on pay day. Many of them have all this money piled up, but they never really get to enjoy the fruits of their labor because their labor takes up most of their lives.

Many of them hate their jobs because they aren't really passionate about what they do. Is there a worse feeling than doing something you hate? Eventually this hatred will cause stress and in the long run, it will have lasting effects on your health.

6. You are more inclined to work later hours.

When you work somewhere that you are passionate about, putting in later hours isn't as much of a burden as it is when you don't like what you are doing. To you, putting in the extra hours doesn't hurt as much because you don't feel like you are forced to do it, which makes the experience that much more enjoyable.

Every industry has a busy season and without a doubt there will come a time when you will need to put in the extra hours. Will it be easier for you to work longer on something you can relate to or something you can't stand doing?

7. You are willing to go above and beyond the call of duty.

Certain obligations at your work will require you to go above and beyond the call of duty. In certain times during the busy seasons, you may be asked to do certain tasks that are not part of your everyday schedule. It is much easier for you to put in the extra work if it's something you actually care about. Because you are passionate about your job, you will be willing to put in the extra effort to go beyond what is required of you.

8. No obstacle will stop you from achieving success.

When you really enjoy what you do, nothing will stop you from getting your work done. Because you are passionate about what you do, you feel unstoppable and nothing can obstruct you from achieving greatness. Your passion ignites your work, and like a rocket, it accelerates you past road blocks that may come about. Any obstacle that comes your way is accepted and fought off with a creative solution.

9. Our working careers will consume most of our lives, so we might as well do something we enjoy.

You will spend a majority of your life working and there is no other way around this fact unless you are born into a wealthy family or marry rich. For the rest of us who weren't fortunate enough, we will be spending a good portion of our lives working in order to make ends meet.

There is no way around this, so we might as well accept the cards we are dealt. Many people go about this the wrong way because they feel like work is something they have to do rather then something they can enjoy. Once you realize that your career should be something you enjoy, then you will lead a more happy and fulfilling life.

10. You will get more fulfillment when you finally make it.

There are few feelings better than achieving a level of success you set out for yourself. Nothing like crossing off your bucket list of goals you set out for yourself to achieve. When you finally reach the pinnacle, it is that much more enjoyable knowing you got there doing something you love. Remember work doesn't have to be something that you hate doing, stay true to yourself and always do what makes you happy.

（来源：https://wenku.baidu.com/view/3c0ab63e227916888486d7fe.html）

3.8 主题拓展资源

英语文章：毕业啦！职场前辈给新人的10条忠告

每年的六月宣告着毕业季的到来。散伙饭吃了，毕业照拍了，毕业生们收拾好行囊，准备迈入社会，在各自的舞台上演炙热的故事。

面对全新的挑战，职场新人们多少会感到紧张和迷茫。不如来听听领英上的职场前辈们总结的10条职场生存法则，你一定会有所收获。

1. Remember These Four Words 记住这四个词

Be positive, principled, proactive, and productive.

乐观、讲原则、主动、高效。

—Rakesh N.

2. Discover Yourself 挖掘自己

Consider this job a journey to learn about yourself. The purpose is to grow as a human being; to discover what you're good at, what you love to do, and what you dislike.

把这份工作看作是一次了解自己的旅程。目的是实现个人成长；去发现你擅长什么，喜欢做什么，不喜欢什么。

3. Be Open to Change 勇于改变

Don't get discouraged when a job you really want does not pan out for you. It just opens up doors to other opportunities.

当你真正想做的工作并不适合你时，不要灰心。它只是为其他机会打开了大门。

—Mitchell M.

4. Don't Hide from Mistakes 不要逃避错误

Be honest. Not sure about something? Ask questions. Screwed up? Own up!

诚实点。有什么不懂的尽管问。搞砸了要承认！

I've always valued someone willing to learn, and we do that in different ways. I'll always highly regard someone willing to be honest about their mistakes because we learn from those just as much as our successes!

我一直很看重愿意学习的人，学习的方式有很多种。我非常重视那些愿意诚实面对自己错误的人，因为我们从这些错误中学到的东西和从成功中学到的一样多！

——Samantha DM.

5. Prepare for the Future 为未来做好准备

Develop good time management habits early on. Your workload will only increase with time, and so will your responsibilities. Be ready when they do.

尽早养成良好的时间管理习惯。你的工作量只会随着时间的推移而增加，你的责任也会随之增加。做好准备迎接它们。

——Alicia M.

6. Learn from Everything 从周围的一切学习

Remember every moment is an opportunity to learn from everyone around you, no matter their title.

记住，每时每刻你都有机会向周围的人学习，不管他们是什么职级。

Pay attention when things go well; pay extra attention when they don't, and watch how people react to it. Build relationships with the people who face problems by being their solution.

事情进展顺利时要留心；不顺利的时候要更加留心，并观察人们的反应。与面对问题想办法解决的人来往。

——Anita S.

7. Make Connections 建立人脉

Your biggest asset is your network.

你最大的资本就是你的人际关系。

——Eddie M.

8. Keep Your Own Counsel 隐藏自己的想法

Don't assume that a co-worker won't repeat your criticisms of a colleague. When asked how you feel about individuals in the office, be open and vague with your answers.

不要以为同事不会把你对另一个同事的批评外传。当有人问你对办公室里的人有何看法时，回答要诚恳但有所保留。

Always reserve judgment on your co-workers until you have enough time to make up your own mind.

在你有足够的时间下定主意之前，不要轻易评价你的同事。

—Nicholas G.

9. Utilize Your Co-workers 利用好你的同事

Don't be intimidated by your colleagues and superiors!

不要被你的同事和上级吓到！

Remember that they were once in your shoes when they began their careers. Leverage their knowledge and experience and find ways to take what worked for them and adapt it to work for you.

记住，他们刚刚开启职业生涯时，也曾站在你的位置上。利用他们的知识和经验，并找到他们行之有效的工作方法，加以调整，为你所用。

—Lauren L.

10. Treat Everyone with Respect 尊重每个人

Speak when you walk into the office every day. Say good morning to your boss and peers as you walk past their offices, smile at janitors and receptionists in your office.

每天走进办公室时打个招呼。路过老板和同事的办公室时，向他们问好，对办公室的管理员和接待员微笑。

Treating people with humanity and integrity is most important.

以博爱和正直的态度待人是最重要的。

—Brittany K.

（来源：https://language.chinadaily.com.cn/a/202106/21/WS60cfd684a31024ad0baca3cb.html）

第三单元　关心公益，注重诚信
（Unit 3 Advertising）

1. 思政主题：关心公益，注重诚信

2. 意义

本单元的主题是广告，两篇课文分别是关于公益广告和商业广告。教师可借助本单元的学习，帮助学生树立公益意识，注重诚信，拒绝虚假广告。

3. 教学设计与思政元素的融入

Passage A

3.1 Warm-up 环节

英文视频1：请系好安全带——英国安全驾驶公益广告

英文视频2：华为 Ascend P6 广告英文版

教师引导学生观看两个英文广告，了解公益广告和商业广告的不同特点。

视频1：

Embrace life. Always wear your seat belt.

（来源：https://tv.sohu.com/v/dXMvMTIzNTg5ODAvNTc5Mzc5My5zaHRtbA==.html）

视频2：

Beauty is all around us. Sometimes it can be seen in the capture of a moment. Sometimes it can be seen in the celebration of joy. Sometimes it can be expressed in art, in precision, in the pinnacle of perfection. Beauty is divine elegance. Huawei Ascend P6, elegance with edge. Make it possible. HUAWEI.

（来源：https://v.qq.com/x/page/m0655q05q2g.html）

3.2 Discussion 环节

英语文章：What Is Public Service Advertising?

什么是公益广告？它的运作机制是怎样的？教师可引导学生阅读本文章，并启发学生讨论公益广告在当今社会的作用。

Public service advertising is designed to inform the public on issues that are frequently considered to be in the general best interests of the community at large. Typically, it reflects a political viewpoint, philosophical theory, religious concept or humanitarian notion. It is also commonly referred to as a public service announcement (PSA) or a community service announcement. The ads are usually broadcast on radio or television, but may also appear in newspapers or magazines. They are prevalent in industrialized countries throughout the world.

PSAs are commonly aimed at altering public attitudes by raising consciousness about particular issues. Health, conservation and safety themes are prevalent in many PSAs. The public service advertising campaigns are often sponsored by trade associations, civic organizations, non-profit institutions or religious groups. The U.S. military, in addition to paid advertising, regularly produces PSAs as part of their recruitment efforts.

Some PSA ads use celebrity spokespersons to garner attention. Others attempt to appeal to the masses through portraying risks and issues relevant to ordinary men, women and children. A common misconception about PSA work is that it includes political campaign ads, which are actually privately funded.

Most public service advertising involves joint efforts of the private and public sectors. Non-profit groups and government agencies commonly team up with private mass media, promotion and advertising firms to produce spots for radio, television and print media. Most commonly, the non-profit agency creates the message and an advertising firm develops the campaign, polishes it to meet industry standards and plans its distribution, all free of charge. Television and radio stations usually broadcast these ads at no charge, and magazines and newspapers customarily publish them for free as well.

In recent years, it has become commonplace for U.S. television stations to feature public service advertising spots immediately following a broadcast that has focused on an issue considered sensitive and of concern to many members of the general public. These PSA broadcasts generally offer addresses, Web sites and toll-free telephone numbers for information sources. Some of the topics focused on in the PSAs have included rape, child abuse, domestic violence, AIDS and civil rights.

Public service advertising was once a requirement for U.S. radio and television stations to receive their broadcast licenses from the Federal Communications Commission. The stations agreed to air a predetermined number of PSAs, which they would normally broadcast during off-peak hours to avoid interference with paid advertisements from sponsors. The deregulation of the broadcasting industry in the 1980s eliminated this obligation.

（来源：https://www.infobloom.com/what-is-public-service-advertising.htm）

3.3 Critical thinking 环节

英语新闻：How Volunteers Kept Wuhan Running During the 76-day Lockdown

2020年新冠肺炎疫情暴发之初，在武汉为期11周的封锁期间，由于旅行限制和公共交通关闭，去医院、购买杂货和购买药品等基本需求无法得到及时供应，直到来自各行各业的人自愿提供帮助，维持了城市的供应和运营。

As Wuhan lifts its quarantine starting from midnight on Wednesday, Hu Jing, a volunteer at Donghulu residential compound in Wuchang district of Wuhan is now busier than ever.

She had to get in touch with all residents heading out of Wuhan, informing them they need to have their travel documents ready and green health code at hand for security check. She reminded that permission must be obtained from the neighborhood community in the respective city they are traveling to, or else if they leave, it would be hard to come back.

For the 55,000 people estimated to be leaving Wuhan by train on Wednesday after a 76-day lockdown, now is the time that they have longed for. But to make their much-anticipated return an orderly process, volunteers like Hu have been on high alert, weary that ease in travel restrictions would lead to a resurgence of infections.

During the 11-week coronavirus lockdown, they are the ones who kept the city supplied and running. With travel restrictions and public transport shutdown, basic needs like going to the hospital, buying groceries and purchasing medicines are left unattended, until volunteers from all walks of life mobilized to offer their help.

Volunteers first sprang up at hospitals, the epicenter of the public health crisis, like 28-year-old Hainan native, Tang, who volunteered to work at Xiehe Dongxihu Hospital shortly after the lockdown was in place. Though not a medical professional, he offered to help maintain order at the crowded hospital main hall at the height of the epidemic outbreak in Wuhan, directing patients to their respective hospital wards.

He offered to join as a temporary worker at the hospital after seeing his wife, who worked at the hospital, was under immense strain on resources. Due to the sharp surge in confirmed cases, hospitals were overwhelmed with patients and most were severely under-staffed. "I did not think much when I first joined; after all, my wife was already there," he said.

Across Wuhan, hundreds of thousands of volunteers from all walks of life emerged in the aftermath of the coronavirus outbreak. On February 23, authorities from the epidemic control and prevention headquarters issued a notice, calling for city-wide recruitment of volunteers.

In one day, more than 10,000 registered, and in three days, around 20,000 joined the neighborhood communities' epidemic control and prevention efforts responsible for meeting the basic needs of residents under lockdown.

Thirty-two-year-old Yang Zhen was among them. The community where he was posted at, Tong'anli residential compound, was home to at least 50 households of foreign residents. Stuck in the city with no prospect of returning home, and no neighbor who speaks the local language, volunteers like Yang offered them a lifeline.

With most people staying home, Yang was in charge of buying groceries for the residents. He was also the go-to person when foreign residents face difficulty of withdrawing money from bank accounts, or when their health code would not work. Asked repeatedly by anxious foreign residents when the lockdown would be lifted, he sought to reassure them again and again that the time will come.

Seniors, people with disability, and children in poverty draw the most attention from the volunteers. Hu, volunteer at Donghulu residential compound, said she would call seniors aged over 85 at the residential compound twice a day to check in on their health and shrinking food supplies. Whenever government-subsidized meat and vegetable are sold, volunteers would first prioritize the need of low-income residents at the residential compound.

The job has its own risks. "It was tough before when there were a lot of infected people and close contacts in the community," said Wu Fan, a 42-year-old government worker turned volunteer. From mid-February, the situation began to improve after all infected patients had been admitted to designated facilities and their close contacts quarantined.

To stay safe while making those deliveries, Wu would leave the items at the door without interacting with the residents. "I usually hanged the shopping bag on the door knob, sprayed it with disinfectant alcohol and then knocked on the door," he said.

He took extra precautions when delivering supplies for quarantined households. "In that case, I put the items on the floor and stepped back two meters when someone answered the door."

Since late March, daily fatalities in Wuhan had fallen to single-digit and each household is permitted to have one resident leave the residential compound for maximum of two hours. But restarting will be a slow process, particularly at a time when the risk of transmission from asymptomatic carriers and people who tested positive after recovering still exist.

On Tuesday, authorities from Hubei epidemic control and prevention headquarters said that after Wuhan reopens, curbs on movement in and out of residential compound will stay while barriers that close off residential compound may be lifted if necessary.

"We call on residents to stay alerted. Don't go out unless necessary and wear mask," said Luo Ping, public health official from Wuhan epidemic control and prevention headquarters.

During the lockdown period, Wu's team of volunteers helped over 300 households in the community purchase medicines and medical supplies, delivering more than 10,000 items including medicines, disinfectant alcohol and face masks, according to a resident surnamed Wan, who cited a detailed record of the volunteers' work from the neighborhood committee.

"They fearlessly put themselves at risks to help the neighbors," Wan said.

Yet Wu insisted that all the work he has done was insignificant compared to what the city endured. "Because we, the people of Wuhan, are all in the same boat. We should look out for one another," said Wu. "Although I can't help on the frontline like the medical workers, I want to be brave like them."

（来源：https://news.cgtn.com/news/2020-04-08/How-volunteers-kept-Wuhan-running-during-the-76-day-lockdown--PwwIMftHSU/index.html）

3.4 主题拓展资源

英文视频1：CCTV 空巢老人公益广告

（来源：https://v.youku.com/v_show/id_XNjQ0ODcwNzA0.html）

英文视频2：《保护动物，拒绝杀害》周杰伦保护野生动物公益广告

（来源：https://www.iqiyi.com/w_19ru197avh.html）

英语文章3：Chongqing's 'Shared-grannies' Tend Children after School

A team of senior women in Southwest China's Chongqing serving as "shared-grannies" to help working parents pick up their children from school and accompany the kids with their homework, has received a lot of likes and comments online lately.

The team of "shared-grannies" from the Shipingcun community in Chongqing's Jiulongpo district consists of nine female retirees, mostly empty-nesters. They shoulder the responsibility as volunteers taking care of 25 pupils in the community.

Working parents of the children who are not able to pick up their kids from school at 3 pm and have no relatives or friends to assist are in desperate need of a temporary guardian. The volunteers can spare the time and energy for the family and ease their loneliness by participating in the job.

Deng Lihong, 66, is a public-spirited member of the team who signed up for the program as soon as she saw the recruitment advertisement. Every workday, she picks up the children from school, and stays with them while they finish their homework and play in the community room until their parents pick them up.

"I feel young with the kids and my retired life's meaningful," she beamed.

"The program started in April and the team is still expanding," Cao Yidan, chairman of Chongqing Amber Social Work Service Center, said.

"The deed is great and worth promoting in other places in the country," a netizen said on social media platform Sina Weibo.

"We mobilize the retired senior women in the community to participate in this public service. The interactions between the families in need and 'shared grannies' are mutually beneficial. The sense of fulfilment and happiness means a lot to them," Peng Mei, secretary of the Party committee of Shipingcun community, said.

The "shared-grannies" program began in the Jifu community in Wuhou district of Chengdu, capital of Southwest China's Sichuan province in 2019, and has created a new mode of public welfare — taking care of the young and lifting the spirits of older residents.

"To be engaged", or "the positive way of retirement", for a retiree is thought to have practical, psychological and sociological significances.

（来源：https://www.chinadaily.com.cn/a/202106/23/WS60d31aeea31024ad0bacb0bb_2.html）

Passage B

3.5 Warm-up 环节

英语视频：华为广告歌曲英文版 *Dream It Possible*

教师播放本广告歌曲视频，激发学生的学习兴趣，并引导学生关注此类广告的特点和作用。

I will run, I will climb, I will soar

I'm undefeated

Jumping out of my skin pull the chord

Yeah I believe it

The past is everything we were don't make us who we are

So I'll dream until I make it real and all I see is stars

It's not until you fall that you fly

When you dreams come alive you're unstoppable

Take a shot chase the sun, find the beautiful

We will glow in the dark turning dust to gold

And we'll dream it possible

Possible

And we'll dream it possible

I will chase I will reach I will fly

Until I'm breaking until I'm breaking

Out of my cage like a bird in the night

I know I'm changing I know I'm changing

In into something big better than before

And if it takes, takes a thousand lives

Then it's worth fighting for

It's not until you fall that you fly

When you dreams come alive you're unstoppable

take a shot chase the sun find the beautiful

We will glow in the dark turning dust to gold

And we'll dream it possible

It possible

From the bottom to the top

We're sparking wild fire's

Never quit and never stop

The rest of our lives

From the bottom to the top

We're sparking wild fire's

Never quit and never stop

It's not until you fall that you fly

When you dreams come alive you're unstoppable

Take a shot chase the sun find the beautiful

We will glow in the dark turning dust to gold

And we'll dream it possible

Possible

And we'll dream it possible

（来源：https://www.iqiyi.com/w_19rukfddy9.html）

3.6 Discussion 环节

英语文章：American Brand La Mer Accused of False Advertising

美国品牌 La Mer 被指控做虚假广告。教师可引导学生阅读本文章，并组织学生讨论：怎样看待广告中的虚假广告现象？如何辨别虚假广告？

An American cosmetic brand, La Mer, was accused by a beauty blogger with one million followers on Weibo, Twitter-like social media in China, of false advertising on its Chinese website.

On September 26, the blogger, Dr Big Mouth, whose real name is Hao Yu, said that La Mer, owned by Estee Lauder Companies, has made an exaggerated and false advertising. It claimed the product could restore the skin and even heal burn scars. While, the introduction of the product on Chinese website is also different from the one in the US.

The statement of charges posted by the blogger.

On its Chinese website, La Mer claimed that the key ingredients in the products, Miracle Broth™, could restore the skin and even help heal burn scars. However, on its US website the company merely said that the active cell-renewing ingredients in Miracle Broth "soothes, moisturizes and heals away dryness", revealing a natural and healthy-looking radiance.

The introduction of the ingredient in its US website which said the Miracle

Broth could soothe the skin and heal away dryness.

"Obviously, it is a discrimination against Chinese consumers", Hao wrote on his Weibo on Wednesday, "I didn't oppose the product, but rather its dishonesty."

The introduction of the ingredient in its US website which said the Miracle Broth could restore and heal the scar.

Its Moisturizing Matte Lotion, running from 260 US dollars to 2,095 US dollars for a 16-ounce jar, made a fancy tale about its inventor.

A German rocket scientist named Max Huber, spent 12 years finding ways to heal and restore his burned face in a lab accident. Then he found the answer in the "pristine waters of a nutrient-rich kelp forest in the Pacific" and invented the cream.

The accusation by the blogger has triggered a heated discussion and speculation in China, with over 30,000 comments under the blogger's post. Some people thought the exaggerated or false advertising make the customer confused.

"I once asked the sales person in store in the US and she said the crème cannot restore the scar," said Yanianyanian under the post of the blogger.

"I have used La Mer for over five years, which cost me over 50,000 yuan (around 7,261 US dollars). I didn't find anything special inside the product, but the advertising motivates me to use it everyday," said I am a teddy bear named Woody on Weibo.

In response, the public relations department at Estee Lauder's office in Shanghai said in a statement that "La Mer is committed to the highest standard of craftsmanship and quality of ingredients. We sincerely invite you to experience our product in store".

"The core function of La Mer's products is to soothe and to moisturize the skin," Sun at the brand's Public Relations department said. "if your skin condition is out of control, we suggest you to see a doctor".

（来源：https://news.cgtn.com/news/3d3d514e336b444e7a457a6333566d54/in dex.html）

3.7 Critical thinking 环节

英语文章：Celebrity Brands Should not Fool Consumers

网红冰淇淋钟薛高被称为"冰淇淋中的爱马仕"，自2018年初成立以来，由于其高端的市场定位，一直很受欢迎。文章中指出，在这个直播流行的时代，流行互联网名人推广的"高端冰淇淋"噱头确实引起了足够的关注。从某种意义上说，钟薛高的人气是基于疯狂的市场营销。2019年，该公司因虚假广告被上海市场监管部门处以两次罚款。

教师可引导学生阅读本文章，并启发学生思考：如何看待当下的网红品牌广告？这些广告跟传统的商业广告有什么不同？

The self-proclaimed star ice cream brand Zhong Xue Gao issued an apology on Friday, constituting a sharp contrast to the previous arrogant remarks by its founder defending the products' high prices.

In the public apology made on social platforms, the ice cream maker said past mistakes can be corrected but not erased and two administrative punishments in the early stage of entrepreneurship constantly remind the company to communicate with clients more carefully, accurately and responsibly.

The apology came just hours before June 18, the 618 shopping festival in China.

Perhaps it is time for celebrity brands to reflect the essence in building a trusted brand: the hearts of consumers are won through quality rather than pricing, fame, livestreaming, capital or marketing.

Dubbed the "Hermes of ice cream", Zhong Xue Gao has been popular since its establishment in early 2018 due to its premium market position and Chinese origins.

Zhong Xue Gao framed itself with the Chinese elements. With its name sounding like "Chinese style of ice cream" in Chinese, its ice cream comes in the shape of traditional Chinese roof tile and the character "hui", meaning to return.

Yet it is the most expensive Chinese ice cream to date. For example, the most expensive product the company has sold is Ecuador Pink — made of pink cocoa powder extracted from a plant growing in the South American country and Japanese shaddock juice. The Ecuador Pink was sold at 66 yuan ($10.30).

Even the company's more standard range of ice creams is usually sold at a price range of 15 to 20 yuan, four to five times the price of most local competitors. In a recent interview, the company founder Lin Sheng defended the high price by saying "This is its price. Take it or leave it."

However, Zhong Xue Gao's high price does not seem to purely come from its self-claimed cost of authentic making process. The company was fined twice by the Shanghai market supervision authority in 2019 for false advertising.

One item the supervision body said, among other false advertising, was that the ad for its milk-flavored ice creams boasting it did not contain a single drop of water contradicted the product ingredient label which listed water.

The gimmick of "high-end ice cream" promoted by popular internet celebrities did bring enough attention in this era of livestreaming. In a sense, Zhong Xue Gao's popularity is based on crazy marketing.

If the cost comes from frenzy publicity instead of the raw materials production and labor, then consumers deserve to know the truth before making their choice to buy it or not.

Celebrity brands should not fool consumers. To stay popular for long and go far, company must treat consumers sincerely and provide products with reasonable price and value for money. False publicity through marketing can only bring short-term profits, but will eventually be rejected and resented by the consumers.

（来源：https://global.chinadaily.com.cn/a/202106/19/WS60cd50fea31024ad0baca209.html）

3.8 主题拓展资源

英语视频： TED 演讲 We're Building a Dystopia Just to Make People Click on Ads

So when people voice fears of artificial intelligence, very often, they invoke images of humanoid robots run amok. You know? Terminator? You know, that might be something to consider, but that's a distant threat. Or, we fret about digital surveillance with metaphors from the past. *1984*, George Orwell's *1984*, it's hitting the bestseller lists again. It's a great book, but it's not the correct dystopia for the 21st century. What we need to fear most is not what artificial intelligence will do to us on its own, but how the people in power will use artificial intelligence to control us and to manipulate us in novel, sometimes hidden, subtle and unexpected ways. Much of the technology that threatens our freedom and our dignity in the near-term future is being developed by companies in the business of capturing and selling our data and our attention to advertisers and others: Facebook, Google, Amazon, Alibaba, Tencent.

Now, artificial intelligence has started bolstering their business as well. And it may seem like artificial intelligence is just the next thing after online ads. It's not. It's a jump in category. It's a whole different world, and it has great potential. It could accelerate our understanding of many areas of study and research. But to paraphrase a famous Hollywood philosopher, "With prodigious potential comes prodigious risk."

Now let's look at a basic fact of our digital lives, online ads. Right? We kind of dismiss them. They seem crude, ineffective. We've all had the experience of being followed on the web by an ad based on something we searched or read. You know, you look up a pair of boots and for a week, those boots are following you around everywhere you go. Even after you succumb and buy them, they're still following you around. We're kind of inured to that kind of basic, cheap manipulation. We roll our eyes and we think, "You know what? These things don't work." Except, online, the digital technologies are not just ads. Now, to understand that, let's think of a physical world example. You know how, at the checkout counters at supermarkets, near the cashier, there's candy and gum at the eye level of kids? That's designed to make them whine at their parents just as the parents are about to sort of check out. Now, that's a persuasion architecture. It's not nice, but it kind of works. That's why you see it in every supermarket. Now, in the physical world, such persuasion architectures are kind of limited, because you can only put so many things by the cashier. Right? And the candy and gum, it's the same for everyone, even though it mostly works only for people who have whiny little humans beside them. In the physical world, we live with those limitations.

In the digital world, though, persuasion architectures can be built at the scale of billions and they can target, infer, understand and be deployed at individuals one by one by figuring out your weaknesses, and they can be sent to everyone's phone private screen, so it's not visible to us. And that's different. And that's just one of the basic things that artificial intelligence can do.

Now, let's take an example. Let's say you want to sell plane tickets to Vegas. Right? So in the old world, you could think of some demographics to target based on experience and what you can guess. You might try to advertise to, oh, men between the ages of 25 and 35, or people who have a high limit on their credit card, or retired couples. Right? That's what you would do in the past.

With big data and machine learning, that's not how it works anymore. So to imagine that, think of all the data that Facebook has on you: every status update you ever typed, every Messenger conversation, every place you logged in from, all your photographs that you uploaded there. If you start typing something and change your mind and delete it, Facebook keeps those and analyzes them, too. Increasingly, it tries to match you with your offline data. It also purchases a lot of data from data brokers. It could be everything from your financial records to a good chunk of your browsing history. Right? In the US, such data is routinely collected, collated and sold. In Europe, they have tougher rules.

So what happens then is, by churning through all that data, these machine-learning algorithms — that's why they're called learning algorithms — they learn to understand the characteristics of people who purchased tickets to Vegas before. When they learn this from existing data, they also learn how to apply this to new people. So if they're presented with a new person, they can classify whether that person is likely to buy a ticket to Vegas or not. Fine. You're thinking, an offer to buy tickets to Vegas. I can ignore that. But the problem isn't that. The problem is, we no longer really understand how these complex algorithms work. We don't understand how they're doing this categorization. It's giant matrices, thousands of rows and columns, maybe millions of rows and columns, and not the programmers and not anybody who looks at it, even if you have all the data, understands anymore how exactly it's operating any more than you'd know what I was thinking right now if you were shown a cross section of my brain. It's like we're not programming anymore, we're growing intelligence that we don't truly understand.

And these things only work if there's an enormous amount of data, so they also encourage deep surveillance on all of us so that the machine learning algorithms can work. That's why Facebook wants to collect all the data it can about you. The algorithms work better.

So let's push that Vegas example a bit. What if the system that we do not understand was picking up that it's easier to sell Vegas tickets to people who are bipolar and about to enter the manic phase. Such people tend to become overspenders, compulsive gamblers. They could do this, and you'd have no clue that's what they were picking up on. I gave this example to a bunch of computer scientists once and afterwards, one of them came up to me. He was troubled and he said, "That's why I couldn't publish it." I was like, "Couldn't publish what?" He had tried to see whether you can indeed figure out the onset of mania from social media posts before clinical symptoms, and it had worked, and it had worked very well, and he had no idea how it worked or what it was picking up on.

Now, the problem isn't solved if he doesn't publish it, because there are already companies that are developing this kind of technology, and a lot of the stuff is just off the shelf. This is not very difficult anymore.

Do you ever go on YouTube meaning to watch one video and an hour later you've watched 27? You know how YouTube has this column on the right that says, "Up next" and it autoplays something? It's an algorithm picking what it thinks that you might be interested in and maybe not find on your own. It's not a human editor. It's what algorithms do. It picks up on what you have watched and what people like you have watched, and infers that that must be what you're interested in, what you want more of, and just shows you more. It sounds like a benign and useful feature, except when it isn't.

So in 2016, I attended rallies of then-candidate Donald Trump to study as a scholar the movement supporting him. I study social movements, so I was studying it, too. And then I wanted to write something about one of his rallies, so I watched it a few times on YouTube. YouTube started recommending to me and autoplaying to me white supremacist videos in increasing order of extremism. If I watched one, it served up one even more extreme and autoplayed that one, too. If you watch Hillary Clinton or Bernie Sanders content, YouTube recommends and autoplays conspiracy left, and it goes downhill from there.

Well, you might be thinking, this is politics, but it's not. This isn't about politics. This is just the algorithm figuring out human behavior. I once watched a video about vegetarianism on YouTube and YouTube recommended and autoplayed a video about being vegan. It's like you're never hardcore enough for YouTube.

So what's going on? Now, YouTube's algorithm is proprietary, but here's what I think is going on. The algorithm has figured out that if you can entice people into thinking that you can show them something more hardcore, they're more likely to stay on the site watching video after video going down that rabbit hole while Google serves them ads. Now, with nobody minding the ethics of the store, these sites can profile people who are Jew haters, who think that Jews are parasites and who have such explicit anti-Semitic content, and let you target them with ads. They can also mobilize algorithms to find for you look-alike audiences, people who do not have such explicit anti-Semitic content on their profile but who the algorithm detects may be susceptible to such messages, and lets you target them with ads, too. Now, this may sound like an implausible example, but this is real. ProPublica investigated this and found that you can indeed do this on Facebook, and Facebook helpfully offered up suggestions on how to broaden that audience. BuzzFeed tried it for Google, and very quickly they found, yep, you can do it on Google, too. And it wasn't even expensive. The ProPublica reporter spent about 30 dollars to target this category.

So last year, Donald Trump's social media manager disclosed that they were using Facebook dark posts to demobilize people, not to persuade them, but to convince them not to vote at all. And to do that, they targeted specifically, for example, African-American men in key cities like Philadelphia, and I'm going to read exactly what he said. I'm quoting.

They were using "nonpublic posts whose viewership the campaign controls so that only the people we want to see it see it. We modeled this. It will dramatically affect her ability to turn these people out."

What's in those dark posts? We have no idea. Facebook won't tell us.

So Facebook also algorithmically arranges the posts that your friends put on Facebook, or the pages you follow. It doesn't show you everything chronologically. It puts the order in the way that the algorithm thinks will entice you to stay on the site longer.

Now, so this has a lot of consequences. You may be thinking somebody is snubbing you on Facebook. The algorithm may never be showing your post to them. The algorithm is prioritizing some of them and burying the others.

Experiments show that what the algorithm picks to show you can affect your emotions. But that's not all. It also affects political behavior. So in 2010, in the midterm elections, Facebook did an experiment on 61 million people in the US that was disclosed after the fact. So some people were shown, "Today is election day," the simpler one, and some people were shown the one with that tiny tweak with those little thumbnails of your friends who clicked on "I voted." This simple tweak. OK? So the pictures were the only change, and that post shown just once turned out an additional 340,000 voters in that election, according to this research as confirmed by the voter rolls. A fluke? No. Because in 2012, they repeated the same experiment. And that time, that civic message shown just once turned out an additional 270,000 voters. For reference, the 2016 US presidential election was decided by about 100,000 votes. Now, Facebook can also very easily infer what your politics are, even if you've never disclosed them on the site. Right? These algorithms can do that quite easily. What if a platform with that kind of power decides to turn out supporters of one candidate over the other? How would we even know about it?

Now, we started from someplace seemingly innocuous — online aels following us around — and we've landed someplace else. As a public and as citizens, we no longer know if we're seeing the same information or what anybody else is seeing, and without a common basis of information, little by little, public debate is becoming impossible, and we're just at the beginning stages of this. These algorithms can quite easily infer things like your people's ethnicity, religious and political views, personality traits, intelligence, happiness, use of addictive substances, parental separation, age and genders, just from Facebook likes. These algorithms can identify protesters even if their faces are partially concealed. These algorithms may be able to detect people's sexual orientation just from their dating profile pictures.

Now, these are probabilistic guesses, so they're not going to be 100 percent right, but I don't see the powerful resisting the temptation to use these technologies just because there are some false positives, which will of course create a whole other layer of problems. Imagine what a state can do with the immense amount of data it has on its citizens. And here's the tragedy: we're building this infrastructure of surveillance authoritarianism merely to get people to click on ads. And this won't be Orwell's authoritarianism. This isn't "1984." Now, if authoritarianism is using overt fear to terrorize us, we'll all be scared, but we'll know it, we'll hate it and we'll resist it. But if the people in power are using these algorithms to quietly watch us, to judge us and to nudge us, to predict and identify the troublemakers and the rebels, to deploy persuasion architectures at scale and to manipulate individuals one by one using their personal, individual weaknesses and vulnerabilities, and if they're doing it at scale through our private screens so that we don't even know what our fellow citizens and neighbors are seeing, that authoritarianism will envelop us like a spider's web and we may not even know we're in it.

So Facebook's market capitalization is approaching half a trillion dollars. It's because it works great as a persuasion architecture. But the structure of that architecture is the same whether you're selling shoes or whether you're selling politics. The algorithms do not know the difference. The same algorithms set loose upon us to make us more pliable for ads are also organizing our political, personal and social information flows, and that's what's got to change.

Now, don't get me wrong, we use digital platforms because they provide us with great value. I use Facebook to keep in touch with friends and family around the world. I've written about how crucial social media is for social movements. I have studied how these technologies can be used to circumvent censorship around the world. But it's not that the people who run, you know, Facebook or Google are maliciously and deliberately trying to make the country or the world more polarized and encourage extremism. I read the many well-intentioned statements that these people put out. But it's not the intent or the statements people in technology make that matter, it's the structures and business models they're building. And that's the core of the problem. Either Facebook is a giant con of half a trillion dollars and ads don't work on the site, it doesn't work as a persuasion architecture, or its power of influence is of great concern. It's either one or the other. It's similar for Google, too.

So what can we do? This needs to change. Now, I can't offer a simple recipe, because we need to restructure the whole way our digital technology operates. Everything from the way technology is developed to the way the incentives, economic and otherwise, are built into the system. We have to face and try to deal with the lack of transparency created by the proprietary algorithms, the structural challenge of machine learning's opacity, all this indiscriminate data that's being collected about us. We have a big task in front of us. We have to mobilize our technology, our creativity and yes, our politics so that we can build artificial intelligence that supports us in our human goals but that is also constrained by our human values. And I understand this won't be easy. We might not even easily agree on what those terms mean. But if we take seriously how these systems that we depend on for so much operate, I don't see how we can postpone this conversation anymore. These structures are organizing how we function and they're controlling what we can and we cannot do. And many of these ad-financed platforms, they boast that they're free. In this context, it means that we are the product that's being sold. We need a digital economy where our data and our attention is not for sale to the highest-bidding authoritarian or demagogue.

So to go back to that Hollywood paraphrase, we do want the prodigious potential of artificial intelligence and digital technology to blossom, but for that, we must face this prodigious menace, open-eyed and now.

Thank you.

（来源：https://www.ted.com/talks/zeynep_tufekci_we_re_building_a_dystopia_just_to_make_people_click_on_ads）

第四单元　灾难与救援
（Unit 4 Calamities and Rescues）

1. 思政主题：抗疫勇士，新时代的英雄

2. 意 义

本单元的主题是"灾难与救援"。在思政教学中，教师可引导学生就2020年起困扰全球的新冠肺炎疫情这一公共卫生灾难进行讨论和反思，重点放在中国政府积极及时的援救措施上。歌颂中国在世界舞台的大国担当、在国内万众一心齐抗议的决心；颂扬医护人员的大无畏精神，引导学生了解和体会疫情当下的中国速度、中国精神、中国信念，致敬抗疫英雄，建立制度自信，激发学生的民族自豪感。

一场疫情，无数城市，亿万人民。当我们的正常生活因疫情几近停摆，当我们的心态随着各种消息起起伏伏，有这样一群人，他们奔赴在一线，用自己的力量全力战疫，维持我们生活的正常运转：他们是与病毒抗争的医护人员，是近在身边的社区工作人员与志愿者，是城市公共交通的维护者……是每一个站在抗疫第一线的普通人。来时风雪满城，归去花开锦绣。这是一场所有人为所有人的战役，感谢所有医护人员的坚守与奉献，感谢每一位在岗位上默默付出的普通人。

医护人员：Brave Medics Guard Lives

Medical staff in Wuhan and Beijing faced different challenges during the COVID-19 outbreak. But the hard work of the medics in both cities is valued equally, as they rose to the challenge of treating patients struck down by the new virus.

冲锋向前，义无反顾，这是奋战在抗疫第一线的医护群像的真实写照。他们也是普通人，也会恐惧，也有担忧，但他们仍旧选择了坚守岗位、抗击病毒。是他们不分昼夜的辛劳与牺牲，击退了病毒，守护了生命。

社区工作人员与志愿者：Community Workers Keep Daily Life Moving

In Wuhan, a city under a near-total lockdown, community workers delivered essentials like food and medicine. In Beijing, although the lockdown was less stringent, they played a key role in keeping vulnerable people safe. In both cities, these community workers shared a belief in the importance of helping others with the challenges of daily life in difficult times.

居家隔离，切断病毒传播链，这是抗疫的重要举措，也给社区工作人员和志愿者带来巨大考验：要保证日常生活必需的食物、药品，要处理各种突发状况……他们尽全力维持着社区人民生活的正常运转，不辞劳苦。

城市公共交通维护者：Diligent Staff Protect Public Transportation

A city's public transportation network is like the arteries that move life-sustaining blood to the body's vital organs. During the epidemic, public transport in Wuhan had to shut down, and in Beijing, service levels were reduced. But as the outbreak was brought under control, thousands of staff worked quietly behind the scenes to ensure that commuters returning to work could do so safely using public transport once more.

公共交通网是维持城市运转的重要动脉，疫情期间，交通卡口是疫情防控的重要环节；疫情得到控制后，确保交通有序恢复也是对城市的重要考验，数千名公共交通工作人员在幕后默默工作，维持着武汉和北京两座城市交通的正常运转。

（来源：外研社高等英语资讯）

3. 教学设计与思政元素的融入

Passage A

3.1 Warm-up 环节

英文文章：Best of Times, Worst of Times

本文以一个美国人的视角，通过数据和对比，描述了中国在抗疫过程中的担当和作为。教师可以让学生在课前阅读本文材料，课堂上参与讨论：Why do you think the author addresses in this essay "No place but China has the ability to competently test the population of a city of nine million people in a mere five days"?

For many of us, 2020 has been the strangest year of our lives, given the shock caused by COVID-19. I'm reminded of the memorable opening of Charles Dickens's great novel, *The Tale of Two Cities*: "It was the best of times, it was the worst of times, it was the age of wisdom, it was the age of foolishness." November perfectly illustrates the contradictions.

This month, in much of the world, one or more successive waves of the corona virus continue to wreak havoc. People are dying and economies are comatose. Yet, in China and a few other countries, personal lives and economic activities have returned to near normalcy. With the imminent promise of effective vaccines, all countries have the prospect of being part of a community of a shared healthy future for mankind in 2021.

At the same time, however that many countries are floundering and/or have given up on confronting the virus, others have bound themselves together in the Regional Comprehensive Economic Partnership (RCEP), reorienting the global compass needle from West to East in what is now not only the Chinese Century, but the Asian Century. This is a genuine pivot, a game-changer and a sign of things to come.

As an American, I've always looked forward to November, but not this year. I'm under a second COVID-19 lockdown in Vienna. The charms of the city like the Golden Hall and Empress Sisi's Hofburg Palace are off-limits to all. Tourism is nonexistent and so the revenue that helps power Austria's economy. Having failed to arrest the virus like China has, the government here has the near-impossible task of finding the microscopic sweet spot balancing the public's health and that of its economy. Virtually all of Europe, Latin America and beyond are in the same boat.

Back in the US, we celebrate Thanksgiving Day on the fourth Thursday in November. It's the most family-oriented holiday of the year and usually the most traveled, although a pale truncated version of China's Spring Festival. But this year it's difficult to be truly thankful, even given the promise of numerous vaccines from the US, China, the World Health Organization (WHO)'s COVAX accelerator and elsewhere.

The fact is that after more than a quarter of a million deaths and almost 12 million cases, many avoidable, US numbers are dramatically accelerating, not abating. The current administration continues to fail to address this calamity. The deeply divided country doesn't even have an officially declared winner of the November 3 presidential election.

China seems like it's in another galaxy; life there is so normal. China has virtually no COVID-19 cases, and those that exist, virtually all foreign in origin, are dealt with speed and efficiency to prevent further spread. No place but China has the ability to competently test the population of a city of nine million people in a mere five days as was done in Qingdao last month.

As a consequence, China's economy has largely recovered and is robust. In fact, despite COVID-19, China's first centennial goal of building a moderately prosperous socialist society in all respects is on track to being accomplished by year-end as is its second centennial goal of becoming a great modern socialist country by 2049.

With the prospect of the country's implementation of China's 14th Five-Year Plan in tandem with the dual circulation paradigm, under the leadership of President Xi Jinping and the Communist Party of China, the country appears to be the only major economy poised for growth this year. Even in this most troubled time, China's future promises to be bright.

Despite the global gloom, even when tempered by the prospect of global normalcy by this time next year, the virtual RCEP signing ceremony was definitely a transformative milestone. It's one of those rare events that demarcate one era from another. As Chinese Premier Li Keqiang said: "Under the current global circumstances, the fact the RCEP has been signed after eight years of negotiations brings a ray of light and hope amid the clouds." He said RCEP also represented "a victory of multilateralism and free trade."

RCEP's 15 Asia-Pacific countries encompass some 2.2 billion people and 30 percent of the world's economic output. It is bigger than both the region of the US-Mexico-Canada Agreement and the European Union.

RCEP is the first multilateral trade deal for China, the first bilateral tariff reduction arrangement between Japan and China, and the first time China, Japan and South Korea have joined in a single free-trade agreement.

Although some experts downplay its significance, I believe RCEP is nothing short of a game-changer. RCEP is expected to eliminate a range of tariffs on imports within 20 years. The 500+ page agreement includes provisions on intellectual property, telecommunications, financial services, e-commerce and professional services.

Never mind that it will make trading for members significantly easier, it will also mean nonmember countries and their enterprises will be economically disadvantaged. For the US, being on the outside means it loses considerable influence and the ability to shape trade in the Asia-Pacific region and beyond. The US Chamber of Commerce, representing large American business interests, said on Monday that its members were concerned that the US is being left behind as economic integration accelerates across the Asia-Pacific region.

Similar to the economic integration of the European Union begun under its predecessors like the European Coal and Steel Community and the European Economic Community, RCEP is expected to improve relations among its member states by creating economic interdependence as companies invest in each other's countries. It could also add $209 billion annually to world incomes and $500 billion to world trade by 2030.

RCEP also has serious implications for integrating its member states into China's Belt & Road Initiative. Of particular import, as the coronavirus rages on, will be an emphasis on a Health Silk Road, particularly in Southeast Asia, to prevent supply shortages as were seen earlier this year, as well as to promote high-tech in the public health arena.

（来源：https://www.chinadaily.com.cn/a/202011/25/WS5fbdf34e a31024ad0ba9 661b.html）

3.2 Discussion 环节

英文视频：Brave Medics Guard Lives 勇敢的医护人员捍卫生命

通过观看本视频可以更深入地了解到新冠肺炎疫情暴发之时中国政府积极及时的救援措施，以及医护人员不忘初心、坚守岗位的大无畏奉献精神。观看视频后，教师可以引导学生去讨论：Who else have you seen that have played their part and have taken responsibility during the pandemic? What kind of spiritual strength do you see in them?

China became embroiled in an intense battle against the novel corona virus epidemic at the start of 2020. With the city of Wuhan in the central Chinese province of Hubei as the epicenter, tens of thousands of medics came from across China to help Wuhan fight against the virus.

This is Lu Rong, a doctor at intensive care unit of Wuhan No.1 Hospital. She started to treat COVID-19 patients from February. She took care of two critically ill patients during her shift, which started at six a.m. every day. Lu Rong has worked as an ICU doctor for four years. At first she was worried. It was her sense of duty that kept her going.

Medical staff worked in places of danger to guard the city and its people. We also cannot forget their sacrifices. They're constantly in the thoughts of their families too. Despite the difficulty of the situation, the medics treated each patient as their own family. They even drew pictures on their protective suits to cheer up sick children. Under their care, more and more patients recovered.

Wuhan was reborn. Medical workers from across China can now return home. It was snowy and windy when they came to Wuhan. When they left, it was already spring. The city's cherry blossoms are blossoming, as the medics board the train that take them home.

China's capital city Beijing sent many medics to Wuhan to support the fight against COVID-19. But many remained at their posts to guard the safety of Beijing. Besides the designated hospitals for COVID-19 patients, another important task for doctors and nurses in Beijing was epidemic prevention.

Her name is Hao Xiaofeng. She is a doctor at the eye hospital of China Academy of Chinese Medical Sciences. She did not take a break from her work during the epidemic. "When the corona virus broke out, all of us are nervous. But we are doctors. We need to see our patients. Ophthalmology was one of the susceptible departments, but the risk of infection can be reduced so long as you take good protective measures."

The pharmacists in the hospital were busy preparing traditional Chinese medicines for patients each day. Such a scene could be witnessed in many hospitals across Beijing. Doctors here have provided medical services to residents in their neighborhood. They provide thoughtful services for residents, especially senior citizens who are unable to leave their homes.

This is the West Branch of the Affiliated Beijing Chaoyang Hospital of the Capital Medical University. To treat COVID-19 patients and protect others in the hospital, doctors worked diligently to test the patients for the novel corona virus.

Such a busy work cannot continue without the support of the medical workers' families. In both cities, hardworking medics spend day and night to guard people's lives. This is a tale of two cities under pandemic.

（来源：http://chinaplus.cri.cn/special/A-Tale-of-Two-Cities-under-Pandemic）

扩展阅读：

"共和国勋章"获得者钟南山院士敢医敢言，强调严格防控，领导撰写新冠肺炎诊疗方案，在疫情防控、重症救治、科研攻关等方面作出杰出贡献。耄耋之年的钟老，一句"把最重的病人都送到我这儿来"感动无数国人。教师可以引导学生讨论：What have you learned from Dr. Zhong Nanshan?

Zhong Nanshan: A Respiratory Expert Bearing the Nation's Trust

"Bring all critically ill patients to me."

During the Severe Acute Respiratory Syndrome (SARS) outbreak in 2003, caused by a coronavirus, Chinese pulmonologist Zhong Nanshan helped the country control the epidemic with his expertise and transparency.

Around 17 years later, he again spearheaded the country's fight against the outbreak of a new coronavirus that causes COVID-19, which has been declared a pandemic by the World Health Organization (WHO).

When a medical team was constituted under Zhong to control the pandemic, people recalled the doctor's bold decisions in taming SARS. A section of doctors believed the disease to be chlamydia, a sexually transmissible bacterium, but Zhong found major loopholes in their claim.

Chlamydia causes upper respiratory tract inflammation, but a considerable number of patients admitted to the hospitals were showing no such conditions. Moreover, antibiotics like Tetracycline, the most effective drug to deal with bacteria-induced infections, had no effect on SARS patients.

Concerned over the prevailing confusion and fatalities caused by the unknown disease, Zhong announced that it was untenable to draw conclusions on the cause of the disease merely by observing virus samples under an electron microscope. In addition to specific structural features, genome sequence analysis is equally important to identify a pathogen, he added.

He decided to tell the truth to people. Zhong confessed that he didn't know the cause and had no idea about the transmission route of the new virus. His announcement created panic among people, but the entire conundrum ended with his landmark statement, "Bring critically ill patients to me."

"At that time, I would think that solving problems for patients, winning respect from the society could give me a sense of pride and satisfaction, that's one of the reasons I love being a doctor," said Zhong.

Patients poured in from across the region. While providing treatment to patients, he also had an additional responsibility of doing research work to understand the etiology of the virus and effective medication.

With an advanced understanding of the disease, Zhong and his team changed remedies based on different symptoms. His region soon had the lowest fatality rate and many countries followed up their treatment regimen.

Growing up in a family of medical professionals, with his parents being world-renowned medical experts, Zhong grew up listening to the challenges of the medical profession. Today, he is also known as China's Dr. Anthony Fauci.

The 84-year-old elderly was nominated the Medal of the Republic in August, the country's highest honor established last year to recognize the exemplary and outstanding contributions towards the nation's development.

（来源：https://news.cgtn.com/news/2020-09-08/Zhong-Nanshan-A-respiratory-expert-bearing-the-nation-s-trust-TBcBq2soqk/index.html）

3.3 Critical thinking 环节

英语文章： Virus Shouldn't Separate China from the World

本文讲述了一位毕业于北京大学的以色列留学生 Raz Galor 在新冠肺炎疫情期间，尽全力去帮助中国的故事。阅读本文后，教师可以引导学生去思考和讨论：Why is Galor so determined to help China? What's your opinion?

Raz Galor, an Israeli alumnus of Peking University, has warmed many Chinese hearts by helping organize medical relief for Wuhan — capital of Hubei province and epicenter of the novel coronavirus outbreak — and other neighboring areas.

Galor, a 26-year-old Israeli social media celebrity, has more than 1.3 million fans on Weibo — where he is better known by his Chinese name Gao Yousi — thanks to his videos on YChina, a program highlighting expat life in China.

A recent video showing him send 100,000 surgical masks to China went viral on social media. In an exclusive conversation with *China Daily* Galor shares his experience of collecting and shipping these medical requirements from Israel.

Helping hands 7,000 km away from China

Galor first got to know that medical supplies were in short supply in Hubei on Jan 25, or *Chuyi*, the first day of the Chinese Lunar New Year. He was in Tel Aviv but decided to do something to help the country that was his home for 12 years. "The least we could do was to send medical supplies," Galor said. Within hours he and a friend got cracking. "We tapped people on the streets, pharmacies, hospitals and businessmen to get enough supplies."

They thought 5,000 was a decent number of surgical masks to arrange in a small country like Israel. However, in a very short time, they managed to collect a lot more. "We ended up getting 100,000 masks. And some other things too."

His father, Amir Gal Or, chairman of Infinity and Innovation and president of the China-Israel Chamber of Commerce, who has contacts in the medical, business and public relations industries, also stepped in to help.

"China has helped Israel so many times. So it was only natural that we do everything possible, there was no question about that," Amir said. That sure helped.

With help from the China-Israel Chamber of Commerce, Galor's team reached out to people who guided them on how to purchase quality medical supplies.

"Israel's largest hospital, Sheba Hospital, referred us to their warehouse, a company called Kodam Medicom," said Galor, emphasizing how lucky they were. "Very lucky indeed. The last 100,000 masks were available for sale at the hospital. We also got 50,000 pairs of gloves and a couple of medical robes."

In fact their difficulties began after they had collected all the medical equipment, on Jan 31, when the World Health Organization declared the outbreak a global health emergency and many airlines called off their flights to China.

"There was no way to get to China," said Galor. They made phone calls to whoever they thought could help but got no guarantees. "Flights were getting cancelled by the hour. Nobody could tell us how or when we would be able to send the materials."

But they kept trying and finally reached Cainiao, Alibaba's logistic platform operator, who offered to ship their supplies to China for free via Moscow.

Galor breathed easy only three days later when the medical consignment was all packed up and ready at the airport warehouse to be sent to China.

"I barely slept those days. I was very nervous," Galor said. "I was worried all our effort would ultimately go to waste."

Some 100,000 surgical masks, 50,000 pairs of medical gloves and 7,000 surgical gowns finally arrived in Huanggang, the second-worst hit city in Hubei, on Feb 9.

Being able to help from 7,000 kilometers away made Galor realize that difficulties are no obstacle "if you really have a good heart and want to help people".

Anti-China movements not really helping

In a video from Tel Aviv, Galor said he and his friends are paying close attention to the epidemic situation and want to do all they can for their Chinese friends.

"Whenever an individual, community or country faces a problem and lacks basic equipment, or needs psychological support, the people who really care should stand by them," Galor said, adding that the anti-China sentiment around the globe is "not really helping".

"We shouldn't let the virus separate China from the world." Any behavior to stigmatize China and Chinese culture is "very disgusting". He hoped people would try "to create another voice that shows the real situation and tells us to be more open to solutions than to separations".

Quoting John Lennon he said he hoped, or imagined, "all the people... sharing all the world".

To give a voice to the voiceless

The popular YChina program Galor anchors showcases a vibrant China to the world through discussions by expats about Chinese culture and latest trends in the country.

After graduating from Peking University, Galor spent more than a decade studying and working in China. He realizes China is one of the cultures most likely to be stereotyped "because of how different and unique and, maybe, mysterious and complicated it is".

What struck him most about China were the people he met there, the truly ordinary people. "If my team and I try to make the world understand China better, we will definitely have to start with the stories, the untold stories of its people," seldom reported by the media.

"But it's only through these people that you can really get a grasp of the real China," Galor said. In fact that is the reason why his work often focuses on unknown groups. "Giving a voice to the voiceless," he quotes Joaquin Phoenix, who just won the Oscar for Best Actor in a Leading Role for Joker, to explain what his team is doing for China. He wants to help "the world see a more diverse and real side of China".

Galor also wants everybody to pay special attention to the medical staff working on the front line in the fight against the epidemic. "It's they who are fighting day and night to save our lives," he said. "We won't notice how much they make an impact on our lives until we see it."

（来源：中国日报微信公众号）

3.4 主题拓展资源

英语文章：Zhang Boli: Traditional Chinese Medicine Offers Oriental Wisdom in the Fight Against COVID-19

　　致力于中医药现代化研究的张伯礼院士一直是推动中医药事业传承创新发展的关键人物。疫情发生后，他用国医济世，主持研究制定中西医结合救治方案，指导中医药全过程介入新冠肺炎救治，取得显著成效，为疫情防控作出重大贡献。

　　Over the past few months, Zhang Boli, 72, has helped the world recognize the power of Traditional Chinese Medicine (TCM) by leading an expert team to treat COVID-19 infections in Wuhan, China's frontline in the battle against COVID-19.

　　Zhang, head of Tianjin University of Traditional Chinese Medicine, arrived in Wuhan, capital of central China's Hubei Province on January 27, the third day of China's Lunar New Year and five days into the mega city's lockdown for epidemic control.

　　COVID-19 patients in Wuhan, the epicenter of the outbreak in China, have received treatment in collective isolation and under classified management, according to decisions made by the Central Guidance Team. Zhang and other experts in TCM strongly advised the use of traditional medicine on all of the isolated patients.

　　With the approval of the Central Guidance Team, Zhang and 208 other experts formed a TCM medical team and started treating patients at a makeshift hospital in Wuhan's Jiangxia District. They decided to apply a comprehensive treatment solution primarily using the Qingfei Paidu Decoction (Lung Cleansing and Detoxifying Decoction) and Xuanfei Baidu Formula, complemented by Tai Chi, Baduanjin and acupuncture therapy.

　　Meanwhile, TCM experts studied the details of 1,000 patients in varying conditions from nearly 20 hospitals across the country and giving direction to TCM treatment. Under Zhang's guidance, his team also evaluated the clinical efficacy of various TCM treatments and carried out drug screening and development.

　　According to China's National Administration of TCM, at least six TCM drugs have proven effective in fighting COVID-19, with an overall effectiveness rate of over 90 percent among 74,187 COVID-19 patients across the nation as of March 24.

The National Administration of Traditional Chinese Medicine has said China has shared TCM therapy, effective prescriptions and clinical experience for dealing with COVID-19 with more than 80 countries and regions.

The Lianhua Qingwen capsule, a recommended patent TCM for the treatment of COVID-19, has received marketing approvals in more than 10 countries and regions.

"Chinese medics have relied on joint consultations between TCM and Western medicine experts in treating COVID-19. Regardless of national boundaries, I hope TCM can help more and more people worldwide," Zhang said.

Back in 2003, Zhang had to call on authorities to get TCM involved in the fight against SARS. This time in Wuhan, TCM was used earlier, but still, it wasn't at the very beginning. Zhang said China must have more confidence in its own culture and medicine during a public health crisis.

"China should take TCM into consideration for a rapid response system, so it can be put into use in the first place in case of an emergency, being used alongside Western medicine therapy as a major force," Zhang said.

Zhang called on the nation to establish a more efficient reporting system so that if a health emergency should happen, information can be passed on to the Chinese Center for Disease Control and Prevention in the shortest possible time.

The doctor hopes he won't see a major epidemic for years to come – but if that happens, China should make sure there are enough resources and capacity to produce more supplies. He expressed belief TCM can play a bigger role in saving more people in time.

（来源：https://news.cgtn.com/news/2020-09-08/Zhang-Boli-TCM-offers-oriental-wisdom-in-the-fight-against-COVID-19-TBUF02mexq/index.html）

Passage B

3.5 Warm-up 环节

双语视频：世界卫生组织总干事高级顾问布鲁斯·艾尔沃德感谢武汉人民所做的贡献

2020年2月24日晚，中国—世界卫生组织新冠肺炎联合专家考察组在北京举行新闻发布会。联合专家考察组外方组长、世界卫生组织总干事高级顾问布鲁斯·艾尔沃德（Bruce Aylward）有一段陈述，在现场引起一阵掌声。布鲁斯·艾尔沃德说："我们要认识到武汉人民所做的贡献,世界欠你们一份情。当这场疫情过去,希望有机会代表世界再一次感谢武汉人民。"现场的翻译在翻译这段话时几度哽咽。教师可在课上给学生播放这段视频,重温2020年武汉作为一个英雄城市为全世界新冠疫情的防控所作出的贡献和牺牲。

Twenty-five years ago, I visited Wuhan to assess the capacity to eradicate, it was at that time another virus, a dangerous virus.

The Wuhan I found was a fair bit smaller than today, but it was a bustling, energetic, lively place filled with wonderful people with a great spirit as it went about trying to eradicate the disease I was working on at the time.

But when Doctor Liang and I arrived in Wuhan two nights ago, it was a very different place. The city of skyscrapers, giant auto routes and a gorgeous hypermodern train station was silent. It was a ghost town.

And behind every window of these skyscrapers we drove past, there were people. There were 15 million people who were staying put in one place for weeks at a time to stop this disease.

And if we spoke with people we were working with in Wuhan, they said, "This is our duty. We have to protect the world from this disease. This is our role. We are playing our role."

And I just thought it's so important that we recognize that to the people of Wuhan, it is recognized, the world is in your debt. And when this disease finishes, hopefully, we will have a chance to thank the people in Wuhan for the role that they played in it, because many of us, many of the people here have suffered but the people of that city have gone through an extraordinary period.

25年前,我曾经到过武汉,评估当地消除另外一种危险病毒的能力。

那时的武汉也许比现在小很多,但车水马龙,熙熙攘攘,是一个充满活力的地方。人们斗志昂扬地忙着根除我当时所研究的那种疾病。

但两个晚上前,我和梁教授到达武汉的时候,这里已经变得完全不一样。这座有着许多高楼大厦、宽敞的高速公路、现代化的火车站的城市,变得沉寂,仿佛是一座空城。

我们途经一座座高楼大厦,窗户后面,有1500万武汉人,他们几个星期都待在屋里,这一切只是为了阻止病毒的传播。

当我们与共事的武汉人说起这件事时,他们告诉我们:"这是我们的责任,我们必须保护世界不被这个疾病侵害,这是我们的职责所在,我们正在做自己应当做的。"

我想这一点很重要，我们必须认识到，对武汉人民而言，世界欠你们一份情。当疫情结束时，希望我们有机会能够感谢武汉人民，为他们的付出和行动，这里的很多人都经受了苦难，但那座城市的人民所经历的是一场异乎寻常的磨难。

（来源：中国日报双语新闻）

3.6 Discussion 环节

双语文章：携手抗疫 共克时艰——习近平主席在二十国集团领导人特别峰会上的发言 Working Together to Defeat the COVID-19 Outbreak

2020年3月26日，国家主席习近平在北京出席二十国集团领导人应对新冠肺炎特别峰会并发表题为《携手抗疫 共克时艰》的重要讲话。面对突如其来的新冠肺炎疫情，中国政府尽显大国风范，始终把人民生命安全和身体健康摆在第一位，中国人民不畏艰险，奋力打响了这场抗击疫情的人民战争。在世界舞台上，充分展现了大国的责任与担当。教师可以引导学生学习习近平主席重要讲话中的金句，思考并讨论：Facing pandemic, what do you think a responsible country should do in today's globalized world?

尊敬的萨勒曼国王，

Your Majesty King Salman bin Abdulaziz Al Saud,

各位同事：

Dear Colleagues,

大家好！首先，我谨对萨勒曼国王和沙特方面为这次会议所做的大量沟通协调工作，表示衷心的感谢！

It is good to join you. Let me begin by expressing my sincere appreciation to His Majesty King Salman and Saudi Arabia for having done tremendous work of communication and coordination to make this summit possible.

面对突如其来的新冠肺炎疫情，中国政府、中国人民不畏艰险，始终把人民生命安全和身体健康摆在第一位，按照坚定信心、同舟共济、科学防治、精准施策的总要求，坚持全民动员、联防联控、公开透明，打响了一场抗击疫情的人民战争。经过艰苦努力，付出巨大牺牲，目前中国国内疫情防控形势持续向好，生产生活秩序加快恢复，但我们仍然丝毫不能放松警惕。

Facing the COVID-19 outbreak that caught us all by surprise, the Chinese government and Chinese people have been undaunted as we took on this formidable task. From day one of our fight against the outbreak, we have put people's life and health first. We have acted according to the overall principle of shoring up confidence, strengthening unity, ensuring science-based control and treatment and imposing targeted measures. We have mobilized the whole nation, set up collective control and treatment mechanisms and acted with openness and transparency. What we fought was a people's war against the outbreak. We have put up a strenuous struggle and made tremendous sacrifices. Now the situation in China is moving steadily in a positive direction. Life and work are quickly returning to normal. Yet, there is no way we will lower our guard or relax control.

在中方最困难的时候，国际社会许多成员给予中方真诚帮助和支持，我们会始终铭记并珍视这份友谊。

At the most difficult moment in our fight against the outbreak, China received assistance and help from a lot of members of the global community. Such expressions of friendship will always be remembered and cherished by the Chinese people.

重大传染性疾病是全人类的敌人。新冠肺炎疫情正在全球蔓延，给人民生命安全和身体健康带来巨大威胁，给全球公共卫生安全带来巨大挑战，形势令人担忧。当前，国际社会最需要的是坚定信心、齐心协力、团结应对，全面加强国际合作，凝聚起战胜疫情强大合力，携手赢得这场人类同重大传染性疾病的斗争。

Major infectious disease is the enemy of all. As we speak, the COVID-19 outbreak is spreading worldwide, posing enormous threat to life and health and bringing formidable challenge to global public health security. The situation is disturbing and unsettling. At such a moment, it is imperative for the international community to strengthen confidence, act with unity and work together in a collective response. We must comprehensively step up international cooperation and foster greater synergy so that humanity as one could win the battle against such a major infectious disease.

在此，我愿提出以下四点倡议。

For that to happen, I would like to put forth four proposals.

第一，坚决打好新冠肺炎疫情防控全球阻击战。国际社会应该加紧行动起来，坚决遏制疫情蔓延势头。我愿在此提议，尽早召开二十国集团卫生部长会议，加强信息分享，开展药物、疫苗研发、防疫合作，有效防止疫情跨境传播。要携手帮助公共卫生体系薄弱的发展中国家提高应对能力。我建议发起二十国集团抗疫援助倡议，在世界卫生组织支持下加强信息沟通、政策协调、行动配合。中方秉持人类命运共同体理念，愿同各国分享防控有益做法，开展药物和疫苗联合研发，并向出现疫情扩散的国家提供力所能及的援助。

First, we need to be resolute in fighting an all-out global war against the COVID-19 outbreak. The community of nations must move swiftly to stem the spread of the virus. In this regard, I propose that a G20 health ministers' meeting be convened as quick as possible to improve information sharing, strengthen cooperation on drugs, vaccines and epidemic control, and cut off cross-border infections. G20 members need to jointly help developing countries with weak public health systems enhance preparedness and response. I propose a G20 COVID-19 assistance initiative for better information sharing and policy and action coordination with the support of the World Health Organization. Guided by the vision of building a community with a shared future for mankind, China will be more than ready to share our good practices, conduct joint research and development of drugs and vaccines, and provide assistance where we can to countries hit by the growing outbreak.

第二，有效开展国际联防联控。病毒无国界。疫情是我们的共同敌人。各国必须携手拉起最严密的联防联控网络。中方已经建立新冠肺炎疫情防控网上知识中心，向所有国家开放。要集各国之力，共同合作加快药物、疫苗、检测等方面科研攻关，力争早日取得惠及全人类的突破性成果。要探讨建立区域公共卫生应急联络机制，提高突发公共卫生事件应急响应速度。

Second, we need to make a collective response for control and treatment at the international level. This is a virus that respects no borders. The outbreak we are battling is our common enemy. All must work together to build a strongest global network of control and treatment that the world has ever seen. China has set up its online COVID-19 knowledge center that is open to all countries. It is imperative that countries pool their strengths and speed up research and development of drugs, vaccines and testing capabilities in the hope to achieve early breakthrough to the benefit of all. Discussions are also needed regarding the establishment of regional emergency liaison mechanisms to enable quicker response to public health emergencies.

第三，积极支持国际组织发挥作用。中方支持世界卫生组织发挥领导作用，制定科学合理防控措施，尽力阻止疫情跨境传播。我建议，二十国集团依托世界卫生组织加强疫情防控信息共享，推广全面系统有效的防控指南。要发挥二十国集团的沟通协调作用，加强政策对话和交流，适时举办全球公共卫生安全高级别会议。中国将同各国一道，加大对相关国际和地区组织的支持力度。

　　Third, we need to support international organizations in playing their active roles. China supports WHO in leading the global efforts to develop science-based and proper control and treatment and minimize cross-border spread. I call on G20 members to enhance anti-epidemic information sharing with the support of WHO and to promote control and treatment protocols that are comprehensive, systematic and effective. The G20 platform for communication and coordination may be used to increase policy dialogue and exchange, and a high-level meeting on international public health security may be convened in due course. For China, we will be happy to join other countries and scale up support for relevant international and regional organizations.

　　第四，加强国际宏观经济政策协调。疫情对全球生产和需求造成全面冲击，各国应该联手加大宏观政策对冲力度，防止世界经济陷入衰退。要实施有力有效的财政和货币政策，促进各国货币汇率基本稳定。要加强金融监管协调，维护全球金融市场稳定。要共同维护全球产业链供应链稳定，中国将加大力度向国际市场供应原料药、生活必需品、防疫物资等产品。要保护妇女儿童，保护老年人、残疾人等弱势群体，保障人民基本生活。中国将继续实施积极的财政政策和稳健的货币政策，坚定不移扩大改革开放，放宽市场准入，持续优化营商环境，积极扩大进口，扩大对外投资，为世界经济稳定作出贡献。

　　Fourth, we need to enhance international macro-economic policy coordination. The outbreak has disrupted production and demand across the globe. Countries need to leverage and coordinate their macro policies to counteract the negative impact and prevent the world economy from falling into recession. We need to implement strong and effective fiscal and monetary policies to keep our exchange rates basically stable. We need to better coordinate financial regulation to keep global financial markets stable. We need to jointly keep the global industrial and supply chains stable. What China will do in this regard is to increase its supply of active pharmaceutical ingredients, daily necessities, and anti-epidemic and other supplies to the international market. What's more, we also need to protect women, children, the elderly, people with disabilities and other vulnerable groups, and provide for people's basic needs. China will continue to pursue a proactive fiscal policy and prudent monetary policy. We will continue to advance reform and opening-up, widen market access, improve the business environment, and expand imports and outbound investment to contribute to a stable world economy.

我呼吁二十国集团成员采取共同举措,减免关税、取消壁垒、畅通贸易,发出有力信号,提振世界经济复苏士气。我们应该制定二十国集团行动计划,并就抗疫宏观政策协调及时作出必要的机制性沟通和安排。

I want to call on all G20 members to take collective actions — cutting tariffs, removing barriers, and facilitating the unfettered flow of trade. Together, we can send a strong signal and restore confidence for global economic recovery. The G20 needs to draw up an action plan and promptly set up communication mechanisms and institutional arrangements for anti-epidemic macro policy coordination.

同志们,

Dear Colleagues,

值此关键时刻,我们应该直面挑战、迅速行动。我坚信,只要我们同舟共济、守望相助,就一定能够彻底战胜疫情,迎来人类发展更加美好的明天!

Now is a crucial moment, a time for us to rise up to challenge and act with swiftness. I am convinced that through solidarity and mutual assistance, we will prevail over this outbreak and we all will embrace a brighter future for mankind!

谢谢大家。

Thank you.

(来源:中国日报双语新闻)

3.7 Critical thinking 环节

双语文章(节选):"中国通"库恩:抗击疫情,没有哪个国家比中国做得更好

"其他地方都不可能像中国一样!"世界知名中国问题专家、中国友谊改革奖章获得者罗伯特·库恩点赞中国担当,直言:"中国的动员能力在全球医疗史上是空前的。"面对国际上阴谋论者对中国提出的质疑,库恩坚定地表示:"历史将会感谢中国在全球战疫中起到的先锋作用。"教师可以带领学生阅读库恩的文章节选,之后就库恩在文中的观点引导学生进行讨论。

I take it seriously when the Standing Committee of the Politburo of the Communist Party of China, China's highest authority, called the epidemic "a major test of China's system and capacity for governance" — a phrase of such significance that in my 30-plus years of watching China, I do not recall the like.

中共中央政治局常委会,中国的最高决策机构将这次疫情称为"对我国治理体系和能力的一次大考"。我在中国30多年来,还没有过这样的经历。

Let me explain why I was confident that China would overcome the epidemic. Three reasons: China's commitment, China's competence, and readiness to change and improve.

我来解释下我为什么相信中国能战胜疫情，有三个原因：中国的投入、中国的国力以及改变、进步的意愿。

China's commitment to fight the coronavirus was exemplified by the country's astonishing mobilization to stop the spread. The government issued strict and resolute diréctives and the whole country marched to this music.

中国通过动员全国，阻止扩散，展现了在疫情方面的重大投入。政府发布了严格的指令，全国上下都步调一致。

This is China's monumental "whole of society" commitment. China's mobilization is unprecedented in global health history. Nowhere could it work like it works in China.

中国全社会的投入是历史性的，中国的动员能力在全球医疗史上也是空前的，其他地方都不可能像中国一样。

And the reason it works relates to how the Party system works. It is the same commitment and mobilization that the Party has been using to win the battle against poverty, since around 2012, lifting the final 100 million poor people out of absolute poverty.

而中国之所以能做到，跟党的制度有关。中国共产党在扶贫攻坚战时也展现了同样的投入和动员能力。自2012年来，中国让超过一亿人脱离贫困线。

China's competence to fight the virus is exemplified by the country's implementation of its commitment: locking down Wuhan, a metropolis of 11 million people, and other cities, perhaps 60 million or more people in Hubei province and other places; constructed hospitals of 1000 beds, literally on green fields and literally in just days; house-to-house temperature checks; the Party's grid management system of social control; postponing the return to work after the Lunar New Year break of hundreds of millions of travelers.

中国对疫情的有效遏制展现在全国上下的身体力行中：封闭了1100万人口的武汉以及湖北省内省外城市，总人口数超过6000万；仅仅十几天在一片空地上建起了1000个床位的医院；挨家挨户测量体温，网格化的社会监督管控，推迟数亿人春节假期后的复工时间。

China's readiness to change and improve is a critical part of its governance system.

中国改变和进步的意愿是他们治理体系中至关重要的一部分。

When I discuss the five or so primary reasons for China's remarkable development over the past four decades, I always include the Party's willingness, albeit sometimes out of necessity, to admit and correct errors. I admire leadership's forthright acknowledgement of "shortcomings and deficiencies".

我在说到过去四十年来中国突飞猛进的五个主要原因时，总会提到中国共产党愿意主动认错并且改正，虽然有时对自己过于苛刻。我对于国家领导人坦率地承认"缺点和不足"这一点深表敬佩。

To stop the spread of virulent diseases, early action is essential. But how to develop an early warning system? The challenge is handling an avalanche of information, from diverse public and private sources and of variegated and uncertain quality.

要阻止疫情扩散，一定要尽早行动。但怎么建立预警体系？真正的挑战在于如何处理大量来源不一、质量参差不齐的信息。

President Xi Jinping called for "fighting the outbreak in an open and transparent manner". Transparency is the key.

习近平主席呼吁，"以公开透明的方式抗击疫情"。透明是关键。

"人类命运共同体"造福全球

A propos of the pandemic, President Xi Jinping's repeated call to build "a community with a shared future for all humanity" is a grand vision with multiple applications. For seven years, it has driven foreign policy, especially the Belt and Road Initiative, helping to rectify global imbalances.

面对疫情，习近平主席不断呼吁构建"人类命运共同体"，这一造福全球的愿景。七年来，该理念推动了以"一带一路"为代表的中国外交政策，促进了全球平衡发展。

While fighting disease or controlling pandemics have always been a "shared future" benefit, it was always tucked within lists of other benefits, such as climate control, preventing terrorism, interdicting drugs, and the like.

能够对抗疫情、控制传染，是"共同未来"愿景的优势之一。除此之外，还有其他益处，比如在气候控制、防止恐怖主义、禁止毒品方面等。

Few ever imagined that a real pandemic could become so grave so fast. But as the pandemic has burst into planetary consciousness, it demonstrates viscerally the global criticality of "shared future" thinking.

几乎没人能想到疫情会这样地迅速恶化。但随着全球各国对疫情逐渐重视起来，"共同未来"这一理念的重要性便不言而喻。

By sending "battle-tested" medical teams to countries suffering under the siege of contagion, China brings to bear experts with contemporary, front line, epidemic experience.

中国派遣"久经沙场"的医疗团队到别国，支援抗疫，为当地带来了具备当代流行病前沿经验的专家。

China's evolved know-how in fighting and containing the novel coronavirus, especially the selfless work of dedicated Chinese healthcare and logistics professionals, can enable other countries to benefit from China's experience.

中国在对抗、控制新冠疫情方面的经验不断深化，尤其是医护人员、后勤人员的无私奉献，使其他国家也从中获益。

控制争端比控制疫情更具有挑战性

There is a problem, though. Emotions worldwide are frayed, rubbed raw by the pandemic's daily-life disruptions, with economic devastation threatening to exceed that of the 2008 global financial crisis.

但问题依然存在。目前全球的情绪都很紧张。疫情对日常生活造成影响，加上可能比2008年更严重的经济危机，大家都很脆弱。

In this toxic psychological environment, when non-stop news, especially in social media, amplifies scurrilous, unsubstantiated rumors by insensitive officials or block-brained conspiracy theorists, attitudes harden and antagonisms ossify. Indigenous nationalism flares in vicious circles.

在情绪如此紧张的环境下，新闻的不断轰炸，尤其是社交网络上将官员无心的言论放大为谣言，或是冥顽不化的阴谋论者都让人们变得冷漠、敌对。极端国家主义滋生。

It takes no cleverness to inflame feelings with glib rhetoric or political insults. Rational people must work together, not allow fringe invective to erode the capacity to fight a common enemy.

阴阳怪气、含沙射影、煽动情绪并不需要什么智慧。理性的人们要联起手来，不要让仇恨的言论影响对疫情的抗争。

Containment of the polemic will be more challenging than containment of the corona-virus. If so, Chinese views of America, and American views of China, are only going to deteriorate further, to the detriment of all.

控制争端将比控制新冠疫情更具挑战性。如此下去，中美对对方的态度看法只会恶化，危及全球。

Enlightened leadership should temper, not inflame, indigenous nationalism. We cannot allow mutual exhaustion to be our last hope. This is why the recent Xi-

Trump phone call was so important.

优秀的领导人应该缓和而不是煽动极端国家主义。我们不希望看到两败俱伤。这就是为何习近平主席和特朗普总统的通话至关重要。

历史将会感谢中国

China's vision of "a community with a shared future for humanity", exhorting all nations to act for the common good, fits our turbulent times.

中国构建"人类命运共同体"的愿景，呼吁所有国家共同发展，正是动荡的当下亟需的。

China's vision is a universal message shared by many cultures. China's challenge is to express the vision in language with which other cultures can identify and feel comfortable supporting.

中国的这个愿景也得到了许多文化的认可。中国面对的挑战，是让其他文化都对这个愿景感同身受。

To be clear, read literally and without bias, a "community with a shared future for humanity" is a powerful exhortation that should benefit the world. This is why the phrase should be protected and enriched by also allowing other, diverse English phases to represent the original Chinese.

客观公正地解读，"人类命运共同体"这个呼吁十分有力，而且能让全世界受益。因此要保护、发扬好这个理念，同时用多样的英语翻译表达中文原本的意思。

The objective is to enable the global community to take collective ownership of the grand vision. Given the global pandemic, the global community must take collective ownership. What China seeks is what humanity seeks, especially with the pandemic, and it behooves people of goodwill everywhere to work together to transform rhetoric into reality.

这个理念旨在呼吁国际社会共同致力于实现这个伟大愿景。考虑到当下的疫情，国际社会也必须如此。中国的目标就是全人类的目标，尤其是疫情当前，世界各地的友好民众也都应该齐心协力实现这个愿景。

Future historians may well look upon China's fight against the coronavirus as a turning point in worldwide efforts to contain outbreaks of novel diseases and stop their spread, which globalization and ubiquitous air travel has made vital.

未来的历史学家会将今天中国对疫情的斗争视为全球范围内遏制新冠疫情暴发、扩散的重要转折点。全球化和便捷的空中交通也是至关重要的。

History may well thank China for pioneering how to deal with virulent contagions in a globalized world.

历史将会感谢中国在全球化的世界中抗击疫情起到的先锋作用。

（来源：https://mp.weixin.qq.com/s/58pPE1tYE3DwDq6CMCVzNg）

3.8 主题拓展资源

双语文章：《抗击新冠肺炎疫情的中国行动》白皮书（节选）

国务院新闻办公室于2020年6月7日发布《抗击新冠肺炎疫情的中国行动》白皮书。选文如下：

抗击新冠肺炎疫情的中国行动
Fighting Covid-19 China in Action

新型冠状病毒肺炎是近百年来人类遭遇的影响范围最广的全球性大流行病，对全世界是一次严重危机和严峻考验。人类生命安全和健康面临重大威胁。

The Covid-19 global pandemic is the most extensive to afflict humanity in a century. A serious crisis for the entire world, and a daunting challenge, it poses a grave threat to human life and health.

这是一场全人类与病毒的战争。面对前所未知、突如其来、来势汹汹的疫情天灾，中国果断打响疫情防控阻击战。中国把人民生命安全和身体健康放在第一位，以坚定果敢的勇气和决心，采取最全面最严格最彻底的防控措施，有效阻断病毒传播链条。14亿中国人民坚韧奉献、团结协作，构筑起同心战疫的坚固防线，彰显了人民的伟大力量。

This is a war that humanity has to fight and win. Facing this unknown, unexpected, and devastating disease, China launched a resolute battle to prevent and control its spread. Making people's lives and health its first priority, China adopted extensive, stringent, and thorough containment measures, and has for now succeeded in cutting all channels for the transmission of the virus. 1.4 billion Chinese people have exhibited enormous tenacity and solidarity in erecting a defensive rampart that demonstrates their power in the face of such natural disasters.

新冠肺炎疫情是新中国成立以来发生的传播速度最快、感染范围最广、防控难度最大的一次重大突发公共卫生事件，对中国是一次危机，也是一次大考。中国共产党和中国政府高度重视、迅速行动，习近平总书记亲自指挥、亲自部署，统揽全局、果断决策，为中国人民抗击疫情坚定了信心、凝聚了力量、指明了方向。在中国共产党领导下，全国上下贯彻"坚定信心、同舟共济、科学防治、精准施策"总要求，打响抗击疫情的人民战争、总体战、阻击战。经过艰苦卓绝的努力，中国付出巨大代价和牺牲，有力扭转了疫情局势，用一个多月的时间初步遏制了疫情蔓延势头，用两个月左右的时间将本土每日新增病例控制在个位数以内，用3个月左右的时间取得了武汉保卫战、湖北保卫战的决定性成果，疫情防控阻击战取得重大战略成果，维护了人民生命安全和身体健康，为维护地区和世界公共卫生安全作出了重要贡献。

The Covid-19 epidemic is a major public health emergency. The virus has spread faster and wider than any other since the founding of the People's Republic in 1949, and has proven to be the most difficult to contain. It is both a crisis and a major test for China. The Communist Party of China (CPC) and the Chinese government have addressed the epidemic as a top priority, and taken swift action. General Secretary Xi Jinping has taken personal command, planned the response, overseen the general situation and acted decisively, pointing the way forward in the fight against the epidemic. This has bolstered the Chinese people's confidence and rallied their strength. Under the leadership of the CPC, the whole nation has followed the general principle of "remaining confident, coming together in solidarity, adopting a science-based approach, and taking targeted measures", and waged an all-out people's war on the virus. Through painstaking efforts and tremendous sacrifice, and having paid a heavy price, China has succeeded in turning the situation around. In little more than a single month, the rising spread of the virus was contained; in around two months, the daily increase in domestic corona-virus cases had fallen to single digits; and in approximately three months, a decisive victory was secured in the battle to defend Hubei Province and its capital city of Wuhan. With these strategic achievements, China has protected its people's lives, safety and health, and made a significant contribution to safeguarding regional and global public health.

中国始终秉持人类命运共同体理念，肩负大国担当，同其他国家并肩作战、共克时艰。中国本着依法、公开、透明、负责任态度，第一时间向国际社会通报疫情信息，毫无保留同各方分享防控和救治经验。中国对疫情给各国人民带来的苦难感同身受，尽己所能向国际社会提供人道主义援助，支持全球抗击疫情。

Having forged the idea that the world is a global community of shared future, and believing that it must act as a responsible member, China has fought shoulder to shoulder with the rest of the world. In an open, transparent, and responsible manner and in accordance with the law, China gave timely notification to the international community of the onset of a new corona-virus, and shared without reserve its experience in containing the spread of the virus and treating the infected. China has great empathy with victims all over the world, and has done all it can to provide humanitarian aid in support of the international community's endeavors to stem the pandemic.

当前，疫情在全球持续蔓延。中国为被病毒夺去生命和在抗击疫情中牺牲的人们深感痛惜，向争分夺秒抢救生命、遏制疫情的人们深表敬意，向不幸感染病毒、正在进行治疗的人们表达祝愿。中国坚信，国际社会同舟共济、守望相助，就一定能够战胜疫情，走出人类历史上这段艰难时刻，迎来人类发展更加美好的明天。

The virus is currently wreaking havoc throughout the world. China grieves for those who have been killed and those who have sacrificed their lives in the fight, extends the greatest respect to those who are struggling to save lives, and offers true moral support to those who are infected and receiving treatment. China firmly believes that as long as all countries unite and cooperate to mount a collective response, the international community will succeed in overcoming the pandemic, and will emerge from this dark moment in human history into a brighter future.

（来源：https://language.chinadaily.com.cn/a/202006/08/WS5ed de063a310 834817251871.html）

第五单元 成功之路

（Unit 5 Ways to Success）

1. 思政主题：什么是成功？人生路上，如何获得成功？

2. 意义

本单元的主题是成功的途径。每个人对于"成功"有着不同的理解。比尔·盖茨曾在对大学生的建议中提出了受到良好的教育对于走向成功的重要性；超人扮演者 Christopher Reeve 的事迹说明坚定的信念、顽强的意志力和心中的爱是战胜困难、获取成功的关键。在授课过程中，教师可以启发学生围绕"什么是成功"从多个角度，就"如何获取成功"等话题展开思考和讨论。

We cannot travel every path. Success must be won along one line. We must make our business the one life purpose to which every other must be subordinate.

我们不可能把每条路都走一遍。必须执着于一条道路才能获得成功。我们必须有一个终生追求的目标，其他的则从属于这个目标。

I hate a thing done by halves. If it be right, do it boldly. If it be wrong, leave it undone.

我痛恨做事半途而废。如果这件事是对的，就大胆勇敢地去做；如果这件事不对，就不要去做。

The men of history were not perpetually looking into the mirror to make sure of their own size. Absorbed in their work they did it. They did it so well that the wondering world sees them to be great, and labeled them accordingly.

历史长河中的伟人并不是靠终日瞻观镜中的自己来衡量自身的形象的。他们的形象来自对事业全身心的投入与追求。他们是如此的卓越超凡，于是芸芸众生觉得他们很伟大，并因此称他们为伟人。

To live with a high ideal is a successful life. It is not what one does, but what one tries to do, that makes a man strong. "Eternal vigilance," it has been said, "is the price of liberty." With equal truth it may be said, "Unceasing effort is the price of success." If we do not work with our might, others will; and they will outstrip us in the race, and pluck the prize from our grasp.

为崇高的理想而活着是一种成功的生活。使人变强大的，不是这个人做了什么，而是他努力尝试去做什么。有人说过，"恒久的警惕是自由的代价"，那同样也可以说，"不懈的努力是成功的代价。"倘若我们不尽全力工作，别人会尽全力，随后他们将在竞争中超越我们，从我们手中夺取胜利的果实。

Success grows less and less dependent on luck and chance. Self-distrust is the cause of most of our failures. The great and indispensable help to success is character.

成功越来越不依赖于运气和巧合。丧失自信是我们失败的主要原因。性格是取得成功不可或缺的重要助力。

——欧内斯特·海明威

（来源：https://fitjoy.cc/on-achieving-success.html）

青年有着大好机遇，关键是要迈稳步子、夯实根基、久久为功。心浮气躁，朝三暮四，学一门丢一门，干一行弃一行，无论为学还是创业，都是最忌讳的。

With more opportunities, young people should make their steps steady, lay a solid foundation and make unremitting efforts. It is no good for study or running a business if one works intermittently, or chops and changes.

——习近平主席2014年五四青年节在北京大学师生座谈会上的讲话

希望你们保持对知识的渴望，保持对探索的兴趣，培育科学精神。

I hope you will stay hungry for knowledge, keep your interest in scientific exploration and foster your scientific spirit.

——2016年12月28日，习近平主席回信北京市八一学校科普小卫星研制团队学生

希望越来越多的青年人以你们为榜样，到基层和人民中去建功立业，让青春之花绽放在祖国最需要的地方，在实现中国梦的伟大实践中书写别样精彩的人生。

I hope that more young people will follow your steps to establish educational careers at the grassroots level, blossom in the places where you are most needed, and live a splendid life while turning the Chinese dream into reality.

——2014年5月3日，习近平主席给河北保定学院西部支教毕业生群体代表回信

（来源：中国日报双语新闻）

3. 教学设计与思政元素的融入

Passage A

3.1 Warm-up 环节

双语视频：What Is Success?

每个人对成功的理解都不尽相同。究竟什么是成功呢？一些人经常认为成功就是要在地位和金钱方面取得成就。但其实成功有很多方向。看过这个视频，也许你会找到一些新思路：只要我们摒弃社会的固有成见，就可以在很多其他方面获得成功。教师可以在播放视频后，引导学生讨论并说出自己对"成功"的定义。

In our societies, we use the word "success" a lot. And we think we know just what it means: money, status, fame, and power. But take a look at the dictionary, and things start to look, thankfully, a lot more complicated, because success is, in truth, rather more neutral and less valuated than we tend to assume.

It just means doing anything well, expert at something, and that might include a lot of different activities: running 100 meters, for sure, selling your App for a lot of money, but also stranger, less heralded things, like listening a lot very attentively to a child, or being extremely kind to strangers, or filling your mind with interesting ideas and associations, or knowing just when to put an arm around someone when it's too much for him. People who triumph here are also big success stories.

No one can be successful at everything; whatever they tell us, it's almost impossible to succeed with a career and a family, or with popularity and integrity. There are always sacrifices.

It's great to be successful. It's even better to make sure you follow it: your own distinctive and not necessarily always obvious path to the success that can truly fulfill you.

在我们的社会中，我们经常使用"成功"这个词。我们认为我们知道什么是成功：获得金钱、声望、名誉和权利。但字典中的解释让"成功"这个词显得更加令人深思。成功这个词其实比我们一贯认为的更加中性，没那么功利。

成功只意味着在一件事情上做得好，擅长于某件事情，因此你可以在很多方面上获得成功。100米跑得很快算是成功，卖App赚了很多钱也是成功。但还有更奇怪的，不那么明显的成功，比如非常耐心地去聆听孩子的话，或者对陌生人十分友善，又或者脑子里有很多有趣的点子和想法，又或者懂得如何去安慰快崩溃的人，在这些方面有出色表现的人也是成功的。

想要在所有方面都成功是不可能的，不管他们怎么谈论平衡，想要在事业和家庭同时都表现出色是几乎不可能的，直率和受人欢迎也很难兼得，生活中总是有牺牲。

做个成功人士当然很好，但更好的是在你自己独特的领域获得成功。这也许并不是世俗上显而易见的那种成功，而是那种能够真正实现你自我价值的成功。

（来源：https://www.bilibili.com/video/BV1VW411s7un?from=search&seid=15389108882805519747）

3.2 Discussion 环节

英文视频：What's Education for? 教育是为了什么？

比尔·盖茨曾在对大学生的建议中提出，受到良好的教育对于走向成功十分重要，以劝诫大学生要珍惜时光，努力学习。你是否也认为教育对于一个人的成长和成功有助力作用？对于你而言，你想从教育中获得一些什么呢？观看本视频后，请与你的同学们一起讨论吧！

Everyone agrees that education is hugely important. The thing is we're not particularly sure what we want from it. The aim of education should be to prepare us for the challenges of adult life. Yet from this perspective, it's clear that schools fail all but a tiny portion of their students. Whether in highly academic private schools or in deprived government-run ones, trouble-dealing with life's challenges remains very wide spread indeed. Human ingenuity, energy, goodwill, and talent is being lost on an industrial scale.

To get more ambitious about education doesn't necessarily mean spending more money, building more schools, employing more teachers or making exams more difficult. Rather, it should mean focusing more on the real purpose of education. There are two fundamental tasks it should help us with: working and sustaining good relationships. In order to address these needs a future national curriculum might specify that the following subjects be studied. Firstly, capitalism. A conspiracy of silence exists around the economic system we live within. We find it hard to change its bad sides or defend its strengths because we simply don't fully understand how it works. A subject like maths should be geared to teaching its number one utility for 99% of the population: dealing with money. Such classes would demystify the global economy by teaching students the importance of the means of production and how profits are made. The role of cash-flow, HR leadership, marketing, and competition would also be studied.

In a perfect school system you'd also then study a really big second subject: yourself. Young students would be introduced to the idea that we humans are extremely prone to misunderstanding ourselves. They would be taken through the concepts of delusion, defensiveness, projection and denial in everyday life. Individual tutors would be on hand to help students towards personality maps with particular attention paid to their neurosis and fears. Doing this would ensure that students learn a lot about how complex they truly are and what types of people they would be best suited to hang out with.

A crucial unit would be devoted to career self-knowledge. What job are you best suited to? Students would spend three hours a week exploring what they might do with their futures. Then we would study relationships. Being intensely aware of the social and individual cost of every unhappy relationship, an ideal education system would emphasize the acquisition of skills that help people to live better together. There would be units on kindness and forgiveness as well as on anxiety-reduction techniques.

In this educational utopia it wouldn't only be children who would go to school but adults as well. Schooling would be for life. Education wouldn't just be taking place in classrooms. Media and arts would be made to maximize their teaching potential and help to teach people what they actually need to learn.

We're so hung up on the challenges of running a massive education system. We're failing to pinpoint the real source of its problems. These are primarily about money, salaries or discipline. These are only a consequence of a more fundamental problem. Right now and with no-one quite meaning for this to happen, we've simply got the wrong curriculum.

（来源：https://www.bilibili.com/video/BV12a4y1e7RP/?spm_id_from=333.788. recommend_more_video.2）

3.3 Critical thinking 环节

双语视频：Will Smith's Secret to Success

在获取成功的路上，你是如何看待失败的？中国有"失败是成功之母"的谚语，视频中的威尔·史密斯也有话要说。他认为失败是他成功的秘诀，人越多经历失败，越容易获得成功。你同意他的观点吗？请观看本视频后，与同学们一起思考和讨论吧！

You know it's always a little bit frustrating to me when people have a negative relationship with failure. Failure is a massive part of being able to be successful. You have to get comfortable with failure. You have to actually seek failure. Failure is where all of the lessons are.

You know, when you go to the gym and you work out, you're actually seeking failure. You wanna take your muscles to the point where you get to failure because that's where the adaptation is. That's where growth is.

Successful people fail a lot. They fail a whole lot more than they succeed but they extract the lessons from the failure and they use that, the energy and they use the wisdom to come around to the next phase of success. You've gotta take a shot. You have to live at the edge of your capabilities. You gotta live where you're almost certain you're gonna fail. That's the reason for a practice.

Practice is controlled failure. You're getting to your limit. Getting to your limit, getting to your limit... You can't lift that, you can't do that. Until you get to the point that all of a sudden your body makes the adjustment and then you can do it.

Failure actually helps you to recognize the areas where you need to evolve. So, fail early, fail often, fail forward.

当人们对失败持消极态度时，我总是感到有点沮丧。失败是成功的重要组成部分。你必须坦然面对失败。你必须寻求失败。失败是所有经验的所在。

你知道吗？你去健身房锻炼，实际上是在寻求失败。你想把你的肌肉锻炼到你做不到的程度，因为那样你才可以适应。这就是成长所在。

成功人士经常失败。他们失败的次数比他们成功的次数多得多，但是他们从失败中吸取教训，并利用这些教训，他们的精力和智慧，走向成功的下一个阶段。你得试一试。你必须处于你的能力极限。你必须处于几乎肯定会失败的地方。这就是实践的原因。

实践是可控的失败。你将达到你的极限。无数次达到极限。你抬不起来，你做不到。直到你的身体突然做出调整，然后你就能做到了。

失败实际上帮助你认识到自己需要发展的领域。所以，尽早失败，经常失败，并在失败中前进。

（来源：https://www.bilibili.com/video/BV14t411q74y?from=search&seid=2744329506921528128）

3.4 主题拓展资源

英文视频：It's Possible

著名励志演说家 Les Brown 小时候是个孤儿，上学时曾被学校贴上"智力低下"的标签，几乎毁了他的前程。但他没有放弃自己，没有向生活低头。请同学们在学习或生活感到艰难时，听听他的演讲，一定会收获很多启发和正能量！

It's hard. Easy is not an option. It's hard living. Life is hard.

See, it's hard when you are 49 years old and working on a job for 17 years, and they come in and tell you "you're finished" and give you one week's severance pay. And you have to start all over again. It's hard when you are married and raising children and your children are crawling and your husband dies unexpectedly. It's hard handling just the tragedies of life. It's hard when you're working on something and you put everything you have in it and it doesn't work out you lose your money and other people's money. It's hard.

It was rough when I lost my job and I could not find a job. It was humiliating and embarrassing borrowing money and then I couldn't pay the money back when I told them I would. That's rough. How people look at you, how they respond to you, it's very hard. It's humiliating.

Here's what I discovered that happens to you in life that you will go through things and while you're going through them, you can't understand why it's happening to you. But after you go through it you get back and you look at it and you say, "Oh, now I understand why I needed that lesson". Have they ever happened to you? Raise your hand. If they ever happened to you — that I couldn't understand it then but after I got through it, then I saw that was preparing me for bigger and better things. That as you go through the challenges of life and you look at it and embrace whatever comes to you, don't run from it, step toward it. Don't try and duck it like most people do.

See, most people want it easy. See, if you easy come, easy what, easy go. But when you go at what you're going to deal with and you deal with the difficulties of it, when you handle those hard things close at hand making those hard decisions right now that you don't want to make. Learning those things that you don't like to do but you know that in order for you to get where you want to go, this is one of the hoops that you have to flip through.

And I'm saying to you whatever you got to do, do it because if you don't, life is going to whoop you until you surrender. And say it's okay, all right, all right, all right, all right, I cooperate. OK, I'll learn, OK. It had wear me out a long time.

So if it's hard then, do it hard. Now what are you — how do you hang in there doing the hard difficult times, Les? You must have faith. You've got to believe in yourself. You've got to believe in your abilities. You've got to believe in your service, your company, your ideas unquestionably.

You've got to have faith and that faith gives you patience. That it's not going to happen as quickly as you want it to happen. A lot of things are going to happen that will catch you off guard. And so therefore you've got to deal with and handle it as it comes.

And not only that, but that faith and patience drives you into action. You've got to keep moving and keep plugging away.

In the Far East, they have something that's called the Chinese bamboo tree. The Chinese bamboo tree takes five years to grow. And when they go through a process of growing it, they have to water and fertilize the ground where it is every day. And it doesn't break through the ground until the fifth year, okay? But once it breaks through the ground within five weeks, it grows 90 feet tall.

Now the question is does it grow 90 feet tall in five weeks or five years? The answer is obvious: it grows 90 feet tall in five years, because at any time had that person stopped watering and nurturing and fertilizing that dream, that bamboo tree would have died in the ground. And I can see people coming out talking to a guy out there watering and fertilizing the ground that's not showing anything: "Hey what are you doing? You've been out here a long time, man! And the conversation in the neighborhood is: you're growing a Chinese bamboo tree, is that right?"

"Yeah, that's right."

You know, that's how people are going to do to you. So how long you've been working on this? How long have you been working on your dreams and you have nothing to show. This is all you got to show. People are going to do that to you. And some people, ladies and gentlemen, they stop because they don't see instant results.

It doesn't happen quickly, they stop. Oh, no, no, no, you've got to keep on watering your dream and when it began to happen, they stopped laughing. They say, "Look, whoa, look here, it's — look up, hey man, you know, huh I know you could do it. Look, you've got a job here."

See, during those hard times we didn't know how you're going to make payroll, during those times when you failed and things didn't work out they were nowhere to be found. But you know what I discovered? When you are working at your dream, somebody said the harder the battle the sweeter the victory. Always sweet to you. It's good to you.

Why? See, when it's hard and there's a struggle, see what you become in the process is more important than the dream. That's far more important. The kind of person you become, the character that you build, the courage that you develop, the faith that you're manifesting, oh, it's something that you get up in the morning, you look yourself in the mirror, you're different kind of person, you walk with a different kind of spirit.

And people know that you know what life is, that you have embraced life. You know it was hard but you did it hard.

（来源：https://www.bilibili.com/video/BV1AD4y1Q7TU?from=search&seid=9338734625931575492）

Passage B

3.5 Warm-up 环节

英语文章：Five Powerful Ways to Build Unbreakable Self-Discipline

知识经济时代，终身学习已经成为了每个人的必修课[①]。当前世界范围内正在发生一场以学生为中心的高等教育变革。大学教育的目标从向学生传递知识逐渐转向了引导学生自律学习的意识和行为，以实现终身学习的能力。"自律是一个人对自我意识、行为进行规划并执行的过程。"[②] 一个自律的学习者，不需要外因的驱动就能主动去探究自己所需的信息。他们有着内在的学习动机，并能回顾、监测自己的想法和行为，及时反思，并提出更好的学习策略[③]。

"在知识日新月异的今天，高层次人才必须具备自我驱动、持续学习、终生学习的能力，才能持续保持突出的工作能力。高层次人才从事的工作往往具有前沿性和探究性，需要长期、高度专注地主动思考；必须有强大的自我驱动能力作为后盾，才能保证其在工作中能迎难而上，在同困难搏击的过程中完成工作任务。"[④] 然而惰性使然，在你的学习生活中，有没有出现过类似的情况呢？单词书买了一本又一本，却没有一本能背完……说好早睡早起，却总是戒不掉熬夜赖床的坏习惯……总有人野心勃勃地立下目标，却半途而废。要知道，生活中的成功来自你始终如一的努力。正如富兰克林曾经说过："谁能珍惜时间，谁能坚持点滴积累，谁就能成就大业，铸造辉煌。"[⑤] 那么，要想成为一个自律的人，从而获取成功，你首先需要明白下面5个道理。

Your life is up to you

No matter what your goals are in life, there is one great law that you need to obey in order to be successful: No one else is going to climb the ladder of success for you. No one else is responsible for your health, wealth, happiness, or success. From the day you leave your parents' house and start to make your own choices,

---

[①] 联合国教科文组织国际教育发展委员会. 学会生存[M]. 北京：教育科学出版社, 1996:223.
[②] 屈丽娜. 自律性对学生学习的影响分析[J]. 华东理工大学学报（社会科学版）, 2017(2).
[③] 王卫杰, 等. 基于自律学习者培养的PBL教学探索[J]. 黑龙江高教研究, 2020(1).
[④] 刘辉, 等. "双一流"建设下拔尖博士研究生自我驱动能力培养研究[J]. 教育教学论坛, 2020(19).
[⑤] 尹申. 成功有学问[M]. 北京：中国戏剧出版社, 2002.

you are responsible for your life and the choices you make. You choose the job you work in, the person you live with, and how much you exercise every day. Only you can choose how you spend your time, and the decisions you make on a consistent basis will make or break your life.

If you want a better life, you need to make better decisions. You can blame other people for your lack of results or happiness all life long, but it doesn't change anything. Only you can change your life by changing the choices you make. Take responsibility for everything in your life, even if you can't directly influence it. Even if it's not in your direct control, you can always choose how you respond.

The biggest enemy to success

According to motivational speaker Brian Tracy, the biggest enemy to success is the path of least resistance. If you choose what is fun and easy over what is necessary, you will never reach the levels of success and happiness you are capable of achieving in your life. That's because every great victory requires great sacrifice. If success was easy, everybody would be successful. But because success in any area of your life requires hard work and sacrifices, most people will never reach their full potential.

Whenever you decide not to do what you should be doing, you not only waste your opportunity to grow as a person, but you also lose confidence in yourself. You start to see yourself as lazy and unsuccessful, and that self-image will become a successful prophecy.

To achieve any goal you have, there are only three things you need: A clear vision for what it is you want, a plan to get there, and massive action consistently repeated over time! While the first two parts are the easy parts of the equation, most people struggle with the last part: Hard work.

There is nothing that you can't achieve with hard work, so it is necessary that you build the habit of choosing what is hard and necessary over what is fun and easy to do. Doing this is probably the surest way to succeed in life.

Create your future

To quote Abraham Lincoln, "The best way to predict the future is to create it." If you ever wonder where you will be 10 years from now, look at your current life. What actions are you taking to make your goals reality? How many books are you reading to grow as a person, and how many new things are you learning? Which people are you associating with? Are you putting in the effort necessary to achieve your goals today?

People often think that their lives will suddenly change through some magical event in the future, but that is not the case. Your life changes only to the extent that you change. If you are not happy with your current circumstances, are you taking actions to change them? If not, you are just daydreaming. Nothing will ever change if you don't change what you do daily. As Aristotle noted over 2,000 years ago, "We are what we repeatedly do. Excellence then, is not an act, but a habit."

A great way to actively create your future is to ask yourself: If I have already achieved my goals, how would I act on a daily basis? What books would I read, how often would I work out, and how would I spend my time at the office?

Once you answer these questions, you know what to do.

Failure is part of success

In life, nothing worth having comes easy. You have to make sacrifices in the form of time, effort, pain, and hard work if you want to succeed. There will be many setbacks, and any time you get close to finally succeeding, there will be some more adversity testing how bad you really want it. Only after passing one more test, and then another, will you be able to succeed.

The great tragedy of life is that most people give up right before achieving success. They already made it to the five-yard line, and all they need is one final push to make the touchdown and bring home the sweet victory. But right before they do that, there is one final obstacle standing in their way — one last failure that they need to overcome. Way too many people give up right then and there, without realizing how close they are.

If you just take one thing from this post, let it be this: Whenever you encounter failure and adversity, keep going! Success is supposed to be hard because that's what makes it so special. If it was easy, anybody could do it.

The only way to grow as a person is by facing the biggest challenges in life and enduring long enough to succeed. No matter how long it takes or how hard it gets, always remember the words of motivational speaker Les Brown: "It's not over until I win!"

Never give up

To make sure that you stay strong in the face of adversity, make sure to resolve in advance how you will respond once it occurs. You need to have a plan for what to do when all hell breaks loose, or else it is too easy to just give up. When writing your goals, commit to making them come true, no matter how hard it may be. Determine how you will respond to failures and setbacks so you can bounce back stronger and better than ever before.

If you make this commitment and never break it, you will succeed at anything you set your mind to. Maybe not immediately, but definitely.

（来源：https://language.chinadaily.com.cn/a/202111/03/WS6181d105a310cdd39bc72eb3.html）

3.6 Discussion 环节

英语文章：Following His Own Path, Blind Chinese Viola Player Will Attend Top UK College

这是一个先天性失明的18岁中国盲人男孩克服重重困难，通过顽强的拼搏，最终考取了英国伯明翰皇家艺术学院中提琴专业的励志故事。教师可在学生阅读完本文后，引导学生思考和讨论：Why did the boy succeed? What can we learn from him?

"Although I can't see the world, I will let the world see my hard work," said Wang Zi'an. Blind since birth, the 18-year-old from Guangdong Province was told he could only be a masseur, but chose instead to play the viola. His persistence has paid off as he was recently accepted to one of the most prestigious music colleges in the UK.

This autumn, Wang Zian will start his music education at the Royal Birmingham Conservatoire. Now he is studying English and learning personal skills to help look after himself, including how to cook.

The expectations have never been high for him, especially from his teachers. When he was 10 years old, the teachers in his school told the group of blind students that being a "blind masseur is your only career option for your future." Defying this advice, Wang decided to bet on himself and focused on music instead.

Wang started playing instruments when he was just five, progressing from a keyboard to the piano and then to the viola. His parents always encouraged him, telling him that "you have the right to choose what you want to do and there is nothing can stop you to do."

With the 88 black and white keys etched in his mind, Wang says he feels happiest when he's playing the piano.

While learning, whenever he came across a difficult song, his teacher would tape his hand to the keyboard. Sometimes his fingers bled, and he would cry, but never give up.

Though Wang did learn the skills of a masseur, he hated hearing the repeated message from his instructors: "Massage is your only way out in your future."

In the atmosphere his parents created for him, Wang led a normal life. He fought with other children and took the subway, watched movies and went to the park, all of which helped drive his musical ambitions.

At the age of 13, Wang caught the attention of a viola teacher. When the teacher asked Wang what music meant to him, his answer was an emphatic, "my whole life!"

Under the teacher's advice and training, Wang started his viola education. His poor vision actually made him more sensitive to the string instrument. Wang recorded each class so he could go back and listen to his progress.

According to the Guangzhou-based news website Dayoo.com, more than 200 students from China applied for the Royal Birmingham Conservatoire last year, with only about a dozen accepted, including Wang.

Wang hopes his experiences could inspire others to believe in themselves, rather than listening to others in deciding what to do with their lives.

（来源：https://news.cgtn.com/news/776b544f35677a6333566d54/index.html）

3.7 Critical thinking 环节

双语视频：The Perfectionism Trap 完美主义陷阱

相信一些人有过这样的经历：你给自己定了个完美的目标，坚持一段时间后觉得达不到自己的期待或期望，随之而来的失败感、挫败感、无力感，让你屡屡产生放弃的念头。其实这是完美主义的表现。我们往往会忽略一件事：完美主义很有可能会让你裹足不前。坦然地去接受自己的不完美，之后轻松地去工作，持续地去努力，才是获取成功的重要方法。看过视频后请大家思考：Do you have perfectionist tendencies? Do you want to get rid of it?

We typically aim for a particular career because we have been deeply impressed by the exploits of the most accomplished practitioners in the field. We formulate our ambitions by admiring the beautiful structures of the architect tasked with designing the city's new airport, or by following the intrepid trades of the wealthiest Wall Street fund manager, by reading the analyses of the acclaimed literary novelist or sampling the piquant meals in the restaurant of a prize-winning chef.

We form our career plans on the basis of perfection. Then, inspired by the masters, we take our own first steps and the trouble begins. What we have managed to design, or make in our first month of trading, or write in an early short story, or cook for the family, is markedly and absurdly, beneath the standard that first sparked our ambitions.

We who are so aware of excellence end up the least able to tolerate mediocrity, which in this case, happens to be our own. We become stuck in an uncomfortable paradox; our ambitions have been ignited by greatness, but everything we know of ourselves points to congenital ineptitude.

We have fallen into what we can term "the Perfectionism Trap", defined as a powerful attraction to perfection shorn of any mature or sufficient understanding of what is actually required to attain it. It isn't primarily our fault.

Without in any way revealing this, or even perhaps being aware of it, our media edits out billions of unremarkable lives and years of failure, rejection and frustration even in those who do achieve, in order to serve us up a daily curated selection of peak career moments, which thereby end up seeming not like the violent exceptions they actually are, but like a normal baseline of achievement.

It starts to appear as though "everyone" is successful because all those who we happen to hear about really are successes — and we have forgotten to imagine the oceans of tears and despair that necessarily surround them.

Our perspective is imbalanced because we know our own struggles so well from the inside, and yet are exposed to apparently pain-free narratives of achievement on the outside. We cannot forgive ourselves the horrors of our early drafts — largely because we have not seen the early drafts of those we admire.

We need a saner picture of how many difficulties lie behind everything we would wish to emulate. We should not look, for example, at the masterpieces of art in a museum. We should go to the studio and there see the anguish, wrecked early versions and watermarks on the paper where the artist broke down and wept. We should focus on how long it took the architect before they received their first proper commission (they were over 50), we need to dig out the early stories of the writer who now wins prizes and examine more closely how many failures the entrepreneur had to endure.

We need to recognize the legitimate and necessary role of failure, allow ourselves to do things quite imperfectly for a very long time — as a price we cannot avoid paying for an opportunity one day, perhaps in many decades, to do something that others will consider a spontaneous success.

我们之所以想从事特定职业是因为受到成功的鼓舞。我们的理想，源自欣赏设计出美丽的建筑，负责新机场建造的建筑师，或是追随华尔街最富有的财务经理，完成一笔笔了不起的交易，又或是阅读畅销作家的分析报告，或者求教于获奖无数的名厨，得到美味佳肴的配方。

我们以完美为积木，建造出理想的职业城堡。受到大师启发，我们踏出第一步，开始一段荆棘之路。我们渴望的设计蓝图、第一个月的成交数、撰写短篇故事草稿，或是为家人煮顿饭，门槛可说是既明显又荒谬地低于初衷。

我们患得患失，其实最后只是折磨看似平庸的自己。这情形每天都在你我生活中上演。我们陷入不自在的矛盾中；伟大点燃野心的熊熊大火，但我们明知自己资质驽钝。

我们落入了"完美主义陷阱"——这是一种对完美主义强烈的追求，但同时又缺乏了对于达到目标所需要的完整或充分的认知。但这不全是我们的错。

在未深陷完美主义陷阱或是自己还未察觉时，媒体报道已删剪了太多成功者不为人知的背后辛酸与无数次失败，遭受拒绝与沮丧之情的媒体只是报道成功人士在职业高峰期的每日计划，最终看起来不像是血泪奋斗史，而像是关于成就的常见心路历程。

一开始塑造人人皆可成功，因为我们平常听到的例子就是如此，而我们忘了去思考成功者背后的泪水与挥之不去的绝望。

我们的认知过于偏颇，因为虽然自己了解内心的苦闷，却又同时被外界宣扬的"成功，毫不费力"的糖衣所影响。我们无法谅解自己早期工作遇到的波折，原因在于没有看到仰慕者过去辛勤付出的足迹。

我们需要一张更加理智的画面，记录下自己努力走过的路。举个例子，我们该欣赏的不是博物馆里的杰作；而是去参观艺术大师的工作室里，那些在早期充满愤怒、弄得残破不堪的初稿与纸上留下来的水印，都是艺术家经历崩溃与痛哭后的写照。我们应该着重在建筑师花多少时间才谈成了第一笔生意（大多都超过50岁了）。我们应该试着挖掘那些得奖的畅销作家早期作品、研究创业者遭遇过多少次失败。

我们必须正视"失败"的存在与其存在的必要，包容自己有一段不完美的人生阶段。"台上一分钟，台下十年功"，或许数十年后，回首过往，大家才会看到我们的"必须非常努力，才会看起来毫不费力"。

（来源：https://www.bilibili.com/video/BV18s411M73r/?spm_id_from=333.788.recommend_more_video.2）

3.8 主题拓展资源

双语文章：Good Mistakes 有益的错误

有句话说："如果你没犯错误，说明你没有尽力。"所以，勇往直前，去犯错误吧。然后学习、成长，直到最后取得成功。

It's good to make mistake, and here is why.

First of all, mistakes are a clear sign that you are trying new things. It's always good to try new things because when you are trying new things you are growing. If you never try anything new, how can you improve? How can you expand? How can you innovate? The simple answer is "You can't". Look around you. With very few exceptions, either everything you see in your physical world or every single detail of every single thing is the result of someone trying something new.

Another good thing about mistakes is this: when you are making mistakes, you are learning. Consider this: Edison failed 10000 times before he perfected the light bulb. when asked how it felt to fail that many times, he remarked that he hadn't failed 10000 times, but rather had learned 10000 things that didn't work.

Finally, when you make a mistake you are much closer to success. Why?

Because when all is said and done, you will have tried some finite number of things before you succeeded, Every time you made a mistake you eliminated one of those things and are one step closer.

But this all doesn't mean that you should forget ahead with disregard for the consequences of a mistake. Quite the contrary, when you try something new you have to be willing to set some reasonable limits so that in the event that it doesn't work out the way you want it to, you will be in a position to try again.

We all have limited resources in the form of time and money so don't blow them all on one approach to a problem. Realize that it probably won't be perfect the first time and allocate these resources appropriately so you can learn, modify, and try it again. Only by embracing and using your mistakes in this way can you make significant advances in your business and your career.

There is an old axiom that goes, "If you're not making mistakes, you're not trying hard enough."

So go forth and make mistakes. And learn. And grow. And prosper.

犯错是大有裨益的，原因有以下几点：

首先，错误清楚地表明你正在尝试新鲜事物。尝试新事物总是好的，因为你会在这一过程中不断成长。如果从不尝试任何新鲜事物，你怎么能进步？如何能发展？又何以创新？答案很简单："你不能。"看看周遭，几乎无一例外，你在客观世界看到的每一件事，或是每一件事的每一个细节都是有人在尝试事物的结果。

犯错的另一个好处是：犯错的过程也正是你学习的过程。想想看，爱迪生在改进电灯泡前失败了一万次。当被问到失败那么多次，感觉如何时，爱迪生说自己并没有失败一万次，而是获知了一万个并不奏效的事物。

最后一点，犯错之前正是你更为接近成功之日。这是为什么呢？

因为在成功前，当该说的说了，该做的做了，你所要进行的尝试是有限的。每犯一次错误，那些所要做的尝试就会减少一个，从而你离成功也就更近一步。

所有这些并不意味着你就该一个劲地往前冲，而不用考虑每一个错误的后果。恰恰相反，在尝试新事物时，你得主动设定一些合理的限度，以便当事态不尽如人意时，你能够再试一次。

在时间和金钱方面，我们的资源都是有限的，所以不要在一棵树上吊死，不要把所有的时间和金钱都投入到一个问题的解决途径上。要明白，第一次可能不会尽善尽美，要合理分配这些资源，这样你就能够学习、改进，并再次尝试。只有以这种方式欣然接受并利用你的错误，你才能在业务和事业上取得重大进步。

有句话说："如果你没犯错误，就说明你没有尽力。"

所以，勇往直前，去犯错误吧。然后学习、成长，最后成功。

（来源：http://kekenet.com/Article/200912/91308.shtml）

第六单元　体育与健康

（Unit 6 Sports and Health）

1. 思政主题：无所畏惧，顽强拼搏的运动精神

2. 意义

本单元聚焦"运动精神"相关话题的学习探讨。教师可以从女排精神，奥运赛场上我国体育健儿们的拼搏精神入手，选取与主题相关的思政素材，鼓励

学生向运动健儿们学习，在人生的赛场上全力以赴的拼搏奋斗，最终突破自我，创造奇迹。

3. 学习设计与思政元素的融入

Passage A

3.1 Warm-up 环节

电影《夺冠》：人生不是一定会赢，而是要努力去赢

电影《夺冠》(原名《中国女排》)讲述中国女排从1981年首夺世界冠军到2016年里约奥运会"中巴大战"的历程，诠释了几代女排人历经浮沉却始终不屈不挠、不断拼搏的传奇经历。文章通过解析电影英文名称 *Leap* 一词的内涵，带领学生感受中国女排的力量与精神，帮助学生正确认识体育精神，树立正确的世界观、人生观和价值观，实现课程思政育人。

《夺冠》(原名《中国女排》)提档国庆，上映13天，票房破5亿元，热议不断：有人赞它叙事精彩，感染力强，令人心神激荡；有人斥它删减更名，流于表面，缺乏深层次的挖掘和捕捉……"一千个观众眼中有一千个哈姆雷特"，视角与喜好不一，自然众说纷纭。

电影虽然更名，但从未失却它的精神内核，从它一直未变的英文名称——*Leap* 即可看出。

1) Leap：中国女排飞跃扣球的飒爽英姿

Leap 一词既可为动词，也可为名词。在《朗文当代高阶英语辞典》中，当 leap 为动词时，其基本意思为 to jump high into the air or to jump in order to land in a different place，即"跳，跳跃"。

eg. She leapt over the fence. 她跳过篱笆。

还有一层意思为 to move very quickly and with a lot of energy，即"猛冲"。

eg. I leapt up the stairs three at a time. 我一步三级地冲上楼。

《夺冠》选用"Leap"一词作为电影英文名称，精准传神地刻画出女排运动员飞跃扣球、坚毅拼搏的飒爽英姿。

2) Leap：中国女排的巨大飞跃

当 leap 为名词时，有 a big jump "跳跃"和 a large increase or change "剧增，激增；剧变"等意思。

eg. ① He threw a stick into the river and the dog went after it in a flying leap. 他把一根枝条扔到河里，那条狗一个飞跃追了过去。

② the huge leap forward that took place in 1980s 发生在20世纪80年代的巨大飞跃

"跳跃"与"剧变"恰好契合了中国女排30余年跌宕起伏的发展脉络。

中国女排并非一帆风顺，一直闪耀在光里。沉寂的七八十年代，她们在临时搭建的竹棚馆里反复训练、突破极限，再苦再累也从不停歇，才拼出了后来的"五连冠"；挫败的2013年，她们坚毅隐忍、奋力拼搏，终于在2016年的里约奥运会逆风翻盘。Leap一词简洁有力地将中国女排坚毅、果敢、隐忍、拼搏的力量浓缩其中，肯定了中国女排一次次在赛事中夺冠，取得飞跃进步的伟大意义。

有人问郎平："女排精神是什么？"

郎平说："女排精神不是赢得冠军，而是有时候知道不会赢，也竭尽全力。是你一路虽走得摇摇晃晃，但站起来抖抖身上的尘土，依旧眼中坚定。人生不是一定会赢，而是要努力去赢。"

时代在变，教练在变，队员在变，对手在变。但女排精神历经岁月洗礼，历久弥坚。这是一代又一代女排人用鲜血和汗水浇灌出的硕果。正如片中所说："中国女排，不是你，不是我，而是我们。"

（来源：外研社高等英语资讯）

英语文章：Teenage Divers Win Gold

"00后"奥运小将展现的是当代中国年轻人的新风貌，赛场上他们坚毅果敢、敢拼敢干，赛场下他们热爱生活、自信满满，这是专属于年轻人的精气神！中国"00后"运动员用自信乐观、敢于拼搏的姿态，让世界看到了中国更加昂扬的年轻一代。

Teenage diving phenoms Chen Yuxi and Zhang Jiaqi summoned the courage of youth to win a diving gold on Tuesday and keep Team China in the hunt to top the medal table at the Tokyo 2020 Olympic Games.

Chen and Zhang executed five near flawless dives to capture the women's synchronized 10-meter platform competition on Tuesday.

The result was widely anticipated despite the duo's relative lack of experience in competition at the international level; Chen is 15 and Zhang 17.

Zhang sees their youth as an advantage. "We are short and light, and this means that our entry (to the water) is better than the others. Our weakness is we are inexperienced," she said, adding that they had learned from the experiences of previous generations of Chinese divers.

Chen said she felt pressure because of the pair's age and lack of experience, but, she added, "We have nothing to lose, and we are brave enough to face any challenges".

The teenage duo finished with 363.78 points, well ahead of silver medalists Jessica Parratto and Delaney Schnell of the US with 310.80 points. Team Mexico won the bronze with 299.70 points.

On the shooting range, student athlete Yang Qian won her second gold medal at the Tokyo Olympics together with Yang Haoran in the 10-meter air rifle mixed event.

Pang Wei and Jiang Ranxin won gold in the 10m air pistol mixed competition after showing true team spirit.

Both the gold medals are the first China has won in the two events at an Olympics. Yang Qian became the first shooter representing Team China to claim multiple gold Olympic medals after winning the women's individual 10m air rifle on Saturday.

"I am very happy. It is special to win an event like this," Yang Qian said, adding that "I thank my country for helping me and giving me all the support."

Yang Haoran admitted the pair were a bit nervous at first. "In the beginning we weren't doing so well, but we kept trying and at the end we were doing great," he said.

Kuo Hsing-chun of Chinese Taipei won the women's weightlifting 59-kilogram gold medal with a total lift of 236kg, bringing the first gold to Chinese Taipei on Tuesday.

（来源：中国日报双语新闻）

3.2 Discussion 环节

双语视频：电影片段《卡特教练》——你们和冠军没有什么不同，因为你们做到超越自己了！

视频节选自电影《卡特教练》，虽然球队在比赛中失利，但他们坚持不放弃的精神比胜利更值得赞扬。视频时长3分30秒，教师可在授课时请学生观看，思考并讨论电影片段中所传达的核心思想，从而加深对课文主题的理解。

Our deepest fear is not that we are inadequate.

我们最大的恐惧并不是因为我们不够好。

Our deepest fear is that we are powerful beyond measure.

我们最大的恐惧是我们自己超乎想象的能力。

It is our light, not our darkness that most frightens us.

我们害怕的不是黑暗的那一面而是我们的光明的一面。

Your playing small does not serve the world.

畏缩的态度不能改变世界。

There is nothing enlightened about shrinking,

隐藏自己内心的潜能,

so that other people won't feel insecure around you.

并不会让你身边的人觉得更有安全感。

We are all meant to shine, as children do.

我们都应该发挥自己内心的潜能,就像小孩子那样。

It is not just in some of us; it is in everyone.

每个人都一样。

And as we let our own light shine,

当我们让自己发光时,

we unconsciously, give other people permission to do the same.

我们不自觉地影响到身边的人,让她们也能这么做。

As we are liberated from our own fear,

我们不但摆脱了自己的恐惧,

our presence automatically liberates others.

我们的存在也自然地解放了别人。

(来源:https://www.bilibili.com/video/BV1PE411w7Cj?from=search&seid=791 3484165078905330)

3.3 Critical Thinking 环节

英文视频:科比励志演讲,曼巴精神永不息!

视频盘点了科比·布莱恩特10条经典语录,从中可以窥见曼巴精神的实质内涵和科比的职业信条。视频时长7分钟,教师可以安排学生观看,深刻感受体育竞技精神,同时思考:What values do you think people can cultivate by playing sports?

(来源:https://www.bilibili.com/video/BV1W7411H7Lg/?spm_id_from=333.788.videocard.0)

3.4 主题拓展资源

英文视频：科比曼巴精神系列纪录片

从不退却，从不放弃，从不逃遁，在困难中创造奇迹，这就是曼巴精神。教师可将该系列纪录片提供给学生观看，让学生通过观看科比事迹充分了解并体会运动精神。

（来源：https://space.bilibili.com/285680112/channel/detail?cid=55919）

双语文章：残奥会故事：为什么一个项目会产生多枚金牌？

从第二次世界大战的伤兵到全球第三大体育赛事，残奥会激发了一场全球运动，不断改变着世界对残障、多样性和人类潜能的看法。教师可推荐学生课后观看，感受体育竞技精神对人的激励作用，深入理解文章主题。

1948年7月29日，因第二次世界大战终止的奥运会在伦敦恢复举办，同日在英国中南部的一家医院里，也举办了一场运动会，参赛的是16名脊髓受伤的"二战"老兵。

当所有人都认为他们只能躺在床上时，举办这场运动会的神经学教授、"残奥会之父"路德维希·古特曼（Ludwig Guttmann）却坚持将体育运动引入残疾治疗，这便是现代残疾人体育运动的雏形。

On 29 July 1948, the day of the Opening Ceremony of the London 1948 Olympic Games, Dr. Guttmann organized the first competition for wheelchair athletes, a milestone in Paralympic history. They involved 16 injured servicemen and women who took part in archery.

1960年，来自23个国家的400多名运动员在罗马举行了第一届残奥会，之后残奥会每隔四年举办一届，和奥运会同年举行。

It later became the Paralympic Games which first took place in Rome, Italy, in 1960 featuring 400 athletes from 23 countries. Since then they have taken place every four years.

自2004年雅典残奥会以来，中国代表团在每届残奥会上都占据金牌榜榜首位置。中国代表团在雅典残奥会摘得63金、北京残奥会89金、伦敦残奥会95金、里约残奥会107金，中国代表团在残奥会上的表现是当之无愧的王者！

China have been the country with most gold medals at each Paralympic Games since Athens 2004. They won 63 in the Greek capital city, followed by 89 at Beijing 2008, 95 at London 2012 and 107 at Rio 2016.

为保证比赛的公平性，赛前会对参赛选手的残疾情况和运动能力进行评估,并根据具体项目的要求将残疾程度或运动能力相近的选手分在一组进行比赛,这一过程称为"分级"。

一个项目会分出多个竞赛组别,这就是为什么残奥会上一个项目会产生多枚金牌。

Classification determines which athletes are eligible to compete in a sport and how athletes are grouped together for competition. In Para sports, athletes are grouped by the degree of activity limitation resulting from the impairment.

以田径项目为例,项目分级由前缀字母 T 或 F+ 数字的形式组成,前缀 T 代表"径赛"(Track)和跳跃项目,F 代表"田赛"(Field)。径赛运动级别以英文字母 T 加一个双位数字表示,十位数值代表残疾类型(impairment types),个位数值代表残疾程度,数值越低表示残疾情况越严重。

Athletes are assessed and then placed into competition categories, called sport classes, according to how much their impairment affects sports performance. The numerical figure in Para athletics classification represents the level of impairment; the lower the number within each impairment type, the more severe the impairment.

在田径项目中,盲人运动员会由引跑员用弹性绳带引领着在跑道上飞驰,引跑员就是他们的眼睛,为他们保驾护航。

Track events involve athletes with a wide range of impairments, including physical, intellectual, or vision impairment. In the sports class for vision impairments, athletes are allowed to compete with their guide-runners. The teamwork between the athletes and their guides is an important element of the race.

在游泳项目中,选手通常从跳台入水,无法起跳入水的运动员可以提前进行入水准备。仰泳等从水中出发的比赛,运动员在预备阶段应握住握手器,身体不便的运动员可以借助皮带、用嘴叼住绳子或毛巾等辅助手段。每位视障运动员会配有一位助手,在靠近转向点或终点时用提示棒敲打运动员的头部或身体进行提醒。

Swimmers can use different starting methods according to their impairment. Athletes with vision impairment may locate themselves in the pool by touching the lane rope with their body. For these athletes, a person known as a "tapper" may tap them to let them know that they are approaching the turn(s) or finish of the race.

匈牙利运动员帕尔·塞克斯是至今为止唯一一名包揽了奥运和残奥奖牌的选手。他曾在1988年汉城(现首尔)奥运会获得击剑铜牌,1991年遭遇车祸之后,他转而成为一名残奥选手,并在1992年巴塞罗那残奥会获得轮椅击剑金牌。

Hungarian Pal Szekeres became the first and so far only athletes to win Olympic and Paralympic medals after taking wheelchair fencing gold at Barcelona 1992. He had won bronze at the Seoul 1988 Olympics as a professional fencer before suffering a bus accident in 1991.

霍金曾在伦敦残奥会的致辞中说到:"残奥会意在改变我们对世界的观念,我们都与众不同,世界上本没有标准或普通人,但我们拥有同样的人类精神。"

"The Paralympic Games are all about transforming our perception of the world. We are all different. There is no such thing as a standard or run of the mill human being. But we share the same human spirit."

（来源：中国日报双语新闻）

英文文章：社评：东京奥运闭幕，中国收获成熟与自信 China Embraces Sporting Spirit

中国代表团不仅交出了一份亮眼的成绩单,而且彰显了和成绩一样令人可喜的奥林匹克精神和中华体育精神,以优良表现践行了"更快、更高、更强、更团结"的奥林匹克格言,展示出大国大团、文明之师的良好形象,并体现出中国青年一代使命在肩、奋斗有我的精神风貌。

The Tokyo Olympics concluded on Sunday. The sports event has undoubtedly offered the world a stage on which to come together, after being divided for so long for various reasons.

As the COVID-19 pandemic is still raging around the world, credit goes to the International Olympic Committee, Japan, and all the organizers and participants for ensuring the Games went ahead. They have left us with countless unforgettable memories, breathed new life into the Olympic spirit, and enabled us to appreciate the charms of sportsmanship and the beauty of humanity.

Since the country won its first gold medal in the Los Angeles Olympic Games in 1984, the Chinese people have long regarded the Games as a marker for the country's development.

However, since then, the Chinese people's attitude toward the Olympics has also changed, and this was particularly evident during the Tokyo Olympics. While Chinese people still see the Olympics as an arena for competition, and Chinese athletes' winning performances as bringing honor to the country, they have also demonstrably enjoyed the events for the sporting contests they are.

So it has been common for the Chinese audiences to wholeheartedly applaud strong performances by athletes wherever they are from, and feel sorry for those who fall short of success, send their best wishes for a quick recovery to those injured during an event, and to be moved by any kindness and encouragement the athletes may have shown one another.

That change partly stems from the improvement in China's national strength and image, as Chinese people are more confident about the country's place in the world, and no longer view the Games from the previous perspective.

Their support for Chinese athletes has gone beyond seeing them solely as fighters for the glory of the nation, but also as athletes chasing their own dreams, whether that be winning a medal or achieving a personal best. That explains why some athletes have won broad support and the hearts of the nation even though they have not won medals.

It is also good to see some athletes, particularly those of the younger generation, regard the Games as more than just a stage on which to struggle for national pride, but also as one on which they can display their own professionalism and commitment, and at times personal charms.

Aug 8 is now earmarked as National Fitness Day, which is part of the country's efforts to improve people's health and well-being. The country's economic rise has laid a solid foundation on which to carry out its national fitness program and that will greatly enlarge the talent pool for the national teams. And the application of advanced technologies, new materials and rational training methods will make the training of young athletes easier and more rewarding.

As the boundary between winners and losers in the Games blurs, the Olympics is achieving larger-than-life effects in the world's most populous country. It is to be hoped that the Beijing Winter Olympics next year can serve to unite the world again, and see the nation again embracing the Olympic spirit.

（来源：https://mp.weixin.qq.com/s/YLGmf8aGpaeuS6IQhV0lIQ）

Passage B

3.5 Warm-up 环节

双语视频：电影《阿甘正传》经典片段

视频为电影《阿甘正传》的经典片段之一，阿甘向一位老人讲述了自己3年2个月14天16小时的跑步经历以及这一经历中发生的种种事情。时长7分钟，教师可在面授课时安排学生观看，请学生思考并讨论支撑阿甘坚持跑步的信念是什么，他这一行动又对他人产生了什么样的积极影响。

（来源：https://www.bilibili.com/video/BV1xW41197Hs?from=search&seid=13811682524011634107）

3.6 Discussion 环节

英文视频：Most Beautiful and Respect Moments in Sports

视频盘点了体育运动中最"美"的几个时刻，教师可以通过播放此视频，让学生总结竞技体育"美"在何处，明晰正确的竞技观念。

（来源：https://www.bilibili.com/video/av60109893/）

6.7 Critical thinking 环节

英文文章：How to Show Good Sportsmanship

文章从对手、队友和运动本身三方面介绍了如何展现良好的运动精神。教师可参考文章观点备课，或安排学生课前阅读，增加对团队运动精神的理解。

Being a respected athlete isn't just about having the most talent or the best skills. It's also about being a good sport and treating teammates, coaches, opponents, and game officials with respect. Showing good sportsmanship may seem difficult at times, but if you just remember to put your team first, you'll be on the right track.

Method One: Interacting with Opponents

1.Don't trash talk. When your competitive juices start flowing, it may be tempting to call members of the other team names or make fun of them. But you can't win a game by running your mouth, and it only makes you look desperate. Focus on outperforming your opponent on the field or court, not on landing a good insult.

2.Control your temper. In the heat of a game, it can be easy to lose your cool, particularly if you've just gotten elbowed or the other team keeps scoring on you. Don't let your anger affect your behavior, though. Sports are supposed to be fun, so don't lose sight of the big picture just because things are going your way.

Retaliating against another player if they've hit, pushed, elbowed, or otherwise tried to injury you is never a good idea. You'll only wind up penalizing your own team.

Avoid any violent confrontations with other players. If someone threatens you or you're worried a situation is going to escalate, talk to the officials or a coach.

3.Respect the other team's effort. Whether they're outplaying you or unable to keep up with your team, it's important to recognize that they've put in plenty of hard work to prepare for the game, just like your team has. Having respect for the other team is crucial to good sportsmanship.

You may actually be able to learn something from your opponent, so keep an open mind. If they're playing better than you are, you may be able to pick up some pointers for the next game.

4.Be gracious in victory and defeat. When you win a big game, it's easy to get carried away in your celebration. However, if you're a good sport, you don't gloat over a victory or try to make your opponents feel bad about their performance. Conversely, if you lose, you shouldn't pout or downplay the other team's victory.

Whether you win or lose, get in the habit of congratulating the other team. It shows that you value the game itself and the effort that goes into it just as much as an actual victory.

Method Two: Relating to Teammates

1.Listen to your coach. He or she is looking out for the good of the team, and sometimes, that means your role may be reduced or changed. Showing good sportsmanship means placing the team's needs above your own, so you should trust the coach's judgement.

If you disagree with a decision that the coach has made, have a polite discussion with him or her. Don't start an argument or sulk over it.

If the coach decides that someone else should start in your place, it's normal to get upset. However, you must realize that it's for the good of the team, and channel your frustration into working hard at practices so you're ready to go for the next game.It's often little things that show you're a team player, such as always arriving at practice on time or helping to clean up afterward.

Because the behavior of every team member reflects on the team, you shouldn't accept unsportsmanlike conduct from your teammates. Firmly but politely remind them that their behavior affects the entire team.

2.Support your teammates. Being a good sport means that you're just as happy with their success as your own. Cheer on your teammates when they're performing well, and offer encouragement to teammates who may have made a mistake or are in a slump.

Be willing to share your knowledge of the game with your teammates. If there is someone who is struggling with a particular part of the game that you excel at, offer some tips and suggestions to help him or her improve.

You should be receptive when teammates point out ways in which you can improve your skills too. Not everyone is good at the same aspects of a game, and you should take advantage of your teammates' expertise to improve your skills.

Method Three: Playing the Game with Good Sportsmanship

1. Familiarize yourself with the sport. Whether you're playing for a school team, in a league, or just with your friends, you can't be a good sport if you don't understand the game that you're playing. You should learn not only what it takes to be successful in that particular sport, but what you're allowed to do and what you'll be penalized for.

You can find the rules and guidelines for most sports by doing a basic online search.

If you're new to sport, you may want to purchase a guidebook that provides all the rules and regulations, as well as tips on how to successfully play the game.

Don't be afraid to ask questions. Friends, family members, teammates, and coaches who are familiar with the game can help you understand it better because they have firsthand experience with the sport.

In addition to following the rules, it's important to respect the sport. You shouldn't show off obnoxiously when you're successful because that puts yourself ahead of the game.

2.Play fair. Once you understand the rules and regulations of the sport, it's important to always abide by them. That means that you shouldn't look for ways to cheat or bend the rules to give yourself a competitive edge. You'll find that winning doesn't mean as much if you have to play dirty to do it.

3.Respect the officials. Sometimes, it can be difficult not to take it personally when a referee, umpire, linesman, and other official makes a call that goes against you during a game. However, it's important to remind yourself that they are there to ensure that the game is played properly, so it's their job to enforce the rules.

In some cases, an official will make an error, and their call may be wrong. Avoid arguing over a missed or incorrect call, and understand that everyone makes mistakes.

If you're concerned with the calls that an official is making, bring it to your coaches' attention. They'll know the best way to address the situation, which may include lodging a formal complaint.

（来源：https://www.wikihow.com/Show-Good-Sportsmanship）

3.8 主题拓展资源

英文文章 1：What Is the Future for Sprinter Su Bingtian?

2020年东京奥运会赛场上，苏炳添吸引了无数人的目光。人们为他在东京奥运会上创造历史骄傲，也关心他之后的职业生涯。苏炳添接受了央视《面对面》栏目的专访，回答了网友们关心的一些问题。

This summer, Su Bingtian attracted the attention of countless people. While being proud of his achievement at the Tokyo Summer Olympics, people also appear concerned about his future career. How much further can the 32-year-old Asian athlete run on the track? Su recently gave an interview to CCTV, and relevant details have become trending topics on weibo.

"I was so thrilled that I wanted to cry."

In the afternoon of August 1, Su Bingtian broke the Asian record with a score of 9.83 seconds at the men's 100-meter semi-final at the Tokyo Summer Olympics. Ranking first among all the runners who advanced to the final, Su was the first Chinese athlete to enter the men's 100-meter final in the Games.

Su Bingtian said, "All the runners in our group were very competitive. I didn't expect that I could make it. I was so thrilled that I wanted to cry."

In the men's 100-meter final, Su eventually finished sixth in the men's race at the Tokyo Summer Olympics with the score of 9.98 seconds. If his score had been 9.83 seconds in the final, Su would have won the silver medal.

"When I entered the final, I guess I could not win a medal," Su explained. "At that time, my goal was to pass anyone I could pass. My final score was 9.98 seconds, which is already beyond what many Asians could achieve. I'm more happy than regretful."

"That is my major shortcoming."

During the interview, Su Bingtian analyzed that other runners grabbing the run during the 100-meter final didn't have much impact on him. In addition, the process of the 100-meter race enabled Su Bingtian to identify his current shortcomings more clearly.

Su introduced that the interval between the semi-final and the final of the 100-meter race is less than 3 hours. With too many things to prepare, he had little time to rest.

Su confessed, "The semi-final put too much burden on my body and I was not sure how much I could recover for the final. After the final, I felt that we compete not only for the ability of one particular field, but for the comprehensive ability. At present, my shortcoming lies in how to try my best in the final after two hours of rest after the semi-final."

"We didn't show our best."

In the men's 4 × 100 meter relay preliminaries on August 5, the Chinese men's team, consisting of Tang Xingqiang, Xie Zhenye, Su Bingtian and Wu Zhiqiang, advanced to the final with the top record of 37.92 seconds. However, the Chinese team finished 4th with 37.79 seconds in the final, missing out on an Olympic medal.

Su Bingtian said, "We were able to reach the national record despite two major mistakes, showing that we still need improvement. According to our current ability, it is very likely for us to reach the score of 37.50 seconds or so."

"I will run as long as I can."

In Su's opinion, the results he achieved in the Tokyo Summer Olympics may not be the peak of his career. "I would like to make a better run in the future. It is said what I achieve is already beyond the limit of the Asian people. I totally disagree with that."

Su Bingtian said he is not sure whether he will participate in the Paris Olympics yet. "For me, I will run as long as I can. If I can still run in 2024, of course I will take the gauntlet. But I may also choose to retire if I can't run anymore."

（来源：中国日报双语新闻）

英文文章2：Superb Commentaries at the Olympic Games

奥运神仙解说词引关注，网友：这就是中国式浪漫。

2020东京奥运会里，一句句"神仙解说词"引发网友关注。那些或激昂或失意的赛场时刻配合着中国式浪漫的精辟之词，无不让人觉得：运动之美，竞技精神之魅，语言可表，中文可达。

During the 2020 Tokyo Olympic Games, the superb sports commentaries were full of Chinese romance, attracting attention of netizens.

To Yang Qian:

除却君身三重雪，天下谁人配白衣。

After a fierce competition, shooter Yang Qian, an athlete of generation Z, claimed the first gold medal of the Tokyo Olympics with a victory in women's 10m air rifle on July 24.

We praised her calm bravery on the field, and we were also fond of her ingenuous and adorable style. She represents a promising future.

To Sun Yiwen who claimed a gold medal in women's fencing individual:

一剑光寒定九州。

Sun Yiwen wins the first gold medal of women's fencing individual in Chinese history at the Tokyo 2020 Olympic Summer Games on July 25.

Leading by only one point in the last 12 seconds, Sun Yiwen outplayed the opponent with slick techniques and a good mentality. The last point of her game rewrites the history of the Chinese fencing team and makes her dream to be a cornerstone member of the team, come true. "When I had to face the overtime, I told myself it's OK and I could make the match-winning point," said Sun. "I don't think too much about the results, and I just do as I have practiced so many times."

To Chen Yuxi and Zhang Jiaqi who dominated the women's synchronized diving 10m platform:

雏凤清于老凤声。

Chen Yuxi and Zhang Jiaqi dominated the women's synchronized diving 10m platform, winning the gold medal at the Tokyo Olympic Summer Games on July 27.

Although both are generation Z (Chen is 15 and Zhang is 17), they continue writing the legend of Chinese diving. "We have nothing to lose, and we are brave enough to face any challenges." They did achieve their goals and won applause from all over the world.

To Rowing — Women's Quadruple Sculls:

一棹逍遥天地间。

The Chinese rowers safely bagged the women's quadruple sculls gold medal with a world best time of 6 minutes and 5.13 seconds on July 28.

Chen Yunxia, Zhang Ling, Lyu Yang and Cui Xiaotong established a convincing lead before the final 500m and updated its Olympic best time set on home soil at the 2008 Olympic games. They achieved first place thanks to their perseverance, determination, confidence in each other, and the pursuit of the sport.

To Pang Wei and Jiang Ranxin:

一个是老骥伏枥志在千里，一个是旭日东升未来可期。

One is like an old steed that lies in the stable yet still aspires to gallop thousands of miles. The other one is like the sunrise whose future is promising.

Pang Wei and Jiang Ranxin won the 10m air pistol mixed team gold medal on July 27. "We are confident. For me, I see the first Olympic Games as a chance to develop myself, so I don't feel much pressure," said 21-year-old Jiang. Pang, who referred to Jiang as"niece" because he is 14 years older than Jiang, said he had firm belief in his partner. "We support and trust each other. Even before the match I knew she would be doing great, so I told myself I couldn't be too bad," said Pang.

To Ma Long:

一个时代的开启不会轻易落下帷幕。漂亮的离场并不只是在巅峰退役，也有绝地求生，也有从零开始。你永远不要低估一颗冠军的心。

The beginning of an era will not end easily. Departure not only means retirement at the top, but also to fight the impasse and start from the scratch. You should never underestimate the heart of a champion.

Ma Long won the gold medal in the men's singles final of the table tennis competition against his teammate Fan Zhendong on July 30. Against ages, against injuries, against all odds, Ma Long finally made it. "Never underestimate the heart of a champion." Former Houston Rockets coach Rudy Tomjanovich's famous quote has turned out to be true once again. Ma, captain of the all-leading Chinese table tennis team, won back-to-back Olympic titles in the men's singles event after overcoming Fan Zhendong, also from China, on Friday. It was a feat that no male player has ever achieved before. "First, I have to keep a winning mentality. This is the most precious thing which is also the reason why this team offers huge support to me. I think I can continue to play and compete with those rivals," he said.

To Fan Zhendong:

尽管今天依旧没能翻越马龙这座高山，但是也请樊振东回头望望，这一路走来，都是风景。

Fan, although you didn't defeat Ma Long, who claimed gold medal in the competition, please look back and you'll see the sceneries along the way.

Fan claimed the silver medal in the men's singles final of the table tennis. He showed the audience his consummate skill and imperturbable mentality. Ma Long said the future of Chinese table tennis belongs to Fan.

To Sun Yingsha:

少年负壮气，奋烈自有时。

Sun Yingsha claimed the silver medal in the women's singles table tennis on July To Xiao Ruoteng:

胸有惊雷而面如平湖。

Chinese gymnast Xiao Ruoteng compared himself to a vinyl record.

The 25-year-old man from China's capital Beijing has suffered from serious shoulder injuries which prevented him from practicing difficult movements, and he has spent a lot of time receiving medical treatment. Before the Tokyo Olympics, he received cortisone shots. "The most important occasion is coming. I will show the world the best of me," said Xiao. Have you been impressed by any live commentaries? Share your experience with us in the comment area.

（来源：中国日报双语新闻）

双语文章3：每周健身几次最有效果？关于健身的11个错误观念

无论你健身是为了变苗条、改善心情，还是拥有一身健美的肌肉，都要有正确的心态和方法。

也许经常有一些过来人给你一些诚恳的建议，但这些建议不一定都是对的，比如，早上锻炼是最好的，举重可以把脂肪变成肌肉。真相到底是怎样的呢？

Myth #1: To stay in shape, you only need to work out once or twice a week.

流言1：为了保持体形，你只需要一个礼拜锻炼一次或者两次。

Truth: Once or twice a week won't cut it for sustained health benefits.

事实：一周一到两次的锻炼不会给身体健康带来持久的回报。

"A minimum of three days per week for a structured exercise program" is best, Shawn Arent, an exercise scientist at Rutgers University, recently told Business Insider.

罗格斯大学的运动科学家肖恩·阿伦特近日告诉商业内幕网说："对一个结构合理的锻炼计划来说，一周至少要锻炼3次"才是最佳的。

"Technically, you should do something every day, and by something I mean physical activity — just move. Because we're finding more and more that the act of sitting counteracts any of the activity you do."

"严格来说，你每天都要练点啥，也就是说要活动一下。因为我们越来越清楚，久坐是会抵消掉你的锻炼成果的。"

Myth #2: The best time to work out is first thing in the morning.

流言2：早上锻炼是最好的。

Truth: The best time for a workout is whatever time allows you to exercise most consistently. Ideally, you want to make physical fitness a daily habit, so if late-night trips to the gym are your thing, stick with it. If you prefer a morning run, do that instead.

事实：锻炼没有最好的时段，无论什么时候都行，只要你能坚持。理想的情况下，你要让健身成为你的日常习惯，所以如果你喜欢晚上去健身房，那就坚持晚上去。如果你喜欢晨跑的话，那就晨跑。

Myth #3: Weight lifting turns fat into muscle.

流言3：举重能把脂肪变成肌肉。

Truth: You can't turn fat into muscle. Physiologically speaking, they're two different tissues. Adipose (fatty) tissue is found under the skin, sandwiched between muscles, and around internal organs like the heart.

事实：脂肪是不会变成肌肉的。从生理学方面来说，这完全是两种不同的组织。脂肪组织被夹在皮肤和肌肉中间，还会包裹在心脏等器官的外部。

Muscle tissue — which can be further broken down into three main types — is found throughout the body.

而肌肉组织可以被细分为3个主要类型（平滑肌、心肌和骨骼肌），分布于全身。

What weight training really does is help build up the muscle tissue in and around any fat tissue. The best way to reduce fat tissue is to eat a healthy diet that incorporates vegetables, whole grains, lean proteins and healthy fats like olive oil and fish.

举重真正能做到的是帮你锻炼脂肪组织内部和周围的肌肉组织。减脂的最佳途径是吃健康的膳食：蔬菜、粗粮、瘦肉蛋白，以及橄榄油和鱼这样的健康脂肪。

Myth #4: Puzzles and games are the best "brain workout" around.

流言4：解谜和游戏是最佳的"大脑锻炼"方式。

Truth: Plain old physical exercise seems to beat out any type of mental puzzle available, according to a wealth of recent research.

事实：根据多项近期的研究结论，普通的身体锻炼似乎能打败任何种类的脑力游戏。

Two new studies published last spring suggest that aerobic exercise — any activity that raises your heart rate and gets you moving and sweating for a sustained period of time — has a significant, overwhelmingly beneficial impact on the brain.

去年春天发表的两个研究结果表明，能让你心跳加快、挥汗如雨的有氧运动对大脑有着显著的、绝对有益的影响。

"Aerobic exercise is the key for your head, just as it is for your heart," wrote the authors of a recent Harvard Medical School blog post.

"有氧运动对你的心脏很重要，对大脑来说也一样重要，"近期哈佛大学医学院的博文中写道。

Myth #5: Exercise is the best way to lose weight.

流言5：锻炼是减肥的最佳方式。

Truth: If you're looking to lose weight, you shouldn't assume that you can simply "work off" whatever you eat. Experts say slimming down almost always starts with significant changes to your eating habits.

事实：如果你想要减肥，你就不要用"我吃下去的卡路里都能燃烧掉"来自我催眠。专家表示，瘦下来主要靠明显改变自己的饮食习惯。

"In terms of weight loss, diet plays a much bigger role than exercise," University of Texas exercise scientist Philip Stanforth tells Business Insider.

得克萨斯州立大学的运动科学家菲利普·斯坦福斯说："在减肥这方面，饮食比锻炼重要得多。"

That said, being active regularly is an important part of any healthy lifestyle.

即便如此，定期锻炼在任何健康的生活方式中都是很重要的一部分。

And when it comes to boosting your mood, improving your memory, and protecting your brain against age-related cognitive decline, research suggests exercise may be as close to a wonder drug as we'll get.

当谈到改善情绪、增强记忆力以及预防大脑因年老产生认知衰退时，研究人员表示，锻炼可能是我们最唾手可得的"灵丹妙药"。

Myth #6: Sit-ups are the best way to get six-pack abs.

流言6：想要六块腹肌，就做卷腹。

Truth: As opposed to sit-ups, which target only your abdominal muscles, planks recruit several groups of muscles along your sides, front, and back. If you want a strong core — especially the kind that would give you six-pack-like definition — you need to challenge all of these muscles.

事实：卷腹只能针对你的腹部肌肉，而平板支撑则要用到你侧面、正面和背部的几组肌肉。所以如果你想拥有强壮的核心肌肉，尤其是想要练出6块腹肌，你需要锻炼到所有的这些肌肉。

"Sit-ups or crunches strengthen just a few muscle groups," write the authors of the *Harvard Healthbeat* newsletter.

《哈佛健康节拍通讯》的作者写道："卷腹只能锻炼到少数几个肌肉群。"

"Through dynamic patterns of movement, a good core workout helps strengthen the entire set of core muscles you use every day."

"通过有活力的运动模式，一组高质量的核心肌肉锻炼有助于增强你日常会用到的整个核心区的肌肉。"

Myth #7: Weight training is for men.

流言7：举重是男人的项目。

Truth: Weight training is a great way to strengthen muscles, and has nothing to do with gender. That said, women produce less testosterone on average than men do, and studies suggest that hormone plays a role in determining how we build muscle.

事实：举重是加强肌肉的好途径，而且和性别无关。不过，女性产生的睾丸素平均要比男性少，研究指出睾丸素有助于塑造肌肉，所以女性也就不太容易练成筋肉人。

Myth #8: It takes at least two weeks to get "out of shape".

流言8："身材走形"至少需要两周时间。

Truth: In most people, muscle tissue can start to break down within a week without regular exercise.

事实：大多数人一周不进行规律锻炼的话，肌肉组织就会开始分解。

"If you stop training, you actually do get noticeable de-conditioning, or the beginnings of de-conditioning, with as little as seven days of complete rest," Arent said. "It very much is an issue of use it or lose it."

"如果7天内完全休息不进行锻炼的话，肌肉减少或者肌肉开始减少是显而易见的，"阿伦特表示，"要么练它，要么失去它。"

Myth #9: Running a marathon is the ideal way to get fit.

流言9：跑马拉松是健身的理想方式。

Truth: Not ready to conquer a marathon? No problem. You can get many of the benefits of long-distance running without ever passing the five-mile mark.

事实：跑不了"全马"？没关系的。就算你跑不到8公里，长跑也是好处多多。

Running fast and hard for just 5 to 10 minutes a day can provide some of the same health outcomes as running for hours can.

每天高强度地跑5到10分钟所带来的某些好处和连续跑上数小时是一样的。

In fact, people who run for less than an hour a week — as long as they get in those few minutes each day — see similar benefits in terms of heart health compared to those who run more than three hours per week.

实际上，每周跑不到一小时（只要他们能每天都跑几分钟）给心脏健康带来的益处和每周跑三小时以上的差不多。

Plus, years of recent research suggest that short bursts of intense exercise can provide some of the same health benefits as long, endurance-style workouts — and they also tend to be more fun.

此外，持续数年的近期研究也表明，短时间的高强度训练能带来和长时间的耐力训练一样的健康益处，而且也更有意思。

Myth #10: Keeping a food diary is a reliable way of monitoring and controlling what you eat.

流言10：记录食物流水账在监督和控制饮食上很可靠。

Truth: Even when we're making an effort to be conscious about what we're putting into our bodies and how active we're being, we often give ourselves more credit than we deserve.

事实：即使我们努力记下自己的食量和运动量，但其实由于我们经常对自己太过于信任了而无法达到预期效果。

"People tend to overestimate their physical activity and underestimate how much food they eat," says Stanforth.

"人们倾向于高估自己的运动量和低估自己摄入的热量，"斯坦福斯说道。

"They consistently think they've worked out more and consistently think they've eaten less."

"人们总是认为自己练得多而吃得少。"

Myth #11: Sports drinks are the best way to re-hydrate after a workout.

流言11：运动饮料是锻炼后补充水分的最佳饮品。

Truth: Most sports drinks are just sugar and water.

事实：大多数的运动饮料都是糖水。

Instead, experts recommend refuelling with plain old water and high-protein snack, since studies suggest protein helps recondition muscles after a workout.

相反，专家推荐喝白开水和高蛋白零食补充能量，因为研究表明在锻炼后补充蛋白质能够帮助修复肌肉。

（来源：中国日报双语新闻）

第七单元　家庭关系
（Unit 7 Family Ties）

1. 思政主题：血浓于水，亲情无价

2. 意义

本单元的主题是家庭关系。中华民族历来重视家庭。正所谓"天下之本在国，国之本在家"。尊老爱幼、妻贤夫安，母慈子孝、兄友弟恭，家和万事兴等中华民族传统家庭美德，铭记在中国人的心中，融入中国人的血脉中，是支撑中华民族生生不息、薪火相传的重要精神力量，是家庭文明建设的宝贵精神财富。

家庭是社会的基本细胞，是人生的第一所学校。不论时代发生多大变化，不论生活格局发生多大变化，我们都要重视家庭建设、注重家庭、注重家教、注重家风……使千千万万个家庭成为国家发展、民族进步、社会和谐的重要基点。

Family is the basic cell of society and the first school of our life. No matter how time has changed, the family value, family education and family building must be stressed ... so that the millions of families become important points for national development, ethnical progress and social harmony.
　　　　　　　　　　　　——习近平主席在2015年春节团拜会上的讲话

广大家庭都要重言传、重身教，教知识、育品德，身体力行、耳濡目染，帮助孩子扣好人生的第一粒扣子，迈好人生的第一个台阶。

Parents should instruct their children through word and deed, giving them both knowledge and virtue and practicing what they teach. They should help their children button the first button in their lifetime and take the first step on the ladder of life.
　　　　　　——习近平主席2016年12月在会见第一届全国文明家庭代表时的讲话

中华民族历来重视家庭，家和万事兴。

Family has always been valued by the Chinese people and harmony in a family makes everything successful.
　　　　　　　　　　　　——习近平主席在2018年春节团拜会上的讲话

发扬光大中华民族传统家庭美德，促进家庭和睦，促进亲人相亲相爱，促进下一代健康成长，促进老年人老有所养。

Chinese traditions and virtues of family harmony and affection should not be forgotten so as to ensure that the young grow up healthily and senior citizens are taken care of.

——习近平主席2015年在春节团拜会上的讲话

父母在，不远游，游必有方。

Children should not travel far while their parents are alive. If they have no choice but to do so, they must retain some restraint.

——《论语·里仁》

慈者，父母之高行也。

To be kind to one's children is the highest virtue of being a parent.

——《管子》

仁者人也，亲亲为大。

Benevolence is the characteristic element of humanity, and the great exercise of it is in loving relatives.

——《中庸》

夫孝，德之本也，教之所由生也。

Filial piety is the root of all virtue, and the stem out of which grows all moral teaching.

——《孝经》

今之孝者，是谓能养。至于犬马，皆能有养，不敬，何以别乎？

Nowadays, to provide parents with enough food is considered being filial. But dogs and horses are also providing to that extent. Without respect, what is the difference?

——《论语》

老吾老，以及人之老；幼吾幼，以及人之幼。

Show reverential respect to the aged of your own and extend the respect to the aged of others; cherish the children of your own and extend the love to the children of others.

——《孟子》

天地之性，人为贵。人之行，莫大于孝。
Of all natures produced by Heaven and Earth, man is the noblest. Of all the actions of man there is none greater than filial piety.

——《孝经》

首孝悌，次谨信。
Respect elders and parents, and be trustworthy and prudent.

——《弟子规》

很多时候不是我们去看父母的背影，而是承受他们追逐的目光，承受他们不舍的，不放心的，满眼的目送。最后才渐渐明白，这个世界上，再也没有任何人，可以像父母一样，爱我如生命。
Most of the time, we don't go to see our parents' backs, but to bear their chasing eyes, bear their reluctant, uneasy, eyeful watching. Finally, I gradually understand that there is no one in the world who can love me like my parents.

——龙应台《目送》

父母之年，不可不知也，一则以喜，一则以惧。
It is always better for a man to know the age of his parents. In the one case such knowledge will be a comfort to him; in the other, it will fill him with a salutary dread.

——《论语·里仁》
（来源：外研社高等英语资讯）

3. 教学设计与思政元素的融入

Passage A

3.1 Warm-up 环节

双语视频：《游子吟》 Song of the Parting son
《游子吟》是唐代诗人孟郊创作的一首五言诗。这是一首对母爱的颂歌。全诗共六句三十字，采用白描的手法，通过回忆一个看似平常的临行前缝衣的场景，凸显并歌颂了母爱的伟大与无私，表达了诗人对母爱的感激以及对母亲深深的爱与尊敬之情。此诗情感真挚自然，虽无藻绘与雕饰，然而清新流畅，淳朴素淡的语言中蕴含着浓郁醇美的诗味，千百年来广为传诵。教师可在课上分享本视频，引导学生一起体会母爱之伟大。

From the threads a mother's hand weaves,

A gown for parting son is made.

Sewn stitch by stitch before he leaves,

For fear his return be delayed.

Such kindness as young grass receives,

From the warm sun can't be repaid.

（来源：https://news.cgtn.com/news/2020-05-10/Mastering-Chinese-Poetry-Ep-10-Song-of-the-Parting-Son--QnorHalGJq/index.html）

3.2 Discussion 环节

英文视频：Young Chinese Mothers Struggle with Balancing Family and Work

教师可引导学生探讨：你的母亲是否也像文章中的这位妈妈一样，一边在职场奋力打拼，一边尽心尽力地操持着家中的大事小情？你印象中的妈妈是什么样的？

This Sunday marks Mother's Day, a day dedicated to honoring motherhood and showing love for mothers. A lot of young Chinese mothers who were born in the 1980s, are facing anxiety and pressure while also trying to maintain some personal time.

It is always tough for Xu Lujie to say goodbye to her son before leaving, whether he is awake or still sleeping.

Due to the high cost of living in Shanghai, the family needs both incomes to provide the best for their son. And she has to spend 40 minutes commuting each way to work.

The baby brings much happiness to the family, but Xu has also felt increasing anxiety since the birth of her child.

"The pressure is quite obvious because I always communicate about it with my colleagues who are also young mothers. We try to offer our babies the best of everything, in terms of eating, clothing and the most important thing — education," said Xu.

Since she needs to work, Xu Lujie asked her parents-in-law to come to take care of the baby while she is out of the house.

"Mothers all love their children, but today's young mothers shoulder a lot of pressure. They need to pay the mortgage together and pick quality schools for the children," said Zhang Cui'e, Xu's mother-in-law.

In addition to paying off a 4 million RMB mortgage over the next 30 years, Xu and her husband are working hard to take care of both of their parents, as well as their son. Experts say a growing number of young mothers who were born in the 1980s face similar difficulties.

"In sociology, we have a special term for them, which is the sandwich generation. It means they have to satisfy competing needs both from their children and their parents," said Dr. Li Jinzhao with the Beijing Foreign Studies University.

Back home after work, Xu will spend her precious time with the baby. Work and family have taken up the major part of her day. Experts say balancing her personal needs with those of her family, requires plenty of support.

"I am also working in the financial sector and it is very busy, and generally it is my wife and parents who take care of the baby. I believe the whole family particularly me, should give her more support," said Dai Yunfeng, Xu's husband.

Every Thursday and Saturday, Xu Lujie goes for a run. She said running is the best way for her to relieve the pressure.

"I think each young mother should find her own way of relieving anxiety. For example, running, yoga and doing some exercise to ease the pressure," she said.

Many young mothers in large cities are struggling to balance their work, personal life and family. They hope to set a good example for their children by pursuing positive lifestyles.

（来源：https://news.cgtn.com/news/3d3d674d3251444e77457a6333566d54/index.html）

英文文章： Chinese Father Donates Skin to Save Severely Burned Daughter

父爱如山。和母亲温润如玉的爱相比，父亲的爱深沉而坚定。关键时刻，父亲愿用自己的一切换取子女的幸福。教师可以请同学们阅读本文，而后请每个同学谈谈自己所感受到的父爱。

A father from central China's Henan Province has drawn public attention for repeatedly donating his skin to his severely burned daughter since he couldn't afford the expensive price of skin grafts needed for her surgery.

The 17-year-old girl, named Li Chenxi, who lost 80 percent of her skin due to a gas explosion at home on October 3, was in critical condition and had to undergo skin grafting surgery to survive.

Li's father, Li Zhifeng, was told by the hospital he must pay 300,000 yuan (43,431 U.S. dollars) to buy the skin needed for the emergency transplant surgery. However, unable to afford the expensive medical cost, Li decided to donate his own skin to save his daughter.

Zheng Guohong, Li's mother, said that they had spent over 1.6 million yuan to pay for the medical treatment by mortgaging their house and borrowing money from relatives. Fortunately, thanks to the money donated by the public, hope was restored once again.

Up until now, they still need around 700,000 yuan for further treatment.

Zheng said her husband had donated his scalps for six or seven times, and he would wait for the skin to grow back before donating it again.

Li's father first donated the skin of his left leg and later donated skin from his left arm for his daughter's surgery. Covered by the gauze bandage, his wound was deep purple after undergoing surgery.

"I could take the physical pain, but I'm heartbroken for my daughter. I hope she could get better soon," said Li's father.

"My daughter's life has just started, and I would do whatever I could to save her — no matter how painful it is," Li's father told *China News Service*.

However, his daughter remained unaware of what her father had done for her because her parents didn't want her to be worried. Li's father asked his wife to tell their daughter that he had been away to another city to work while he actually underwent surgery in the same hospital.

According to the doctor, Li has undergone over 17 surgeries, and she was described as a girl with a strong will since she would even comfort her parents not to worry about her.

The doctor said Li was recovering now and she would be in good health if the next surgery goes on smoothly.

Skin grafting is a type of surgery that involves skin transplantation to treat burns, trauma or other kinds of skin loss. Around the world, the cost of skin grafting surgery is relatively high; thus, for poverty-stricken family, it would be a disaster to face such an operation.

（来源：https://news.cgtn.com/news/3d3d414d3251444e31457a6333566d54/index.html）

3.3 Critical thinking 环节

英文文章：Don't Ignore Parent's Advice

随着时代的发展，越来越多人都认为，老人家的智慧都是老旧的，早已不适用于这个社会了。随着年龄的增长，代沟的存在，你是否也会觉得自己的见识越来越多，因而对父母的建议越来越无法接纳、越发感到不耐烦了呢？其实，父母的建议往往来自他们日积月累的人生经验，我们若能辩证地听取、采纳，一定能从中获取不少人生智慧。

Whenever our parents gives advice, children thinks that parents don't know anything about new fashion and living style. Whenever parents gives advice, children generally try to ignore it and make sure that their parents understand that children want to live life their own way.

Ignoring parent's old logical advice and giving weird expressions might harm you only, their advice will surely help you somewhere and that time you will feel guilty that you never listened to what they want you to teach.

Here are few points which shows that why you need to listen to your parent's advice:

1. World changed to worst: Most common excuse for ignoring your parent's advice and doing what your friends say to you is generation gap. I agree that world is changing and you need to change with time but you must listen to your parents also. Your parents might not know about computers or latest technologies but they have more experience about life. They know that life is getting tough for kids to handle. Your parents love you and thus want to save you from changing world, where others can trap you in different kind of problems.

2. Know world: There are so many news everyday about problems with teen occurring due to few innocent mistakes. You might get confused while taking decisions about your life. Who you should listen to? Your parents or friends? Your parents and friends can be right or wrong but it's up to you what you want from your life and you must have ability to take your decision about fashion, drugs or adventures in life. Best way to take decision is to think about best and prepare for worst. Once you analysis best and worst, you will never feel sorry for your

decision.

3. Parents love you: Simple reason why parents want to help you in taking decisions is because they love you. They don't want that the mistakes which they did in their life, you should repeat it. They want you to live your life with happiness always without regretting anything in life because of wrong decision. If your parents are successful, they might have knowledge and experience. Don't be biased while they advice you about life and success, their advice will surely help you somewhere in life.

4. Think of past, before ignoring your parent's advice: There are lots of reasons and proofs in your life which shows that you must listen to your parent's advice. They always advice you to study well but you always ignore. When you get fewer marks and face problems in getting jobs, you remember your parent's advice. They might have scolded you while teaching you manners and etiquettes, but because of those manners only you are well known in your college or office. Thus always listen to parent's advice and then take decisions.

God wants you to be perfect and thus created parents to make you perfect and save you from ruining your life.

（来源：https://www.letstalkrelations.com/dont-ignore-parents-advice.html）

英文文章：How to Improve Communication with Your Parents

时代在发展，年轻一代与老一代在思想方法、价值观念、生活态度、兴趣爱好等方面存在代沟在所难免。如何与父母进行有效的沟通是我们每个人人生中必要的功课。教师可以与学生分享本文，之后讨论：Are there generation gaps in your family? What do you think are the effective ways to communicate with your parents?

The relationship between parents and their sons and daughters can deteriorate due to a lack of proper communication. When children become adults, they often find they have stopped having meaningful conversations with their parents. Conflict often arises from parents thinking they know what is best for their offspring who often want something different in life. It is important to work on achieving healthy communication with your parents to maintain a strong relationship with them.

Step 1

Make time to have meaningful conversations with your parents. One of the biggest threats to parent-child communication is generational differences in communication. The newer generations often reach out to others through technology, such as text messages, online chats or email. There is much less face-to-face contact. Although the older generation is catching on, most still prefer a personal conversation or phone call. Consider that your parents' generation has a stronger need for person-to-person conversation. Take the time to sit down and have a few minutes of conversation with them every day. If you live some distance away, make it a goal to call them at least three times a week or video chat frequently. Keep in mind that text messages can often be misinterpreted by the receiver because there is no tone or facial expression to provide context.

Step 2

Be open and honest with your parents. Families often stop communicating because it is easier to ignore an issue than to have a conversation about it. If an issue is important to you, bring it up to your parents. Bottling up emotions or annoyances can deteriorate the relationship that you have with them. Always communicate your feelings in a calm and neutral tone. Avoid getting trapped in the blame game. Use "I" statements that talk about how you feel, and avoid "you" statements that point fingers at other people. Allow time for them to respond and share how they feel.

Step 3

Use the PEN method to facilitate difficult conversations with your parents. The PEN (pause, empathy, needs) method was developed to prevent conflict and violence when communicating. If a certain conversation with your parents is taking a turn for the worse, start by taking pause. Practice deep breathing, excuse yourself for a couple of minutes or drink a cold glass of water if you are becoming agitated. When you are ready to continue with the conversation, listen to your parents' needs or wants and empathize with them. Inform them that although you understand their point of view, you also have your own needs and wants. The next step is to express your perspective and ask them to try and empathize with you as well.

Step 4

Don't just talk about the difficult stuff. Talk to your parents about your everyday life, funny experiences and other trivial things. Encourage them to share how their day went or what they are working on. Most of your conversations with your parents should be light-hearted, humorous and spontaneous. You don't want to talk to them only when you are faced with an issue. Regular communication about the less important things will make the difficult conversations much easier.

（来源：https://oureverydaylife.com/improve-communication-parents-124 21.html）

3.4 主题拓展资源

双语文章：常有父亲陪伴的孩子智商更高 Children Who Spend Time with Their Fathers Have a Higher IQ

耶鲁大学一项持续12年的研究表明：成长过程中有父亲积极参与的孩子其智商高，他们在学校里的成绩往往更好，将来走向社会也更容易成功。世界卫生组织最新研究成果也表明，平均每天能与父亲共处两个小时以上的孩子，要比其他孩子智商高。因为性别差异，父母亲的养育方式不同。父亲的角色，对孩子的学习、性格、情感、品质、体质等方面都有不可替代的影响。

Children who spend large amounts of time with their fathers have higher IQs, according to a new study. Strong fatherly involvement in their early life can also improve a child's future career prospects, the research shows.

Academics at the University of Newcastle, who carried out the study, also found that men tended to pay more attention to their sons than their daughters. The researchers warned that it was not enough for parents to live together, but that a father should be actively involved in a child's life to benefit their development.

The study looked at more than 11,000 British men and women, born in 1958. The scientists asked their mothers how often the father of their child took part in activities with them, including reading, organizing outings and general "quality time". The findings, published in the journal *Evolution and Human Behaviour*, show that those children whose fathers spent more time with them had a higher IQ and were more socially mobile than those who had received little attention.

The differences were still detectable by the age of 42. Dr Daniel Nettle, who led the research, said: "What was surprising about this research was the real sizeable difference in the progress of children who benefited from paternal interest and how thirty years later, people whose dads were involved are more upwardly mobile." "The data suggest that having a second adult involved during childhood produces benefits in terms of skills and abilities that endure throughout adult life," he added.

Jon Davies, chief executive for Families Need Fathers, said: "We hope that research like this will lead to the government to reconsider how poorly served separated families often are and how a child needs a father as well as mother."

一项新研究显示，经常与父亲在一起的孩子智商更高。另外，孩子在早年若常有父亲相伴，他们的职业前景也更为光明。

纽卡斯尔大学的科学家们在研究中还发现，相较于照料女儿，父亲在儿子身上花的精力更多。研究人员指出，为了孩子的身心成长，家庭圆满还不够，父亲的付出才是关键。

该研究调查了1.1万多名生于1958年的英国男女。科学家们询问了这些调查对象的母亲，关于孩子的父亲是否常常参与阅读、远足等家庭活动。本研究刊登在《进化与人类行为》上。结论称，与缺少父爱的孩子相比，经常与父亲在一起的孩子智商更高，前途也更为光明。

即便受调查对象已年过不惑，他们之间仍存在这种差别。牵头本研究的丹尼尔·内特博士表示："这次调查让我们大吃一惊，父亲的付出竟能在孩子的成长中产生如此大的影响，甚至改变了他们三十年后的未来。""数据显示，孩子在成长中若有除母亲之外的第二位成人相伴，他们的技能和能力会有大幅提升，使他们受益终生。"

"父亲力量"组织的主管乔恩·戴维斯说："我们希望这项研究能让政府意识到，单亲家庭现状堪忧，孩子的成长需要父母同时相伴左右。"

（来源：http://language.chinadaily.com.cn/2016-01/08/content_22992122.htm）

Passage B

3.5 Warm-up 环节

英文歌曲 + 电影混剪视频

我们往往要等到长大后，才会渐渐懂得父母的不易。这是一个有关父母、成长、理解的电影混剪，配乐是 Sasha Alex Sloan 的原创歌曲 *Older*。涉及的经典影片包括 *Lady bird*（《伯德小姐》）、*Boyhood*（《少年时代》）、*A perfect world*（《完美的世界》）、*Wonder*（《奇迹男孩》）、*Love, Simon*（《爱你，西蒙》）。让我们一起回顾电影中的感人片段，反思那个或许曾经叛逆的自己，以及父母给予我们的无私的爱：Parents are not heroes. They just love us.

I used to shut my door

When my mother screamed in the kitchen

I'd turn the music up

Get high and try not to listen

To every little fight

Cause neither one was right

I swore to never be like them

But I was just a kid back then

The older I get, the more that I see

My parents aren't heroes, they're just like me

And loving is hard, it don't always work

You just try your best not to get hurt

I used to be mad, but now I know

Sometimes it's better to let someone go

It just hadn't hit me yet

The older I get

I used to wonder why

Why they could never be happy

I used to close my eyes

And pray for a whole 'nother family

Where everything was fine

One that felt like mine

I swore to never be like them

But I was just a kid back then

The older I get, the more that I see

My parents aren't heroes, they're just like me

And loving is hard, it don't always work

You just try your best not to get hurt

I used to be mad, but now I know

Sometimes it's better to let someone go

It just hadn't hit me yet

The older I get

我曾紧关房门

只留妈妈独自在厨房叫喊

我把音乐开得超大声

尝试沉浸其中而不理会妈妈的声音

大大小小的争吵

我们都不承认是自己错了

我发誓永远不会变成像他们一样的人

但那时我年纪尚小，无能为力

年纪渐长，阅历增多
我明白父母也不是神，我们都只是普通人
爱一个人很难，并不总是顺风顺水
你只能竭尽所能保护自己不受伤害
我曾无法理解，但现在我明白
有时候放下是更好的选择
当时的我阅历尚浅
长大后才明白这一切
我曾感到困惑
为何父母总是无法绽放笑颜
我只好闭上双眼
祈祷可以生活在另一个家庭
另一个事事如意的家庭
另一个让我有归属感的家庭
我发誓永远不会变成像他们一样的人
但那时我年纪尚小，无能为力
年纪渐长，阅历增多
我明白父母也不是神，我们都只是普通人
爱一个人很难 并不总是顺风顺水
你只能竭尽所能保护自己不受伤害
我曾无法理解，但现在我明白
有时候放下是更好的选择
当时的我阅历尚浅
长大后才明白这一切

（来源：https://www.bilibili.com/video/BV1ap4y1C7Cp）

3.6 Discussion 环节

双语视频：Parents and Anxiety 父母与焦虑

为人父母是一些人毕生的功课。可以说，父辈母辈也是在不断的学习中渐渐成长和成熟起来的。一些父母出于对孩子无限的爱，在养育过程中不免会充满了焦虑。选取这个视频并非想要让我们去吐槽自己的父母，而是引导大家一起去学习和理解父母焦虑的原因和表现，从而通过不断学习，让自己在面对下一代时成为不再焦虑的父母。教师可以引导学生来讨论：Are your parents anxious? Are you anxious about parenting?

Anxiety is an issue that is being brought to light more and more frequently in mainstream media, which can really help those that suffer from this issue. People often see anxiety as just something that everyone experiences, but it's important to recognize that there's a difference between the occasional bout of nerves and the debilitating symptoms of those that suffer from anxiety as an actual mental illness.

Graham Davey is an experimental psychopathology. He researches mental health in labs and in particular tries to get a better understanding of the causes of anxiety based problems through controlled experimentation. Davey has spoken a lot about the phenomenon of helicopter parents. As Davey explains, it's only natural for parents to want to do the best for their kids, particularly in terms of health and education, but helicopter parents probably overdo this. Davey elaborates further saying in life everyone will be faced by threats and challenges at some point and will need to know how to deal with these when they arise. Kids whose parents shield them from every kind of challenge even challenges they face in education run the risk of growing up anxious largely because their parents protective behavior has prevented them from practicing suitable coping responses and has conveyed to them that maybe there is something frightening about those things their parents have been shielding them from. Along with helicopter parents you have snowplow parents. Snowplow parents are probably the worst observed Davey. By removing everything in life that might be a potential obstacle to their child, they never allow their children to learn how to cope with their own obstacles in life.

"I suspect many helicopter parents are themselves anxious people who are genuinely attempting to do the best for their kids", says Davey when discussing what makes helicopter parents so protective. But as a result they're not allowing their offspring to find out about the world and how to cope with it. Davey points out that kids don't come with manuals. Every parent has a different way of raising kids, but it's been proven time and again that over-protection is a downside and doesn't allow children to develop coping mechanisms later in life.

Davey is quick to point out what a major influence a parent can have on the mental health of their children. Parents can be quite subjective about what issues they consider important in their children's lives, explains Davey. But arguably more important than this is the way these issues are dealt with. Negative parenting for example is particularly problematic and a common source of mental health problems in offspring. Negative parenting includes disciplining strategies such as threatening a child "you stop crying or I'll give you something to cry about" or attending to the child only when they're doing something wrong.

Studies have shown that about 30% of our anxiety can be traced to our own genetics, but the other 70% is influenced by experience and upbringing. Even 10 month old babies can pick up on negative behaviors from a parent and avoid things that their parents have behaved negatively towards. Davey explains this probably stays with kids through their childhood and is likely to override any contrary explanations given by the parent.

Vicarious learning is a significant way in which children pick up anxieties throughout childhood. Many non-Human animals also learn their fears by watching other con-specifics behaving fearfully, so it's quite a common mechanism in nature. A parent will need a very convincing argument to dissuade an offspring not to be fearful of something they've seen someone else behaving fearfully of too. Graham clearly shows how parents have a massive impact on what experiences children will take from the world around them. If you convince a child that something should be feared, even if you don't intend to, then they will be more likely to fear it as well.

It is good to allow a child to experience things in their own way instead of removing all risks that they may face. Although it is understandable to want to protect your child, parenting is a difficult thing. But as long as you're there for your child and ready to help when needed, you'll be just fine.

焦虑这个问题越来越频繁地被主流媒体提及，这的确帮助到了很多焦虑者。人们经常认为焦虑是每个人都经历过的，但是，认识到偶尔的精神紧张与焦虑症患者饱受折磨的精神衰弱症状有区别很重要。焦虑症是真正的心理疾病。

Graham Davey 是一名实验心理学家，他在实验室研究心理疾病，特别是基于对照实验研究造成焦虑症的原因。Davey 已经对"直升机父母"的现象发表过很多看法。正如 Davey 所说，家长们想要给孩子最好的，特别是健康与教育方面，这是最正常不过的了。但是直升机父母可能会表现的过分。Davey 进一步阐释说，生活中每个人都会在某时面临威胁和困难，当它们来临时都需要知道怎么样处理。那些父母帮着处理困难甚至帮着处理学习困难的孩子，就有患焦虑症的危险。主要是因为他们父母的保护行为已经阻止了他们实践合理的应对反应，这也使他们以为父母不让他们处理的困难很可怕。

除了直升机父母，还有一种"扫雪机父母"。据 Davey 观察，扫雪机父母可能是最差的。他们清除孩子生活中所有可能的障碍，从不允许孩子学习如何处理他们生活中的困难开始。

当讨论到"是什么让直升机父母过度保护孩子"时，Davey 说："我认为很多直升机父母本身就焦虑，他们真的想要给孩子最好的，但结果是他们不允许孩子发现世界并应对世界。"Davey 指出孩子并不是一出生就带着手册，每个父母都有自己养育孩子的方式，但是无数次实践证明，过度保护有其不足之处。这阻止了孩子在未来生活中形成应对问题的能力。

Davey 很快指出父母可以带来的最大的影响是孩子的心理健康方面，他解释说，父母对孩子认为重要的事情有很强的主观性，但是可能比这更重要的是他们处理这些事的方式，比如消极养育特别容易出问题，也是后代心理疾病的普遍诱因。消极养育包括纪律策略，比如威胁孩子"别哭了，再哭我就揍你"或者只关心孩子的错处。

研究发现大约30%的焦虑可以在遗传中找到踪迹，但是剩下的70%是被经历和抚养方式所影响的。10个月大的孩子就可以辨识出父母的消极行为，并且避免做父母已表现过消极反应的行为，Davey 解释说，这可能伴随着孩子的童年时期，并会对父母给出的相反解释无动于衷。

替代学习是孩子童年时期发展焦虑的重要方式。很多非人类灵长类动物也是通过观察同类表现害怕才学到害怕的，所以这是大自然中的普遍机制。父母将需要一个非常有说服力的观点去劝阻孩子不要因看到别人表现害怕自己也害怕。Graham 清楚地表明父母对孩子在世界上的经历有巨大的影响。如果你让孩子相信某事是可怕的，即使你并不是有意为之，他们也可能会更害怕。

尽管想要保护孩子是可以理解的，但最好的方式是允许孩子以自己的方式处事，而不是去帮清除掉他们可能面对的危险。抚养孩子很难，但是只要你在孩子身边并在孩子需要时给他提供帮助，你就已经做的很好了。

（来源：https://www.yxgapp.com/parents-and-anxiety/）

3.7 Critical thinking 环节

英文文章: How China Is Solving Pension Fund Challenge Amid Population Aging

随着老龄化社会的到来，老龄人口严重增加，我国面临的人口老龄化问题越来越严峻。如何解决人口老龄化对养老金的挑战，引起国人的热切关注。教师可以引导学生在阅读完本文后，思考并讨论：What should family members do to face the challenge of population aging?

The phrase "poor generation of the 1980s" has been buzzing on Chinese social media this week after an article sparked public anger by saying that the country's pension fund will run out by 2035, which means the generation born after the 1980s will have no pensions when they retire at 55 for women or 60 for men.

The article was cited in a report by the World Social Security Center at the Chinese Academy of Social Sciences. The report states that the current pension fund for urban workers will have difficulty maintaining a balance in the next few years within the upcoming three decades before it starts to plunge. Moreover, the deficit will expand until the pension fund surplus runs out by 2035.

"Of course, aging is the main reason for the problem. When fewer people pay pensions and more people take benefits, the surplus of the pension fund can't last long," said Wu Gangliang, an expert from the China Enterprise Reform and Development Society.

China is accelerating into an aging society, with 17.9 percent of the total population aged 60 or above, and 11.9 percent aged 65 or above, according to 2018 figures from the National Bureau of Statistics. Standards set by the UN state that when the population of seniors aged 65 or above hits seven percent, the country can be defined as aging.

Japan, for example, is known as a super-aging society as its senior population aged 65 or older accounted for 28.1 percent in 2018, a record in the country's history, which experts say will hamper the nation's productivity due to snowballing social security costs and a labor shortage. Is China facing the same problem?

The China National Committee on Aging (CNCA) predicted that the population of seniors aged 60 and over is expected to peak at 487 million around 2050, nearly 35 percent of the total population.

Despite the issue of aging, another reason for the problem is the Chinese government lowering pension contributions from enterprises from 20 percent to 16 percent this May to reduce the tax burden on businesses and boost the real economy. How can this problem be resolved? The transfer of state assets is one primary option.

"State assets, seems to me, is the best funding source. Our state assets are huge... The total value is somewhere between 60 to 70 trillion yuan. According to government plans, 10 percent of them will be transferred to the pension fund. That is a huge amount of money. Seven trillion in all is enough to cover any pension shortfall," said Wu.

The expert also elaborated on the viability of the state assets transfer, telling CGTN that the Chinese people are the final and true owners of the state assets, so using such assets as the source of pension fund is logical and reasonable. He added that China's state-owned enterprises (SOEs) have always been criticized for having single shareholders. So the transfer will, to some extent, improve the governance structure of SOEs by bringing in more shareholders.

"After transferring the shares or equities, another agency (National Council for Social Security Fund) will become their new major shareholder. The diversification is expected to improve the governance structure of SOEs," Wu said.

Chinese Premier Li Keqiang also said the government would increase the total amount of the social security fund by transferring state assets to guarantee the safety of pension during the first session of the 13th National People's Congress in March. The work will fully unfold this year, according to the State Council last week.

Transferring state assets is a viable solution, but not a panacea. The best way is to boost the economy, in turn allowing more enterprises to make pension contributions, according to the expert.

China has taken many other measures to address the funding challenge, including allocating a portion of central government funds to make up for the local pension deficit, in a country where pension contributions are collected and managed by local governments. Authorities are also allowing Chinese couples to have their second child to enlarge the labor force and to cut enterprise taxes to increase employment.

"The claim that the generations born after 1980 will have no pension once they retire is totally a misunderstanding of the pension system and irresponsible," said Zhang Yinghua, researcher of the World Social Security Research Center for the Chinese Academy of Social Sciences.

He explained that there was no surplus of pension fund when the system was founded in 1996. At that time, local governments paid annual pensions to retirees with the money they collected the same year from laborers and there was no surplus, but kept a balance.

The surplus of China's pension fund went up steadily since the establishment of the pension system, but because of aging, the reserve began to decrease in 2014, which will eventually run out by 2035 if all else remains unchanged.

"The calculation is true (the surplus of pension fund will run out by 2035), but it's normal and doesn't mean the local governments can't pay pensions to the people born after 1980 when they retire. Because the governments could keep a balance then, they're capable of doing it in the future," Zhang said.

（来源：https://news.cgtn.com/news/2019-07-18/How-China-is-solving-pension-fund-challenge-amid-population-aging-IpbZp0rK7e/index.html）

3.8 主题拓展资源

英文文章：Chinese President Stresses Familial Virtues

天下之本在家。党的十八大以来，习近平总书记高度重视家庭建设问题，在许多场合作出一系列重要论述。他指出，不论时代发生多大变化，不论生活格局发生多大变化，我们都要重视家庭建设，注重家庭、注重家教、注重家风。

Chinese President Xi Jinping on Monday called for efforts to enhance virtue and civility in Chinese families and make them "an important foundation" for national development, progress and social harmony.

People from all walks of life should work for "a new trend toward socialist family values" featuring love for the nation, family and one another, devotion to progress and kindness, and mutual growth and sharing, said President Xi Jinping when meeting with attendees at a Beijing conference to honor model families across the nation.

President Xi Jinping, also general secretary of the Communist Party of China (CPC) Central Committee, said the Chinese nation has always valued the family.

"Traditional family values have been engraved on the minds and melted into the blood of the Chinese people," President Xi Jinping said.

Describing them as important spiritual power supporting the Chinese nation, President Xi Jinping said virtue is a precious treasure for promotion of family harmony.

President Xi Jinping hoped that families would value education and their own familial culture.

Calling families as "cells of society," President Xi Jinping went on, "a prosperous, strong nation, the great national rejuvenation and the happiness of the people are embodied by the happiness of tens of thousands of families and the better life of hundreds of millions of people."

Only by realizing the Chinese dream of national rejuvenation can the dreams of families come true, President Xi Jinping added, calling on households, more than 400 million of them, to integrate their love for the family with their love for the nation.

President Xi Jinping said though family education had many aspects, the most important was in character building, stressing sound moral values should be passed down to children from an early age.

Efforts should be made to "guide children to develop the trait of integrity, help them cultivate beautiful minds and ensure their healthy growth, so that they can be useful to the nation and the people," President Xi Jinping said.

He called on households to nurture and practise socialist core values, encouraging family members, especially the younger generation to love the Party, the motherland, the people and the Chinese nation.

"Family is not only the dwelling of people's body, but also the home of people's hearts," President Xi Jinping said.

A family may thrive with a good culture while a bad culture may bring trouble to themselves and to society, President Xi Jinping said.

He called on all Chinese families to promote fine family culture and sustain the good social ethos.

The president called on leading officials to take the lead in maintaining the family virtues and learning from role models such as Jiao Yulu, Gu Wenchang and Yang Shanzhou.

Leading officials and cadres at all levels should teach their children and families to be law-abiding, frugal and self-reliant, President Xi Jinping said.

He urged CPC and governmental organizations to cultivate good culture among families and help families in difficulties.

Liu Yunshan, a member of the Standing Committee of the Political Bureau of the CPC Central Committee, also met with the participants and attended the conference.

Liu at the conference stressed the important role of family culture in the country's development, national progress and social harmony, calling for promotion of socialist core values and the understanding of Chinese dream.

Monday's conference was the first of its kind to honor model families selected nationwide. A total of 300 model families won this honor in a selection that highlights patriotism, observation of law, ethics, harmony, honesty, professional spirit, thrift and commitment to public welfare.

Vice Premier Liu Yandong read the decision to honor these model families at the conference. Liu Qibao, head of the Publicity Department of the CPC Central Committee, presided over the event.

（来源：http://www.chinadaily.com.cn/china/2016-12/13/content_27648200.htm）

英文视频：For Parents, Happiness Is a very High Bar

随着时代的进步，做个好父母的门槛仿佛也越来越高。建立在爱这个基础上的过度焦虑和过度养育是否合理，是否有利于新时代孩童的成长？这个视频也许会带来更多的启发。

When I was born, there was really only one book about how to raise your children, and it was written by Dr. Spock.

No, it was Benjamin Spock, and his book was called "*The Common Sense Book of Baby and Child Care.*" It sold almost 50 million copies by the time he died. Today, I, as the mother of a six-year-old, walk into Barnes and Noble, and see this. And it is amazing the variety that one finds on those shelves. There are guides to raising an eco-friendly kid, a gluten-free kid, a disease-proof kid, which, if you ask me, is a little bit creepy. There are guides to raising a bilingual kid even if you only speak one language at home. There are guides to raising a financially savvy kid and a science-minded kid and a kid who is a whiz at yoga. Short of teaching your toddler how to defuse a nuclear bomb, there is pretty much a guide to everything.

All of these books are well-intentioned. I am sure that many of them are great. But taken together, I am sorry, I do not see help when I look at that shelf. I see anxiety. I see a giant candy-colored monument to our collective panic, and it makes me want to know, why is it that raising our children is associated with so much anguish and so much confusion? Why is it that we are at sixes and sevens about the one thing human beings have been doing successfully for millennia, long before parenting message boards and peer-reviewed studies came along? Why is it that so many mothers and fathers experience parenthood as a kind of crisis?

Crisis might seem like a strong word, but there is data suggesting it probably isn't. There was, in fact, a paper of just this very name, "*Parenthood as Crisis,*" published in 1957, and in the 50-plus years since, there has been plenty of scholarship documenting a pretty clear pattern of parental anguish. Parents experience more stress than non-parents. Their marital satisfaction is lower. There have been a number of studies looking at how parents feel when they are spending time with their kids, and the answer often is, not so great. Last year, I spoke with a researcher named Matthew Killingsworth who is doing a very, very imaginative project that tracks people's happiness, and here is what he told me he found: "Interacting with your friends is better than interacting with your spouse, which is better than interacting with other relatives, which is better than interacting with acquaintances, which is better than interacting with parents, which is better than interacting with children, who are on par with strangers."

But here's the thing. I have been looking at what underlies these data for three years, and children are not the problem. Something about parenting right now at this moment is the problem. Specifically, I don't think we know what parenting is supposed to be. Parent, as a verb, only entered common usage in 1970. Our roles as mothers and fathers have changed. The roles of our children have changed. We are all now furiously improvising our way through a situation for which there is no script, and if you're an amazing jazz musician, then improve is great, but for the rest of us, it can kind of feel like a crisis.

So how did we get here? How is it that we are all now navigating a child-rearing universe without any norms to guide us? Well, for starters, there has been a major historical change. Until fairly recently, kids worked, on our farms primarily, but also in factories, mills, mines. Kids were considered economic assets. Sometime during the Progressive Era, we put an end to this arrangement. We recognized kids had rights, we banned child labor, we focused on education instead, and school became a child's new work. And thank God it did. But that only made a parent's role more confusing in a way. The old arrangement might not have been particularly ethical, but it was reciprocal. We provided food, clothing, shelter, and moral instruction to our kids, and they in return provided income.

Once kids stopped working, the economics of parenting changed. Kids became, in the words of one brilliant if totally ruthless sociologist, "economically worthless but emotionally priceless." Rather than them working for us, we began to work for them, because within only a matter of decades it became clear: if we wanted our kids to succeed, school was not enough. Today, extracurricular activities are a kid's new work, but that's work for us too, because we are the ones driving them to soccer practice. Massive piles of homework are a kid's new work, but that's also work for us, because we have to check it. About three years ago, a Texas woman told something to me that totally broke my heart. She said, almost casually, "Homework is the new dinner." The middle class now pours all of its time and energy and resources into its kids, even though the middle class has less and less of those things to give. Mothers now spend more time with their children than they did in 1965, when most women were not even in the workforce.

It would probably be easier for parents to do their new roles if they knew what they were preparing their kids for. This is yet another thing that makes modern parenting so very confounding. We have no clue what portion our wisdom, if any, is of use to our kids. The world is changing so rapidly, it's impossible to say. This was true even when I was young. When I was a kid, high school specifically, I was told that I would be at sea in the new global economy if I did not know Japanese. And with all due respect to the Japanese, it didn't turn out that way. Now there is a certain kind of middle-class parent that is obsessed with teaching their kids Mandarin, and maybe they're onto something, but we cannot know for sure. So, absent being able to anticipate the future, what we all do, as good parents, is try and prepare our kids for every possible kind of future, hoping that just one of our efforts will pay off. We teach our kids chess, thinking maybe they will need analytical skills. We sign them up for team sports, thinking maybe they will need collaborative skills, you know, for when they go to Harvard Business School. We try and teach them to be financially savvy and science-minded and eco-friendly and gluten-free, though now is probably a good time to tell you that I was not eco-friendly and gluten-free as a child. I ate jars of pureed macaroni and beef. And you know what? I'm doing okay. I pay my taxes. I hold down a steady job. I was even invited to speak at TED. But the presumption now is that what was good enough for me, or for my folks for that matter, isn't good enough anymore. So we all make a mad dash to that bookshelf, because we feel like if we aren't trying everything, it's as if we're doing nothing and we're defaulting on our obligations to our kids.

So it's hard enough to navigate our new roles as mothers and fathers. Now add to this problem something else: we are also navigating new roles as husbands and wives because most women today are in the workforce. This is another reason, I think, that parenthood feels like a crisis. We have no rules, no scripts, no norms for what to do when a child comes along now that both mom and dad are breadwinners. The writer Michael Lewis once put this very, very well. He said that the surest way for a couple to start fighting is for them to go out to dinner with another couple whose division of labor is ever so slightly different from theirs, because the conversation in the car on the way home goes something like this:

"So, did you catch that Dave is the one who walks them to school every morning?" Without scripts telling us who does what in this brave new world, couples fight, and both mothers and fathers each have their legitimate gripes. Mothers are much more likely to be multi-tasking when they are at home, and fathers, when they are at home, are much more likely to be mono-tasking. Find a guy at home, and odds are he is doing just one thing at a time. In fact, UCLA recently did a study looking at the most common configuration of family members in middle-class homes. Guess what it was? Dad in a room by himself. According to the *American Time Use Survey*, mothers still do twice as much childcare as fathers, which is better than it was in Erma Bombeck's day, but I still think that something she wrote is highly relevant: "I have not been alone in the bathroom since October."

But here is the thing: Men are doing plenty. They spend more time with their kids than their fathers ever spent with them. They work more paid hours, on average, than their wives, and they genuinely want to be good, involved dads. Today, it is fathers, not mothers, who report the most work-life conflict.

Either way, by the way, if you think it's hard for traditional families to sort out these new roles, just imagine what it's like now for non-traditional families: families with two dads, families with two moms, single-parent households. They are truly improvising as they go.

Now, in a more progressive country, and forgive me here for capitulating to cliché and invoking, yes, Sweden, parents could rely on the state for support. There are countries that acknowledge the anxieties and the changing roles of mothers and fathers. Unfortunately, the United States is not one of them, so in case you were wondering what the U.S. has in common with Papua New Guinea and Liberia, it's this: We too have no paid maternity leave policy. We are one of eight known countries that does not.

In this age of intense confusion, there is just one goal upon which all parents can agree, and that is whether they are tiger moms or hippie moms, helicopters or drones, our kids' happiness is paramount. That is what it means to raise kids in an age when they are economically worthless but emotionally priceless. We are all the custodians of their self-esteem. The one mantra no parent ever questions is, "All I want is for my children to be happy." And don't get me wrong: I think happiness is a wonderful goal for a child. But it is a very elusive one. Happiness and self-confidence, teaching children that is not like teaching them how to plow a field. It's not like teaching them how to ride a bike. There's no curriculum for it. Happiness and self-confidence can be the byproducts of other things, but they cannot really be goals unto themselves. A child's happiness is a very unfair burden to place on a parent. And happiness is an even more unfair burden to place on a kid.

And I have to tell you, I think it leads to some very strange excesses. We are now so anxious to protect our kids from the world's ugliness that we now shield them from "*Sesame Street*." I wish I could say I was kidding about this, but if you go out and you buy the first few episodes of "*Sesame Street*" on DVD, as I did out of nostalgia, you will find a warning at the beginning saying that the content is not suitable for children. Can I just repeat that? The content of the original "*Sesame Street*" is not suitable for children. When asked about this by *The New York Times*, a producer for the show gave a variety of explanations. One was that Cookie Monster smoked a pipe in one skit and then swallowed it. Bad modeling. I don't know. But the thing that stuck with me is she said that she didn't know whether Oscar the Grouch could be invented today because he was too depressive. I cannot tell you how much this distresses me. You are looking at a woman who has a periodic table of the Muppets hanging from her cubicle wall. The offending muppet, right there.

That's my son the day he was born. I was high as a kite on morphine. I had had an unexpected C-section. But even in my opiate haze, I managed to have one very clear thought the first time I held him. I whispered it into his ear. I said, "I will try so hard not to hurt you." It was the Hippocratic Oath, and I didn't even know I was saying it. But it occurs to me now that the Hippocratic Oath is a much more realistic aim than happiness. In fact, as any parent will tell you, it's awfully hard. All of us have said or done hurtful things that we wish to God we could take back. I think in another era we did not expect quite so much from ourselves, and it is important that we all remember that the next time we are staring with our hearts racing at those bookshelves. I'm not really sure how to create new norms for this world, but I do think that in our desperate quest to create happy kids, we may be assuming the wrong moral burden. It strikes me as a better goal, and, dare I say, a more virtuous one, to focus on making productive kids and moral kids, and to simply hope that happiness will come to them by virtue of the good that they do and their accomplishments and the love that they feel from us. That, anyway, is one response to having no script. Absent having new scripts, we just follow the oldest ones in the book — decency, a work ethic, love — and let happiness and self-esteem take care of themselves. I think if we all did that, the kids would still be all right, and so would their parents, possibly in both cases even better.

Thank you.

对于父母而言，幸福是个非常高的标准

我出生那会儿，只有一本书是讲述育儿经的，它的作者是斯波克医生。谢谢大家配合。非常高兴看到你们的热情。

事实上是本杰明·斯波克，他的著作叫《斯波克育儿经》。他离世时，该书已畅销接近5000万册。如今，作为一名6岁孩子的母亲，我走进巴诺书店时，看到了这个书架。书架上形形色色书籍多得令人惊讶。有关"环保地"养育小孩的，有关养育"无麸质"小孩的，有关养育"百病不侵"小孩的，这些书，在我看来，让人感觉有些不自在。还有关于如何让孩子学会两种语言的书籍，即使在家里你只会用一种语言跟孩子沟通。有教你培养孩子金融思维的书，也有培养孩子科学头脑的书，还有培养孩子成为瑜伽大师的书。除了教小孩如何拆除核弹，其他似乎应有尽有。

所有这些书籍可谓用心良苦。我深信其中也有许多优秀作品。但把它们整合起来的话，非常遗憾，当我看着那一架子书时，我看到的不是它们会为我带来什么帮助，我看到的是焦虑。我看到了一座高耸的糖果色的碑，集聚着整个社会的恐慌，这不禁让我深思，为何养育子女会有如此多的苦恼，会如此让人困惑？这可是一件人类薪火相传了上千年的事情，为何今天却让人摸不着头脑呢？那时，可没有育儿论坛，也没有专家特地来研究。为何有这么多人会把为人父母当作一种危机？

说是危机，看似言重了，但有数据表明这么说并不为过。事实上，1957年就有文章以此命名，《视为人父母如危机来临》在此后的50多年里，诸多学术论文一五一十地反映了父母的苦恼。有孩子的夫妇的压力要高于那些没有孩子的夫妇，前者对婚姻的满意度更低。有很多课题研究父母与孩子共度时光时的感受，而结论往往并不理想。去年，我与专家马修·柯林沃斯有过一次交谈，他正在研究一个极富于想象力的追踪人们幸福感的项目，他与我分享了研究成果："与朋友来往获得的快乐高于与配偶来往获得的，高于与其他亲属来往获得的，高于与点头之交来往获得的，高于与父母来往获得的，高于与子女来往获得的，与子女来往的快乐跟与陌生人的差不多。"

事实是这样的。我对这些数据的前因后果做了为期3年的研究，我发现问题不在于孩子，而是在于如今养育孩子的理念和方法。具体说来，我认为我们没有理解育儿的真正意义。"育儿"这个动词，在20世纪70年代才开始流行。

作为父母，我们的角色已经发生了变化。孩子们的角色也发生了变化。养育儿女，宛如一场即兴表演，但这场表演没有剧本。如果你是一名响当当的爵士音乐家，即兴演奏也会很棒，但对普通大众而言，说是危机也无可厚非。

　　我们为何会陷入这种状况？没有指引，我们如何在育儿的浩瀚世界中做到游刃有余？从头说起吧，育儿理念发生过一次历史性的转变。这个转变就发生不久，在这之前，孩子自小就劳作，主要在农场，也在工厂、车间、矿山。孩子被当作经济资产。到了"进步时代"，对孩子的这种看法终结了。

　　我们认为小孩也有权力，明令禁止雇佣童工，我们将他们的教育放在首位，因而学习便成了孩子们的新任务。幸好如此。但是，这样会让父母更加迷茫于自己应该扮演的角色。曾经的观念也许不太符合伦理道德，但它是互惠的。我们提供给孩子衣、食、住，以及基本的道德教育，他们则提供经济收入作为回报。

　　一旦孩子们不再自小就工作，从经济学角度来看，育儿的理念便发生了变化。引用一位非常有天分但又"无情"的社会学家的话，孩子"经济上一文不值，感情上珍贵无比"。孩子们从此不为我们工作，我们便要开始为他们张罗。因为仅仅数十年一过，事实已经浮现在眼前：如果我们想让孩子成功，学校教育是不够的。如今，各种课外活动成了孩子们的新功课，更是我们的新功课，因为正是我们把他们拉入足球训练场。堆积如山的作业是孩子们的新任务。也是我们的任务，因为我们得检查作业。大约3年前，一位得克萨斯州女士向我倾吐了一些事情，我听了后心都碎了。她在不经意间说到，"家庭作业是第二顿晚餐。"现在，中产阶级将所有的时间、精力和资源完全投入在小孩身上，哪怕他们能够给予的东西越来越少。而今，母亲们陪在孩子身边的时间多于1965年，那时大多数女士还都是不用工作的。

　　假如知道该为孩子准备些什么，父母们适应这个新的角色或许会容易得多。这也是现代育儿令人困惑的另一原因。我们不知道究竟哪一种智慧，如果有的话，适用于自己的孩子。世界变化得如此日新月异，凡事难以预料。我年轻的时候也是一样。在我小的时候，特别是在高中时，有人告诉我要是不懂点日语的话，我将来会迷失在新的全球经济环境中。但日语，恕我冒昧，并没有显现出如此重要的作用。如今，又有一些中产阶级的父母，他们痴迷于让小孩学习中文，也许，他们是预料到了什么，但没人能确定。既然我们无法预知未来，但想当称职的父母的话，我们就得尝试着为小孩准备一切，来应对将来的不时之需，希望总有一分努力会有用武之地。我们教小孩下棋，认为可以培养他们的问题分析能力。我们为他们报名参加团体运动，认为可以培养他们的团队合作能力，你懂的，当他们去哈佛商学院读书时就用到了。我们试着将他们培养成一名富有金融思维、科学思维、生态友好而且无麸质的小孩，那么，借此机会告诉大家，小时候，我不是生态友好或无麸质的孩子。我吃了一罐又一罐的通心面和牛肉。结果呢？一切正常。我纳税，有稳定的工作。还被邀请来做 TED 演讲。但现在的前提是，对我和我那个时代的人而言足够好的东西，如今已不再足够了。所以，我们才一窝蜂地涌向那个书架，因为我们觉得，凡事不尝试一番，就相当于什么都没做，就是没有履行对孩子应尽的义务。

所以我们就很难扮演好今天的父母的角色。让问题更为复杂的是，我们还扮演着丈夫和妻子的新角色，因为现在大多数女士们已进入职场。我想，这可能是另一个人们把做父母视如危机的原因。爸爸、妈妈忙于养家糊口，又没有标准、剧本、指引，小孩出生后可该怎么办。作家迈克尔·刘易斯曾经一语中的。他说最能引起夫妻争吵的方法，是与另一对夫妇共进晚餐，而且他们的职业还与自己的略有不同。晚餐过后，驱车回家途中的对话一般会是："喂，难道你没有发现是大卫每天早晨送小孩上学吗？"在这样一个崭新的社会，没有成文规定谁该做什么，夫妇便争吵起来了，而且双方各自的抱怨都合乎情理。母亲在家时，往往承担多项家务，而父亲在家时，同一时间做的事情通常是一件。随便看看哪户人家，有意思的是爸爸通常每次只做一件事情。事实上，加州大学洛杉矶分校最近就中产阶级家庭里最常见的现象做了一项调查。猜猜结果如何？父亲独自一人在一个房间里。《美国人的时间安排调查》表明，母亲在照顾小孩上所花费的时间是父亲的两倍，这一比例虽然低于艾尔玛·邦贝克的描述，但我认为这跟她写的一些东西还是息息相关："10月份以来，我就没一个人在卫生间待过。"

但事实是：男士们的付出也不少。他们陪伴孩子度过的时间要多于他们的父亲陪伴自己的时光。他们的平均工作时间要多于妻子，而且他们不仅想要把工作做好，在家也想做一个好父亲。如今，是父亲，而不是母亲，更多地抱怨工作生活失衡问题。

不管怎样，顺便说一下，如果传统家庭适应这些新角色都较难的话，试想一下，非传统家庭将会怎样？两个父亲的家庭，两个母亲的家庭，单亲家庭。他们真的是走一步，看一步。

如今，在一个制度更先进的国度，不好意思，又提到老生常谈的问题了，是的，要说到瑞典，在那里，父母可以依靠国家的福利。很多国家已经认识到了父母的担忧，以及他们不断变化的角色。不幸的是，美国不在其中，因此，如果要问美国与巴布亚新几内亚和利比里亚有何共性的话，答案是：我们都没有带薪产假政策。已知的奉行无薪产假的国家有8个，我们赫然在列。

在这样一个困惑丛生的年代，只有一个目标是所有父母一致同意的，无论母亲是虎妈还是嬉皮妈妈，是直升机父母的还是无人机父母，孩子们的幸福是首要的。这也就是在一个把孩子看作"经济上一文不值，感情上珍贵无比"的时代里，养育孩子的意义所在。我们是孩子的自尊的守护者，有这样一句父母都不会质疑的祈祷，"保佑我的子女们幸福快乐。"不要误会我的意思：我认为幸福对孩子们是一个再好不过的目标。但事情没这么简单。让孩子幸福与自信，不同于教他们如何犁地。也不同于教他们如何去骑车。没有教程告诉我们如何实现它。幸福与自信是随着其他事物而生的，而不是作为一种目标，强加到他们身上。孩子的幸福，让父母来承担是不公平。但如果让孩子来承担的话，更不公平。

我必须要告诉你们，为了让孩子幸福，我们有时会反应过度。我们现在总是急于让小孩远离社会上的是非之物，甚至不让他们观看《芝麻街》。我希望我是在开玩笑，但是，如果你去买几张《芝麻街》最初几集的 DVD 光盘，我之前是出于怀旧目的买的。你会发现片头的的警告语，提示说本片少儿不宜。是真的，昔日的《芝麻街》居然是少儿不宜的节目。《纽约时报》就此事进行采访时，该节目的制片人给出了种种解释。原因之一是饼干怪兽在剧中抽过烟斗，然后把烟斗吃掉了。这是个负面形象。我不太明白。但是让我印象深刻的是，她说她不知道 Oscar the Grouch（《芝麻街》中的角色）放到今天是否能被创作，因为它性格太悲观了。我简直无法形容这句话让我多伤心。你现在看到的是一位将经典布偶主题的元素周期表挂在墙上的女士。这个心情不愉快的布偶，就在这儿。

这是我儿子出生那天拍的照片。当注射吗啡后，我感觉就像高高飞翔的风筝一样。我做了个意料之外的剖腹产手术。在还没有醒麻的时候，我第一次抱着他，就有了个清晰的想法。我靠近他耳边，轻轻说，"我会非常努力地去做到不伤害你。"这是希波克拉底的誓言，我浑然不觉地说了这句话，但是现在，在我看来这句誓言是比幸福更容易实现的一个目标。事实上，每位父母们都知道，这是相当难的。我们都说过或做过一些让人伤心的事情，我们恳请上帝让我们将其收回。我想，未来有一天，我们不再对自己有过高的期望，更重要是，我们都要提醒自己记住我们看着那些满满的书架时内心的焦虑。虽然我确实不知道该如何去为世界制定新的标准，但我确实认为，当我们竭力追求培养幸福快乐的小孩时，我们或许承担着错误的思想负担。我觉得更好的目标，容我说，也是更有效的目标，那就是注重培养富有创造力和品德高尚的孩子，然后只要祝福他们幸福，通过他们的德行善举、他们的才能成就以及感受到我们对他们的爱。总之，这也是一种对现实的答复。没有新的剧本，那么就沿用书中最古老的箴言吧——保持礼貌，职业道德，爱——幸福与自尊将自然成长。

337

我想如果我们都做到了这一点，孩子们就会幸福成长，父母也不用说了，可能对双方都更好。

谢谢大家。

（来源：https://www.ted.com/talks/jennifer_senior_for_parents_happiness_is_a_very_high_bar/transcript）

第三章

《大学体验英语》综合教程第三册

第一单元　关爱我们的地球
（Unit 1　Caring for Our Earth）

1. 思政主题：全球变暖，保护地球，人与动物和谐共生

2. 意义

本单元关注全球气候变暖、人与自然的关系。气候变暖是一种和自然有关的现象，是由于温室效应不断积累，导致地气系统吸收与发射的能量不平衡，能量不断在地气系统累积，从而导致温度上升，造成全球气候变暖。

由于人们焚烧化石燃料，如石油、煤炭等，或砍伐森林并将其焚烧时会产生大量的二氧化碳，即温室气体导致地球温度上升，即温室效应。全球变暖会使全球降水量重新分配、冰川和冻土消融、海平面上升、物种灭亡、山火频发、疾病快速蔓延、出现干旱洪涝热浪极端天气等等，不仅危害自然生态系统的平衡，还影响人类健康，甚至威胁人类的生存。

人与自然应该和谐共生。我国"十三五"规划中提出了"创新、协调、绿色、开放、共享"的"五大发展"理念，强调"绿色发展"，指出了当前在我国大气、水、土壤污染问题仍旧严峻的现状，加快建设资源节约型、环境友好型社会，推进绿色低碳循环发展，是为国家乃至全球的生态安全做贡献。教师可将这一理念融入单元教学设计，带领学生探讨近年来中国环境污染防治的积极举措与成效，引导学生对环境保护、生态价值观、人类命运共同体等主题进行思考与讨论，体现外语课程思政育人价值。

习近平总书记曾在领导人气候峰会上发表题为《共同构建人与自然生命共同体》的讲话中提到：

人类进入工业文明时代以来，在创造巨大物质财富的同时，也加速了对自然资源的攫取，打破了地球生态系统平衡，人与自然深层次矛盾日益显现。近年来，气候变化、生物多样性丧失、荒漠化加剧、极端气候事件频发，给人类

生存和发展带来严峻挑战。新冠肺炎疫情持续蔓延，使各国经济社会发展雪上加霜。面对全球环境治理前所未有的困难，国际社会要以前所未有的雄心和行动，勇于担当，勠力同心，共同构建人与自然生命共同体。

Since time of the industrial civilization, mankind has created massive material wealth. Yet, it has come at a cost of intensified exploitation of natural resources, which disrupted the balance in the Earth's ecosystem, and laid bare the growing tensions in the human-nature relationship. In recent years, climate change, biodiversity loss, worsening desertification and frequent extreme weather events have all posed severe challenges to human survival and development. The ongoing COVID-19 pandemic has added difficulty to economic and social development across countries. Faced with unprecedented challenges in global environmental governance, the international community needs to come up with unprecedented ambition and action. We need to act with a sense of responsibility and unity, and work together to foster a community of life for man and nature.

坚持人与自然和谐共生。"万物各得其和以生，各得其养以成。"大自然是包括人在内一切生物的摇篮，是人类赖以生存发展的基本条件。大自然孕育抚养了人类，人类应该以自然为根，尊重自然、顺应自然、保护自然。不尊重自然，违背自然规律，只会遭到自然报复。自然遭到系统性破坏，人类生存发展就成了无源之水、无本之木。我们要像保护眼睛一样保护自然和生态环境，推动形成人与自然和谐共生新格局。

We must be committed to harmony between man and nature. "All things that grow live in harmony and benefit from the nourishment of nature." Mother nature is the cradle of all living beings, including humans. It provides everything essential for humanity to survive and thrive. Mother nature has nourished us, and we must treat nature as our root, respect it, protect it, and follow its laws. Failure to respect nature or follow its laws will only invite its revenge. Systemic spoil of nature will take away the foundation of human survival and development, and will leave us human beings like a river without a source and a tree without its roots. We should protect nature and preserve the environment like we protect our eyes, and endeavor to foster a new relationship where man and nature can both prosper and live in harmony.

坚持绿色发展。绿水青山就是金山银山。保护生态环境就是保护生产力，改善生态环境就是发展生产力，这是朴素的真理。我们要摒弃损害甚至破坏生态环境的发展模式，摒弃以牺牲环境换取一时发展的短视做法。要顺应当代科技革命和产业变革大方向，抓住绿色转型带来的巨大发展机遇，以创新为驱动，大力推进经济、能源、产业结构转型升级，让良好生态环境成为全球经济社会可持续发展的支撑。

We must be committed to green development. Green mountains are gold mountains. To protect the environment is to protect productivity, and to improve the environment is to boost productivity — the truth is as simple as that. We must abandon development models that harm or undermine the environment, and must say no to shortsighted approaches of going after near-term development gains at the expense of the environment. Much to the contrary, we need to ride the trend of technological revolution and industrial transformation, seize the enormous opportunity in green transition, and let the power of innovation drive us to upgrade our economic, energy and industrial structures, and make sure that a sound environment is there to buttress sustainable economic and social development worldwide.

（来源：中国双语日报新闻）

3. 教学设计与思政元素的融入

Passage A

3.1 Warm-up 环节

英文视频：An Inconvenient Truth

通过展示世界各地冰川地貌在短短数十年内缩小乃至消失的过程，揭示了温室效应已经引发了全球气候深刻变化这一难以忽视的真相，时长2分30秒。单元面授课时，教师可用几分钟时间请学生观看并思考视频中所揭露问题产生的原因以及对人类生活的影响。

All this time what I have seen all these years is that it just keeps going up, it is relentless and now we are beginning to see the impact in the real world. This is mount Kilimanjoro thirty years ago and more recently a friend of mine just came back from Kilimanjoro with a picture he took a couple months ago. Another friend Lonnie Thompson studies glacier. Here is Lonnie with the last sliver of one of the once mighty glaciers. Within a decade, there will be no more snow of Kilimanjoro. This is happening in glacier national park. I climb to the top in nineteen ninety-eight with one of my daughters. Within fifteen years, this will be a park formerly known as glacier. Here is what has been happening year by year to the Columbia glacier.

It just retreats every single year and it's a shame cause these glaciers are so beautiful but for those who go up to see them, here is what they see every day now. In the Himalayas, there is a particular problem because there are forty percent of all the people in the world who get their drinking water from rivers and spring systems that are fed more than half by the melt water coming off the glaciers. And within this next half century those forty percent of the people on earth are going to face a very serious shortage because of this melting.

Italy. The Italian Alps, same site today. A postcard from Switzerland throughout the Alps were seen the same stories. It's also true in South America. This is Peru fifteen years ago and the same glacier today. This is Argentina twenty years ago, same glacier today. Seventy five years ago in Patagonia, tip of South America, this vast expanse of ice is now gone. There is a message in this, it is worldwide and the ice has stories to tell us.

（来源：https://v.qq.com/x/page/a3077j3s4n2.html）

3.2 Discussion 环节

双语文章：Global Warming 全球变暖

联合国气候变化科学机构——政府间气候变化专门委员会（The Intergovernmental Panel on Climate Change，简称 IPCC）发布了一份报告，揭示了全球变暖即将带来的灾难性后果，并呼吁各方为遏制全球变暖采取必要的行动。教师可以让学生阅读文章后讨论：What are the consequences of global warming? What should be done to reduce global warming?

《纽约时报》（*The New York Times*）称，该报告是由来自40多个国家的91名科学家在分析了6000多份科学研究后撰写的。

据分析，照现在的趋势发展下去，2040年将会出现重大灾难，美国、中国、孟加拉国、埃及、印度等5000万人的家园将受到洪水的影响，损失预计高达5.4万亿美元（约合37万亿人民币，即中国2016年国内生产总值的一半）。

"It's telling us we need to reverse emissions trends and turn the world economy on a dime," said Myles Allen, an Oxford University climate scientist and an author of the report.

牛津大学气候科学家、该报告的作者迈尔斯·艾伦说："这告诉我们，需要立即扭转排放趋势，转变世界经济发展方式。"

但联合国最新的研究表明，升温2℃所产生的不良后果可能比预期的更严重，全球升温幅度必须控制在1.5℃以内。

1.5℃和2℃明明没有很大差别。但研究表明，这0.5℃的温差看似微不足道，实则会影响到数亿人的生活。

一起来看看德国之声（Deutsche Welle）的报道：

In a plus 1.5℃ world, sea level rise would be 10 centimeters (3.94 inches) less than with 2℃, exposing about 10 million fewer people in coastal areas to risks such as floods, storm surges or salt spray damaging crops.

在升温1.5℃时，海平面上升高度将比在升温2℃时少上升10厘米（3.94英寸），沿海地区受洪水、风暴潮及盐雾等灾害破坏庄稼所影响的民众也会减少约1000万。

全球变暖后果比预期的严重。

根据2015年签署的《巴黎协定》（Paris Agreement），与工业化前相比，全球升温幅度要被控制在2℃以内，最好能低于1.5℃。

Over past years, global warming has ravaged the oceans' richest ecosystems, with bleaching events across the tropics. At 1.5℃, we can expect to lose between 70 and 90 percent of our reefs. But 2℃ of warming would see them virtually wiped out — a loss of at least 99 percent.

在过去几年中，全球变暖摧毁了海洋最丰富的生态系统，"漂白"现象在整个热带地区蔓延。在升温1.5℃时，我们可能会失去70%至90%的珊瑚礁。但升温2℃则会让它们几乎全部消失——至少损失99%。

此外，温度升高不仅会对沿海地区造成威胁，对北极乃至整个地球都将带来毁灭性的灾难。

At 1.5℃ we can expect to see an ice-free Arctic summer once a century. At 2℃, that risk shoots up to once every decade.

在（升温）1.5℃时，每隔一个世纪就会出现一个无冰的北极夏季。在（升温）2℃时，这种风险飙升至每十年出现一次。

需要强调的是，目前人类活动已经使全球变暖了大约1℃，并且正在以每十年约0.2℃的速度上升，距离1.5℃的警戒值越来越近。

据德国之声报道，近几年，极端天气（extreme weather）已经愈加频繁，海平面的加速上升也已经造成了部分岛屿的淹没。

While 2004 to 2010 saw oceans rise by about 15 millimeters in total, this value doubled for 2010 to 2016. Tropical regions in the western Pacific are especially affected, threatening many of the coastal areas and low-lying islands with submersion by the end of the century.

2004年至2010年海洋总体上升了约15毫米，但这一数字在2010年至2016年翻了一番。西太平洋热带地区受到的影响尤其大，许多沿海地区和低洼岛屿在本世纪末将面临被淹没的威胁。

斐济、图瓦卢等低洼岛屿国家已被迫改变食物种植方式，甚至搬迁整个村庄以求生存。

仍有机会降低全球变暖造成的影响

IPCC报告明确指出，人类需要在气候保护方面采取更多有效措施，将升温幅度控制在1.5℃以内。

"Limiting global warming to 1.5℃ would require rapid, far-reaching and unprecedented changes in all aspects of society."

"将全球变暖限制在1.5℃，将需要在社会各个方面进行快速、深远、前所未有的变化。"

首要目标是转变能源结构，减少碳排放。

In order to limit global warming to 1.5 degrees, we would need to cut global emissions 45 percent by 2030 (compared to 2010 levels), and bring them to net zero by 2050.

为了将全球变暖限制在1.5℃，我们需要在2030年之前将全球排放量减少45%（与2010年相比），并在2050年之前将其降至零净值。

路透社（Reuters）相关报道称，清洁能源的使用应大幅增加。

The draft says renewable energies, such as wind, solar and hydro power, would have to surge by 60 percent from 2020 levels by 2050 to stay below 1.5℃ "while primary energy from coal decreases by two-thirds".

该草案称，为使升温幅度保持在1.5℃以下，在2050年之前，风能、太阳能和水力发电等可再生能源必须在2020年的水平上提高60%，而"煤炭能源需减少三分之二"。

除了通过改变能源结构减少碳排放，也可以通过重新造林（reforestation）、"负排放"（negative emissions）技术等手段减少大气中的碳含量。负排放，即使用碳捕获和储存（carbon capture and storage）等技术从大气中去除二氧化碳。但迄今为止，这种技术仅限于小规模应用，且运行结果有好有坏。

不过，正如《纽约时报》所指出的，要遏制全球变暖，解决技术难题易，解决政治问题难。

国际气候研究中心的研究主任格伦·彼得斯（Glen Peters）一针见血地指出，比负排放技术更难搞定的，是各国的政治家。

"Engineers can figure out how to remove carbon dioxide from the atmosphere," Peters said. "It's a lot harder to get rid of Trump — or to get India or Brazil, say, to prioritize climate over everything else."

"工程师可以弄清楚如何从大气中去除二氧化碳，但要搞定特朗普，或者让印度和巴西把气候问题放在最优先位置，那就更难了。"

世界自然基金会（WWF）气候变化首席顾问斯蒂芬·科尼利斯（Stephen Cornelius）也表示，能不能实现减排目标，主要看各国政府的政治意愿（political will）。

"We need to push governments, so they know this is important, so that they have that mandate to act."

"我们需要鞭策政府，让他们知道事态的严重性，让他们采取行动。"

节能减排，抑制全球变暖，任重而道远。

比世界末日更可怕的，是我们明知道如何避免灾难，却不付诸实践。

（来源：中国日报双语新闻）

3.3 Critical thinking 环节

英文视频：Planet Earth Is You

近5分钟的英文视频，通过展示人类出于一己之欲肆意破坏自然生态、伤害其他生物的多个片段，传达了"破坏大自然就是伤害我们自己"这一观点，提醒人们警惕自食其果，呼吁提高保护地球的意识。教师可请学生观看视频，结合单元主题思考人类是该战胜自然还是崇拜自然，亦或是平衡人与自然。

Humans,
what an incredible word.
We are considered the most intelligence species on the planet.
However,
we are the worst.
What are we doing in this world?
Who brought us here?
What's our mission on this planet?
Maybe we will never understand it,
but it seems,
the only mission is continue with its destruction.
Have you ever considered that this planet does not belong to us?
Either way, its care is in our hands.
They were here already before us,

and we are nothing but their guests.
We came in, invaded their territory,
and we are destroying their home.
They've been tolerant.
We've been forgiven countless times,
but we keep ignore their situation.
We've been their kidnappers,
their killers,
however,
they accept us as their owners.
We are the only species that attacks, destroys, annihilates, contaminates and extinguishes just for ambition,
or just live better.
The world is yours,
is ours,
it's for all of us.
However, remember it's their world too.
We have to understand that they can't do anything to save their life,
much less,
to save their planet.
Planet earth is dying,
We are destroying it in a savage way.
But he's hungry for love,
he's getting weak,
and despite it all,
he keeps giving to us generously,
the best experience since we arrived on it.
The planet has been the best house for species.
If we were given the capacity to speak, think, create, build and help,
why do we remain silent, ignorant, destroy and kill it?
Open your eyes,
you are dying too,
along with your planet,
the only planet in all solar system that we were given to privilege to live.

We are billions on this planet.

We are thinking of these, rational, dominate,

why we haven't notice it?

We are capable of conquering countries,

the moon,

even planets,

however, we are not capable of conquering our own hearts.

Touch your heart,

feel what it's trying to say,

listen to what it's yearning for.

Let's understand that we have to co-exist on the same planet,

start by changing yourself,

engage yourself,

make sure your children know it and understand it,

and remind those who have forgotten.

When the day human stop existing,

and another species find our planet,

they will see that we are species that failed, fell down.

But get up and fix our mistakes,

the planet is not the same anymore.

We can not wait any longer,

everybody knows what we have to do.

Our time is now,

the future of the planet is still in your hands.

Help him.

Let's help him,

because planet earth is you.

（来源：https://v.qq.com/x/page/p0161vcv0dw.html?）

3.4 主题拓展环节

英语视频：TED 演讲应对气候变化刻不容缓

视频中，气候研究员 Alice Bows-Larkin 通过细致描述气温升高2℃至4℃后世界将发生的巨大变化，阐明应对气候变暖已是刻不容缓，呼吁大众提高对全球气候变暖问题的关注。该素材有助于学生进一步思考作为世界公民对环境保护的责任，深化对课文内容的理解。

（来源：https://www.ted.com/talks/alice_bows_larkin_climate_change_is_happening_here_s_how_we_adapt#t-118845）

Passage B

3.5 Warm-up 环节

英语视频：绿水青山就是金山银山

视频时长约4分30秒，简述了习近平总书记的生态文明观。围绕"绿水青山就是金山银山"这一主题，清晰梳理了中国多年来应对环境污染的积极举措和取得的傲人成果，学生可通过观看本视频，深刻了解中国的生态价值观。

Humans and nature live together. For China, establishing an ecological civilization is a fundamental strategy in achieving sustainable development. We want mountains of gold and silver but not at the cost of lucid waters and lush mountains. We would rather have lucid waters and lush mountains than mountains of gold and silver, because lucid waters and lush mountains are invaluable assets.

Every major city in China lies on a river. However, in 2013, studies revealed a shocking statistic that China's ten biggest waterways were polluted for over half of their combined length. Of all China's rivers, the one that gives rise to the greatest concern is its Mother River, the Yangtze River. President Xi has visited the river numerous times. He has called for a major effort to protect it and for a ban on large-scale construction along its course. Insisting on ecology first and green development, the development path of the Yangtze Economic Belt is becoming clear. Today, the Yangtze River is generally in good condition. The water quality of the Yellow River and two other key waterways, Heilongjiang River and Nenjiang River, has been improving.

The Three-North Shelter Forest Program has been a great success in global ecosystem governance. Returning the Grain Plots to Forestry Project has created more than thirty million hectares of forest and grasslands in the past twenty years. China adheres to green development, and by doing so, it is helping the entire world. In spring 2019, the results of a NASA environmental study were published: From 2000 to 2017, China had been responsible for about a quarter of the new green area created worldwide. This made it the world's biggest contributor.

The main idea of green development is to solve how man and nature exist in harmony. Builders of the Hong Kong-Zhuhai -Macao Bridge have made a promise that its construction would not force the dolphins from their natural habitat. That promise has evidently been kept. Many of China's cities are rapidly being covered in green. China's environmental protection revolution has been transforming the country's economic and energy structures. China must be a beautiful place covered with green hills and clear rivers and filled with nostalgic memories.

（来源：http://www.chinareports.org.cn/yszx/duoyu/20191024/11584.html）

3.6 Discussion 环节

英文文章: What Is Environmental Sustainability and Sustainable Development?

面对日益严峻的环境和资源问题，"可持续"已经被越来越频繁地讨论，并且被更广泛地实践着。通过本文，教师可引导学生思考：你能为环境可持续与可持续发展做什么？

While it may seem that environmental sustainability and sustainable development are one in the same, there is quite a few ways in which they diverge in their goals. They do have the same overall goal that of conserving natural resources and creating more energy efficient projects and practices — but the two groups that are focused on them may find themselves in disagreement about what the priorities of actions are. Having a better understanding of how they are different and the same can help you do know how to navigate dealing with both.

What is Environmental Sustainability?

The goal of environmental sustainability is to conserve natural resources and to develop alternate sources of power while reducing pollution and harm to the environment. For environmental sustainability, the state of the future — as measured in 50,100 and 1,000 years is the guiding principle. Many of the projects that are rooted in environmental sustainability will involve replanting forests, preserving wetlands and protecting natural areas from resource harvesting. The biggest criticism of environmental sustainability initiatives is that their priorities can be at odds with the needs of a growing industrialized society.

What is Sustainable Development?

Sustainable development is the practice of developing land and construction projects in a manner that reduces their impact on the environment by allowing them to create energy efficient models of self-sufficiency. This can take the form of installing solar panels or wind generators on factory sites, using geothermal heating techniques or even participating in cap and trade agreements. The biggest criticism of sustainable development is that it does not do enough to conserve the environment in the present and is based on the belief that the harm done in one area of the world can be counter balanced by creating environmental protections in the other.

According to Brundtland Commission in its 1987 report *Our Common Future*, "Sustainable development is development that meets the needs of the present, without compromising the ability of future generations to meet their own needs."

Sustainable development has 3 goals: to minimize the depletion of natural resources, to promote development without causing harm to the environment and to make use of environmentally friendly practices.

When are the goals of each not in agreement?

The goals of the two groups diverge when it comes to the development of endangered areas. For instance, there will be disagreements when it comes to developing construction practices on a wetland. The environmental sustainability focus would argue that the preservation of the wetland is more important than everything else.

Sustainable development will show that by incorporating preservation areas, and contributing to the overall preservation of a different wetland area that the damage is balanced out. Sustainable development will also argue that the local economic benefits will lead to more funding to create environmental protection areas elsewhere.

What are the current practices that seek a balance?

Resolving these differences can be difficult. Very often, money and economy will prove to be the deciding factor. This doesn't mean that one side loses and one side wins, but the environmental factors can influence the development design to create an approach that provides the best of both worlds, without completing adopting one approach over the other. The environmental sustainability plans may show the sustainable development engineers that there are aspects of their design that can be improved to lessen the impact of the project on the wetland area that would still be in existence. Through committing funds and development to protected areas that are not a part of the development, environmental sustainability projects that emphasize conservation and public education can advance further than they would have on their own.

What can be done to promote greater attention to both?

The best approach is to educate the consumers, and the industry, to leave behind an either/or approach to development and conservation and to take on a balanced ratio approach that seeks the best of both worlds. This is very hard to do as it requires an element of sacrifice be adopted by the present society. To this end you need both of the sides to come together to commit to creating regulations, incentive programs and tax credits that promote sustainable development while defining priorities for conservation in different areas that will also feed back into the local communities.

More research and development is also needed in the areas of sustainable development to create better engineering and construction options that are more in keeping with environmental sustainable goals. In the end, no one can afford to lose sight of the fact that the environment as we know it is steadily eroding and the future of everyone is dependent on the care we take today to preserve the resources that we know, so we have time to develop better ways of living in the world.

（来源：https://www.conserve-energy-future.com/what-is-environmental-sustainability-and-sustainable-development.php）

3.7 Critical thinking 环节

双语文章：China's Green Development Wins Recognition, Creates New Opportunities 绿色发展赢得共识 创造机遇

经济发展会不会以牺牲环境为代价？习近平总书记指出："绿水青山就是金山银山"，经济的高质量发展不能以牺牲环境为代价，这在当代中国已经成为共识。近年来，中国坚持走生态优先、绿色发展之路，这不仅没有阻碍经济发展，反而给经济发展创造了新的机遇。

China's economic growth has long impressed the world with its blistering speed. Now its accelerating green transformation is expected to offer inspiring lessons in coordinating the economy and the natural environment.

长期以来，中国经济的快速增长给世界留下了深刻印象。现在，中国的绿色转型正在加速发展，有望在协调经济和自然环境方面给人们提供积极经验。

Ant Forest, a green initiative on the world's leading payment platform Alipay, last week won the 2019 UN Champions of the Earth award for turning the "green good deeds of half a billion people" into real trees planted in some of China's most arid regions.

上周，蚂蚁森林因将"5亿人的绿色善行"转化为在中国最干旱地区种植树木，赢得了2019年联合国"地球卫士奖"。蚂蚁森林是全球领先的支付平台——支付宝发起的一项环保行动。

It was not the first time that China won the UN's highest environmental honor for outstanding contributions in terms of a positive transformative impact on the environment.

这并不是中国第一次因对环境产生积极的变革影响，作出突出贡献而获得联合国最高环境荣誉。

Last year, the Zhejiang green rural revival program won the award for inspiration and action for its work to regenerate polluted waterways and damaged lands. In 2017, the Saihanba afforestation community was recognized in the inspiration and action category for transforming degraded land in northern China into a lush paradise.

去年，浙江绿色乡村复兴项目（"千村示范万村整治"工程）因其对受污染的水道和受损土地的修复工作获得"地球卫士奖"中的"激励与行动奖"。2017年，中国北部的塞罕坝机械林场因退耕还林也获得这一奖项。

The awards came amid China's solid progress in curbing pollution, which is a key part of China's "three tough battles" that also include forestalling and defusing major risks and targeted poverty alleviation.

与此同时，中国在控制污染方面取得了坚实的进展，这是中国"三大攻坚战"的关键部分，另外两项是防范化解重大风险和精准脱贫。

The importance attached to the environment is now greater than ever. Policymakers have reiterated that China's modernization is characterized by harmonious coexistence between man and nature.

人们对环境的重视程度比以往任何时候都要高。政策制定者重申，中国现代化的特点是人与自然和谐共处。

China's economic growth has come without negative consequences for the environment and climate. In the late 1970s, China's economy began expanding, and the expansion accelerated in the following decades, during which problems of environmental pollution also increased.

中国的经济增长也给环境和气候带来了负面影响。20世纪70年代末，中国经济开始发展，并在随后的几十年加速，在此期间，环境污染问题也日益严重。

To strike a balance between economic boom and environmental burden, the country has strived to wean its economy off excessive environment-damaging development and advance well-coordinated environmental conservation.

为了在经济繁荣和环境负担之间取得平衡，中国努力使经济减少对环境的过度破坏，并促进得以协调发展的环境保护。

In the 1980s, China enshrined environmental protection as a fundamental national policy. The sustainable development strategy was formulated and put into practice in the 1990s. Since 2012, the development of an ecological civilization has gained greater momentum. Now the country follows a maxim illustrated in the catchphrase: "Lucid waters and lush mountains are invaluable assets."

20世纪80年代，中国把环境保护作为一项基本国策。可持续发展战略是在20世纪90年代制定并实施的。2012年以来，生态文明建设取得新进展。如今，中国遵循的理念是："绿水青山就是金山银山。"

The connection between China's pollution and economic growth has been weakening since 1995, according to new international research published in the *Science Advances* journal that was based on statistics including economic growth and environmental conditions in China during the 1977—2017 period.

发表在《科学进展》期刊上的一项最新国际研究显示，自1995年以来，中国的污染与经济增长之间的联系一直在减弱。该研究基于1977年至2017年间中国经济增长和环境状况统计数据。

Researchers from five countries also point out that increased environmental awareness and investments in China over the past decade have produced results.

来自5个国家的研究人员还指出，过去10年中国环境意识的提高和投资都取得了成效。

Air quality in China continued to improve with more cities reporting a drop in major pollutant indicators. Surface water quality kept improving in general. In terms of soil pollution control, the country had reduced solid waste imports by 46.5 percent last year.

随着更多城市报告主要污染物指标下降，中国空气质量继续改善。地表水水质总体上一直在改善。在土壤污染控制方面，中国去年减少了46.5%的固体废物进口。

Vigorous environmental protection has injected impetus into related sectors. Total revenue of China's environmental protection industry is expected to surpass 2 trillion yuan in 2020, up from 1.5 trillion yuan in 2018, according to estimates by the China Association of Environmental Protection Industry.

强有力的环境保护促进了相关领域的发展。据中国环境保护产业协会估计，到2020年，中国环保产业总收入有望超过2万亿元人民币，高于2018年的1.5万亿元人民币。

Green finance also took off. In 2018, the country issued a total of 31.2 billion dollars in green bonds, remaining the world's second-largest green bond market, according to the China Central Depository & Clearing Co. and Climate Bonds Initiative.

绿色金融也开始腾飞。根据中央国债登记结算有限责任公司和气候债券倡议组织的数据，2018年，中国共发行了312亿美元（约合人民币2224亿元）的绿色债券，仍然是全球第二大绿色债券市场。

The country announced a plan in 2016 to establish a national green finance mechanism, becoming the first country in the world to do so. It also helped push green finance to be included on the G20 agenda.

2016年，中国成为全球首个宣布建立国家绿色金融机制计划的国家。中国还推动绿色金融纳入二十国集团议程。

In recent years, China has adhered to the path of giving priority to ecology and green development, said Minister of Ecology and Environment Li Ganjie. "Ecological and environmental protection has become an important force and a key to promoting high-quality economic development."

时任生态环境部部长李干杰表示，近年来，中国坚持走生态优先、绿色发展之路。"生态环境保护已成为推动经济高质量发展的重要力量和抓手。"

（来源：https://language.chinadaily.com.cn/a/201910/04/WS5d969990a310cf3e3556ebac.html）

3.8 主题拓展资源

双语文章：山东的这个小渔村环境有多美？每年成千上万只天鹅来度假！

2018年6月，习近平总书记在山东省威海市考察时强调，良好生态环境是经济社会持续健康发展的重要基础，要把生态文明建设放在突出地位。

黄海之滨的山东省威海市荣成，因生态环境优美，每年10月至来年的4月，成千上万只天鹅从西伯利亚地区、蒙古国等地飞到这里，越冬栖息，使荣成成为有名的"天鹅之乡"。

在这群美丽的天鹅中，有一只环志标号A97的天鹅，来自蒙古国北部的湿地，因连续多年来荣成烟墩角过冬，成为烟墩角的"常客"和游客们的"老朋友"，也成为"天鹅爷爷"曲荣学最牵挂的一只天鹅。

On the brick wall at the gate of Qu Rongxue's house is a list, carved by Qu, of the dates in recent years of the annual arrival of "A97", which, though having wings, is not a plane. It's a whooper swan.

曲荣学家门口的砖墙上刻着一些数字，这些数字是近几年曲荣学记录的 A97 每年到达荣成的日子。尽管 A97 也有翅膀，但这只 A97 可不是飞机，它是一只大天鹅。

Once October arrives, Qu begins to watch for the arrival of his white swan friend. He will walk along the bay, which is around five meters away from his home in a coastal fishing village, and look for the swan every day until he finds it.

每年一进入十月份，居住在海边渔村的曲荣学就会开始寻找他的白天鹅朋友。他会沿着距离家门口 5 米之外的海湾边走边寻找这只天鹅，直到找到它。

"If I don't see her, I will become worried about whether she got hurt or died on her way here. A97 will come as long as she is alive, because the living environment here is so good," said Qu, who believes that the swan, whose gender has not been determined, is a female.

"如果我找不到她，我会担心她是不是受伤了或者在飞来的路上遇到了意外。只要 A97 活着，她便会飞来，因为这里的生活环境实在是太好了，"曲荣学说。尽管 A97 的性别并没有得到确认，但是曲荣学认为它是一只"母天鹅"。

Attracted by the abundant supply of fresh water, aquatic plants and fish, shrimp and seaweed, the whooper swans migrate from the Siberian region, the Inner Mongolia autonomous region and China's north-eastern regions to stay for the winter along the bay, making it China's largest winter habitat for whooper swans. As a result, the bay has become known as "Swan Lake".

被这里充沛的水源、丰美的海藻和鱼虾吸引，天鹅们每年从遥远的西伯利亚地区、蒙古国地区以及东北地区飞到这片海湾越冬，使这片海湾成为中国最大的大天鹅栖息地。因此，这片海湾便有了"天鹅湖"的美誉。

For people driving along the coastline of Rongcheng, flocks of swans can be seen foraging for food, preening and flapping their wings.

行驶在荣成的海岸，可以看到成群的天鹅在湖、湾里觅食、梳理羽毛、拍打翅膀嬉戏。

Qu has been taking care of the swans since the late 1980s, when he spotted a couple of them along the bay. Amazed by the big white birds, he began feeding them corn. He also has taken injured swans to his home to treat them until they recover and can live on their own on the bay.

自 20 世纪 80 年代在海湾里发现了几只天鹅，曲荣学便开始照料天鹅。他被这些美丽的天鹅吸引，开始喂它们玉米。发现受伤的天鹅，他会带回家悉心照料，直到它们康复，回到海湾自己生活。

"Some swans are even moving to lakes in the urban area as water quality there becomes very good," he added.

曲荣学说，随着水质不断改善，来到荣成的天鹅数量也不断增加。

优良环境带来舒适栖息地

威海市高度关注生态环境建设。这里的环境空气质量连续两年达到国家二级标准，位居山东省第一位。

威海市加大人工湿地和生态河道建设力度，目前有国家级湿地公园2个，省级湿地公园6个。

作为威海所辖县级市，荣成着力打造"绿水青山"与"金山银山"互融共赢的宜居之地，为天鹅营造了舒适的栖息环境。

Since a campaign was launched in 2015 to improve sewage treatment and river water quality, the quality of offshore waters is now rated Grade II, the second-highest in China's five-level rating standard for water quality, which means the water is drinkable after treatment.

2015年，荣成市开始实施规模化污水治理和水质改善工程，近岸海域水质常年国家二级标准以上。在中国，水质分五个等级标准，二级表示水质经常规净化处理即可供生活饮用。

Qu Xuejun, Party chief of Yandunjiao village, said: "Years ago, sewage from our village was discharged into rivers and the sea. But now we have 27 facilities to treat sewage, which has completely stopped sewage discharge."

烟墩角村党支部书记曲学军介绍，几年前，村里的污水直接流到河里海里。现在，村里建设了27处污水处理设施，完全阻止了污水排放。

With the improvement of the environment, the number of whooper swans has reached nearly 10,000, compared with fewer than 2,000 at the end of the 1990s.

荣成天鹅国家级自然保护区统计数字显示，随着环境不断变好，来这里越冬栖息的天鹅数量不断增加，由20世纪90年代的2000只左右增长到现在的上万只。

Besides whooper swans, there are more than 150 species of birds living in the zone, mostly migratory birds including Oriental storks.

除了天鹅，还有150余种鸟类生活在保护区，这些鸟类大部分为迁徙鸟类，包括东方白鹳。

天鹅火了乡村旅游

每年,大量海内外的摄影师和游客来到烟墩角村看天鹅。

The village of Yandunjiao, whose history dates back more than 400 years, has also benefited from the efforts. The village, whose seaweed-thatched houses have walls made of thick stone or earthen blocks, has drawn an increasing number of tourists. Photographers and tourists from China and abroad flock there each winter to see the swans.

有着400多年历史的烟墩角村便受益于当地环境保护措施。烟墩角用海草做屋顶和用土坯砖块砌起来的海草房吸引了越来越多的游客。每年,海内外的摄影师和游客来到这里看天鹅。

Yu Haiyang, a native of Yandunjiao, returned to the village in 2014 from Singapore to help his family run hostels for the tourists.

烟墩角村的于海洋2014年从新加坡回到村里和家人一起经营民宿。

"The time-honored, seaweed-roofed houses, the elegant swans, the ocean and the good environment — all of these are what people dream of," said Yu, 30, who added that he can earn around 150,000 yuan each winter.

"历史悠久的海草房、优雅的天鹅、海洋以及优美的环境,这些都是人们向往的。"30岁的于海洋说,每个冬季他有大约15万元的收入。

"When the sun rises, casting golden glows, Swan Lake is so beautiful," said Angeline Lew, a photographer from Singapore.

"早上,太阳升起,阳光洒在湖面,天鹅湖格外美。"来自新加坡的摄影师Angeline Lew说。

"Years ago, I couldn't sleep because the swan's calls were so loud," Qu said. "But now that I am used to it, I can't sleep well without their calls."

"多年前,天鹅叫吵得我睡不着觉;现在已经习惯了,反而是听不到天鹅叫会睡不着觉。""天鹅爷爷"曲荣学说。

随着天气变暖,这群美丽的精灵陆续北飞回迁。目前,聚集在荣成天鹅湖的天鹅已不多。

天鹅迁徙路途遥远,愿它们平安顺利返乡!

(来源:中国日报双语新闻)

第二单元　诺贝尔奖获得者的科学家精神
（Unit 2　Nobel Prize Winner）

1. 思政主题

诺贝尔奖科学家勇攀高峰、敢为人先的创新精神，追求真理、严谨治学的求实精神，淡泊名利、潜心研究的奉献精神等。

2. 意义

本单元内容是从诺贝尔奖导入，谈到爱因斯坦的童年经历，引发学生对科学家特质的思考。教师可围绕"科学家"这一话题，引入新时代"科学家精神"，引导学生对"科学有无国界""科学发展的最终目的"以及"中国在诺奖获奖艰难的原因"等问题的思辨和探究。

教师可结合中国首位女性诺贝尔医学奖得主屠呦呦的短片、被授予"共和国勋章"的钟南山、"人民英雄"张伯礼、陈薇等科学家的人文关怀和中国精神，选取与主题相关的思政素材，引导学生不仅体会科学家精神，更能意识到中国的科学发展要为老百姓服务，要为国家服务，努力培养他们的中国精神、中国力量和中国担当。科学是第一生产力，科学是为了促进人类和自然的发展，从积极层面上来说，科学是没有国界的，科学发现的成果应该造福于全人类。但是从消极层面上来说，科学如果被用于摧毁自然的发展和阻碍人类的进步，那它就是有国界的。

科学是人类探索自然又变革自身的伟大事业，科学家是科学知识和科学精神的重要承载者。习近平总书记指出："中国要强盛、要复兴，就一定要大力发展科学技术，努力成为世界主要科学中心和创新高地。"他强调："希望广大院士弘扬科学报国的光荣传统，追求真理、勇攀高峰的科学精神，勇于创新、严谨求实的学术风气，把个人理想自觉融入国家发展伟业，在科学前沿孜孜求索，在重大科技领域不断取得突破。"这一重要论述，体现了党中央对科学家群体的殷切期望，而要激励和引导科技工作者追求真理、勇攀高峰，真正把学问和人格融合在一起，就必须重视对科学家精神的培育和弘扬。

习近平总书记表示，为了中国的经济社会发展和人民生活的改善，需要的科技解决方案比以往任何时候都要多，中国需要弘扬新时代科学家精神。新时代科学家精神包括胸怀祖国、服务人民的爱国精神，勇攀高峰、敢为人先的创新精神，追求真理、严谨治学的求实精神，淡泊名利、潜心研究的奉献精神，集智攻关、团结协作的协同精神，甘为人梯、奖掖后学的育人精神。这些精神特质，既有在科学的发生、发展中积淀的品格、方法和规训，又强调社会责任、人文关怀等伦理维度，体现了中国传统科技文化中物我合一、理实交融的天人观，是仰望星空的真理追求和检视内心的人文关怀的统一。

Xi Jinping Stresses Science and Technology for Economic Development

Scientific and technological solutions are needed for China's economic and social development, and the improvement of people's livelihoods, more than ever before, Chinese President Xi Jinping said on Friday.

Xi Jinping, also general secretary of the Communist Party of China (CPC) Central Committee and Chairman of the Central Military Commission, made the remarks when chairing a symposium of scientists on the development of science and technology during the 14th Five-Year Plan (2021—2025) period.

The 14th Five-Year Plan period will be the first five years of China's new journey toward fully building a modern socialist country and march toward the second centenary goal.

Historical achievements and revolutions in science and technology have been made since the 18th National Congress of the CPC, Xi Jinping said, and China has taken innovation as the primary driving force for development.

Noting the fight against COVID-19, the president expressed thanks to scientific and technological workers for their efforts in the research and development of treatments as well as vaccine development, prevention and control, and works in other important areas.

He highlighted the urgency and importance of accelerating scientific and technological innovation to better promote development during the 14th Five-Year Plan period and beyond.

Xi Jinping stressed several aspects in further developing science and technology, such as improving the environment for science and technology innovation to stimulate creativity, setting up national laboratories to form China's laboratory system and tackling core technologies in key areas.

Universities and colleges should play an important role in scientific research, the president added, highlighting the importance of training innovative talents. Increasing investment in basic research and providing necessary policy support in fiscal, financial and tax fields are also important, he said.

Efforts are needed to unleash the huge potential of innovation by deepening reform of the science and technology system, Xi Jinping noted, calling for efforts to strengthen international cooperation, integrate into the global innovation network and enhance capacity for scientific and technological innovation through open cooperation.

（来源：https://news.cgtn.com/news/2020-09-11/Xi-Jinping-stresses-science-and-technology-for-economic-development-THDgyIm3Ys/index.html）

3. 教学设计与思政元素的融入

Passage A

3.1 Warm-up 环节

英文文章：Nobel Prizes: Rewarding the World's Best and Brightest

文章介绍了诺贝尔奖的由来及评选过程，诺贝尔奖设立的目的是表彰在物理学、化学、和平、生理学或医学以及文学上"对人类作出最大贡献"的人士。文章还介绍了一些具有特殊意义创造了历史的诺贝尔获奖者。通过阅读文章，学生可以对诺贝尔奖有所了解。

The Nobel Prize — around the world, these two words evoke greatness, accomplishment, a unique contribution to humanity. As the 2019 laureates are about to be announced, what is the story behind the Nobel Prize, who are some of its most prominent recipients and how are they chosen?

A testament to greatness

The prize is the brainchild of Alfred Nobel, a Swedish inventor and businessman born in 1833, who is credited with inventing dynamite and reportedly held 355 patents on everything from explosives to barometers and artificial rubber.

Upon his death in 1896, he ordered that his entire fortune of 31 million Swedish krona — about 1.8 billion krona or 182 million U.S. dollars in today's money — be used to set up five prizes for "those who, during the preceding year, shall have conferred the greatest benefit to humankind."

These became the Nobel Prizes, which are awarded every year, most famously for Peace and Literature, but also Physics, Chemistry and Physiology or Medicine.

In 1968, an additional prize was added, for Economic Sciences, following a donation by Sweden's central bank to the Nobel Foundation.

How is the Nobel Prize awarded?

Although rumors about potential laureates circulate ever year, the selection process is notoriously secretive and shortlists of nominees are not made public.

A year before the prizes are announced, Nobel Committees invite select figures from each field — including university professors and former laureates — to submit nominations. After a long evaluation process and consultations with experts, each committee submits a list of final candidates.

The prizes for Physics, Chemistry and Economic Sciences are then decided by the Royal Swedish Academy of Sciences, while the Literature and Medicine prizes are decided by separate Swedish institutions.

The Peace Prize differs from the others in that it is determined by a Norwegian Nobel Committee and given out at a ceremony in Oslo, not Stockholm.

Since 1974, a new rule states that no prize can be awarded posthumously.

Laureates are awarded a medal, a diploma and prize money, which in 2019 will be nine million krona (913,000 U.S. dollars) — to be divided equally if a prize is shared.

Some numbers

Since 1901, a total 590 Nobel Prizes have been handed out to 935 laureates — some prizes have been shared between two or more people. Only 51 laureates have been women.

Not just individuals have been recognized: out of the 935 laureates, 27 were organizations, such as the International Atomic Energy Agency (IAEA), the European Union, the Intergovernmental Panel on Climate Change (IPCC) or Doctors without Borders.

In 118 years, there have been only three years when no Nobel Prizes were given out in any category: from 1940 to 1942. On other occasions, academies and committees have not awarded one or the other Prize for lack of a suitable recipient.

Big names

Many Nobel Prize winners have become household names — Peace laureates like Mother Teresa, Martin Luther King Jr. and Nelson Mandela, or Literature winners like Kazuo Ishiguro, Ernest Hemingway and George Bernard Shaw. But some have also made history while remaining in the shadows.

First woman: Marie Curie shared the 1903 Nobel Prize in Physics with her husband Pierre and fellow Frenchman Henri Becquerel for their work on radioactivity. She was also the first person to receive a second Nobel Prize, this time in Chemistry in 1911.

Youngest winner: Malala Yousafzai, the Pakistani teenager who became a global icon for children's education after being shot by the Taliban, was awarded the Nobel Peace Prize in 2014 at age 17.

Oldest winner: Arthur Ashkin was 96 years old when he received the Nobel Prize in Physics in 2018 for developing "optical tweezers."

Three-time winner: the International Committee of the Red Cross (ICRC) won the Nobel Peace Prize in 1917, 1944 and 1963, the only laureate to achieve that feat. Separately, its founder Henri Dunant, also won it in 1901.

Two-time winners: besides Curie, three other scientists won double Nobels: John Bardeen in Physics in 1956 and 1972; Frederick Sanger in Chemistry in 1958 and 1980; and more unusually, Linus Carl Pauling for Chemistry in 1954 and then Peace in 1962 for his efforts to ban nuclear weapons. The UN Refugee Agency UNHCR also took home the Peace Prize twice, in 1954 and 1981.

Successful relatives: Pierre and Marie Curie were not the only celebrated scientists in their family: their daughter Irene and her husband Frédéric Joliot also won a Nobel Prize in Chemistry in 1935. Dutch brothers Jan and Nikolaas Tinbergen were awarded Nobel Prizes separately, for Economic Sciences in 1969, and Physiology or Medicine in 1973. Six father-son pairs have also received the honor, either together or separately, over the years.

First Chinese: Yang Chen Ning and Lee Tsung Dao were awarded the Nobel Prize in Physics in 1957 for their work on elementary particles.

First Chinese woman: Tu Youyou won the Nobel Prize in Physiology or Medicine in 2015 for discovering a new treatment for malaria.

Other notables:

Albert Einstein: perhaps the most famous scientist of all, he won the Nobel Prize in Physics in 1921 "for his services to Theoretical Physics."

Winston Churchill: the former British prime minister won a Nobel Prize in 1953, unusually, in Literature.

Luc Montagnier and Françoise Barré-Sinoussi received the Nobel Prize in Physiology or Medicine in 2008 for discovering the human immunodeficiency virus (HIV), and shared the prize with Harald zur Hausen, who discovered the human papillomavirus (HPV) that causes cervical cancer.

Bertha von Suttner: the second woman after Marie Curie to win a Nobel Prize — for Peace in 1905 — von Suttner was not only a prominent anti-war campaigner but also a close friend of Alfred Nobel and is credited with convincing him to set up the Peace Prize.

2019 laureates

The 2019 recipients are being announced on October 7-14, starting with Physiology or Medicine, followed by Physics, Chemistry, Literature, Peace and Economic Sciences.

The prizes will then be handed out, as is the tradition, at two ceremonies in Stockholm and Oslo on December 10, the anniversary of Alfred Nobel's death.

（来源：https://news.cgtn.com/news/2019-10-07/Nobel-Prizes-Rewarding-the-world-s-best-and-brightest-KB2f6mzI08/index.html）

3.2 Discussion 环节

英文视频：诺贝尔大会授予屠呦呦2015年医学奖回顾

2015年10月5日17时30分，诺贝尔奖生理学或医学奖一半授予了中国女科学家屠呦呦，以表彰她发现青蒿素——治疗疟疾的新方法，每年数百万感染者从中受益。视频时长3分24秒，可以请学生回顾一下诺贝尔大会对屠呦呦的介绍以及宣告大奖得主时的画面，引导学生思考"屠呦呦获奖重大意义"（比如：中国第一位诺贝尔生理学或医学奖；第一位中国女性获奖；世人再一次把目光聚焦到中医学等）。

And then we proceeded to the focus of this year's glories.

So from the left we have William C. Campbell born in 1931 Ireland, now professor emeritus at the Drew University, Madison. New Jersey, US. In the middle, Satoshi Omura born 1935 in Japan, a scientist at the Kitasato Institute. And now professor emeritus at Kitasato University, Tokyo, Japan. And to the right Youyou Tu born in 1930 in China trained in traditional Chinese medicine, and now chief professor to China Academy of Traditional Chinese Medicine in Beijing, China.

Globally around half a million people, most of them children, die every year in malaria. After entering the human body, the parasites first infected liver cells. Thereafter they enter red blood cells and multiply destroying the cells, causing recurrent fever attacks. The life of the parasite is maintained by new blood sucking mosquitos.

To tackle the challenge of developing new malaria therapies, Youyou Tu in

China trained in pharmacy and part of a big national project turned to traditional herbal medicine in thousand year of literature.

She discovered that the plant Artemisia annua, sweet wormwood appeared in hundreds of recipes. She therefore tested an extra from the plant on mice with malaria and found a clear effect on the parasites.

But the results were inconsistent. Tu then decided to visit the ancient literature again. In a seventeen hundred year old book, she discovered a recipe that inspired her to develop a new method to extract the active substance. It turned out to be a great success.

Hundred percent of the malaria parasites in infected mice and monkeys were killed. This was a genuine breakthrough in the discovery of artemisinin, and a turning point in finding a new drug to combat malaria.

And Nobel Assembly at Karolinska Institute has today awarded the 2015 Nobel Prize in Physiology and Medicine, with one half joint to Willian C. Campbell and Satoshi Omura for their discoveries concerning a novel therapy against infection caused by roundworm parasites, and the other half to Youyou Tu, for her discoveries concerning a novel therapy against malaria.

（来源：https://www.bilibili.com/video/BV1Js41127ju?from=search&seid=3376363297773439261）

3.3 Critical thinking 环节

英文文章：China's Top Respiratory Experts Recommended for Highest State Honor

Scientific and technological solutions are needed for China's economic and social development, and the improvement of people's livelihoods, more than ever before, Chinese President Xi Jinping said.

中国国家主席习近平主席表示，为了中国的经济社会发展和人民生活的改善，需要的科技解决方案比以往任何时候都要多。学生阅读完国家最高荣誉获得者的科学家们和国家最高科学技术奖获得者袁隆平院士的文章后，思考：

1）获国家最高荣誉的科学家们为中国，乃至世界作出了杰出的贡献，引导学生归纳出新时代"科学家精神"的内涵有哪些？

2）引导学生思考"科学无国界、科学家有祖国"。热爱祖国的人，才拥有完整人格。没有人格，学问越大，对社会的危害也越大；没有人格，也不可能有真学问。这就是人格与学问之间深刻的辩证法。追求知识和真理是中国科学家的初心，服务经济社会发展和广大人民群众亦是中国科学家的初心。

Zhong Nanshan, a top respiratory expert who identified the SARS virus in 2003 and is currently leading the Chinese government's efforts in the fight against COVID-19, was recommended for the Medal of the Republic, a working committee for honor-granting said on Monday.

This is the second time the Medal of the Republic is being given out after the country honored a number of exemplary figures in 2019 for their outstanding contributions to the People's Republic's development since its founding in 1949.

What's more, national honorary titles, which honor those who make exceptional contributions in specific fields, will be awarded to other three prominent experts at the same time.

Zhang Boli, Zhang Dingyu, and Chen Wei, all of whom played an important role in the fight against COVID-19, have been shortlisted for national honorary titles, the committee said.

Decorated with illustrations of China's national emblem, a five-pointed star, the Yellow River, the Yangtze River, a mountain and orchid flowers, the medal so far has only been conferred on eight people, including Yuan Longping, father of hybrid rice, Tu Youyou, Nobel Laureate in medicine, Yu Min, father of China's hydrogen bomb.

Meet the candidates

Zhong Nanshan: Born in 1936, Zhong was one of the most important figures in fighting the Severe Acute Respiratory Syndrome (SARS) outbreak in 2003. As head of Guangzhou Institute of Respiratory Diseases, he offered to treat all critical SARS cases in Guangdong Province at his institute.

When the COVID-19 outbreak hit China in January, the 84-year-old medical genius chose to work on the front line, saving millions of lives inside and outside of China. He was the first person to publicly warn that the virus can be transmitted from one person to another.

The introductory statement released by the committee lauded Zhong for his courage to speak out.

Zhang Dingyu: As the acting president of one of Wuhan's major hospitals in treating COVID-19 patients, the man who was diagnosed with Amyotrophic Lateral Sclerosis (ALS) in October 2018 chose to stay with his colleagues, and save lives with no looking back.

Zhang Boli: As a candidate for the national honorary title, Zhang directed the country in utilizing Traditional Chinese Medicine (TCM) to defeat the novel coronavirus. He also led the formulation of the TCM treatment protocol for COVID-19 patients.

Having spent 82 days in Wuhan fighting COVID-19, Zhang is in Beijing now as a national lawmaker drawing up proposals to help the country better prepare for epidemics on the legal front.

Chen Wei: Chen is a professor at Academy of Military Medical Sciences. The vaccine co-developed by Chen's team and a Chinese vaccine developer was the first in the country to proceed to the human testing stage in March. The vaccine project that she headed is one of a handful of vaccines that have shown some promise in early human testing prior to much larger trials to demonstrate efficacy.

She is also one of the key leaders in China's Ebola vaccine research.

（来源：https://news.cgtn.com/news/2020-08-03/China-s-top-respiratory-expert-awarded-highest-state-honor-SELoNTUY5a/index.html）

英文文章：Yuan Longping, China's Most Famous "Farmer"

It says every scientist cherishes a childhood dream indicating his or her future success, but for Yuan Longping, dubbed as "father of hybrid rice". The dream is that he cultivates rice as plump as peanuts, and farmers can relax in the cool shadow of big rice plants.

Yuan, 71, won a 5 million yuan State Supreme Science and Technology Award today, known as the Nobel Prize in China, for his outstanding achievements in breeding high-yield hybrid rice, which has substantially increased China's grain output.

Yuan came up with the idea of hybridizing rice for the first time in the world in 1960s. Since then, 50 percent of China's total rice cultivation fields have grown such rice, which added some 300 billion kilograms to the country's grain output.

Furrows grown on his sunburnt face, a slim figure and coiled-up trousers legs would confuse foreign reporters who came to interview the most famous scientist in China, who would rather be called "a farmer."

Indeed, like many Chinese farmers, Yuan in his 70s and has devoted most of his life growing rice in paddy fields, but unlike those farmers, he reaps the seed from experimental fields only for hybridizing rice.

The urbanite-turned-farmer graduated from Southwest Agriculture College in 1953 has his name related to the world's most advanced agricultural technology. Four minor planets, a listed seed company's and a science college in China were named after him, which were the first time that a Chinese scientist's name is valued for its intellectual assets.

By lending his name to the Longping High-tech, a seed company, Yuan obtained a 5 per cent stake, or 2.5 million shares worth 2 million yuan, in the firm.

However, Yuan said his research requires the lifestyle of a farmer, or rather a migrating farmer, as he has conducted extensive research related to the cultivation of new strains of hybrid rice "Super Hybrid Rice" in some 10 provinces.

In the year 1999, more than 300 billion kilograms of grain were increased from about 240 million hectares of hybrid rice, which signified the success of his research. And this made Yuan firmly believe that China can surely feed her 1.2 billion population with her limited cultivated land.

The "Super Rice" yields are 30 percent higher than those of common rice. The record yield of 17,055 kilograms per hectare was registered in Yongsheng County in Yunnan in 1999.

But even after that achievement Yuan won't take a break. He has a dream, more realistic than that of his young age, that popularizing new strains of grain with higher yields around the world can eliminate starvation on earth.

The UN Food and Agriculture Organization (FAO) has vowed to get involved in the work of spreading the coverage of Yuan's high-yield hybrid rice, which it considers the best way to increase the world's grain output.

The FAO's 1991 statistics show that 20 percent of the world's rice output was yielded from 10 percent of the world's rice fields, which grow hybrid rice.

"If the new strain was sown in the rest of the rice acreage, the present grain output around the world can be more than doubled. This can be a solution to the grain shortage," said the unselfish scientist.

In 1980, Yuan went to the United States at the invitation of the International Rice Research Institute to share his knowledge about the cultivation technology of hybrid rice. He was also employed in 1991 as the chief consultant of FAO to bring his research methods to other countries.

With the help of Chinese scientists, the acreage of hybrid rice in Vietnam and

India increased to 200,000 hectares and 150,000 hectares in 1999, respectively.

The rice research costs time to prove its value. At the age of 43, Yuan cultivated the world's first hybrid rice. At that time the country's grain yield was about 4,500 kilogram per hectare.

"The natural disaster and policy miscarriage further deteriorated starvation in China by then," Yuan recalled tearfully.

This is his motivation to stimulate his research. Largely due to his scientific progress, China's total rice output rose from 5.69 billion tons in 1950 to 19.47 billion tons last year. The growth rate of rice output far exceeded the population growth speed.

Some people estimate Yuan's actual fortune might amount to more than 100 million yuan (12 million U.S. dollars), making him one of the richest people in China. But he doesn't know for sure himself, for he seems not to care about his own assets than the rice harvest.

Some people asked him to move the focus of his research from improving amounts of hybrid rice to the quality and taste, which would be easier to do. But the stubborn academician insisted that the amount of hybrid rice's per unit yield still outweighs the quality, for his foremost task is to improve the grain reserve in developing countries.

（来源：https://www.docin.com/p-393556073.html&isPay=1）

3.4 主题拓展环节

BBC 短片双语视频：20 世纪最伟大的科学家之一——屠呦呦

在 2019 年 BBC 发起的 20 世纪最伟大人物评选中，中国首位诺贝尔生理学或医学奖得主屠呦呦与居里夫人、爱因斯坦、艾伦·图灵共同入围最伟大科学家候选名单。视频时长 8 分钟，讲述了屠呦呦临危受命，查遍古籍汲取创新灵感，以身试药，成功提取青蒿素，挽救数百万人生命的传奇故事。学生可通过观看视频，感受屠呦呦对科研的执著，体会成功背后的付出与艰辛，强化脚踏实地、积极进取的奋斗意识。

The envelope was stuffed full of original documents connected to the discovery of artemisinin and one name stood out from the rest — Tu Youyou.

这个信封里装满了与发现青蒿素相关的原始文件，在这些文件中，一个名字映入眼帘，屠呦呦。

Finally, I can piece the whole story together.

于是，我终于得以将整个故事串联起来。

As they scoured the documents, Louis and Su uncovered an incredible story, the story of an exceptional scientist, willing to risk her own life to find a cure for malaria and bring it to the world, the story of Tu Youyou.

在翻阅文件的过程中，路易斯和苏发现了一个不可思议的故事，关于一位伟大科学家的传奇故事：她宁愿冒着自己的生命危险，也要寻找治疗疟疾的方法，并将这份厚礼献给全世界，这就是屠呦呦的故事。

Tu's quest didn't begin in China, but in the jungles of Vietnam, where soldiers on both sides of the war found themselves fighting a third enemy—mosquitoes.

屠呦呦征服疟疾的征程并非始于中国，而是越南的丛林中，当时正值越战，交战双方减员严重，并非因为战斗，而是因为"第三方敌人"——蚊子。

Tens of thousands were left incapacitated after being bitten by the malaria-carrying insects.

成千上万的士兵在被携带疟疾的蚊虫叮咬后，完全丧失行动能力。

In one US army unit, a third of soldiers contracted the disease.

某个美国军团里，有三分之一的士兵都感染上疟疾。

Now, we have no way of estimating how many soldiers died in the North Vietnamese army, but we know the losses were colossal because the Communist Party Chairman, Ho Chi Minh, reached out in desperation to his allies in China, asking for help to find a cure.

虽然我们无法预估因为感染疟疾而导致北越士兵的死亡人数，但我们敢肯定，一定是损失惨重，因为当时的越南主席胡志明在绝望之中，向他的中国盟友伸出了求救之手，希望中国能帮忙找到治疗方法。

Chairman Mao Zedong declared the search for a drug a top priority, and in May 1967, officially launched Project 523.

在毛泽东主席的亲自指示下，研发抗疟药物成为了当务之急，1967年5月，中国政府正式启动"523项目"。

At Beijing's Academy of Chinese Medical Sciences, 39-year-old researcher Tu Youyou decided to scour hundreds of old manuscripts in search of ancient wisdom a traditional herbal remedy that might form the basis of a cure.

在北京的中医研究院中药研究所里，39岁的研究员屠呦呦临危受命，翻查上百份中国古代医学典籍，从中汲取创新灵感，希望能找到一味传统中草药，为治疗疟疾奠定基础。

With over 2,000 preparations to choose from, this was a daunting task.

2000多个关于疟疾的药方需要一一实验排查，这是一项异常艰巨的任务。
Professor Ni Muyun worked closely with Tu on the project.
倪慕云教授与屠呦呦曾在"523项目"上展开密切合作。

Tu Youyou was very self-disciplined. She set an example for the rest of us leading the discussions and inspiring everyone else.
因为她自己也很严格要求自己，处处以身作则，来带动我们大家一起共同来探讨这些问题。

At that time, we were all young, so it was a happy team.
我们都比较低，她自己本身也年轻，所以我们这个团队还是非常和谐的。

Our task was very clear. We had to complete the task.
当时这个任务非常明确，就是交给我们一定要完成这个任务。

Then, with her husband away and her research growing more demanding, Tu was forced to place her children into care.
后来，她的丈夫被下放，但手头的研究项目却让她根本抽不开身，于是，她不得不将自己的孩子们送去寄养。

At that time, we had to overcome the difficulties ourselves.
还是一心一意，当时没有办法，都自己克服困难。

It really was not easy for her. The children were away for so long, it placed a barrier between them.
不容易，很不容易。所以孩子跟她也有一些隔阂，时间比较长。

Tu only saw her daughters once in the next three years and when they finally reunited, the older girl refused to acknowledge the face that she was her mother and the younger one didn't even recognize her.
接下来的三年里，母女三人仅仅见过一次面，直到后来母女重聚，大女儿已经生疏到都不愿意开口叫妈妈，而小女儿甚至都不认识自己眼前的母亲。

Despite the hardship, Tu never gave up hope that a cure was just around the corner.
尽管困难重重，屠呦呦却从不放弃希望，找到治疗方法一定指日可待。

By this stage, she had tested almost 200 compounds with noting to show for it.
此时，她已经对近200种中草药进行了研究，可惜却颗粒无收。

She continued to scour the ancient text.
不服输的屠呦呦继续查阅古代医学典籍。

Then, in a book written in the fourth century by Chinese scholar Ge Hong, she found a preparation that claimed to cure a malaria-like fever.

某天，她在无意间读到晋代葛洪的《肘后备急方》，书中提到一条处方说是能治愈疟疾导致的发热症状。

Take a handful of artemisia annua, soak in two litres of water, extrude juice and take it all.

青蒿一握，以水二升渍，绞取汁，尽服之。

Artemisia was a plant Tu had tested before without success.

屠呦呦之前用青蒿提取物做过试验，但却没有成功。

Then she had an epiphany. By heating the plant to extract the compound, she might have been damaging the drug in the process.

她突然冒出一个灵感，莫非是之前实验时提取过程中的温度过高，而高温可能破坏了药物的效果。

Instead, she decided to try extracting it at a lower temperature mimicking the original formula.

于是，屠呦呦决定改用低沸点溶剂来提取有效物，以此来模仿书中的古方。

She tested it on a cluster of malaria cells.

她将青蒿提取物用于疟疾细胞进行试验。

Every single one was destroyed.

结果发现，对疟疾抑制率高达100%。

But when the team tested the drug on animals, the results were alarming.

可是，当研究小组将青蒿用于动物实验时，结果却令人震惊。

While some of them were cured, others were poisoned.

某些动物得到痊愈，还有某些动物甚至疑似中毒。

Nobody could say whether the drug could be safe in humans.

没人敢说这种药物用于人体是否安全。

What happened next was a little unconventional, scientifically.

接下来发生的事情，从科学角度来看有点不太循规守矩。

You see, Tu was so convinced that the extract would work that she volunteered to test it on herself.

屠呦呦坚信青蒿提取物有效且对人体无毒害，于是，她主动要求在自己身上做试验。

Knowing what was at stake, Tu went into hospital, and over several days, doctors gradually increased the dose.

虽然明知可能会危及生命，屠呦呦还是进了医院。接下来那几天，医生对她进行试药观察并逐渐增加剂量。

She took the extract, she felt fine, but more importantly, they were monitoring her major organs, her heart, her liver, her kidneys, and they were fine too.

她亲自试药，感觉良好。而最重要的是医生一直在观察她内脏器官的各项指标，心脏、肝脏、肾脏，全都没有任何问题。

The test had worked.

实验成功了！

Few people are brave enough to risk their own lives in the hope of saving others.

很少有人会像她这样敢于冒着自己的生命危险，仅仅因为有一线希望能够拯救他人。

Further proof that Tu is worthy of your vote.

这也进一步证明屠呦呦值得你为她投票。

Like any new drug, it would take many years of refinement by Tu and her team before artemisinin could be rolled out worldwide.

与所有新药物一样，屠呦呦和小组成员必须再花上多年时间对药物进行改良，最终才能将青蒿素推广至全世界。

The first tablets were approved in 1986, and in 1999, the World Health Organization added artemisinin to their list of essential medicines.

1986年，青蒿素获得了卫生部新药证书。1999年，世界卫生组织将青蒿素列入"基本药品"目录。

Since then, the number of deaths due to malaria have fallen by almost 50% with several countries eradicating the disease altogether.

从那天起，疟疾造成的死亡人数整整下降了近50%，多个国家甚至彻底根除了这种疾病。

Tu dedicated her life to perfecting the drug, but continued to work in the shadows.

屠呦呦一生致力于继续完善青蒿素，可她却仍然默默坚守，默默耕耘。

Then 40 years after the discovery, Tu was herself discovered by Louis and Su in Washington.

在青蒿素发现40年后，来自美国国家科学院的路易斯和苏终于发现了她。

They wrote about her story in the journal *Cell*.

他们将屠呦呦的故事撰写成文发表在《细胞》杂志上。

And at the age of 84, she was awarded the Nobel Prize for Medicine, the first Chinese person ever to win the award.

84岁高龄的屠呦呦终于获得了诺贝尔医学奖，她也是第一位获得该奖项的中国人。

I'm deeply grateful to my family for their understanding and support. This is not only an honour for myself but recognition and encouragement for all scientists in China.

深深感谢家人一直以来的理解和支持，这不仅是授予我个人的荣誉，也是对全体中国科学奖团队的嘉奖和鼓励。

Tu still lives in Beijing, but prefers to stay out of the spotlight.

屠呦呦现居北京，她依然不喜欢公开场合的聚光灯。

If you measure greatness in terms of the number of human lives saved, then there is no doubt at all that Tu Youyou is one of the greatest scientists of all time.

如果要用拯救了多少人的生命来衡量一个人伟大的程度，那么，毫无疑问，屠呦呦是人类历史上最伟大的科学家之一。

The drugs saved millions of people's lives, people in some of the poorest communities on the planet, millions of children.

她研制的药物挽救了数百万人的生命，包括全世界最贫困地区的人民以及数百万儿童。

When it comes to science icons, there is no doubt at all Tu Youyou is right up there.

当我们提及杰出科学人物时，毫无疑问屠呦呦一定会出现在这个名单中。

So, four people who may have seemed outsiders, a female Polish immigrant, a Jewish refugee, a gay mathematician, and a Chinese woman working almost anonymously, ended up making some of the biggest contributions to the 20th century.

因此，我们挑选出了4位看起来像是"局外人"的科学家，一位是来自波兰的女性移民（居里夫人），一位是犹太难民（爱因斯坦），一位是同性恋数学家（阿兰·图灵），还有一位是此前几乎无人认识的中国女性（屠呦呦），正是他们四位为20世纪的人类做出最伟大的贡献。

But despite their differences, they all shared the intellectual courage to think outside the box and the personal courage to stand firm in the face of adversity.

尽管他们彼此差异巨大，但他们都有跳出固有思维模式的智识和勇气，以及面对逆境依然坚定立场的个人勇气。

（来源：https://v.qq.com/x/page/t0836rgq3dp.html）

Passage B

3.5 Warm-up 环节

英文视频:【Mini BIO】Albert Einstein

Nobel Prize for Physics in 1921 for his theory of photoelectric effect figured out the underpin all of our modern life participated in humanitarian causes warned Roosevelt about the danger of nuclear weapon.

1921年，爱因斯坦因其光电效应理论而获得诺贝尔物理学奖，他发现的基本物理定律支撑着我们现代生活，它们催生了激光、电信、卫星、手机的发明……它们无处不在，爱因斯坦的工作在今天仍有影响，它将继续对后代具有重要意义。他还警告罗斯福注意核武器的危险。教师可以让学生观看视频，引导学生思考：

1）成为"科学家"，他/她们需要具备的一些共同特质。

2）他们的成果应该怎么运用（爱因斯坦对核武器的态度；对人道主义的认同等）。

Albert Einstein not only is one of history's most important physicists, but his quirky personality and fame made him a cultural icon as well, so much so that *Time* magazine even named him person of the century.

The inventions that he came up with, the fundamental laws of physics that he figured out underpin all of our modern day life. They gave rise to the invention of lasers, telecommunications, satellites, cell phones... They are everywhere.

Albert Einstein was born in Ulm, Germany on March 14th, 1879, but spend most of his childhood in Munich before his family moved to Milan, Italy. After graduating from the Swiss Polytechnic Institute at age twenty-one, Einstein had a hard time finding employment.

Einstein tried to apply for multiple academic positions and actually was turned down because of a recommendation letter that one of his teachers wrote for him.

Albert Einstein found full-time work as a patent clerk in Bern, Switzerland in 1902, and soon thereafter married Mileva Maric. They would eventually have two sons together. In 1905, often called Einstein's Miracle Year, he published four hugely important theories, including that of special relativity, or as most people know it, $E=mc^2$.

Einstein faced significant obstacles in his path to successful academic and scientific careers. There were very few Jews in academia in the 1910s, when

Einstein became a professor first in Prague, then in Switzerland and then in Berlin.

Einstein finished formulating what is considered to be his masterpiece, his general theory of relativity in 1915.

General relativity wasn't actually proven until 1919, when Sir Arthur Eddington was able to observe it happen with a solar eclipse. Albert Einstein became instantly world famous. Also, in 1919, Albert Einstein divorced his first wife and married his cousin Elsa Lowenthal.

Adding more luster to his name, Einstein was awarded the Nobel Prize for physics in 1921 for his theory of photoelectric effect.

Einstein came to the United States in 1933 after he had been essentially chased out of Germany by the Nazis. And he became a member of the Institute for Advanced Study in Princeton.

Albert Einstein continued his theoretical studies while living in Princeton and became a US citizen in 1940. In addition to his research, Einstein is also known for his deep commitment to many humanitarian causes and his wry sense of humor.

It is said that Einstein was asked to explain that theory of relativity. He said, "Put your hand on a hot stove for a minute. It seems like an hour. You sit next to a beautiful woman for an hour and it seems like a minute. That's relativity."

Albert Einstein died on April 18th, 1955 at the age of seventy-six.

Every time you pick up a cell phone to answer a call, you are using the laws of quantum mechanics. Every time you look a satellite television image, you are using something that is invoking the theory of relativity. Einstein's work continues to be felt today and it's going to continue to be important for generations to come.

The things I remember about Einstein are more his personality. The man who warned President Roosevelt about the dangers of nuclear weapons. The man who was offered the second Presidency of Israel and turned it down. And he rumpled haired elderly professor, who once was faced with paparazzi, stuck his tongue out, resulting in the most iconic picture of this amazing personality.

（来源：https://www.bilibili.com/video/BV117411k7ku?from=search&seid=178 05615070877910302）

3.6 Discussion 环节

英文文章：Why Can't China Win the Nobel Prize? (2009)
一个国家的科学文化传统对其创新能力和技术发展以及诺贝尔奖的获得起

着相当重要的作用。在中国历史上，科学文化传统有着光明的一面，推动了中华民族的发展和进步。但是，也存在一些不足和缺陷，这可能是中国获得诺贝尔奖的一个不利因素。我们应该客观地看待和对待中国科学文化传统的缺陷和不足。

The scientific and cultural tradition of a country plays a quite important role in its innovation capacity and technological development and the winning of the Nobel Prize. In the Chinese history, there is a bright side in the scientific and cultural tradition, which has boosted the development and progress of the Chinese nation. However, there are some shortcomings and flaws as well, which may be a negative factor for China to win the Nobel Prize. We should view and treat the shortcomings and deficiencies in Chinese scientific and cultural tradition objectively.

The ancient Chinese civilization is brilliant and glorious. There are the Four Great Inventions that Chinese people are still proud of. The Chinese have made outstanding scientific achievements long before the scientific prosperity in the west. China had been the pacesetter in science and technology in the world before the 15th century. There was the Rule of Zhenguan, a period in the Chinese history in Tang Dynasty when over five hundred Japanese students came to Chang'an to study. The ideas in the traditional Chinese culture including system, harmony, and truth-seeking have also exerted momentous impact on modern science and culture in the west. The role of the Chinese nation on the development of human civilization has been well-acknowledged in the world.

Speaking of the Chinese history of science, we must mention Joseph Needham, a British biochemist from Cambridge University. In 1937, he recruited 3 Chinese students: Wang Yinglai (the principal responsible person for the synthetic insulin study in China later), Lu Guizhen and Shen Shizhang. Their talents amazed Joseph Needham so much that he began to develop a yearning for the ancient Chinese civilization. He was already a renowned biochemist then. But he took a lot of efforts in studying Chinese, and was devoted in the study of the Chinese history of science at the cost of giving up his own specialty. In his *Science and Civilization in China*, a masterpiece of more than ten volumes, it was proved with substantial historical data that science and civilization in China had been unmatched by the west from the 3rd century BC to the 13th century; The scientific inventions and discoveries in China far outweighed those in contemporary Europe, which was especially so before the 15th century.

In the feudal society after the Yuan Dynasty, the Chinese rulers neglected science and technology. There used to be a saying that intellectuals ranked "number 9" in terms of social position, slightly higher than a beggar. The long-term examination system had seriously impeded people from the pursuit of science and technology. In the recent four to five hundred years, especially since the late Ming and early Qing Dynasty, the seclusion policy had been implemented by China's feudal Dynasties, which not only closed its door to the world, but also missed the scientific, technological and industrial revolutions in the world. China became poor and weak. It apparently fell behind the tide of development in the world.

In terms of the scientific development in the world, modern science and technology was introduced to China about 100 years ago. At that time, the technological revolution flourished in Europe and the Nobel Prize began to attract the world's attention, whereas there had hardly been any modern technology in China, nor a single university. Some statistics say that there were no more than 10 people in China who understood calculus. China had experienced many vicissitudes during the 100 years, especially before the birth of the new China. China was ravaged by the world powers and there had been endless wars and chaos, which immensely traumatized the Chinese people.

Let us trace back and compare the scientific and cultural thoughts between China and the west. The theories of the natural philosophy of the ancient China and Greece are similar. The ancient Chinese people's understanding of the objective world can be summarized in *Yin* and *Yang*, the Eight Trigrams, and *Wu Xing* (Five Elements), namely, metal, wood, water, fire and earth, whereas the ancient Greeks attributed everything to "Four Causes", i.e., dryness, wetness, coldness, and heat, or water, fire, earth and air. In fact, their common point was that the world was evolved from some material things. However, it turned out that a strict logical system has been gradually formed in the west and resulted in the scientific theories through scientific experiments. However, a social, political and ethical system far from the natural science had come into being in China. Thus, the modern science based on controlled scientific experiments and strict mathematical reasoning was not cultivated in China.

In terms of the comparison between the cultural traditions between China and the west, the western culture is more concrete and precise, which is embodied in strict logical thinking; there is a good tradition in the pursuit of differences and novelties, whereas the traditional Chinese culture tends to be embodied in intuitionistic and analogical thinking, which is fuzzy and inaccurate, and there is a lack of logical and mathematical tradition. Moreover, it is too utilitarian and basic research is neglected. There had been no experimental tradition and a complete scientific system in ancient China, resulting in a loss of position for science and technology and the impetus and mechanism for the boosting of productivity through science and technology.

Joseph Needham, as was previously mentioned, once put forward a question of great significance: why modern science did not occur in China, which was called Needham's Grand Question. He had some well-known ideas to explain it: modern science did not occur in China was because: firstly, there was no view of nature which could facilitate the growth of science; secondly, the Chinese people was so practical that many discoveries were only empirical; thirdly, the examination system in China stifled people's interest in exploring the natural laws; the eight-legged essay smothered the interest of the students in exploring nature and they focused themselves on ancient books and the pursuit of fame and fortune; "to become an official by excelling in one's study" has become the first aspiration of the scholars. In fact, this influence still roots deep in the present Chinese society. The strong official-oriented mentality has exerted severe negative impact on science and innovation.

Why there has been no one from mainland China who won the Nobel Prize has become the contemporary Needham's Question. These two questions are inter-related and quite similar and deserve further reflections. During the anti-Japanese war, Joseph Needham had been the Science Counselor in British Embassy in China. He wrote a book titled *"Science Outpost"*, in which he was fully confident in the future of the Chinese science. It is a pity that there is no Chinese translation of the full text of this book. The objective attitude that Joseph Needham had shown in the study of the Chinese history of science was highly commendable.

It is well-known that Confucianism has exerted the greatest impact on the thinking and behavior of the Chinese people. The conservatism in Confucianism is regarded as the biggest reason that western scientific thinking was difficult to be absorbed in China in the past 300 years. In the traditional Chinese culture, great importance has been attached to conformity. This value has impeded the innovative spirit of the Chinese people. The Chinese people has been brainwashed by ideas such as stressing the past instead of the present, accepting one's fate, being content with the status quo, and going with the stream for a considerable period of time. Moreover, the thinking mode of the Chinese people tends to be empirical. Therefore, the natural phenomenon has been personified and compared to morality. Practicability was overly stressed in research. And there was a lack of in-depth exploration on the theories and laws of the objective things.

Most of the so-called theoretical innovation in China is just the interpretation of the theories of some politicians instead of real innovation. There is some free academic atmosphere in China compared with the situation before the reform and opening-up. However, the mentality of "the ruler guides the subject; the father guides the son and the husband guides the wife" has existed in China for thousands of years, which has severely imprisoned scholars and resulted in the fact that top priority is given to seniority and authority. There is no academic equality, which is not conducive to the full play of the creativity of middle-aged or especially young researchers.

When talking about why there has been no one from mainland China winning the Nobel Prize, Yang Zhenning explicitly pointed out: "the Golden Mean Doctrine is not the best for scientific development. The reason that the Geometric Law of Euclid was not developed in China is that the inquisitive scientific attitude revealed in it deviates from the Chinese cultural tradition which advocates the mean and impugns the maverick. This cultural mechanism is not conducive to the cultivation of maverick scientific talents."

The survey on the American Nobel Prize winner shows that the prize winning is closely related to the continuity of several generations. That is to say that the accumulation and creation of knowledge is not only related to the work of forefathers, but also the intellectual relay of several generations. Some research done abroad has proved that the birth of a Nobel Science Prize winner requires the knowledge acquisition of at least three generations, showing the important role of the social, educational, and research environment including the family education. The impact of the "knowledge heritage" is mainly manifested in the unconscious inheritance of the academic attitude, research methodology and thinking habits of their predecessors.

There are some prominent problems in China such as the insufficient knowledge acquisition of the Chinese scientists and the shortage of scientist groups. Some sampling estimates have done on the middle-aged and senior academicians in the Chinese Academy of Sciences. The result shows that less than 39% of them were born in professional families, and less than 10% of their children are engaged in high-level scientific research. There is a lack of team spirit among Chinese research workers. Many of them look down upon each other and are hard to cooperate with, which is greatly incompatible with the tendency of collective efforts in scientific study. Before Ding Zhaozhong won the Nobel Prize in 1976, not many researchers participated in the experiments of finding the evidences of beauty quark. By 1995, more than two experiment groups comprising of more than 800 people were searching the evidences for top quark. The world in the future is turning into a "research village" where some Chinese phenomena will be hugely unfit, such as the facts that priorities given to seniority and many people would rather be the tail of a lion than the head of a dog.

Nobel Prizes are awarded to the original innovative science and technology which can exert huge impact on human civilization and social progress. Three factors are crucial in the winning of the Nobel Prize: efforts, opportunity and team spirit. Many scientists have realized that cooperating with the Nobel Prize winner or masters of the same level, becoming their students, earnestly study their papers, or make further explorations based on their output is shortcut in winning the Nobel Prize. However, this goal cannot be reached if there is a lack of team spirit.

（来源：http://www.chinadaily.com.cn/life/2009-10/30/content_11569301.htm）

3.7 Critical thinking 环节

英文文章：Why not Nobel Prize for China for Poverty Alleviation

2019年的诺贝尔经济学授予了印度裔经济学家阿比吉特·班纳吉（Abhijit Banerjee）、他的妻子、麻省理工学院的埃丝特·杜弗洛（Esther Duflo）和哈佛大学教授迈克尔·克雷默（Michael Kremer），"他们以实验性的方式缓解了全球贫困"，这在中国引发了一场辩论，有人认为中国的脱贫攻坚应该获得诺贝尔奖，因为它使1亿多人摆脱了极端贫困。中国经济学家表示，"这是两件不同的事情，中国在减贫方面的最大成就在于实践，而诺贝尔奖则授予学者。获得诺贝尔奖并不是衡量一个国家在解决贫困问题上的贡献和成就的标准。无论有没有诺贝尔奖，中国在扶贫方面的建议、实践、研究和成就是世界历史上最辉煌的成就之一，中国人民应该为中国在扶贫方面取得的进步感到自豪。"

"They are two different things," Xu noted that winning the Nobel Prize is not the criteria for judging a country's contribution and achievements in tackling poverty.

This year's Nobel Economics Prize to Indian-origin economist Abhijit Banerjee, his wife Esther Duflo from MIT and Harvard professor Michael Kremer "for their experimental approach to alleviating global poverty" has sparked off a debate in China that it deserves the coveted prize for lifting over 100 million people from extreme poverty. The announcement of the winners of the Nobel prize in economics has set Chinese internet abuzz, with some Chinese netizens posting their support for China to receive the Nobel Economics Prize for lifting more than 100 million people out of extreme poverty and contributing to 70 per cent of worldwide poverty reduction, official media here reported.

The Nobel Economics Prize was viewed more than 25 million times on China's Twitter-like Sina Weibo platform akin to Twitter, state-run Global Times reported on Wednesday. Some users posted that the US trio's experiment in tackling poverty could not compare with China's efforts. "China is best qualified to speak on poverty alleviation. The Chinese government and researchers have done more than just experiments," one post said. Announcing the award for the trio, the Royal Swedish Academy of Sciences said the research conducted by this year's Laureates has considerably improved our ability to fight global poverty.

In just two decades, their new experiment-based approach has transformed development economics, which is now a flourishing field of research." They have introduced a new approach to obtaining reliable answers about the best ways to fight global poverty, it said. Their "research findings – and those of the researchers following in their footsteps – have dramatically improved our ability to fight poverty in practice," it said. Xu Hongcai, an economist with the China Centre for International Economic Exchanges, told the *Global Times* that "China's biggest achievements on poverty alleviation are in practice, while the Nobel Prize is designated to give to academics.

Commentator Sima Nan posted on his Weibo that China's proposal, practice, research and achievements in poverty alleviation were one of the most brilliant successes in world history. Chinese people should be proud of China's poverty alleviation progress and continue the work with or without a Nobel Prize, he posted.

（来源：https://www.financialexpress.com/economy/why-not-nobel-prize-for-china-for-poverty-alleviation-ask-chinese-netizens/1737389/）

3.8 主题拓展资源

双语文章：John B. Goodenough just Became the Oldest Person, at 97, to Win a Nobel Prize 2019诺贝尔化学奖揭晓，97岁获奖者"棒约翰"火了

诺贝尔奖官方网站最新消息，北京时间10月9日，瑞典皇家科学院宣布，将2019年诺贝尔化学奖联合授予美国科学家约翰·B·古迪纳夫、M·斯坦利·惠廷汉姆以及日本科学家吉野彰，以表彰他们在锂离子电池领域的研发工作。古迪纳夫是至今为止最年长的诺贝尔奖获得者。

Most 97-year-olds would probably feel accomplished just getting out of bed in the morning. John B. Goodenough, 97, just won the Nobel Prize in chemistry.

大多数97岁的老年人只要早上能起得了床就会充满成就感。而97岁的约翰·B·古迪纳夫刚刚获得了诺贝尔化学奖。

Goodenough won the award alongside Stanley Whittingham and Akira Yoshino for their contributions to the development of lithium-ion batteries.

今年的诺贝尔化学奖颁发给了古迪纳夫、斯坦利·惠廷汉姆和吉野彰三位获奖者，以表彰他们对锂离子电池发展的贡献。

They will receive equal shares of the 9m Swedish kronor prize, which was announced by the Royal Swedish Academy of Sciences in Stockholm on Wednesday.

周三（10月9日），位于斯德哥尔摩的瑞典皇家科学院宣布，三位获奖者将平分900万瑞典克朗（约合人民币644万元）的奖金。

97岁的约翰·B·古迪纳夫是美国得克萨斯大学奥斯汀分校机械工程系教授、著名固体物理学家，是钴酸锂、锰酸锂和磷酸铁锂正极材料的发明人，锂离子电池的奠基人之一，通过研究化学、结构以及固体电子/离子性质之间的关系来设计新材料解决材料科学问题，被业界称为"锂电池之父"。

Goodenough is the oldest person to win a Nobel Prize. Arthur Ashkin was the previous record holder, having won the Nobel Prize in physics in 2018 at age 96.

古迪纳夫是最年长的诺贝尔奖获得者。之前的纪录保持者是阿瑟·阿什金，他在2018年以96岁的高龄获得了诺贝尔物理学奖。

"Live to 97 (years old) and you can do anything," Goodenough said in a statement. "I'm honored and humbled to win the Nobel Prize. I thank all my friends for the support and assistance throughout my life."

古迪纳夫在一份声明中说："活到97岁，你可以做任何事情。能获得诺贝尔奖，我感到既荣幸又受宠若惊。感谢所有的朋友一直以来对我的支持和帮助。"

Born in 1922 in Jena, Germany, Goodenough earned a Ph.D from the University of Chicago in 1952, according to the Nobel Foundation. He went on to work at the Massachusetts Institute of Technology, then at the University of Oxford, where he served as the head of the Inorganic Chemistry Laboratory, according to the University of Texas at Austin, where he now works.

据诺贝尔奖基金会介绍,古迪纳夫1922年出生于德国耶拿,1952年获得芝加哥大学博士学位。据目前任职的得克萨斯大学奥斯汀分校介绍,古迪纳夫先后在麻省理工学院和牛津大学工作,并曾担任牛津大学无机化学实验室负责人。

It was at Oxford that Goodenough made the groundbreaking discovery that helped him win the Nobel, UT Austin officials said in a news release.

校方在新闻稿中说,正是在牛津大学期间,古迪纳夫取得了突破性的发现,帮助他获得了诺贝尔奖。

Whittingham developed the first functional lithium battery in the early 1970s, but Goodenough was able to double the battery's potential in 1980 by using lithium cobalt oxide as the cathode of a lithium-ion battery, the foundation said. Using Goodenough's cathode as a basis, Yoshino created the first commercially viable lithium-ion battery five years later.

诺贝尔奖基金会称,惠廷汉姆在20世纪70年代初发明了第一块功能性锂电池,但是古迪纳夫在1980年使用钴酸锂作为锂离子电池的正极,使电池的电势翻了一番。五年后,吉野彰以古迪纳夫的发明为基础,制造出了第一块具有商业可行性的锂离子电池。

"Lithium-ion batteries have revolutionized our lives since they first entered the market in 1991," the Nobel Foundation said in a statement. "They have laid the foundation of a wireless, fossil fuel-free society, and are of the greatest benefit to humankind."

该基金会在一份声明中说:"自1991年首次进入市场以来,锂离子电池已经彻底改变了我们的生活,为无线、无化石燃料的社会奠定了基础,人们获益匪浅。"

Lithium-ion batteries have long been tipped for the award, not least since they have proved pivotal in the development of the high-tech world we inhabit.

锂离子电池一直是诺贝尔化学奖的热门,主要是因为锂离子电池在当今高科技世界的发展中起到了关键作用。

From laptops to smartphones, lithium-ion batteries power some of the most commonly used devices. Electric vehicles were made possible because of the development of these batteries, and wireless communication has flourished because of the technology.

从笔记本电脑到智能手机，锂离子电池为一些最常用的设备提供动力。正是由于锂离子电池的发展，人们研发出了电动汽车，无线通信也因为锂离子电池而蓬勃发展。

"The [electric car] batteries no longer weigh two tonnes, but 300kg," said Prof Sara Snogerup Linse, a member of the Nobel committee for chemistry. "The ability to store energy from renewable sources, the sun, the wind, opens up for sustainable energy consumption," she added.

诺贝尔化学奖评选委员会成员萨拉·斯诺格鲁普·林斯教授说："这种（电动汽车）电池的重量不再是2吨，而是300千克。锂离子电池储存来自太阳能、风能等可再生能源的能力为可持续的能源消费打开了大门。"

"I'm extremely happy the lithium-ion batteries (have) helped communications around the world," Goodenough said Wednesday in a conference call with reporters. "We are indeed happy that people use this for good and not evil."

古迪纳夫在周三（10月9日）的记者电话会议上说："我非常高兴锂离子电池帮助全球的人们沟通交流。我们确实很高兴人们用它来做好事，而不是做坏事。"

Even at the age of 97, he continues to develop new polymers and battery concepts with researchers in his lab. He is now largely focused on developing all-solid-state batteries as they can offer better safety, according to Arumugam Manthiram, a longtime colleague from UT Austin.

即使在97岁的高龄，他仍然在实验室里和研究人员一起开发新的聚合物，研究新的电池概念。据他在该校的老同事阿鲁穆加姆·曼迪亚姆说，古迪纳夫现在主要专注于开发全固态电池，因为其安全性更佳。

（来源：https://language.chinadaily.com.cn/a/201910/10/WS5d9ec222a310cf3e3556fb1c.html）

第三单元 知名企业品牌
（Unit 3 Famous Brand Names）

1. 思政主题：企业家精神和社会责任

2. 意义

理解中国企业精神在当代社会发展的价值，学习中国企业家们的创新、执着和敬业的精神，勇于承担社会责任。

3. 教学设计与思政元素的融入

Passage A

3.1 Warm-up 环节

A. 英文文章：China's Young Entrepreneurs: Growing up Through Pain

本篇文章讲述了5位中国青年企业家的创业故事，他们坚守梦想，在磨砺中成长，展现了新一代中国青年创业者敢想敢拼、坚韧不拔的品格。教师可安排学生阅读，感受榜样力量，确定自己的奋斗方向并为之努力，体现外语课程思政价值。

An entrepreneurial fever is sweeping across China. People, especially young college graduates, are being encouraged to create and innovate by starting their own businesses.

Local governments, eager to tap into these creative minds for new growth engines, have promised to help by rolling out favorable policies. Meanwhile, media have shed a bright light on this trend, likening it to a "wave" that would steer the world's second largest economy towards prosperity, at a time headwinds hamper progress.

Headlines about success stories ignite youngsters' ambitions, but dampen the prospects of those who have tried... and failed.

CGTN spoke to three young entrepreneurs in the build-up to China's Youth Day on May 4, about their unfortunate business endeavors in an effort to understand the dark, and often untold, side of the entrepreneurial glory.

For them, to succeed, fall and stand up again is not just about dreams, pride or money; it's also about growing up through pain.

Sleeping to Escape the World

Feng Chi, 26, used to be a role model among young Beijing entrepreneurs. He quit university in junior year to pursue his dream in musical education.

A capital of 300,000 yuan (around 43,500 US dollars) funded his Rock & Roll workshop for school children. The business expanded the following year; but a year later, his start-up went downhill.

"A shortage of qualified trainers" is the culprit, Feng said, and blamed his "inexperience and over-optimism" for the difficulties he faced down the road.

The derailment of Feng's first entrepreneurial attempt guided him to a dark state of mind. His concern over the survival of his workshop soon developed into a deeper fear for the future.

"I began to lose sleep and feared to open my eyes to see the world when I'm up", recalled Feng.

The collapse of one's business not only brings down dreams once thought to be within reach, but also destroys the confidence which had initially gave these entrepreneurs the power to dream.

The blow the failure deals to one's psyche is "harder" than any financial loss, said Zhu Huaiyang, a 26-year-old who used to run a hedge fund in Shanghai before the business crumbled as a result of a "strategic error" that landed Zhu in huge debt.

"You used to believe that the sky was the limit until reality knocked you down," Zhu told CGTN.

"And that's the hardest part of failure."

Zhu said he was too bankrupt to even pay his rent. He was only allowed to stay in his apartment at Lujiazui, Shanghai's financial hub, because the landlord failed to find new tenants as it was Chinese Spring Festival.

The financial hardship remains a sensitive topic for Zhu, who admits being haunted by his sizeable debt.

"It felt like trying to fill a pit, created by a nuclear bomb, with... a shovel."

Interest, while capable of binding people together, can also tear them up. The young adventurers had learned this the hard way.

Li Hang, who is now running a travel agency in Beijing, said his previous attempts to build the business with several friends had cost him both his money and their friendship, after his partners "kicked him out".

"That's betrayal and it hurt me the most," Li said.

Waking up

For Feng, the phase following self-doubt was self-questioning.

"I kept asking myself what I wanted to be," Feng said. "I had to find the answer, otherwise there would be no moving on for me."

The Rock & Roll fan buried his head in books looking for an answer, and undergoing self-help therapy that involved "cornering yourself with tough inquiries until you break down."

The enlightenment Feng had long sought for eventually materialized.

"I stayed in my room, brought out a sheet of paper and began jotting down the things I wanted to become during my life," Feng said. "Eventually I felt I'd touched the softest spot in my heart with one answer after another."

Zhu did not recover from the shock until eight depressing months, marked with repeated "breakdown at the smallest upset," had passed.

Reading was another therapeutic tool. A Zen book written by Kazuo Inamori, a Japanese entrepreneur, left a deep effect on him.

"You have to force yourself to make changes for the better," Zhu summarized his reflection about hard times.

Reading did not reduce debt, but it sure brought down the fear of the future, Feng and Zhu agreed. Having shaken off fear, both were able to leave their houses in the morning, return to the work field more humbled and start meeting people for new business sparks.

Zhu said he had shared his experience with some senior business owners, who told him in return that it is a blessing that he suffered what he went through in his 20s, and that he "would be really devastated had he undergone this hardship in his 40s."

"I didn't feel quite comfortable hearing that," Zhu said, noting that he "forced himself to smile throughout."

Zhu later ventured into the world of Bitcoin, piling up a fortune along the way with a new firm.

Meanwhile, Feng said he had realized that his salvation lied in helping others.

He shook out plans to start a new firm and joined a company that helps start-ups rise up to their challenges, benefitting others from his firsthand experience.

Gains After Pains

Life is bound to be tough for those who think big, Zhu summed up what he had learned from his rough times. "Dreams come true at a cost."

Looking back at their pains, the three young entrepreneurs agreed that making mistakes were the curse and prerogative of youth.

Being young enables one to turn yesterday's mistakes into tomorrow's assets, Li told CGTN.

Like most of young dreamers in China, these entrepreneurs suffered as they attempted to perfect the world, while building a better life. Their failures, they said, instead of dampening their enthusiasm, prepared them better for the challenges ahead.

"One day, I will stand on a global platform to demonstrate to the world what my generation is all about," Zhu envisaged.

"All the failures we have been through will only be the foundation of our legends."

（来源：CGTN）

B. 英语视频：If You Could Start a Business, What Could It Be and Why?
如果可以开一家公司，你会做什么，为什么？BBC 街头采访，时长约 1 分钟，多位受访人分享了自己关于创业的奇思妙想。教师可在面授课时请学生观看视频并尝试回答该问题，开拓思路，引入单元主题。
（来源：https://www.bilibili.com/video/BV1E4411g7v9?from=search&seid=4705856810571951270）

3.2 Discussion 环节

双语视频：The Startup Kids
一部关于互联网行业年轻创业者的纪录片。片中采访了 Vimeo、Soundcloud、Kiip、Dropbox 等企业的创始人，展现他们充满激情与朝气、敢于尝试和冒险的精神。教师可根据学情选取视频片段请学生观看并回答有关大学生创业的问题。
（来源：https://www.bilibili.com/video/av43525671/）

3.3 Critical thinking 环节

英文视频：Should I Quit My Job and Start a Business?

在你决定要创业之前，首先要考虑五个方面：生活费用、创业内容、成本、存款与时间。视频时长10分钟，教师可安排学生观看，结合自身实际思考毕业后是否决定创业，同时为自己的未来职业发展做铺垫。

（来源：https://v.qq.com/x/page/o3077c6l8cy.html）

3.4 主题拓展资源

随着中国经济的高速发展，中国产品和服务已深入世界经济的各个领域，也涌现出一大批被世界所熟知的企业及企业家。作为新时代青年学子，在了解学习国外企业及企业家的同时，也应更多了解中国企业和企业家的风采。教师可安排学生课后观看以下素材，让学生体会中国经济的崛起，感受中国科技与经济巨头的思想与人格魅力，强化民族自豪感，树立正确价值观，体现外语课程思政育人功能。

A. 动画视频："中国新四大发明"名扬海外

中国网购、快递、移动支付、共享经济惠及全中国乃至世界消费者，被誉为中国"新四大发明"。中国企业及企业家向世界展现了鲜活的创造力及强大的实力，视频时长3分钟，学生可通过观看视频了解中国企业的魅力，增强民族自豪感。

（来源：https://haokan.baidu.com/v?vid=8343479769076807470&pd=bjh&fr=bjhauthor&type=video）

B. 英文文章：China Footprint: The Four Major Breakthroughs in Modern China

Ancient China came up with four inventions which had a massive impact on the world-papermaking, gunpowder, printing and the compass.

Fast forward to the 21st Century and four modern-day breakthroughs have revolutionized daily life for millions of people around the country.

First, the high-speed rail network. Connecting most major cities, the high-speed railway system has been praised as fast, comfortable and more punctual than air travel.

Second, mobile payment. This has transformed China into a predominately cashless society, where even credit and debit cards are seldom used. The penetration rate of cellphone payments now stands at 65 percent, with everything from high end department stores right down to street food vendors allowing customers to scan a QR code to pay for goods and services.

Third, the shared bicycle system. This has had a massive impact on the way Chinese people travel and single-handedly sparked a bicycle revival in China. Scan to ride, then lock and leave. No docking stations are needed at all! This phenomenally popular model has even been exported to countries such as Singapore and the UK.

And finally, online shopping. In China, not just clothes and books can be bought at the touch of a button...quite literally everything can be found and bought online. Takeout food, laundry and manicure services, flowers, goods storage. The list is, quite literally, endless.

Of these four areas which have revolutionized life in China, entrepreneur Bruce Nikoo says he has been most impressed by the explosive popularity of mobile payments.

"It is not just money; China is creating lots of foundations and programs, they encourage Chinese enterprises, specifically information and communication technology to invest research and development, the key driver behind the new growth trajectory of China is going to be science, technology and innovation," he said.

However, Nikoo did point out that China has been growing so rapidly in the last four decades that some worry further development might be difficult.

In 2016, the State Council issued a national scientific and technological innovation plan to improve the country's technology and innovation capabilities, and to bring comprehensive innovation capabilities up into the world's top 15 by 2020.

In 2015, 213 billion US dollars were spent on scientific research and experiments. Invention patent ownership reached 630 per million people. In addition, the contribution rate of technology to economic growth increased from 21 percent in 2010 to 55 percent in 2015.

Furthermore, the development of Artificial Intelligence (AI) in China is also thriving. According to Bruce Nikoo, the next wave is going to be AI, and the strategy of every company is going to be an AI first strategy.

（来源：CGTN）

C. 英文文章: Huawei CEO: 90-day License Bears Little Meaning, Huawei Is Ready

The 90-day temporary general license for Huawei "bears little meaning" and Huawei is fully prepared, said Huawei CEO Ren Zhengfei on Tuesday.

Ren made the statement in a group interview with China Media Group, adding Huawei is grateful for U.S. enterprises' contributions to them, and many of his counselors are from U.S. companies such as IBM.

Focus on our own business

What the U.S. government intends to do is beyond our control, and for Huawei, what counts is to make sure the job is properly done, Ren told reporters.

"We received entity control from the U.S. a year ago, but this has no close bearing on U.S. companies, U.S. politicians are the ones to blame, and their actions underestimate our strength," said Ren.

Ren also expressed confidence in Huawei's 5G competence, saying it will not be affected by the restrictions.

He predicted that no other parties would be able to catch up with the company in 5G technology in the next two to three years.

Ren said Huawei's mass production capacity is still very strong and the ban will not cause negative growth for the company.

Say no to politics

Ren insisted Huawei is a commercial company, hence buying its products depends on consumers' preference. It's wrong to connect Huawei's products with politics.

The industry leader's R&D investment in the U.S. abide by local laws, and our use of partner's scientific payoffs entails expenses, which falls under the commercial activity, Ren added.

"Huawei has established some 10 R&D centers across the globe, and we know the beneficiaries of enterprises' overseas investment are global R&D institutions including U.S. higher education institutions. Huawei's achievements in scientific research are the combinations of global sci-tech wisdom and spur multilateral exchanges and mutual benefits," according to the CEO.

Huawei fights for an ideal, rather than deep pockets. That's why the company rejects the inflow of capital. The greediness of capital will undermine the realization of our ideals.

U.S. chips still Huawei's choice

The CEO stressed the company will not rashly or narrowly exclude the use of U.S. chips, and at the same time appealed for the common development of chip technology.

He said Huawei makes half of its chips itself, while the other half come from the U.S., adding that Huawei will not be isolated from the world.

"We can make the same chips like the U.S. counterparts. However, that doesn't mean we will not buy U.S. chips."

"We do need to learn from U.S. technology in terms of width and depth. But in the 5G area, Huawei is at the forefront, although it can't be denied that there is still a huge gap between China and (the) U.S. on the whole," he noted.

"We sacrifice ourselves and families in the pursuit of a dream to stand on top of the world, which would clash with (the) U.S. sooner or later," Ren said.

Do not incite nationalist sentiment

There are currently two main attitudes towards Huawei, Ren said: some bolster the company driven by patriotism, while others deem that Huawei is holding society's patriotic feelings hostage.

Ren urged against inciting nationalist sentiment, arguing that buying Huawei's products should not be tied simply to patriotism.

（来源：CGTN）

Passage B

3.5 Warm-up 环节

双语视频：张瑞敏：一代商骄（The Business Giant of a Generation）

一部关于张瑞敏和海尔集团的纪录片，展现中国企业家的中国企业和企业家的风采，可以作为课文的导入，让学生加深对海尔和张瑞敏的了解。

In 1984, Haier was a small collectively-owned factory with a budget deficit of 1.47 million yuan, and then came Zhang Ruimin.

In 2017, Haier Group's revenue reached 241.9 billion yuan. Its pre-tax profits exceeded 30 billion yuan, with global operating profits increasing by 41 percent.

Over the past 40 years of the reform and opening-up, Zhang Ruimin and Haier's past and future reflect the development and destiny of contemporary Chinese entrepreneurs. There is a simple but difficult truth to be learned: Self-denial is crucial as success requires humility not conceitedness.

Zhang Ruimin once said, "Without the reform and opening-up, there would be no Haier."

Indeed, every stage of the reform and opening-up provided opportunities for Haier to develop. But more importantly, Zhang incorporated the spirit of continuous change and innovation that characterized the reform and opening-up policy into Haier's DNA.

The 40 years of reform and opening-up have created precious opportunities for Zhang and many other Chinese entrepreneurs. The next 40 years will be a greater challenge.

Zhang has one ultimate goal for Haier. "One day, whenever you go anywhere in the world, people would say: 'I know Haier. It is a famous brand.' That's enough."

Zhang is grateful for the past, but yesterday is over and tomorrow will still bring unknown challenges.

（来源：CGTN）

3.6 Discussion 环节

英语文章：The 6 Biggest Challenges Faced by Student Entrepreneurs

大学生创业并非易事，文章列举了大学生创业过程中的6个常见挑战及对策，如优化产品、寻找合作伙伴等。教师可请学生阅读文章，讨论大学生创业可能遭遇的困难，以及应对举措，加深学生对课文主题的理解。

We fund some of the nation's earliest and brightest innovators and entrepreneurs—university students dedicating their time to inventing something new and bringing it to market in order to effect worthwhile social change. This is not an easy proposition. Being an entrepreneur is hard enough in and of itself, let alone doing it as a student who is trying to get a degree at the same time, has no entrepreneurial experience, and is trying to perfect complex new technology, all with the goal of helping people and the planet.

Recently, members of 13 E-Teams we've funded traveled to Cambridge, Massachusetts to get venture development training intended to help with all this. We asked students about the challenges they're facing as they try to develop and commercialize their products.

1. Intellectual property

Every student needs to understand her or his school's Intellectual Property policy (assuming it has one). If you've invented something of real value while in school, it's doubly important. You need to understand your rights and obligations: unlike faculty and graduate researchers, whose contractual relationships with an institution are usually quite formalized, undergraduates and masters students aren't generally regarded as being employed by their university in the traditional sense. Accordingly, student-generated IP can lie outside the boundaries and can raise a unique set of issues about ownership.

Our advice: Learn your school's IP policy. There's a lack of consensus among institutions right now on how to manage IP generated by undergraduates; policies vary. Finding out now can help minimize conflicts down the road. You can also read our article, *Do You Know the Right Answers to These Intellectual Property Questions*?

2. Perfecting the product

E-Teams typically have complex science behind their inventions. Having a great idea but not knowing exactly how to execute on it is a challenge a lot of teams face. Team members from Spinthesis, a North Dakota State University startup, found that perfecting their spider silk replicating technology was one of their biggest challenges. Team member Brad Hoffmann said, "A lot of it is the bio-based materials, so jumping into the biological aspect of everything was the biggest challenge. We're so technically focused that we don't have that knowledge. It was actually a really steep learning curve."

Our advice: E-Teams can leverage their PIs, cohort peers, and other mentors to work through technology challenges.

3. Balancing school with venture

Being an entrepreneur is a time-intensive job, bordering on a life-consuming obsession. Most young entrepreneurs are working on their innovations on top of finishing school, so it's no surprise that balancing the two is a big challenge. For Mary Dwyer and Anushree Sreedhar, leaders of a team from Cooper Union that created a small, fire extinguishing ball called SEAL, they found that a rigorous course load has them struggling to find time to work on their invention.

Our advice: We always point to Covey's Time Management matrix, which helps entrepreneurs identify what's urgent and what's not. Prioritizing is key!

Remember, hundreds of E-Teams before you have found a way to make it work.

4. Staying focused on crucial goals

A student entrepreneur's most limited resource is time. Many of our teams have found it difficult to figure out what really matters for market success, causing them to prioritize ambiguous goals that lead nowhere. Student entrepreneurs can ensure they are optimizing the use of their time by implementing an objectives and Key Results System (OKR). OKRs enable teams to refresh their vision and communicate goals as outcomes, rather than activities. This helps teams prioritize clarity and alignment, and eliminate unhealthy power dynamics.

For Remora, a team based out of UC San Diego, OKRs provided clarity, direction, and transparency. They developed a water vehicle called SeaSkimmers that uses AI to collect waste in seaports, but had difficulty moving forward with their goals. "One of the learnings we were most excited to implement was the OKR framework; our team sat down and spent some time strategizing for our future and using OKRs as a way to concentrate our vision," said Remora team lead, Saakib Akbany.

Our advice: By centering goals around ideal outcomes, student teams can determine what activities are most likely going to help them achieve those results. By giving everyone permission to actively decide what activities best align with key objectives, teams can practice direct communication, foster healthy relationships, and make progress on their goals with clear accountability and direction.

5. Finding the right partners

All businesses need to secure the right partners, like manufacturers, suppliers, or joint technology developers. But alignment between company and partner doesn't always exist.

A team called cerVIA from Columbia has found this out. In trying to develop an imaging tool for low-income countries that increases the accuracy of cervical cancer screenings, Olachi Oleru of cerVIA says that in their search for a manufacturing partner: "Even though we have a very clear idea of what we want the product to look like and what we want it to do, partnering with a bigger manufacturing firm is the best thing for us to do with so little capital. But they want to push their idea onto our product. It's hard to keep the integrity of it."

Our advice: Do extensive due diligence on partners to identify one where there's potential for mutual benefit. Both sides want to gain as much as possible while giving up as little as possible. It's up to the team to decide what's reasonable and what's not.

6. Getting funding

No surprise here — a major challenge E-Teams face is getting funding. This manifests itself in two ways: 1) getting enough pre-seed funding to support prototype development and the earliest stages of venture development, and 2) bridging the gap between fledgling venture and one pulling in significant angel or VC investment dollars.

Many of our teams testify that before they found us, they couldn't find enough funding to make pursuing the idea worthwhile. That was the case for Blu Horizon from the University of Puerto Rico Mayaguez, led by Kevin Olavarría and Abimelec Mercado. Their product, Anani, measures water usage in households and delivers the data to customers in an easily digestible format. Finding good funding is hard for teams, especially in Puerto Rico. Using the Stage 1 E-Team grant money, Kevin and Abimelec traveled to Cambridge to work on market discovery — finding the best market for Anani.

Our advice: Securing major investment money to propel a venture forward remains a big challenge for E-Teams or any other entrepreneur. As you move beyond grants, it's important to line up milestone objectives with funder expectations. Pursue angel investment and early-stage venture capital when there's a clear value proposition, evidence of product-market fit, and an initial, vetted business model.

（来源：https://venturewell.org/five-biggest-challenges/）

3.7 Critical thinking 环节

通过展示中国企业家的风采，教师可以引导学生深层思考：企业家精神在现代社会中的精神内涵：财富是目的还是工具？在当今的历史时期，我们需要构建什么样的企业家信仰体系与价值观体系？

双语视频：李彦宏：作为企业家就要敢冒险

百度掌门人李彦宏是中国科技企业家的代表之一，面对科技领域的变化，他冒险挑战新领域，寻找新的发展发向，带领百度不断发展，展现了中国企业家的挑战精神和气魄。

（来源：https://haokan.baidu.com/v?vid=16473870584389172517&pd=bjh&fr=bjhauthor&type=video）

3.8 主题拓展资源

A. 英文文章: 6 Reasons to Start a Business While in College

文章作者从自身创业经历出发,介绍了6个在学生时期创业的优势,如拥有丰富的校园资源、易于结交志同道合的伙伴等。教师可请学生阅读文章,思考并讨论自己创业的优势是什么。

I started my business in 1999 while a student in college. There were pros and cons, but I'm largely thankful for the experience and would recommend it to other aspiring entrepreneurs. Here are seven reasons why.

1. Low risk, high reward

This isn't to say you should take a casual approach to starting a business. Your years in college will be over before you know it, and suddenly the risks will be larger. You probably have time to start one serious business venture per year of college and within 12 months figure out if it's going to work out or not. Maybe you'll get it right the first time, maybe you'll pivot, maybe you'll quit and start something new. The sooner you can test your ideas, the better.

2. Campus resources

Universities have access to the fastest internet connections, free consulting from professors who often love getting involved in student run startups, meeting rooms, and many other resources you would pay dearly for outside the campus. The truth is you are paying dearly for these campus resources, whether through tuition or taxes, so you might as well take advantage of them.

3. Real-world education

You can only learn so much in the classroom. The startup world is a great bridge between material taught and applied concepts. "There is no better way to accelerate your growth than to build a company," says student entrepreneur Jordan Gonen, a freshman at Washington University in St. Louis. "It is 100X harder than anything that happens in a classroom, but also 100X more valuable than any textbook lesson."

4. Accessible customers

Students are a valuable resource for testing out your ideas. They're cheap, and they tell it like it is, if they don't like what you have to offer. If you can get students to pay for something it's a good sign your product or service is viable. Students are also connectors. They have the power to manufacture virality.

5. Mentoring

When I was a student I could get access to anyone. All I had to do was contact a CEO's assistant and say "I'm a student at BYU and I'm starting a company and I'm interested in getting some advice from so and so." Successful entrepreneurs love to give advice to young entrepreneurs. They'll make time that they wouldn't make for anyone else, and they'll speak more openly with you than anyone else because they don't see you as a threat or someone with an ulterior motive.

6. Co-founders

It's true that college students lack experience, but think about it this way — the successful entrepreneurs of tomorrow are in college today, and when are you going to have a better time to recruit them than today, when they don't yet realize what they're capable of? The next Zuckerberg may be the guy or gal sitting next to you in your finance class looking bored.

7. Career building

Even if you start a business in college and it fails, it's a huge plus on your resume. Starting a business shows that you're proactive, creative, and driven — just the type of employee successful companies are looking for. Startup experience while in college can put you on the fast track to leadership opportunities at another company if you decide you're not ready to be a full-time entrepreneur and want to get some work experience under your belt first.

Are there negatives to starting a business while in college? Sure, you might spend some money launching your business and you'll definitely lose sleep. But these investments will pay off in other ways both tangible and intangible, making it a rewarding experience you'll always be grateful for.

（来源 https://fortune.com/2017/01/23/start-business-college-student-mark-zuckerberg/）

B. 英文文章： 10 Businesses You Can Start from Your Dorm Room

本部分探讨企业家精神和创新创业。企业家精神是企业家组织建立和经营管理企业的综合才能的表述方式，突出表现为创新精神、机会意识、冒险精神三个方面。[①] 在新形势下，如何加强大学生创新精神和创业能力的培养是高校人才培养的战略性问题，也越来越成为我国高等教育改革发展面临的重要任

---

① 孙云龙，刘万兆. 大学生创业教育模式探索——基于企业家精神培养视角[J]. 思想教育研究，2013(11):87-89.

务。[1] 我国于1996年颁布的《关于深化教育改革全面推进素质教育的决定》明确提出："高等学校要重视培养大学生的创新能力、实践能力和创新精神。"[2]

本部分的教学内容可以选取知名企业家的创业经历与杰出成就，特别是中西方不同企业家的案例故事，作为学习素材，激发学生对企业家精神的思考以及对中西方企业家精神差异的思考。教师通过分享这些成功案例和经历，可以激励学生以这些例子为榜样，拓宽视野，树立正确的跨文化意识和创新创业观念。[3] 通过对企业家创新精神、机会意识和冒险精神的深刻领悟，有利于培养大学生的自主创业意识，形成一种敢创业、能创业、创好业的创业精神。[4] 通过正确引导学生认识中国企业精神在当代社会发展的价值，鼓励学生学习中国企业家们的创新、执着和敬业的精神，和勇于承担社会责任的精神。

本篇文章基于大学生的环境和自身特性，为大学生推荐分析了在校期间可以进行的10个创业项目。

What do Microsoft, Dell, Napster and Facebook all have in common? Aside from being among some of the most market-shaking companies of the last quarter century, they were all also created by college students.

Sure, not everyone can be the next Mark Zuckerberg, but starting a small business while in college is definitely possible. There are several options that require little to no startup capital and can be done without an office space. Entrepreneurship in college can help make valuable connections while also generating some income to cover tuition, meals and those very expensive textbooks.

Here are 10 ideas for starting a business from the comfort of your own dorm room.

Information technology (IT) consulting

Information technology is one field where having years of experience can actually work against you. College students typically have the freshest skills in this area and knowledge of the newest technologies. If you don't feel confident promoting yourself as an IT consultant to businesses, put the word out on campus that you're available to help the less tech-savvy majors with their computer issues, and build from there.

---

[1] 周济. 注重培养创新人才，增强高水平大学创新能力 [J]. 中国高等教育，2006(15):4.
[2] 陈希. 将创新创业教育贯穿于高校人才培养全过程 [J]. 中国高等教育，2010(12):4-6.
[3] 张映婷. 英语教学中跨文化教育与创新创业教育双融合的路径探究 [J]. 沈阳工程学院学报（社会科学版），2021(4):116-119
[4] 林银，谢志远. 大学生创业教育中的价值观引导 [J]. 创新与创业教育，2012(4):38-40.

Social media consulting

College students are often on the cutting edge of social-media trends. Use this knowledge and experience to advise companies on their social-media strategy. Take them beyond Facebook and LinkedIn, and introduce them to new channels to get their messages out.

Graphic design

Graphic design consulting relies more on creativity and talent than years of experience. Design majors should grab a portfolio of their best projects from class, print off some impressive looking business cards or feature them on a website, and get started.

Website design

Students are much more exposed to designing websites than ever before. Many have done so for a campus group or club, a fellow student or just a personal blog. Those sites can be used as samples and leveraged in order to branch out to designing websites for a profit.

Photography

Thanks to platforms like Pinterest, Instagram, Snapchat and Facebook, the world has become more accustomed to using images to communicate. With a rise in the need for visual content, there has also been growing sense of comfort with using amateur photographers. Due to advancements in technology, these amateurs have the ability to churn out high-quality work.

Host an event

College students have probably attended their fair share of parties, but putting that party experience to good use is another story. Event planning requires attention to detail, organization, the ability to multitask and creativity. If equipped to handle the job, start a business around campus and become the go-to source for planning campus group or club activities. It's important to note that taking your business outside of school may require special certification.

Personal trainer

Personal trainers have flexible hours and can conduct workouts almost anywhere. Personal training can oftentimes require a certification through an organization such as ACE, but meeting the requirements, such as taking a certification exam and passing CPR/AED courses, may be easier than you think.

Cleaning services

Starting a cleaning business allows students to work flexible hours and doesn't require an office. Not to mention, supplies needed for this business can be purchased at your local grocery store. Many people are willing to pay someone else to do a dirty job. A gold mine for the cleaning business lies within fraternity or sorority houses the day after a big game.

Freelance makeup artist

According to Federal data, women have outnumbered men in American colleges for nearly 35 years. This provides the perfect opportunity to start a small business geared towards the female demographic. Freelance makeup artists can generate revenue in the traditional sense of applying makeup to customers ahead of special occasions. Alternately, one of the newest ways to make money is by providing tutorial videos on social media. Great content that attracts a high number of viewers can turn into YouTube sponsorship dollars.

Landscaping / Snow Removal

Landscaping and snow removal services are great seasonal businesses that can carry over vacation breaks and throughout the semester. Armed with a shovel, garden store equipment and some sturdy boots, students living off-campus or local residents could become very lucrative clients.

Even if a business is started by a student while in college, it's still a real business, with real rewards and risks. No matter what the business or size of the company, it's important to have insurance protection. Things like specialized IT consultant insurance or a more general professional liability policy will help a company stay out of trouble if anything goes wrong. The bottom line is that college entrepreneurship can be a great way to earn some money as well as pave the way for continued career success after graduation.

（来源：https://www.entrepreneur.com/slideshow/306553）

第四单元　克隆与伦理
（Unit 4 Cloning and Ethics）

1. 思政主题：科技与伦理

2. 意义

学生在了解克隆技术发展及应用前景的基础上，思考并讨论克隆技术的利与弊，以及存在的潜在危险和不确定性。科学技术是把双刃剑，如何规范基因编辑是今天人类社会面临的严峻考验之一。人类生殖细胞基因编辑如果缺乏监管和法律、道德和伦理的约束可能带来对人类社会安全危害，甚至给人们的经济和生活造成毁灭性的灾难。

我国高度重视科研伦理和安全问题。2019年1月21日，习近平总书记在省部级主要领导干部坚持底线思维着力防范化解重大风险专题研讨班开班式上发表重要讲话，指出要加快科技安全预警监测体系建设，围绕人工智能、基因编辑、医疗诊断、自动驾驶、无人机、服务机器人等领域，加快推进相关立法工作。

3. 教学设计与思政元素的融入

Passage A

3.1 Warm-up 环节

A. 英语视频：多利羊是怎样诞生的 Cloning Dolly the Sheep

让学生通过多利的诞生，了解克隆技术，并启发学生思考这种技术的发展所带来的启示和可能的应用。

（来源：https://v.youku.com/v_show/id_XNzA3Nzg0Mjcy.html）

B. 双语文章：Can Babies Be Designed? 婴儿可以人工培育吗？

We hear a lot nowadays about designer babies. The idea that parents can choose the genes of their children sounds frightening. The question we have to answer is: how much can we and should we control the creation of designer babies?

What exactly is a "designer baby"? One simple way that parents design their child is by choosing its sex. From a technical point of view, this is very easy. In Europe, it is not legal to do this. But in the United States, people can pay about $ 2,000 to go to a specialized fertility clinic where they can choose the sex of their child.

It is also possible to choose the specific genes that a baby will have. This happens for medical reasons, to avoid certain serious genetic diseases. A lot of people are worried that parents will want to choose their baby's genes for non-medical reasons. The parents may, for example, want to have a child with specific qualities. Some experts believe that this will certainly happen. Professor Lee Silver of Princeton University in the USA says, "Men and women will go to specialized clinics. The doctors will take about 200 eggs from the women. The eggs will be fertilized. Then the doctors will choose the embryo that has the desired genes. They will throw away the other embryos."

In this case, the genes of the baby will have come from the parents. But it is also possible to add genes to an embryo. The baby that grows will then have genes that did not come from its parents, for example, a gene for intelligence or for musical ability.

Nobody has added a gene to a human embryo yet, but scientists have added genes to other animals. Dr Keith Campbell is one of the researchers who cloned Dolly, the sheep. Dr Campbell has also added a human gene to another sheep called Polly. Dr Campbell says, "The way of adding genes to humans is the same as in animals."

If someone tries to add a gene to a human embryo, something terrible could happen. Some of the experiments on animals have in fact produced terrible consequences. In one experiment, scientists added a gene to pigs to make them grow bigger more quickly. But the experiment went wrong — only some parts of the pigs grew bigger and quickly the animals became ill and died.

The problem is that scientists do not know enough about what specific genes do and how different genes work together. Dr Dean Hamer of the National Cancer Institute says, "One gene can do a lot of different things. We can never be sure that we know everything about a particular gene. If we added a gene to a human, the result could be terrible."

If scientists add a gene to a human, that new gene will be passed to future generations. After many generations, this could produce a division in society.

Professor Lee Silver says, "The problem with this technology is that it will make a division between rich and poor. The rich will have good genes. They will be intelligent, beautiful and healthy. The poor will have bad genes."

Dr Hamer is sure that one day scientists really will design human genes. "The question isn't: will we be able to do it?" he says. "The real question now is: what genes are we going to change?"

婴儿可以人工培育吗？

眼下我们听到许多关于人工培育良种婴儿的传闻。这种父母可以为自己的孩子选择基因的想法听上去令人惊恐。我们要回答的问题是：我们能够并应该在多大程度上对婴儿人工培育进行控制呢？

到底什么是"人工培育良种婴儿"呢？父母人工培育婴儿的一种简单办法就是选择性别。从技术角度上讲，这是一件很容易做到的事情。在欧洲这样做是非法的，但是在美国，人们可以支付大约2000美元去一个专门的生育诊所，在那里可以对孩子的性别进行选择。

同时，为婴儿挑选特别的基因也可以实现。这是出于健康考虑，以避免孩子患上某些严重的遗传疾病。很多人担心父母不是出于健康原因去为自己的孩子选择基因。比如，父母可能希望拥有一个具有某种特殊才能的婴儿。有些专家相信这种事情早晚会发生。美国普林斯顿大学李·西尔弗教授说："男人和女人将前往专门诊所。医生将从妇女体内提取大约200个卵子，使这些卵子受精。然后医生将留下带有父母所希望的基因的那个胚胎，把其他胚胎丢弃。"

在这种情况下，婴儿的基因都会来自其父母。但是也有向胚胎中注入其他基因的可能性。于是，这个婴儿长成后会有非其父母的基因，如智力基因或者音乐才能基因。

目前为止，还没有任何人向人类胚胎中注入过基因，但是科学家已经给动物注入了基因。基思·坎贝尔博士是进行多莉羊克隆的研究者之一。他还给另一只羊波莉注入了人类基因。他说："给人注入基因与给动物注入基因的方法是一样的。"

如果有人想要向人类胚胎内注入某一基因，那么可怕的事情可能会发生。实际上，一些对动物的试验已经产生了可怕的后果。在一次试验中，科学家给猪注入了某一基因，以促使其长得更大更快。但是试验却出现了问题——猪只是局部长得更大，然后很快便病死了。

科学家面临的问题是，他们尚不清楚特种基因能起什么作用以及不同的基因之间是如何配合起作用的。美国国家癌症研究所迪安·哈默博士说："一个基因可以做许多不同的事情。我们永远也无法确定我们对某一基因已经了如指掌。如果我们给一个人注入某一基因，其后果不堪设想。"

假若科学家给一个人注入某一基因，那个新基因将会一代代往下遗传。经过若干代，这可能造成社会的差异。李·西尔弗教授说："这一技术的问题在于，它将在富人与穷人之间形成一条鸿沟——富人将拥有好的基因，他们将变得聪明、漂亮和健康；而穷人将只能有不好的基因。"

哈默博士确信，终有一天科学家将真正进行人类基因的培育。他说："问题不在于我们是否有能力去做，而是在于我们将要改变哪些基因。"

（来源：http://www.tingroom.com/lesson/englishsalon1/25651.html）

3.2 Discussion 环节

英语视频：BBC 地平线——克隆人的诞生

结合课文，通过了解 Severino Antinori 团队克隆人的计划引发科学界对于伦理的争论，以及人们对于中国科研人员贺建奎基因编辑免疫艾滋病婴儿事件评论，引导学生思考并讨论克隆人的利与弊，有哪些风险，是否符合伦理，以及我们该如何合理应用克隆技术。

（来源：https://v.qq.com/x/cover/4qjhykh1e71prp7/g0013akjd9p.html）

3.3 Critical thinking 环节

英语视频：TED 演讲：科技新突破：编辑人类 DNA

Jennifer Doudna 是 2020 年诺贝尔化学奖两位获得者之一。她的同事发现并掌握了一项新技术可以进行 DNA 的编辑，这项技术如果运用于人体，它的意义将是非凡的，因为我们将可以按自己的喜好与要求塑造各类人体特质，甚至定制人类。但同时这项技术也会带来道德、伦理等诸多方面的潜在风险和危害。这位科学家呼吁：在没弄清楚这些风险和危害前，暂停这项技术的研发与运用，这是有良知和社会责任的医学专家应有的态度。教师可以引导学生思考：科学家在进行科学研究时是否可以抛开社会责任和法律与道德规范？

A few years ago, with my colleague, Emmanuelle Charpentier, I invented a new technology for editing genomes. It's called CRISPR-Cas9. The CRISPR technology allows scientists to make changes to the DNA in cells that could allow us to cure genetic disease.

几年前，我跟同事 Emmanuelle Charpentier 发明了一个可以编辑基因组的新技术。它叫做 "CRISPR-Cas9"。CRISPR 技术让科学家可以改变细胞里的 DNA，从而让我们能够治愈基因疾病。

You might be interested to know that the CRISPR technology came about through a basic research project that was aimed at discovering how bacteria fight viral infections. Bacteria have to deal with viruses in their environment, and we can think about a viral infection like a ticking time bomb — a bacterium has only a few minutes to defuse the bomb before it gets destroyed. So, many bacteria have in their cells an adaptive immune system called CRISPR, that allows them to detect viral DNA and destroy it.

你可能有兴趣想知道，CRISPR 技术其实来自于一个基础的科学研究，它的主要目的是要了解细菌如何与病毒感染进行对抗。细菌必须在它们的环境里对付病毒。我们可以这么想，病毒感染像是个定时炸弹，细菌在被消灭前，只有几分钟时间可以拆除炸弹。很多细菌在它们的细胞里有一种适应力免疫系统叫做"CRISPR"，它可以使细菌检测到病毒 DNA 并消灭它。

Part of the CRISPR system is a protein called Cas9, that's able to seek out, cut and eventually degrade viral DNA in a specific way. And it was through our research to understand the activity of this protein, Cas9, that we realized that we could harness its function as a genetic engineering technology — a way for scientists to delete or insert specific bits of DNA into cells with incredible precision — that would offer opportunities to do things that really haven't been possible in the past.

CRISPR 系统中，有一部分是一种叫 Cas9 的蛋白质，它能够以特殊的方式寻找出、剪断，最后削弱病毒 DNA。我们的研究主要是想了解 Cas9 蛋白质的活动，我们意识到可以驾驭它的功能，把它当做一种基因工程技术—— 一种可以让科学家用难以置信的精准度来消除或插入特定 DNA 片段到细胞中——这项技术提供了一个前所未有的机会，让我们可以做到在过去根本无法完成的事情。

The CRISPR technology has already been used to change the DNA in the cells of mice and monkeys, other organisms as well. Chinese scientists showed recently that they could even use the CRISPR technology to change genes in human embryos. And scientists in Philadelphia showed they could use CRISPR to remove the DNA of an integrated HIV virus from infected human cells.

CRISPR 技术已经被应用于改变老鼠和猴子细胞里的 DNA，还包括其他有机体。中国科学家最近发现，他们甚至可以利用 CRISPR 技术改变人类胚胎里的基因。费城的科学家证实，他们可以利用 CRISPR 技术从一个受感染的人类细胞中移除 HIV 病毒（人类免疫缺陷病毒）。

The opportunity to do this kind of genome editing also raises various ethical issues that we have to consider, because this technology can be employed not only in adult cells, but also in the embryos of organisms, including our own species. And so, together with my colleagues, I've called for a global conversation about the technology that I co-invented, so that we can consider all of the ethical and societal implications of a technology like this.

这个充满契机的基因组编辑技术，也引发了各种我们必须认真思考的道德争议。因为这种技术不仅可以运用在成人细胞上，也可以用在有机体的胚胎上，包含我们人类自己。所以，我和同事们呼吁，要针对这项技术展开一次全球对话，思考应该赋予这种技术的道德与社会责任。

What I want to do now is tell you what the CRISPR technology is, what it can do, where we are today and why I think we need to take a prudent path forward in the way that we employ this technology.

那么现在，我要告诉你们 CRISPR 技术是什么、它可以做什么、目前的发展状况、以及我为什么认为我们需要一个缜密的思路来运用这项技术。

When viruses infect a cell, they inject their DNA. And in a bacterium, the CRISPR system allows that DNA to be plucked out of the virus, and inserted in little bits into the chromosome — the DNA of the bacterium. And these integrated bits of viral DNA get inserted at a site called CRISPR. CRISPR stands for clustered regularly interspaced short palindromic repeats.

当病毒感染一个细胞，它们会插入自身的 DNA。在一个细菌中，CRISPR 系统可以把病毒的 DNA 拔掉，并且将其中一小段插入染色体内——也就是细菌的 DNA。而这些成簇的病毒 DNA 会被插入一个名为 CRISPR 的位点。CRISPR 意思是"规律成簇的间隔短回文重复"。

A big mouthful — you can see why we use the acronym CRISPR. It's a mechanism that allows cells to record, over time, the viruses they have been exposed to. And importantly, those bits of DNA are passed on to the cells' progeny, so cells are protected from viruses not only in one generation, but over many generations of cells. This allows the cells to keep a record of infection, and as my colleague, Blake Wiedenheft, likes to say, the CRISPR locus is effectively a genetic vaccination card in cells. Once those bits of DNA have been inserted into the bacterial chromosome, the cell then makes a little copy of a molecule called RNA, which is orange in this picture, that is an exact replicate of the viral DNA. RNA is a chemical cousin of DNA, and it allows interaction with DNA molecules that have a matching sequence.

很绕口——这回你们就知道为什么我们要使用 CRISPR 的缩写了。

CRISPR 是一种机制—— 它允许细胞随时记录被感染到的病毒。而且重要的是，这些 DNA 片段会遗传到细胞的后代，所以细胞不只有一代会一直被保护不受病毒感染，好几代细胞都会如此。这允许细胞持有受感染的记录，就像我同事 Blake Wiedenheft 喜欢说的，CRISPR 的基因座其实上就是细胞的一张基因疫苗接种卡。一旦这些片段 DNA 被插入到细菌染色体内，细胞就会复制出一小段叫 RNA 的分子，就是照片上的橘色的部分，它就是病毒 DNA 的复制品。RNA 相当于 DNA 的化学表亲，能够与 DNA 上相同序列的分子产生反应。

So those little bits of RNA from the CRISPR locus associate—they bind—to protein called Cas9, which is white in the picture, and form a complex that functions like a sentinel in the cell. It searches through all of the DNA in the cell, to find sites that match the sequences in the bound RNAs. And when those sites are found—as you can see here, the blue molecule is DNA—this complex associates with that DNA and allows the Cas9 cleaver to cut up the viral DNA. It makes a very precise break. So we can think of the Cas9 RNA sentinel complex like a pair of scissors that can cut DNA—it makes a double-stranded break in the DNA helix. And importantly, this complex is programmable, so it can be programmed to recognize particular DNA sequences, and make a break in the DNA at that site.

所以这些从 CRISPR 基因座转录的 RNA 片段，会与一种叫 Cas9 的蛋白质相结合，也就是照片上白色的部分，这个蛋白质综合体像是细胞的卫兵。它会搜寻细胞里所有的 DNA，找到符合所结合的 RNA 序列的位点。当这些位置被找到—— 就是你们看到的蓝色 DNA 分子，这个综合体会与 DNA 结合，并允许 Cas9 蛋白质像刀一样切断病毒 DNA。这是一次非常精确的截断。所以我们可以把 Cas9 RNA 标记复合体想像成是一把 DNA 剪刀—— 它在 DNA 螺旋结构中，制造了一种 "双股螺旋断裂"。最重要的是，这种复合体是可程式化的，在程式化后可以用来辨认特定的 DNA 序列，并且在 DNA 的特定位置制造一个断裂。

As I'm going to tell you now, we recognized that that activity could be harnessed for genome engineering, to allow cells to make a very precise change to the DNA at the site where this break was introduced. That's sort of analogous to the way that we use a word-processing program to fix a typo in a document.

我现在想要告诉大家，我们已经意识到这个技术，可以被利用于基因工程中，就在我提到过的断裂处使细胞内的 DNA 产生一个非常精准的变化。这个方式有点类似于我们使用文字处理软件在一个文档中修改错字一样。

The reason we envisioned using the CRISPR system for genome engineering is because cells have the ability to detect broken DNA and repair it. So when a plant or an animal cell detects a double-stranded break in its DNA, it can fix that break, either by pasting together the ends of the broken DNA with a little, tiny change in the sequence of that position, or it can repair the break by integrating a new piece of DNA at the site of the cut. So if we have a way to introduce double-stranded breaks into DNA at precise places, we can trigger cells to repair those breaks, by either the disruption or incorporation of new genetic information. So if we were able to program the CRISPR technology to make a break in DNA at the position at or near a mutation causing cystic fibrosis, for example, we could trigger cells to repair that mutation.

我们意识到 CRISPR 系统可以被用于基因组工程的原因是，细胞具有检测损坏的 DNA，并将其修复能力。所以当一个植物或动物细胞在它的 DNA 中检测到双股螺旋断裂时，它可以修复这种断裂，把破裂的 DNA 尾端接合在一起，只在那个位置的序列产生微小的变化，或者也可以借由在该位置处聚集新的 DNA 片段来修复断裂。所以如果我们有一种方式可以引导"双股螺旋断裂"精准地进入 DNA，我们就可以刺激细胞来修复这些断裂，通过破坏或合并新的遗传信息。所以如果我们可以程式化 CRISPR 技术在 DNA 里制造断裂，例如，在囊性纤维化发生突变的位置或附近制造断裂，我们就可以刺激细胞去修复那个突变。

Genome engineering is actually not new, it's been in development since the 1970s. We've had technologies for sequencing DNA, for copying DNA, and even for manipulating DNA. And these technologies were very promising, but the problem was that they were either inefficient, or they were difficult enough to use that most scientists had not adopted them for use in their own laboratories, or certainly for many clinical applications. So, the opportunity to take a technology like CRISPR and utilize it has appeal, because of its relative simplicity. We can think of older genome engineering technologies as similar to having to rewire your computer each time you want to run a new piece of software, whereas the CRISPR technology is like software for the genome, we can program it easily, using these little bits of RNA.

基因工程并不是什么新技术，它在20世纪70年代就发展起来了。我们已经拥有 DNA 测序技术，DNA 复制技术，甚至 DNA 修改技术。这些技术前程无量，但问题是它们要么效率不高，要么操作太复杂，所以大部分科学家们并不在实验室采用这项技术，或是应用于临床。而 CRISPR 的技术相对简单，所以使用它的机会已展露曙光。我们可以想像一下：旧的基因工程技术就好比每次你要安装新的软件，就要把电脑升级一次一样；而CRISPR技术就像基因组的软件，利用这些RNA小片段，我们可以简单地编辑它。

So once a double-stranded break is made in DNA, we can induce repair, and thereby potentially achieve astounding things, like being able to correct mutations that cause sickle cell anemia or cause Huntington's Disease. I actually think that the first applications of the CRISPR technology are going to happen in the blood, where it's relatively easier to deliver this tool into cells, compared to solid tissues.

那么一旦双股螺旋断裂在DNA中发生，我们就可以诱导修复，由此有可能达到惊人的效果，比如，能够修正引起镰刀细胞贫血症，或引起亨廷顿氏病的突变。我认为CRISPR技术的第一项应用会在血液里发生，相对于坚硬组织而言，能更容易地在细胞内导入这项技术。

Right now, a lot of the work that's going on applies to animal models of human disease, such as mice. The technology is being used to make very precise changes that allow us to study the way that these changes in the cell's DNA affect either a tissue or, in this case, an entire organism.

目前，很多工作已经运用在人类疾病的动物模型中，例如，老鼠。这技术已经被用来实现非常精准的改变，使我们能够研究细胞DNA里的变化，不论是对一个组织或像这个案例中的整个有机体。

Now in this example, the CRISPR technology was used to disrupt a gene by making a tiny change in the DNA in a gene that is responsible for the black coat color of these mice. Imagine that these white mice differ from their pigmented litter-mates by just a tiny change at one gene in the entire genome, and they're otherwise completely normal. And when we sequence the DNA from these animals, we find that the change in the DNA has occurred at exactly the place where we induced it, using the CRISPR technology.

在这个案例中，借由在DNA里的小改变，CRISPR技术被用来扰乱关联这些老鼠黑色皮肤的基因。想象一下，这些白色的老鼠与它们有色小同伴不同的原因，仅是由于在整个基因组中的一个小改变，除此之外，它们几乎一模一样。当我们对这些动物的基因进行测序，我们发现了在基因里的变化就精准地发生在我们使用CRISPR技术的地方。

Additional experiments are going on in other animals that are useful for creating models for human disease, such as monkeys. And here we find that we can use these systems to test the application of this technology in particular tissues, for example, figuring out how to deliver the CRISPR tool into cells. We also want to understand better how to control the way that DNA is repaired after it's cut, and also to figure out how to control and limit any kind of off-target, or unintended effects of using the technology.

其他动物，如猴子，作为人类疾病的的试验模型，也正在被应用于这类实验。我们在此发现，可以通过使用这些系统来检测这一技术在特定组织中的运用，以解决诸如"如何传送 CRISPR 工具到细胞中"的问题。我们也想进一步了解如何控制 DNA 在切断后的修复方式，也更想知道如何控制并限制任意一种偏离目标的状况，或者使用这技术时的副作用。

I think that we will see clinical application of this technology, certainly in adults, within the next 10 years. I think that it's likely that we will see clinical trials and possibly even approved therapies within that time, which is a very exciting thing to think about. And because of the excitement around this technology, there's a lot of interest in start-up companies that have been founded to commercialize the CRISPR technology, and lots of venture capitalists that have been investing in these companies.

我想我们会在十年内就看到它在临床上的应用，特别是应用于成人。我认为在这期间，我们很可能会看到临床试验，甚至也有可能是获得批准的治疗方式，想想的确是件令人兴奋的事。另外，因为这项技术的兴起，也涌现了很多初创公司，致力于 CRISPR 技术的商业化，也有很多风险投资家开始为这些公司投资。

But we have to also consider that the CRISPR technology can be used for things like enhancement. Imagine that we could try to engineer humans that have enhanced properties, such as stronger bones, or less susceptibility to cardiovascular disease or even to have properties that we would consider maybe to be desirable, like a different eye color or to be taller, things like that. "Designer humans", if you will. Right now, the genetic information to understand what types of genes would give rise to these traits is mostly not known. But it's important to know that the CRISPR technology gives us a tool to make such changes, once that knowledge becomes available.

但我们也必须要思考一件事，就是 CRISPR 技术能被用在强化性能上。想象一下我们可以尝试设计制造人类，像是拥有更强壮的骨骼，或降低心血管疾病的诱发概率；甚至拥有我们期待已久的特征，像是不同的眼睛颜色，或长得更高。"定制人"，你们也可以这么理解。目前为止，关于哪些类型的基因会有

413

这些特征，相关的基因信息大部分仍是未知的。但对于了解 CRISPR 技术为我们提供了一个可以改变现状的工具这点是很重要的，尤其是当我们获得了这些基因信息之后。

This raises a number of ethical questions that we have to carefully consider, and this is why my colleagues and I have called for a global pause in any clinical application of the CRISPR technology in human embryos, to give us time to really consider all of the various implications of doing so. And actually, there is an important precedent for such a pause from the 1970s, when scientists got together to call for a moratorium on the use of molecular cloning, until the safety of that technology could be tested carefully and validated.

这会引发一系列我们必须仔细考量的道德问题，这也是为什么我跟我的同事们想要呼吁全世界暂缓任何临床上有关 CRISPR 在人类胚胎上的应用，给我们一些时间，让我们认真思考各种不同的 CRISPR 应用。实际上，在20世纪70年代，有一个类似暂缓的重要例子，当时科学家们聚集在一起，呼吁暂缓使用"分子克隆"，直到那个技术可以安全地被小心测试并验证。

So, genome-engineered humans are not with us yet, but this is no longer science fiction. Genome-engineered animals and plants are happening right now. And this puts in front of all of us a huge responsibility, to consider carefully both the unintended consequences as well as the intended impacts of a scientific breakthrough.

虽然经过基因工程改造的人类尚未出现，但这已经不仅仅是科幻小说了。动物及植物的基因改造正在进行中，这也使我们每一个人都面临一项重大责任：认真思考这个科技突破可能会带来的未知后果和可预见的冲击。

（来源：中国日报网）

3.4 主题拓展资源

双语文章：霍金生前最后担忧：超级富豪操纵 DNA 或毁灭人类
Stephen Hawking's Final Fear Revealed — a Terrifying Master Race of Superhumans

著名物理学家霍金的成就有很多，此外，他还是这个世界上最惊世骇俗的预言家。地球将在200年内毁灭，人类要想继续存活只能移民外星球；或许外星生命正盯着我们，可能会为资源入侵地球；2600年地球或将变成"火球"；人工智能可能会导致人类的灭亡……这些都是霍金曾作出的预言。霍金遗作中透露了他生前最大的担忧："超人"的出现或将导致人类逐渐绝迹。

Stephen Hawking's final fear was that DNA manipulation would lead to a master race of superhumans, it has been revealed.

据披露，斯蒂芬·霍金最后的担忧是：操纵 DNA 将催生超级人类优等种族。

The physicist, who died in March aged 76, thought the development could destroy the rest of humanity.

已故物理学家霍金认为这一发展趋势可能毁灭人类。霍金于 2018 年 3 月去世，享年 76 岁。

His last prediction is revealed in a new book of his collected articles and essays called *Brief Answers to Big Questions*.

最近出版的霍金文集《重大问题简答》一书披露了他的最后预言。

He feared rich people would soon be able to edit their children's DNA to improve attributes like memory and disease immunity.

他担心，过不了多久，富人将能够编辑子女的 DNA，提高其记忆力和疾病免疫力。

And he said that would pose a crisis for the rest of the world even if politicians tried to outlaw the practice.

他还说，即使政治家设法用法律禁止这种做法，它仍将对其他人群带来危机。

In an extract published by *The Sunday Times*, he wrote: "I am sure that during this century people will discover how to modify both intelligence and instincts such as aggression."

在《星期日泰晤士报》发表的一篇文章节选中，霍金写道："我敢肯定本世纪之内人们将找到改变智力和攻击性等天性的办法。"

"Laws will probably be passed against genetic engineering with humans. But some people won't be able to resist the temptation to improve human characteristics, such as memory, resistance to disease and length of life."

"人们可能会制定法律禁止人类基因工程。但是，有人肯定抵制不了诱惑，想要改进一些人类特征，比如，记忆力、疾病抵抗力和寿命。"

And he said that would cause huge problems for humans who have not undergone the same process, leaving them unable to compete.

他表示，这将给未修改基因的人带来严重问题，导致他们没有竞争力。

The professor even warned it could lead to the extinction of humanity as we know it.

霍金甚至警告说，这可能导致我们所认知的人类走向灭绝。

He said of normal humans: "Presumably they will die out, or become unimportant."

他谈到普通人是说："他们可能会绝种，或变得可有可无。"

"Instead, there will be a race of self-designing beings who are improving at an ever-increasing rate."

"取而代之的是一种不断加速改进的自主设计人类。"

The Brief History of Time author also refers to techniques like Crispr, which enables scientists to modify harmful genes and add in others.

霍金，《时间简史》的作者，还提到了相关基因编辑方法，比如"规律成簇间隔短回文重复系统（Crispr）"，科学家可以借此修复有害基因并加入其他基因。

And although such procedures could be a boost for medical science, some critics are concerned they could lead to a eugenics-style movement, where the weak are weeded out of society.

尽管这类方法可能促进医学发展，但是一些批评者担心它也可能导致优生学式的运动，弱势群体将被社会淘汰。

The new book, published by Hodder & Stoughton on Tuesday, also collects his writings on what he thought were the big questions facing science and wider society.

新书还收集了霍金的其他文章，涉及他对科学与广义社会所面临的重大问题的思考。这本书由霍德&斯托顿出版公司于10月9日出版。

In it, he examines whether aliens exist, how to colonize space and whether humans will ever go beyond our solar system.

他在书中探究了外星人是否存在，如何开拓太空殖民地以及人类最终是否能够走出太阳系。

（来源：中国日报网）

Passage B

3.5 Warm-up 环节

英文文章： Eyes on China to Strengthen Biotech Ethics Through Legislation

研究员何建奎无视政府禁令，为了追求个人名利而进行研究。涉嫌犯罪的人员将被移交公安部门处理，这不仅表明了我国重视生物技术伦理，也反映了我国认真处理此类案件的决心。弘扬学术道德和科研伦理，这是科技工作者的安身之本。无治理则无伦理，让科技趋利避害，除了寄希望于科学家的道德自觉，更需立法跟进。

A preliminary investigation into claims of genetically edited babies shows that researcher He Jiankui defied government bans and conducted research in pursuit of personal fame and gain, according to Xinhua on Monday. Those suspected of committing crimes will be transferred to the public security department, the report said. He's case has challenged China's code of ethics and regulations. The result not only shows that China values the ethics of biotechnology, but also reflects China's resolution in seriously dealing with such cases.

Science is noble, and it should tally with the morals and interests of human beings. Although he claimed he felt proud of his gene-editing work, he has brought huge uncertainties not only to the two babies, but also to all mankind. It is extremely irresponsible that He has left unknown fears for all human beings to handle. If he only regards science as a stepping stone to fame and defies ethics and bans, then he deserves severe punishment.

He's work has imposed adverse effects on China's scientific ethics. More importantly, it opened a Pandora's Box of human genome editing. Now that there is a "modern-day Frankenstein," our law should keep pace with breakthroughs in the area. Chinese President Xi Jinping said in a speech on Monday that efforts should be made to accelerate establishing an early warning and monitoring system to ensure scientific and technological security, as well as to promote the legislation work concerning artificial intelligence, gene editing, medical diagnosis, autopilot, drones and service robots.

In 2003, China released a document that forbids gene editing of human embryos for reproduction. But it still lacks strong enforcement or punishment. We have to admit that China's current laws and regulations haven't kept pace with rapidly developing science. To make sure that such cases won't happen again, China should treat He's case seriously and promote legislation.

Human genome editing is prohibited by official order in many countries. In Canada, according to the 2004 Assisted Human Reproduction Act, anyone who alters the genome of a cell of a human being is liable to imprisonment for a term not exceeding 10 years. In Australia's Prohibition of Human Cloning for Reproduction Act 2002, a person faces imprisonment up to 15 years if he or she makes heritable alterations to a genome. Nevertheless, the world still lacks a mature model for regulating gene-editing. The whole world is still exploring.

According to He, there is another potential pregnancy, which means there is now another woman carrying a gene-edited baby in China.

What should we do with these babies? Some people suggested that they should be supervised their whole lives, and others believe this is unnecessary as only two or three people's genes won't affect the whole human gene pool. China still needs to solicit professional opinions worldwide. Facing the world's first gene-edited babies, China must be prudent as there's no experience to use for reference.

The world's attention is on China now. As a responsible major country, China must value the ethics of biotechnology, promote legislation, try to reduce uncertainties and close Pandora's Box.

（来源：https://www.globaltimes.cn/content/1136675.shtml）

3.6 Discussion 环节

英文视频：TED 演讲：How AI Can Save Our Humanity

李开复介绍了人工智能在中国的发展，并认为中美两国在人工智能领域的并驾齐驱正将人类带入迅速的科技革命。未来，人工智能将代替人类从事重复性的工作，这促使人们反思人类与人工智能的区别，以及人的价值。他认为，人类区别于人工智能在于人类的创造和爱的能力，并给出未来人类与人工智能合作的四种模式：一是人工智能从事重复性工作；二是人工智能辅助人类完成创造性工作；三是人类以人工智能为分析工具从事人文关怀类工作；四是人类从事兼具同理心与创造性的工作。教师可引导学生讨论中国在人工智能方面的成就，以及人工智能发展对人类工作与自我认知的影响。

（来源：https://www.bilibili.com/video/BV1cW411Z7HV?from=search&seid=1447180979665187348）

3.7 Critical thinking 环节

英语访谈：Leon Wieseltier on the Value of the Humanities

本视频为 Leon Wieseltier（美国评论家、《新共和》杂志编辑）2013年关于"人文学科"价值和意义的采访，其观点深刻完整，与文章主题贴合，具有启发意义。同年，Leon Wieseltier 还在布兰迪斯大学毕业典礼上作了题为《人文学科永不过时》的演讲，同样发人深省。他认为近几十年来，人们被"效用、速度、便捷"等衡量标准所绑架，更关注实效而不是意义，逐渐丧失了对事物背后真假善恶的追诉。他坚定地认为知识并非单纯的数字、信息，而是艺术、自然、人性等的含义表达，坚持人文学科学习，就是在维护建立在真善美基础上的文明的繁荣。教师可以组织学生思考有哪些论据可以佐证 Leon Wieseltier 的观点，并思考这样的想法是否过于夸大事实，也存在相应的弊端？

"Perhaps Culture is Now the Counterculture"

A Defense of the Humanities

On May 19, *New Republic* literary editor Leon Wieseltier spoke at the commencement ceremony of Brandeis University, addressing the graduates as "fellow humanists." Here is a text of his talk.

Has there ever been a moment in American life when the humanities were cherished less, and has there ever been a moment in American life when the humanities were needed more? I am genuinely honored to be addressing you this morning, because in recent years I have come to regard a commitment to the humanities as nothing less than an act of intellectual defiance, of cultural dissidence.

For decades now in America we have been witnessing a steady and sickening denigration of humanistic understanding and humanistic method. We live in a society inebriated by technology, and happily, even giddily governed by the values of utility, speed, efficiency, and convenience. The technological mentality that has become the American worldview instructs us to prefer practical questions to questions of meaning — to ask of things not if they are true or false, or good or evil, but how they work. Our reason has become an instrumental reason, and is no longer the reason of the philosophers, with its ancient magnitude of intellectual ambition, its belief that the proper subjects of human thought are the largest subjects, and that the mind, in one way or another, can penetrate to the very principles of natural life and human life. Philosophy itself has shrunk under the influence of our weakness for instrumentality — modern American philosophy was in fact one of the causes of that weakness — and generally it, too, prefers to tinker and to tweak.

The machines to which we have become enslaved, all of them quite astonishing, represent the greatest assault on human attention ever devised: they are engines of mental and spiritual dispersal, which make us wider only by making us less deep. There are thinkers, reputable ones if you can believe it, who proclaim that the exponential growth in computational ability will soon take us beyond the finitude of our bodies and our minds so that, as one of them puts it, there will no longer be any difference between human and machine. La Mettrie lives in Silicon Valley. This, of course, is not an apotheosis of the human but an abolition of the human; but Google is very excited by it.

In the digital universe, knowledge is reduced to the status of information. Who will any longer remember that knowledge is to information as art is to kitsch — that information is the most inferior kind of knowledge, because it is the most external? A great Jewish thinker of the early Middle Ages wondered why God, if he wanted us to know the truth about everything, did not simply tell us the truth about everything. His wise answer was that if we were merely told what we need to know, we would not, strictly speaking, know it. Knowledge can be acquired only over time and only by method. And the devices that we carry like addicts in our hands are disfiguring our mental lives also in other ways: for example, they generate a hitherto unimaginable number of numbers, numbers about everything under the sun, and so they are transforming us into a culture of data, into a cult of data, in which no human activity and no human expression is immune to quantification, in which happiness is a fit subject for economists, in which the ordeals of the human heart are inappropriately translated into mathematical expressions, leaving us with new illusions of clarity and new illusions of control.

Our glittering age of technologism is also a glittering age of scientism. Scientism is not the same thing as science. Science is a blessing, but scientism is a curse. Science, I mean what practicing scientists actually do, is acutely and admirably aware of its limits, and humbly admits to the provisional character of its conclusions; but scientism is dogmatic, and peddles certainties. It is always at the ready with the solution to every problem, because it believes that the solution to every problem is a scientific one, and so it gives scientific answers to non-scientific questions. But even the question of the place of science in human existence is not a scientific question. It is a philosophical, which is to say, a humanistic, question.

Owing to its preference for totalistic explanation, scientism transforms science into an ideology, which is of course a betrayal of the experimental and empirical spirit. There is no perplexity of human emotion or human behavior that these days is not accounted for genetically or in the cocksure terms of evolutionary biology. It is true that the selfish gene has lately been replaced by the altruistic gene, which is lovelier, but it is still the gene that tyrannically rules. Liberal scientism should be no more philosophically attractive to us than conservative scientism, insofar as it, too, arrogantly reduces all the realms that we inhabit to a single realm, and tempts us into the belief that the epistemological eschaton has finally arrived, and at last we know what we need to know to manipulate human affairs wisely. This belief is invariably false and occasionally disastrous. We are becoming ignorant of ignorance.

So there is no task more urgent in American intellectual life at this hour than to offer some resistance to the twin imperialisms of science and technology, and to recover the old distinction—once bitterly contested, then generally accepted, now almost completely forgotten —between the study of nature and the study of man. As Bernard Williams once remarked, "'humanity' is a name not merely for a species but also for a quality." You who have elected to devote yourselves to the study of literature and languages and art and music and philosophy and religion and history—you are the stewards of that quality. You are the resistance. You have had the effrontery to choose interpretation over calculation, and to recognize that calculation cannot provide an accurate picture, or a profound picture, or a whole picture, of self-interpreting beings such as ourselves; and I commend you for it.

Do not believe the rumors of the obsolescence of your path. If Proust was a neuroscientist, then you have no urgent need of neuroscience, because you have Proust. If Jane Austen was a game theorist, then you have no reason to defect to game theory, because you have Austen. There is no greater bulwark against the twittering acceleration of American consciousness than the encounter with a work of art, and the experience of a text or an image. You are the representatives, the saving remnants, of that encounter and that experience, and of the serious study of that encounter and that experience—which is to say, you are the counterculture. Perhaps culture is now the counterculture.

So keep your heads. Do not waver. Be very proud. Use the new technologies for the old purposes. Do not be rattled by numbers, which will never be the springs of wisdom. In upholding the humanities, you uphold the honor of a civilization that was founded upon the quest for the true and the good and the beautiful. For as long as we are thinking and feeling creatures, creatures who love and imagine and suffer and die, the humanities will never be dispensable. From this day forward, then, act as if you are indispensable to your society, because — whether it knows it or not — you are.

Congratulations.

（来源：https://docs.qq.com/doc/DZnROaWl3b01LdlNU）

3.8 主题拓展资源

英语视频：Why Tech Needs the Humanities

针对青年群体中存在的"年轻人在选择是否上大学、选何种类型的学校、是否选学人文学科课程充满困惑"的现状，本视频中的企业家 Eric Berridge 给出了自己的观点——人文学科背景的员工，可以为科技公司带来创造性和洞察力。本素材可用于引导学生思考与讨论学习人文学科在现实生活中的意义。

You've all been in a bar, right?

But have you ever gone to a bar and come out with a $200 million business? That's what happened to us about 10 years ago. We'd had a terrible day. We had this huge client that was killing us. We're a software consulting firm, and we couldn't find a very specific programming skill to help this client deploy a cutting-edge cloud system. We have a bunch of engineers, but none of them could please this client. And we were about to be fired.

So we go out to the bar, and we're hanging out with our bartender friend Jeff, and he's doing what all good bartenders do: he's commiserating with us, making us feel better, relating to our pain, saying, "Hey, these guys are overblowing it. Don't worry about it." And finally, he deadpans us and says, "Why don't you send me in there? I can figure it out." So the next morning, we're hanging out in our team meeting, and we're all a little hazy ...

and I half-jokingly throw it out there. I say, "Hey, I mean, we're about to be fired." So I say, "Why don't we send in Jeff, the bartender?"

And there's some silence, some quizzical looks. Finally, my chief of staff says, "That is a great idea."

"Jeff is wicked smart. He's brilliant. He'll figure it out. Let's send him in there."

Now, Jeff was not a programmer. In fact, he had dropped out of Penn as a philosophy major. But he was brilliant, and he could go deep on topics, and we were about to be fired. So we sent him in. After a couple days of suspense, Jeff was still there. They hadn't sent him home. I couldn't believe it. What was he doing?

Here's what I learned. He had completely disarmed their fixation on the programming skill. And he had changed the conversation, even changing what we were building. The conversation was now about what we were going to build and why. And yes, Jeff figured out how to program the solution, and the client became one of our best references.

Back then, we were 200 people, and half of our company was made up of computer science majors or engineers, but our experience with Jeff left us wondering: Could we repeat this through our business? So we changed the way we recruited and trained. And while we still sought after computer engineers and computer science majors, we sprinkled in artists, musicians, writers ... and Jeff's story started to multiply itself throughout our company. Our chief technology officer is an English major, and he was a bike messenger in Manhattan. And today, we're a thousand people, yet still less than a hundred have degrees in computer science or engineering. And yes, we're still a computer consulting firm. We're the number one player in our market. We work with the fastest-growing software package to ever reach 10 billion dollars in annual sales. So it's working.

Meanwhile, the push for STEM-based education in this country — science, technology, engineering, mathematics — is fierce. It's in all of our faces. And this is a colossal mistake. Since 2009, STEM majors in the United States have increased by 43 percent, while the humanities have stayed flat. Our past president dedicated over a billion dollars towards STEM education at the expense of other subjects, and our current president recently redirected 200 million dollars of Department of Education funding into computer science. And CEOs are continually complaining about an engineering-starved workforce. These campaigns, coupled with the undeniable success of the tech economy — I mean, let's face it, seven out of the 10 most valuable companies in the world by market cap are technology firms — these things create an assumption that the path of our future workforce will be dominated by STEM.

I get it. On paper, it makes sense. It's tempting. But it's totally overblown. It's like, the entire soccer team chases the ball into the corner, because that's where the ball is. We shouldn't overvalue STEM. We shouldn't value the sciences any more than we value the humanities. And there are a couple of reasons.

Number one, today's technologies are incredibly intuitive. The reason we've been able to recruit from all disciplines and swivel into specialized skills is because modern systems can be manipulated without writing code. They're like LEGO: easy to put together, easy to learn, even easy to program, given the vast amounts of information that are available for learning. Yes, our workforce needs specialized skill, but that skill requires a far less rigorous and formalized education than it did in the past.

Number two, the skills that are imperative and differentiated in a world with intuitive technology are the skills that help us to work together as humans, where the hard work is envisioning the end product and its usefulness, which requires real-world experience and judgment and historical context. What Jeff's story taught us is that the customer was focused on the wrong thing. It's the classic case: the technologist struggling to communicate with the business and the end user, and the business failing to articulate their needs. I see it every day. We are scratching the surface in our ability as humans to communicate and invent together, and while the sciences teach us how to build things, it's the humanities that teach us what to build and why to build them. And they're equally as important, and they're just as hard.

It irks me ... when I hear people treat the humanities as a lesser path, as the easier path. Come on! The humanities give us the context of our world. They teach us how to think critically. They are purposely unstructured, while the sciences are purposely structured. They teach us to persuade, they give us our language, which we use to convert our emotions to thought and action. And they need to be on equal footing with the sciences. And yes, you can hire a bunch of artists and build a tech company and have an incredible outcome.

Now, I'm not here today to tell you that STEM's bad. I'm not here today to tell you that girls shouldn't code.

Please. And that next bridge I drive over or that next elevator we all jump into — let's make sure there's an engineer behind it.

But to fall into this paranoia that our future jobs will be dominated by STEM, that's just folly. If you have friends or kids or relatives or grandchildren or nieces or nephews ... encourage them to be whatever they want to be.

The jobs will be there. Those tech CEOs that are clamoring for STEM grads, you know what they're hiring for? Google, Apple, Facebook. Sixty-five percent of their open job opportunities are non-technical: marketers, designers, project managers, program managers, product managers, lawyers, HR specialists, trainers, coaches, sellers, buyers, on and on. These are the jobs they're hiring for. And if there's one thing that our future workforce needs — and I think we can all agree on this — it's diversity. But that diversity shouldn't end with gender or race. We need a diversity of backgrounds and skills, with introverts and extroverts and leaders and followers. That is our future workforce. And the fact that the technology is getting easier and more accessible frees that workforce up to study whatever they well please.

Thank you.

（来源：https://www.ted.com/talks/eric_berridge_why_tech_needs_the_humanities/transcript）

第五单元　关注终身教育，争当终身学习者
（Unit 5 Lifelong Education）

1. 思政主题：关注终身教育，争当终身学习者

2. 意义

本单元的主题是终身教育。教师可借助本单元的学习，引导学生关注终身教育，鼓励学生成为一名终身学习者。

习近平同志在中央党校2008年春季学期第二批进修班开学典礼上讲到："到了知识经济时代，只有经常不断地抓紧学习、坚持不懈地终身学习，才能够使用一辈子，这也就是人们常说的要活到老、学到老。"

3. 教学设计与思政元素的融入

Passage A

3.1 Warm-up 环节

英语视频：Lifelong Learning

我们这个时代正发生着巨大的变化，自动化、人工智能、在线课程等新兴事物不断改变着我们的生活和学习方式。终身学习变得日益重要。教师可引导学生观看本视频，并启发学生思考终身学习的重要性。

We are living in times of tremendous change with technology and automation and artificial intelligence.The world is changing in ways that our grandparent could never have imagined and our great grandparents would consider this an almost impossible world to understand. So in a very few years, our whole life has changed enormously. What does this do? What it does is make it terribly important that people dedicate themselves to lifelong learning. You can't just go to school as a child or as a young adult and expect you are going to learn all the things that you need in order to do well in this world. You have to keep up with the times. You have to continue to learn all through your life.

（来源：https://www.iqiyi.com/w_19s7izkjpl.html）

3.2 Discussion 环节

英语文章：How to Be a More Curious Person: 7 Tips for Becoming a Lifelong Learner?

怎样才能成为一个终身学习者？本文作者给出了7点建议。教师引导学生阅读本文章，并组织学生讨论：怎样才能成为一名真正的终身学习者。

The other day, I was in the grocery store. I overheard a cart-bound little kid asking his mom question after question. "Mom, why do they put so many apples out at once?" he asked as they browsed the produce section. "Mom, what's Ocean Spray?" he speculated from one aisle over.

His enthusiasm and investigative demeanor got me thinking about my own level of curiosity. After all, in today's fast-paced, innovation-heavy world, what we know today might not be valuable to us in a few weeks, months, or years. And if we want to remain agile, we need to continue to seek out and explore new information, new mediums, and new opportunities.

We need to be more curious.

While it may seem like an innate desire, there's actually a lot you can do to nurture and increase your own curiosity. From asking more questions to embracing the unexpected, the following tips are designed to help you become more curious.

1) Ask every question.

Try as we might, it's impossible to have all the answers, all the time. And while it's easy to default to assumptions when faced with a challenging unknown, it's better to work through knowledge gaps by asking questions.

When we ask questions, we're creating an opportunity to discover new, useful information that can be used to challenge our existing approach, expand our vision, and spark fresh ideas. Questioning allows us to become more insightful.

"People who get insights see something that's a little bit off, and instead of ignoring it, they're curious about it. Curiosity keeps our mind engaged to work out the implications," explains cognitive psychologist Gary Klein.

Don't know what questions to ask? The folks at HopeLab, a research and development organization, created a series of questions for curious leaders. Designed to help people remain both present and open, these prompts promote the importance of curiosity when assessing a situation.

2) Consume content that's outside of your comfort zone.

I never realized how much there was to learn about coffee pots until mine stopped working one morning. It's funny the way that works, isn't it? When we don't have any initial knowledge about something, we're not really curious about it ... that is, until we have to be.

Back in 1994, George Loewenstein, a professor of economics and psychology at Carnegie Mellon University, suggested that curiosity does, in fact, require some initial knowledge. In other words, the more we know, the more we want to know.

So if you're looking to become a bit more curious, you may want to try tapping into some subject matter you don't know much about. Whether you focus on productivity habits, Egyptian pyramids, beer brewing or something entirely different is up to you. The important part is that the content is unfamiliar—basic research will spur you to want to know more.

3) Listen without judgment.

"Curious people are often considered good listeners and conversationalists," explains Ben Dean, Ph.D. in a newsletter for the University of Pennsylvania.

By suspending judgment, you're ultimately allowing yourself to be more receptive to what someone is saying. You're focusing less on what you're going to say next, and more on the words and information they're choosing to tell you — or not tell you.

So next time you're having a conversation with someone, just listen. When you take the time to truly absorb what they are saying, it'll be easier for you to formulate questions, warm up to new perspectives, and learn something new that you may have missed otherwise.

4) Embrace the unexpected.

Many people find themselves plagued by their own doubts, which causes them to miss out on new places, flavors, people, and experiences. But often times, doing something unexpected can trigger a chain of reactions — both positive and negative — that you can learn from and formulate questions based on.

When you're busy worrying about the "what if," you're shutting yourself off from these types of unexpected opportunities. So go ahead, book that plane ticket. Go on that blind date. Say yes to the "chef's special" at a restaurant — even if you're not quite sure how to pronounce it.

Research reveals that surprise can actually drive our motivation to learn, so embrace the unexpected and celebrate whatever the outcome.

5) Try not to dwell on the past.

When you spend all your time worrying about the past, you don't give yourself a chance to be curious about the future. So rather than worrying about what you could have, would have, or should have changed about your last assignment, try to focus on strategies for blowing your next project out of the water.

"The problem for many adults is that we stop being curious about new experiences and are instead focused on understanding what we've already been through," explains David Klow, founder of Skylight Counseling Center.

What new opportunities are out there for you to explore? Is there anyone in your network who can help you get better at XYZ? What conferences can you attend to expand your understanding of the industry you work in? Focus on what's to come, not what's already happened.

6) Gamify learning.

If you tend to view learning as dull or tedious, you'll probably find that training yourself to be more curious isn't easy. As you would imagine, this is a problem that many teachers are forced to overcome when dealing with unmotivated students.

To inspire curiosity and excitement, many teachers have turned to gamification in the classroom. By gamifying lessons, they're able to regain the attention and interest of their students.

Why does this approach work? Games make us "more curious, more determined, and more optimistic," explains game designer and author Jane McGonigal. According to her research, games allow us to try—and try again—without having to worry about failure, which helps to motivate us to keep going.

If you're having trouble staying curious about a subject, try turning your research into a game. Check out Quizlet's game mode to brush up on subjects by completing challenges such speed tests and drag-and-drop matching games.

7) Change your perspective on a situation.

Rather than rest on your laurels when it comes to making decisions or planning projects, allow yourself to view the situation from the perspective of a stranger—or better yet, your buyer persona.

What would they suggest? What concerns would they have? What challenges do they face? Then, look at the situation through the eyes of your competitor, your boss, an industry outsider, etc. and continue the exercise.

"When we are curious about others and talk to people outside our usual social circle, we become better able to understand those with lives, experiences, and worldviews different than our own," explains Emily Campbell, research assistant at UC Berkeley's Greater Good Science Center. More curiosity and empathy is a good thing—it can go a long way to making you a better marketer (and human).

（来源：https://blog.hubspot.com/marketing/be-more-curious-tips）

3.3 Critical thinking 环节

英语新闻：What's Behind Chinese Parents' Anxiety about Education?

2021年，热播剧《小舍得》因为剧中三个家庭不同的教育态度而引发了网友热议。中国父母为什么对孩子的教育如此焦虑？教育的目的是什么？如何实现素质教育？教师引导学生阅读本新闻，并启发学生思考以下问题：

In the news, a reader thinks that education is the enjoyment of lifelong learning, it is not "rote learning to pass an exam 15 hours a day, every day in a bleak" classroom of slogans. Do you agree or disagree? Why?

Editor's note: "*A Love for Dilemma*," a family drama focusing on three families' different attitudes toward children's education, has sparked heated online discussions. Despite the government's move to lighten burden of schoolwork, many parents still send their children to attend various after-school training classes in order to get an edge on exams amid fierce competition. Why are Chinese parents stressed about their child's schooling? What is education for? How can a quality education be achieved? Readers share their opinions.

Jetschin

I think sometimes Chinese parents have somehow transferred their own personal aspirations to their children. Thus, the relentless efforts to study very hard, etc... The intentions may be noble but we need to understand that each child's gifts are different from another, even though all siblings come from the same parent. Perhaps what all parents need to do is to nurture and help refine the gifts of each child so that they can realize their fullest potential.

Neocortex

I'm a student and I know my parents care about me a lot. It is the traditional thinking that they want to decide what's best for their children. But I have learned to ignore my parents and do what's best for myself.

Because the parents worry too much they sometimes put pressure on their children without noticing what they have done. I'm fairly blunt at times and when I counter them they are surprised... somewhat I guess they just want their children to succeed but without knowing the limits of their own children.

TedM

Education is the enjoyment of lifelong learning. It is not rote learning to pass an exam 15 hours a day, every day in a bleak classroom of slogans. Teenage years are a time of excitement and adventure, creativity and challenge; a time in a person's life where he/she can learn more about relationships and enjoy family and friends. Furthermore students need time to "play"; to react and discuss and think about what they have learned. Time to internalize the learning of a broad and balanced curriculum is so lacking at present.

JCQ

I see lots of children from primary school have been sent to extra classes. They often come home at 8 pm and have to finish the homework assigned by teachers. Exhaustion and aversion are often seen in their eyes. Education should help develop their interests instead of depriving them of happiness. The burden on their shoulders is way too much for someone their age. Parents should not push their children too much and insist that good grades mean everything.

Jaaja

Yes, kids in China are in fierce competition, but ultimately for what? Better schools? No — the assumption that better schools open better career opportunities and bring wealth.

Invest in more high quality schools and/or overall in better education from middle schools upwards, so that younger kids won't have so much to compete about. That will not only benefit the young children, but create better adults overall.

Increase pay for less educated people — technicians, engineers and nurses. Not everyone needs to get a Ph.D or any university degree. Increase the value of vocational education.

If that does not help, spread the quality higher education in universities from a handful of elite universities to the whole university network in China.

Simply remove the need for competition in all levels, and educate children to find their own competitiveness through creativity.

（来源：https://www.chinadaily.com.cn/a/202104/24/WS60836d95a31024ad0baba076_1.html）

3.4 主题拓展资源

A. 英语新闻：Lecture Shows "Lifelong Learning Is Value for Money"

The pandemic year of 2020 has shown the only certainty these days is the presence of persistent uncertainty, experts said.

This realization is forcing some Chinese firms to embrace the new year with discussions on serious topics ranging from the Chinese economy to international relations.

Luo Zhenyu, founder of Dedao, a lifelong learning platform, quenched people's thirst for insights, forecasts, estimates and predictions with a four-hour-long New Year's Eve speech in Wuhan, capital of Hubei province, which was hard hit by the COVID-19 outbreak.

"The city epitomizes how Chinese people join forces to combat difficulties and has shaped up to be the symbol of the era," Luo said.

The New Year's Eve speech has become something of a tradition. Titled "Time's Friend", the annual event was the sixth in a row, and is one of Dedao's iconic offerings to keep users "hooked" to the platform.

Luo has pledged to hold the session for two decades. Lecture participants could enroll for any of the conventional online or app-based courses on entrepreneurship, wealth management, psychology and self-enhancement.

"Some members of the audience have already bought the 20-year pass in order to attend the planned series of speeches," Luo said. "I simply provide them a tool through which they believe that lifelong learning is value for money."

This year, Luo's speech touched upon a wide spectrum of issues and new perspectives like understanding China's social fabric, tackling the pandemic and handling hardship and potential of indigenous R&D of key technologies.

He also identified a number of trends such as carbon neutrality and the resurgence of offline business as opportune growth areas that people can leverage in the years to come.

These have undoubtedly helped address anxiety of middle-income earners who are typically Dedao's target audience. Luo's approach of citing entrepreneurs and experts on specific issues has lent credibility and authenticity to his speech, said Cao Lei, director of consultancy Internet Economy Institute.

"For people looking to hone a particular skill or quality, they long for avenues offering multi-skill courses taught by qualified teachers at reasonable prices," Cao said. "Most important of all, they want the platform to be stable. The annual speech serves to create that 'predictable' image."

Dedao started out as an obscure media account, where Luo repackaged complex historical, philosophical or economic topics into a daily 60-second voice message and weekly one-hour video lectures. Soon, they all morphed into a comprehensive knowledge-sharing portal where people pay for a torrent of classes, books and offline events.

Platforms such as Dedao have mushroomed on the back of a trend of people paying for online content they deem useful or valuable.

Data from iResearch forecast the education industry will expand to 4 trillion yuan ($619.2 billion) in 2023. The lifelong education sector will expand quickly as 5G telecom technology can provide educators with an avenue of new possibilities, upgrading e-learning systems, and brightening prospects for the sector.

But concerns linger, with nearly half of respondents to consultancy iiMedia's survey attributing homogeneity of content and lack of practicality as the dual culprits capping both user growth and payment willingness for these platforms.

To overcome the tricky situation, Luo has adopted a two-pronged strategy: offering corporate courses to secure massive and stable sources of users and extending options to offline venues by giving regular lectures at high-end shopping malls to enlist new individual customers.

For instance, in October, the company launched a program dedicated to companies that offer their employees an opportunity to hone a particular skill or simply broaden their horizons in their spare time. Corporate clients can choose from the library of courses, mix and match, and customize their orders.

"Compared with general social media platforms like WeChat and Douyin, traffic growth bottlenecks are plaguing some vertical knowledge-sharing sites, given the fierce competition and explosive growth of the previous years," said Zhang Yi, CEO of iiMedia.

"Attracting top-tier lecturers and influencers to these platforms seems to be a way out to help restore growth and unlock greater potential."

（来源：https://global.chinadaily.com.cn/a/202101/05/WS5ff3bef6a31024ad0baa0732.html）

B. 英语新闻：Working till Late

Initiated in the early days after the founding of the People's Republic of China in 1949, China's retirement policy was developed in line with the nation's social and economic status as well as its people's health and life expectancy at that time. Since the rapid aging of China's population has raised concerns about the sustainability of the current pension system based on a pay-as-you-go approach, further discussions on postponing the retirement age need to be put on the agenda.

People's life expectancy in many countries and regions has been prolonged due to social and economic development, leading to higher burdens on countries' pension systems. Therefore, many developed economies have delayed the age at which people can receive their pension in accordance with their changed social situations. The postponement of the retirement age can help increase the labor force supply as well as productivity.

The requirements for physical conditions, intelligence and working abilities have also changed. The types of jobs and the ages at which people can work have also changed. Therefore, aging does not necessarily mean people lose their entire working capacity once they reach a certain age. People ought to be entitled to choose their retirement age or make decisions with employers jointly. As social pensions are public resources and concern the interests of several generations, the minimum age of receiving pensions, obligations of insurance payment and pension rights need to be clarified based on public consensus and fairness.

The government needs to outline a road map for reform of the retirement policy to make it gradually accepted by the public, the sooner the better. Trials of a flexible retirement system can be launched. Employees and employers need to be granted retirement options. The authorities can also develop regulations on the actual pensions received depending on the age at which a person chooses to retire, it means the minimum retirement age (or age for receiving the full pension) should be redefined. A flexible retirement system can be implemented first in regions with large aging populations and start from people with high academic training and strong skills.

Postponing the retirement age calls for improvement of the current institutional settings. First, China's current law on protecting rights and interests of older people refers to them as citizens over 60. Although the law has stipulated that older people can provide consulting services, participate in the development and application of technologies, and engage in business and productive activities, the rights and interests of people above the mandatory retirement age of participating in social and economic activities need to be clarified during the reforms. The laws and regulations should be expanded to establish clear regulations on social security and injury at work for people who postpone retirement.

Second, the reform will affect labor participation of the generation approaching retirement and the childbearing of the coming generation. It is a common practice in China that grandparents take care of their grandchildren. While China has launched the three-child policy and the postponement of retirement age is expected, the policies may collide with each other due to high costs of bearing and raising children and the lack of public childcare services. Therefore, the government needs to expand social childcare services and introduce supporting policies and public services such as male maternity leave, household tax relief plans and elimination of hidden discrimination on women of childbearing age in the job market to facilitate the launch of new retirement age policies.

Finally, the authorities need to build a lifelong education system. As the development and application of modern technologies represented by artificial intelligence are changing the nature of work, traditional education and training systems can no longer ensure that workers can keep up with technological development and remain competitive in their work. Therefore, lifelong learning has become an important approach to maintaining economic vitality in the new era. The government should play a leading role in promoting lifelong learning, reform the education system for older people, and encourage enterprises and social organizations to participate in lifelong education, especially vocational education for those older adults.

（来源：https://www.chinadaily.com.cn/a/202108/13/WS6115b105a310efa1bd668819.html）

Passage B

3.5 Warm-up 环节

英语新闻: Universities for the Elderly Enrich the Lives of Graying Population

老年大学丰富了老年人的生活。教师可引导学生阅读本新闻，并启发学生思考：如何从老龄化的角度看待终身教育？

One week before the end of her course at a university for the elderly, Wu Yue'e carefully made notes for her speech at the closing ceremony as a student representative.

Wu, 72, has been a student for more than 10 years at Changsha Senior Cadre University in central China's Hunan Province, where she learned a number of new skills including reading and writing Chinese *pinyin*, using traditional Chinese medicine and playing the *erhu*.

Heading back to school for further study and cultural enrichment is becoming a choice of many Chinese senior citizens.

Self-Improvement

Wu, an active participant in all facets of school life, felt the greatest regret that she had not received a full education when she was young.

"I have always loved literature even though I dropped out of school very early," Wu said. Before retirement, Wu was a textile worker who insisted on reading in her spare time. Her favorite book is "*The Count of Monte Christo.*"

After her retirement, she was able to fulfill her dream of studying at the university for the elderly. "I felt the elderly should keep up with the pace of social development, and I haven't done well enough," said Wu, adding that she hopes to improve herself through learning and set a good example for her children.

Yin Jianlin, 57, echoed Wu's views. Five years ago, Yin had just retired from an enterprise where she worked for decades and was unable to adapt to her retired life. "Once a person stops working, the sense of loss comes," Yin said.

In 2015, Yin was enrolled in the university for the elderly to study folk dance and mental health. With the help of the mental health class, Yin accepted her new role in life and learned to control her emotions.

"I used to take care of my family as my sole responsibility. Now I have learned to take care of myself, too," Yin said, adding that whenever she took her schoolbag and headed off for class, she was filled with confidence. "Although we are old, we feel like we are still teenagers when dancing with our classmates."

Caring Family

Although an increasing number of seniors are heading off in pursuit of self-fulfillment, a large percentage of the elderly in China remain the primary caregivers of their grandchildren, whose parents are tied down with their busy work schedules.

Liu Yanping, a 37-year-old psychological consultant, has run parenting education and positive discipline courses for children and parents in primary schools with her team in Changsha since 2014. Liu found that many children rely on their grandparents rather than their parents for learning about the world.

In 2017, Liu and her team set up a course of alternate-generation education at Changsha Senior Cadre University.

Huang Qijian, 60, who attended the alternate-generation education class, has a pair of twin grandchildren. How to properly educate and guide them has become his major concern.

"My educational method is outdated," Huang said. By learning advanced educational concepts and methods in the alternate-generation education class, many old people, like Huang, have learned how to balance the relationships between themselves, their children and their grandchildren. "Having practiced the knowledge learned from the classes, I've found the atmosphere of our family has become warmer and closer," Huang said.

Policies Taking Shape

Since China entered an aging society at the end of the 20th century, the number of elderly and their proportion in the total population have continued to grow.

From 2000 to 2018, the elderly population aged 60 and above increased from 126 million to 249 million, and the proportion of the elderly population in the total population increased from 10.2 percent to 17.9 percent.

It has become a trend for Chinese seniors to enrich their spare time and improve the quality of life in their later years by attending classes in universities for the elderly and participating in community activities.

Statistics from the China Association of Universities for the Elderly show that by the end of 2018, China had 62,000 universities and schools for the elderly, with more than 8 million students attending classes and more than 5 million students participating in distance learning.

In November, the Communist Party of China Central Committee and the State Council jointly unveiled a medium and long-term plan for responding proactively to aging population, proposing to build a social environment marked by filial piety, respect for the elderly and the protection of the aged.

The plan highlights improving the effective supply of labor in an aging society, which requires improving the quality of new members of the labor force, establishing a lifelong learning system for senior citizens, and striving to achieve fuller employment and create better quality jobs.

Yin Jianlin and her classmates were sketching the image of perfect grandparents during a class. After counting more than a dozen qualities representing perfection, all the students gathered to share their feelings.

Some said that perfect grandparents should be literate and good-tempered, while others said a decent appearance is also indispensable. Yin, however, had a different perspective, saying, "there are no perfect grandparents, we can only try our best to be better."

（来源：http://www.xinhuanet.com/english/2019-12/25/c_138655416.htm）

3.6 Discussion 环节

英语文章： Workers Require Lifelong Learning Opportunities
麦肯锡在 *Reskilling China* 报告中预计，到2030年，由于自动化的影响，将有约2.2亿劳动者不得不改换其它工作，其中有多达40%可能是农民工。

他们缺乏提高技能的渠道，也缺乏个人发展机会，这使他们成为就业市场上的弱势群体。教师可引导学生阅读本文，并组织学生讨论："如何从可持续发展的角度看待终身教育？"

In a report released on Jan 12, 2021, McKinsey Global Institute pointed out that China's next challenge is to ensure it has the talent needed for an innovative, digitized, postindustrial economy.

That sheds light on the sustainability of the country's vast, comparatively underdeveloped rural education and vocational training systems. If not addressed, this will hinder the country's development in the near future.

The country has vowed to raise its per capita gross domestic product to 70 percent of developed economies by 2050. That means per capita GDP and income should maintain annual growth rates of at least 4.7 percent and 4.9 percent respectively up till then.

Such a marked increase over three decades will not be possible without a corresponding increase in labor productivity, which can only be realized through improving the quality of the workforce.

The current talent cultivation model in the country lags far behind that requirement, particularly in the countryside, home to about half of the country's working age population.

In its *Reskilling China* report, McKinsey anticipates that about 220 million laborers, about 30 percent of the country's workforce, will have to change their jobs because of the influence of automation by 2030, among which up to 40 percent are likely to be migrant workers.

Their lack of channels for improving their skills and lack of access to personal development opportunities make them a vulnerable group in the job market, which calls for government support.

China needs to refashion its education and skills-development system in the direction so that everyone, everywhere has access to lifelong learning opportunities.

That necessitates a dramatic increase in the government's inputs into education and skills-development, particularly for the country's about 300 million migrant workers.

The advancement of telecommunication technologies will further empower employers to play a leading role in providing training and education to migrant workers.

Now is the time for policymakers to draft the rules and make those initiatives that have proved successful in some places compulsory practices nationwide.

（来源：https://www.chinadaily.com.cn/a/202101/18/WS6004d45ca31024ad0baa329a.html）

3.7 Critical thinking 环节

英语新闻：Transforming World's Largest Workforce into Lifelong Learners

我国经济正迅速从工业主导型向消费、服务和创新主导型转变，同时，我国的人才发展体系也需要转变。教师可引导学生阅读本文，并启发学生思考：要建立终身学习的教育体制，最重要的是什么？

China has made unprecedented investments to bring education to the younger generation over the past 30 years, but now the nation faces a new challenge: ensuring that the whole population has the skills to thrive in a fast-changing economy.

Today, 91 percent of teachers in secondary education hold a bachelor's degree or higher, up from only 24 percent in 2000, and the number of college admissions soared to 9.1 million in 2019, from 3.7 million in 2000. Although gaps in quality and access still need to be filled, the system meets the needs of China's industrial economy.

But China is rapidly evolving away from an economy led by industry to one driven by consumption, services and innovation: a post-industrial economy. A transformation of China's talent-development systems is necessary to turn the world's largest workforce into a nation of lifelong learners.

As in the rest of the world, digital technologies and automation are on the rise, and it changes the type of skills that will be in demand. Digitization and automation have accelerated in response to the COVID-19 pandemic, and therefore the need to reskill and potentially change occupation may have become even more urgent.

Automation will change the skills people need. New McKinsey Global Institute research indicates that 516 billion hours of work activities, assuming each worker works eight hours a day, the equivalent of 87 days on average per worker, may be displaced by automation by 2030 in a midpoint adoption scenario. While the demand for physical and manual skills could fall by 18 percent in the period to 2030, the demand for technological skills could rise by 51 percent. Up to 220 million Chinese workers may need to change occupations by 2030 — that's about 30 percent of the workforce. Particular attention will need to be paid to China's millions of migrant workers who tend to be low-skilled and low-paid with little time or money to devote to training. Yet 22 to 40 percent of their jobs are susceptible to automation.

China needs an ambitious plan for reskilling that centers on what we call the "three Es". Everyone needs access to training, notably China's 775 million workers. By 2030, that implies that the system has to accommodate three times as many people as are enrolled in the education system today. Increasing turnover among the younger generation of workers leads to low investment in training provision by employers. Less than 30 percent of Chinese workers perceive new technical or vocational skills training to be urgent.

Content needs to offer everything — the broad capabilities that equip Chinese people for a fast-evolving economy, notably high cognitive skills (such as critical thinking and decision-making), social and emotional skills (such as interpersonal skills and leadership) and technical skills (such as advanced data analysis) will be in demand. This requires investment in developing different content beyond traditional textbooks, such as case studies and hands-on projects as well as new delivery approaches such as participatory learning and experiential training.

Skills development needs to be available everywhere to all throughout their lives. According to official statistics, only 3 million migrant workers out of a total of 291 million took a vocational and technical program in 2019. And a rural-urban divide in funding and teachers' qualifications needs to be overcome.

Based on surveys of best practices in China and around the world, we identified four levers around which pilot projects can be designed to test what works and what does not.

First, digital technologies. Adoption of digital technologies can enable more engaging multichannel learning and teaching. These technologies can empower content creators to deliver "micro curricula", and make content delivery more exciting and personalized by using tools such as artificial intelligence technologies, augmented and virtual reality, and gamification. More than 900 million people could benefit. China is in a good position to digitize education and training, as it accounted for 56 percent of global venture capital investment in education technology in 2019.

Second, a collaborative skills development ecosystem. Expanded public-private partnerships can help address the gap between workforce skills and what employers need. Enterprises can play a more significant role in vocational education, committing themselves to playing a part in the design of curricula, training and recruiting. We see potential for a coalition of school-industry partnerships with the participation by 300,000 companies.

Third, an enhanced vocational education track. Workers need flexibility in returning to school, receiving retraining, and pursuing higher-skill jobs. China could create multiple entry points while also making the vocational education track more attractive to prospective high school students, for instance by expanding a "3+4" model that enables them to go directly to application-oriented universities. Vocational trainers could collaborate more with companies to gain up-to-date knowledge, and vice versa, more company representatives could come to vocational schools to teach. By 2030, more than 80 percent of vocational teachers could have industry experience in related areas.

Last, shifting attitudes and incentivizing change. To back up such a transformation will require attitudes to change — for everyone to "own" their lifelong learning journeys by using information platforms and a micro-credential system to navigate career options and skills-development paths. Companies can also strengthen the provision of training to develop their own workers, potentially with financial support from the government in the form of co-funding or tax incentives.

Delivering a skills transformation of this scale and pace will be unprecedented. It will require substantial investment, but also a comprehensive approach with the participation of national and local governments, educational institutions, and, crucially, companies. A national leading group could set the strategy with local delivery units delivering it in a way that suits local conditions. Employers, in particular those in the private sector, can also play a crucial role as educators and trainers as well as investors.

China's continued prosperity and economic dynamism as well as the livelihoods of its citizens hinge on wide-ranging reform to the skills of the nation, and the work needs to start now. As the popular saying goes: "It takes 10 years to grow a tree, but 100 years to cultivate people."

（来源：https://www.chinadaily.com.cn/a/202101/13/WS5ffe3d65a31024ad0baa229d.html）

3.8 主题拓展资源

A. 英语新闻: Meeting Challenges of an Aging Society

The population in China is aging rapidly. The proportion of people aged 60 or above is expected to increase to 35 percent by 2050, turning the population into one of the oldest in the world. While aging poses great challenges, if managed well, these can be overcome to create opportunities.

Reforms for fostering labor mobility and upgrading human capital will reduce the labor shortages stemming from an aging population. Greater public and private investments to strengthen elderly care services and facilities will create employment opportunities and improve people's well-being.

Benefits of greater labor mobility

Mobility restrictions in China — the household registration system (*Hukou*) and inability of migrants to claim social security benefits away from home — discourage transfers from provinces where there is a surplus of labor to ones where there is a deficit. Re-allocating labor from low to high-productivity sectors could add several percentage points to GDP growth. And accelerating the ongoing relaxation of the *Hukou* policy and social security reforms for migrant workers to gain access to social services and benefits in their place of residency will remove such institutional mobility barriers.

The benefits of greater mobility can be maximized through increased investments in human capital. Gross enrollment rate in China's senior high schools and the percentage of population with tertiary education in scientific and technical subjects need to increase. The growing digitalization of the economy adds pressure to the task.

While new learning methods should encourage lifelong learning, creativity, innovation, and problem-solving skills, incentives must be introduced for companies to provide on-the-job training, and initiatives to re-train workers whose skills are obsolete to prolong their participation in the labor force.

Increasing female participation in the labor market will also help maintain the labor supply. Although gender gaps in education have largely closed, female workforce participation has declined over the past decade, and women continue to bear a disproportionate responsibility for unpaid care work at home and remain under-represented in scientific research and high-technology industries and services. Policies for equal employment opportunities, increased maternity leave, improved support for childcare, elderly care, and single mothers, are essential to attract and maintain women in the labor force.

Better services and care for the elderly

Under China's 14th Five-Year Plan (2021—2025), development of an efficient long-term care (LTC) system is a government priority. Insufficient elderly care facilities result in unnecessary admissions in acute care hospitals and are a waste of healthcare resources. Improved home and community-based LTC can address this issue. Incentives to develop home and community-based services, such as home help, home care, and home nursing services, and center-based services to support the elderly are critical to meet the "90-7-3 older persons care pattern" launched during the 12th Five-Year Plan (2011—2015) period in which 90 percent of the elderly population should receive home-based care, 7 percent community-based care, and 3 percent institutional care.

More affordable elderly residential care for lower-income households that need assistance is part of the solution. These facilities can be funded by a mix of government support, individual pension contributions, and private sector involvement. This approach is emerging in China but needs to be strengthened. These efforts will benefit from a shift in the role of the government from supplier to regulator for the provision of LTC. Examples of government tasks include setting policies and standards, subsidizing people who cannot afford the private facilities, and incentivizing private sector participation, which can engage in effective models of public-private partnerships.

Incentives and policies need to be improved

At the same time, incentives and policies to retain and train LTC givers must improve. Professions crucial to a well-functioning elderly care system, including nurses, physiotherapists, occupational therapists, nutritionists, medical specialists (that is, neurologists, specialists in geriatrics), social workers, service providers, and managers must expand. The number of professionals in paramedical, medical, social work and elderly care management should also increase, as those will result in better care and improved services for the elderly, as well as significant employment opportunities.

Addressing the needs of an aging society is costly. Public healthcare expenditure in China stands at 2.9 percent of GDP compared with the 6.5 percent average in the Organisation for Economic Co-operation and Development countries, where LTC alone amounts to 1.7 percent of GDP. China has made significant progress in extending health insurance coverage universally, but out-of-pocket payments still account for about half of the total health expenditure, exacerbating the vulnerability of lower-income households. Expanding health insurance coverage, reducing co-insurance rates, and introducing ceilings on maximum out-of-pocket payments are reforms that have proven effective in other countries.

Increased funding should not threaten fiscal sustainability. A more progressive taxation system, the further liberalization of energy and resource prices, and the introduction of environmental and property taxes would increase social spending without straining public finances. Policy reforms, too, can help. Affordable social services, higher pensions, and support to women through subsidies for childcare, baby bonuses, child grants, flexible hours, or part-time work, are key to lift fertility rates mitigating the impacts of an aging society.

While gradual increases in retirement age will strengthen labor supply and support the sustainability of the pension system, which is crucial for the success of a multigenerational workforce, age-friendly policies, such as more flexible work options, retraining, re-skilling, and age-friendly workplaces are important during the transition. Finally, the sustainability of the pension system is critical in an aging society. For that, the introduction of voluntary private pension funds, currently piloted in Zhejiang and Chongqing, needs to progress faster.

（来源：https://www.chinadaily.com.cn/a/202107/30/WS610332f8a310efa1bd6655f6.html）

B. 英语视频：TED 演讲：The Nerd's Guide to Learning Everything Online

This is a map of New York State that was made in 1937 by the General Drafting Company. It's an extremely famous map among cartography nerds, because down here at the bottom of the Catskill Mountains, there is a little town called Roscoe—actually, this will go easier if I just put it up here—There's Roscoe, and then right above Roscoe is Rockland, New York, and then right above that is the tiny town of Agloe, New York.

Agloe, New York, is very famous to cartographers, because it's a paper town.

It's also known as a copyright trap. Mapmakers — because my map of New York and your map of New York are going to look very similar, on account of the shape of New York — often, mapmakers will insert fake places onto their maps, in order to protect their copyright. Because then, if my fake place shows up on your map, I can be well and truly sure that you have robbed me. Agloe is a scrabblization of the initials of the two guys who made this map, Ernest Alpers and Otto Lindberg, and they released this map in 1937. Decades later, Rand McNally releases a map with Agloe, New York, on it, at the same exact intersection of two dirt roads in the middle of nowhere. Well, you can imagine the delight over at General Drafting. They immediately call Rand McNally, and they say, "We've caught you! We made Agloe, New York, up. It is a fake place. It's a paper town. We're going to sue your pants off!" And Rand McNally says, "No, no, no, no, Agloe is real," because people kept going to that intersection of two dirt roads — in the middle of nowhere, expecting there to be a place called Agloe — someone built a place called Agloe, New York.

It had a gas station, a general store, two houses at its peak.

And this is of course a completely irresistible metaphor to a novelist, because we would all like to believe that the stuff that we write down on paper can change the actual world in which we're actually living, which is why my third book is called "*Paper Towns*".

But what interests me ultimately more than the medium in which this happened, is the phenomenon itself. It's easy enough to say that the world shapes our maps of the world, right? Like the overall shape of the world is obviously going to affect our maps. But what I find a lot more interesting is the way that the manner in which we map the world changes the world. Because the world would truly be a different place if North were down. And the world would be a truly different place if Alaska and Russia weren't on opposite sides of the map. And the world would be a different place if we projected Europe to show it in its actual size. The world is changed by our maps of the world. The way that we choose — sort of, our personal cartographic enterprise, also shapes the map of our lives, and that in turn shapes our lives.

I believe that what we map changes the life we lead. And I don't mean that in some, like, secrecy Oprah's Angels network, like, you can think your way out of cancer sense. But I do believe that while maps don't show you where you will go in your life, they show you where you might go. You very rarely go to a place that isn't on your personal map.

So I was a really terrible student when I was a kid. My GPA was consistently in the low 2s. And I think the reason that I was such a terrible student is that I felt like education was just a series of hurdles that had been erected before me, and I had to jump over in order to achieve adulthood. And I didn't really want to jump over these hurdles, because they seemed completely arbitrary, so I often wouldn't, and then people would threaten me, you know, they'd threaten me with this "going on my permanent record," or "You'll never get a good job." I didn't want a good job! As far as I could tell at eleven or twelve years old, like, people with good jobs woke up very early in the morning, and the men who had good jobs, one of the first things they did was tie a strangulation item of clothing around their necks. They literally put nooses on themselves, and then they went off to their jobs, whatever they were. That's not a recipe for a happy life. These people—in my, symbol-obsessed, twelve year-old imagination—these people who are strangling themselves as one of the first things they do each morning, they can't possibly be happy. Why would I want to jump over all of these hurdles and have that be the end? That's a terrible end!

And then, when I was in tenth grade, I went to this school, Indian Springs School, a small boarding school, outside of Birmingham, Alabama. And all at once I became a learner. And I became a learner, because I found myself in a community of learners. I found myself surrounded by people who celebrated intellectualism and engagement, and who thought that my ironic oh-so-cool disengagement wasn't clever, or funny, but like it was a simple and unspectacular response to very complicated and compelling problems. And so I started to learn, because learning was cool. I learned that some infinite sets are bigger than other infinite sets, and I learned that iambic pentameter is and why it sounds so good to human ears; I learned that the Civil War was a nationalizing conflict, I learned some physics, I learned that correlation shouldn't be confused with causation—all of these things, by the way, enriched my life on a literally daily basis. And it's true that I don't use most of them for my "job," but that's not what it's about for me. It's about cartography.

What is the process of cartography? It's, you know, sailing upon some land, and thinking, "I think I'll draw that bit of land," and then wondering, "Maybe there's some more land to draw." And that's when learning really began for me. It's true that I had teachers that didn't give up on me, and I was very fortunate to have those teachers, because I often gave them cause to think there was no reason to invest in me. But a lot of the learning that I did in high school wasn't about what happened inside the classroom, it was about what happened outside of the classroom. For instance, I can tell you that "There's a certain Slant of light, Winter Afternoons —That oppresses, like the Heft of Cathedral Tunes —" not because I memorized Emily Dickinson in school when I was in high school, but because there was a girl when I was in high school, and her name was Amanda, and I had a crush on her, and she liked Emily Dickinson poetry. The reason I can tell you what opportunity cost is, is because one day when I was playing Super Mario Kart on my couch, my friend Emmet walked in, and he said, "How long have you been playing Super Mario Kart?" And I said, "I don't know, like, six hours?" and he said, "Do you realize that if you'd worked at Baskin-Robbins those six hours, you could have made 30 dollars, so in some ways, you just paid thirty dollars to play Super Mario Kart." And I was, like, "I'll take that deal."

But I learned what opportunity cost is.

And along the way, the map of my life got better. It got bigger; it contained more places. There were more things that might happen, more futures I might have. It wasn't a formal, organized learning process, and I'm happy to admit that. It was spotty, it was inconsistent, there was a lot I didn't know. I might know, you know, Cantor's idea that some infinite sets are larger than other infinite sets, but I didn't really understand the calculus behind that idea. I might know the idea of opportunity cost, but I didn't know the law of diminishing returns. But the great thing about imagining learning as cartography, instead of imagining it as arbitrary hurdles that you have to jump over, is that you see a bit of coastline, and that makes you want to see more. And so now I do know at least some of the calculus that underlies all of that stuff.

So, I had one learning community in high school, then I went to another for college, and then I went to another, when I started working at a magazine called "*Booklist*" where I was an assistant, surrounded by astonishingly well-read people. And then I wrote a book. And like all authors dream of doing, I promptly quit my job.

And for the first time since high school, I found myself without a learning community, and it was miserable. I hated it. I read many, many books during this two-year period. I read books about Stalin, and books about how the Uzbek people came to identify as Muslims, and I read books about how to make atomic bombs, but it just felt like I was creating my own hurdles, and then jumping over them myself, instead of feeling the excitement of being part of a community of learners, a community of people who are engaged together in the cartographic enterprise of trying to better understand and map the world around us.

And then, in 2006, I met that guy. His name is Ze Frank. I didn't actually meet him, just on the Internet. Ze Frank was running, at the time, a show called *"The Show with Ze Frank,"* and I discovered the show, and that was my way back into being a community learner again. Here's Ze talking about Las Vegas.

(Video)

Ze Frank: Las Vegas was built in the middle of a huge, hot desert. Almost everything here was brought from somewhere else — the sort of rocks, the trees, the waterfalls. These fish are almost as out of place as my pig that flew. Contrasted to the scorching desert that surrounds this place, so are these people. Things from all over the world have been rebuilt here, away from their histories, and away from the people that experience them differently. Sometimes improvements were made — even the Sphinx got a nose job. Here, there's no reason to feel like you're missing anything. This New York means the same to me as it does to everyone else. Everything is out of context, and that means context allows for everything: Self Parking, Events Center, Shark Reef. This fabrication of place could be one of the world's greatest achievements, because no one belongs here; everyone does. As I walked around this morning, I noticed most of the buildings were huge mirrors reflecting the sun back into the desert. But unlike most mirrors, which present you with an outside view of yourself embedded in a place, these mirrors come back empty.

John Green (the speaker, short as "JG"): Makes me nostalgic for the days when you could see the pixels in online video.

Ze isn't just a great public intellectual, he's also a brilliant community builder, and the community of people that built up around these videos was in many ways a community of learners. So we played Ze Frank at chess collaboratively, and we beat him. We organized ourselves to take a young man on a road trip across the United States. We turned the Earth into a sandwich, by having one person hold a piece of bread at one point on the Earth, and on the exact opposite point of the Earth, have another person holding a piece of bread. I realize that these are silly ideas, but they are also "learny" ideas, and that was what was so exciting to me, and if you go online, you can find communities like this all over the place. Follow the calculus tag on Tumblr, and yes, you will see people complaining about calculus, but you'll also see people re-blogging those complaints, making the argument that calculus is interesting and beautiful, and here's a way into thinking about the problem that you find unsolvable. You can go to places like Reddit, and find sub-Reddits, like "Ask a Historian" or "Ask Science," where you can ask people who are in these fields a wide range of questions, from very serious ones to very silly ones. But to me, the most interesting communities of learners that are growing up on the Internet right now are on YouTube, and admittedly, I am biased. But I think in a lot of ways, the YouTube page resembles a classroom. Look for instance at "Minute Physics," a guy who's teaching the world about physics.

(Video)

Let's cut to the chase. As of July 4, 2012, the Higgs boson is the last fundamental piece of the standard model of particle physics to be discovered experimentally. But, you might ask, why was the Higgs boson included in the standard model, alongside well-known particles like electrons and photons and quarks, if it hadn't been discovered back then in the 1970s? Good question. There are two main reasons. First, just like the electron is an excitation in the electron field, the Higgs boson is simply a particle which is an excitation of the everywhere-permeating Higgs field. The Higgs field in turn plays an integral role in our model for the weak nuclear force. In particular, the Higgs field helps explain why it's so weak. We'll talk more about this in a later video, but even though weak nuclear theory was confirmed in the 1980s, in the equations, the Higgs field is so inextricably jumbled with the weak force, that until now we've been unable to confirm its actual and independent existence.

JG: Or here's a video that I made as part of my show "*Crash Course*," talking about World War I.

(Video)

The immediate cause was of course the assassination in Sarajevo of the Austrian Archduke Franz Ferdinand, on June 28, 1914, by a Bosnian-Serb nationalist named Gavrilo Princip. Quick aside: It's worth noting that the first big war of the twentieth century began with an act of terrorism. So Franz Ferdinand wasn't particularly well-liked by his uncle, the emperor Franz Joseph — now that is a mustache! But even so, the assassination led Austria to issue an ultimatum to Serbia, whereupon Serbia accepted some, but not all, of Austria's demands, leading Austria to declare war against Serbia. And then Russia, due to its alliance with the Serbs, mobilized its army. Germany, because it had an alliance with Austria, told Russia to stop mobilizing, which Russia failed to do, so then Germany mobilized its own army, declared war on Russia, cemented an alliance with the Ottomans, and then declared war on France, because, you know, France.

And it's not just physics and world history that people are choosing to learn through YouTube. Here's a video about abstract mathematics.

(Video)

So you're me, and you're in math class yet again, because they make you go every single day. And you're learning about, I don't know, the sums of infinite series. That's a high school topic, right, which is odd, because it's a cool topic, but they somehow manage to ruin it anyway. So I guess that's why they allow infinite series in the curriculum. So, in a quite understandable need for distraction, you're doodling and thinking more about what the plural of "series" should be than about the topic at hand: "serieses," "seriese," "seriesen," and "serii?" Or is it that the singular should be changed: one "serie," or "serum," just like the singular of "sheep" should be "shoop." But the whole concept of things like 1/2 + 1/4 + 1/8 + 1/16 and so on approaches one, is useful if, say, you want to draw a line of elephants, each holding the tail of the next one: normal elephant, young elephant, baby elephant, dog-sized elephant, puppy-sized elephant, all the way down to Mr. Tusks and beyond, which is at least a tiny bit awesome, because you can get an infinite number of elephants in a line, and still have it fit across a single notebook page.

JG: And lastly, here's Destin, from *"Smarter Every Day,"* talking about the conservation of angular momentum, and, since it's YouTube, cats:

(Video)

Hey, it's me, Destin. Welcome back to *"Smarter Every Day."* So you've probably observed that cats almost always land on their feet. Today's question is: why? Like most simple questions, there's a very complex answer. For instance, let me reword this question: How does a cat go from feet-up to feet-down in a falling reference frame, without violating the conservation of angular momentum?

JG: So, here's something all four of these videos have in common: They all have more than half a million views on YouTube. And those are people watching not in classrooms, but because they are part of the communities of learning that are being set up by these channels. And I said earlier that YouTube is like a classroom to me, and in many ways it is, because here is the instructor — it's like the old-fashioned classroom: here's the instructor, and then beneath the instructor are the students, and they're all having a conversation. And I know that YouTube comments have a very bad reputation in the world of the Internet, but in fact, if you go on comments for these channels, what you'll find is people engaging the subject matter, asking difficult, complicated questions that are about the subject matter, and then other people answering those questions. And because the YouTube page is set up so that the page in which I'm talking to you is on the exact — the place where I'm talking to you is on the exact same page as your comments, you are participating in a live and real and active way in the conversation. And because I'm in comments usually, I get to participate with you. And you find this whether it's world history, or mathematics, or science, or whatever it is.

You also see young people using the tools and the sort of genres of the Internet in order to create places for intellectual engagement, instead of the ironic detachment that maybe most of us associate with memes and other Internet conventions — you know, "Got bored. Invented calculus." Or, here's Honey Boo Boo criticizing industrial capitalism:

"Liberal capitalism is not at all the Good of humanity. Quite the contrary; it is the vehicle of savage, destructive nihilism."

In case you can't see what she says ... yeah.

I really believe that these spaces, these communities, have become for a new generation of learners, the kind of communities, the kind of cartographic communities that I had when I was in high school, and then again when I was in college. And as an adult, re-finding these communities has re-introduced me to a community of learners, and has encouraged me to continue to be a learner even in my adulthood, so that I no longer feel like learning is something reserved for the young. Vi Hart and "Minute Physics" introduced me to all kinds of things that I didn't know before. And I know that we all hearken back to the days of the Parisian salon in the Enlightenment, or to the Algonquin Round Table, and wish, "Oh, I wish I could have been a part of that, I wish I could have laughed at Dorothy Parker's jokes." But I'm here to tell you that these places exist, they still exist. They exist in corners of the Internet, where old men fear to tread.

And I truly, truly believe that when we invented Agloe, New York, in the 1960s, when we made Agloe real, we were just getting started. Thank you.

（来源：https://www.ted.com/talks/john_green_the_nerd_s_guide_to_learning_everything_online?referrer=playlist-the_love_of_lifelong_learning）

第六单元　旅行的意义
（Unit6 Travel around the World）

1. 思政主题：世界那么大，我们一起去看看

2. 意义

本单元聚焦"旅行"相关话题，探讨旅行对于人生的意义。古今中外，不少名家曾发表对旅行的见解。教师可以从古今中外的经典文章中选取与主题相关的思政素材，鼓励学生积极思考旅行的意义。同时，积极引导学生去欣赏和了解中国的壮美山河，增强其民族自豪感和自信心。

Read ten thousand books, travel ten thousand miles.
读万卷书，行万里路。

——［明］董其昌

The world is a book and those who do not travel read only one page.
世界是一本书，不去旅行的人只看到了这本书的一页。

——圣·奥古斯丁

One's destination is never a place, but a new way of seeing things.
旅行的目的地不是某个地方，而是一种看待事物的新眼光。

——亨利·米勒

Travel is fatal to prejudice, bigotry and narrow-mindedness.
旅行是偏见、固执和心胸狭隘的死敌。

——马克·吐温

Travel, in the younger sort, is a part of education; in the elder, a part of experience.
旅行对青年人而言是一种教育；对老年人来说，是一种经历。

——弗朗西斯·培根

3. 教学设计与思政元素的融入

Passage A

3.1 Warm-up 环节

英文视频：Why Do We Travel?

当谈到旅行的原因或目的，人们大多会想到美食和美景。这个英文视频从几个不同的角度，就旅行给人们带来的好处展开了讨论。也许能给大家带来一些新的启发。视频时长约为3分钟，观后可以组织学生一起来讨论：Do you like travelling? Why? What can you get from travelling?

We all need a break from our everyday life. Going on a vacation is fun and fulfilling, but you can gain a lot more by actually traveling, exploring and being present at the places you visit.

Here are some benefits of traveling.

It is better to spend your money on experiences rather than on material things. The memory is a collector like treasures. They will remain forever and will bring you more happiness than some new clothes or other material things. Think how good it will feel when you're old and you look back to see not only in an ordinary routine but also adventures and unique experiences you had gone through, and not only when you're old. Ever a few years from now, you can recall how much fun you have and plan your next adventure. In the end, you will not regret the things you've done, that the things you didn't do.

Traveling is a great opportunity to temporarily get away from your everyday life and look at it from a different point of view. It's so much easier to deal with issues and solve problems when you look at them from the outside. While traveling, you have a lot of time to think without distractions and make healthy decisions. You will have a better perspective and maybe even realize that things are not that bad as you thought. In our everyday life, we're used to doing the same things, meeting the same people, going to the same places. We basically live in our comfort zone. When you travel, you get out of your bubble. You meet new people, other travelers and locals. You're exposed to different cultures. You see different landscapes and views, you experience new things, you learn that the world is diverse and it helps you understand people that are different from you.

Traveling actually makes you smarter. You learn new things all the time. When you travel, you get into unusual situations and face different challenges. It makes you push your limits, handle things better, and come up with creative solutions. After all, the best way to learn is through experience.

Traveling helps you to know yourself better. You're out of your comfort zone and get to see your behavior in different situations, sometimes even extreme ones. You will be surprised to find out new things about yourself that you didn't know and decide what and how to improve.

The best part of traveling is the people you meet along the way. You get to meet new people from countries around the world whom you would never have met in your daily life. You listen to their stories, tell yours. Here are various opinions and experience things together with people. Happiness is greater when shared with others. Traveling may sound scary or too challenging to some people and it's okay. Just remember that you can choose your own kind of travel. It doesn't have to be tracking in the mountains, although that could be fun, but you can do anything: explore cities, do some couch surfing, relax in nature, visit small villages and so on. You will get more confident and learn what is good for you.

Hey, have a nice trip!

（来源：https://www.bilibili.com/video/BV1UJ411s7YQ?from=search&seid=12438175613698885436）

我们都需要从日常生活中解脱出来。度假是件既有趣又充实的事，但通过真正的旅行去探索和体验你的目的地，你会收获更多。

以下是旅行的一些好处。

把钱花在体验上比花在物质上更好。记忆是个像珍宝一样的收藏皿。旅行的记忆将永驻于心，它永远比一些新衣服或其他物质的东西能带给你更多的快乐。当你老了，追忆过往，回过头来看看那些你所拥有的，不仅是一些常规的旅行，还有那些冒险和独特的经历，那种感觉会是多么的快乐！其实，不一定要等到老了，再过几年，你就可以回忆起旅行中经历过的趣事，并策划你的下一次冒险。最终，一些事无论你做没做过，你都不会后悔。

旅行是让人暂时远离日常生活的好机会，去从不同的角度看它。当你置身事外，处理和解决问题就会变得更容易。旅行时，你有了更多的时间去思考，不会分心，更容易做出明智的决定。你会拥有一个更好的视角，甚至可能意识到事情并没有你想的那么糟糕。在我们的日常生活中，我们习惯做着同样的事情，每天遇见同样的人，去同样的地方，我们基本上都生活在自己的舒适区。而旅行时，你会走出自己的堡垒，遇到新的人，其他的旅行者和当地人，你会接触到不同的文化。你看到了不同的风景，体验了新的事物，你就会知道世界是多样的，世界上的人同你是不一样的。

事实上，旅行还会让你变得更聪明。旅行时，你会一直学到新的东西，你会进入不寻常的情况，面临不同的挑战。它会让你挑战自己的极限，把事情处理得更好，最终想出更有创意的解决方案。毕竟，最好的学习方式是通过个人经历而获得的。

旅行可以帮助你更好地了解自己。当你离开舒适区，看到自己在不同情况下的行为，有时甚至是极端的行为，你会为发现了一个未知且全新的自己而感到惊奇，并决定在哪方面去提高自己，怎么提高自己。

旅行中最棒的事情就是你在旅途中遇到的人。你会遇到日常生活中绝不会出现的，来自世界各地的新朋友。你会听到他们的故事，并告诉他们你的故事。和他们在一起，你会收获各种各样的见解和经验。旅行对有些人来说可能是充满恐惧和挑战的，但是没有关系。只要记住，你可以选择自己的旅行方式。你不一定要在山中探秘，虽然那可能会很有趣，但你可以做任何事情：在城市漫步，做个沙发客，在大自然中放松身心，参观小村庄等等。这样，你会变得更加自信，会了解什么是适合自己的。

嘿，祝你旅行愉快！

3.2 Discussion 环节

英文文章：Why Travel — What Is the Purpose of Travel?

通过观看 Warm-up 环节中的视频，同学们应该对旅行给我们带来的种种好处有了更深的了解。教师可以引导学生结合以下文章的阅读，去思考自己的答案：旅行的目的是什么？旅行对于人生而言的意义何在？

Why do people travel?

Have you ever been asked: "Why do you travel?" Maybe you even asked it yourself?

Do you remember your answer? Was it something like:

"Because we love it, It is what we need to do."

For many, answering this question turns out to be difficult. Even if it is somewhat clear to you, explaining it to others — especially to those who are not infected by the travel bug — is a considerable challenge.

"Is it simply a way to relax?" Why not go fishing for a day or book a spa treatment instead?

"Can we reduce it to the adrenaline rush we might feel?" If that is the case, we can also go on a roller coaster ride.

What is the purpose of travel?

As a psychologist, neuron-scientist and someone who loves to travel I had to find a better answer.

According to scientists:

Researcher Filep Sebastian makes a strong case that "a fulfilling travel experience is not only about satisfactions. It is also about how personally meaningful we found our travel activities".

The purpose of travel is connected with building social relationships, opportunities to learn and grow, and commitment. It gives us the chance to be truly engaged in an activity, to develop new skills and to discover new cultures. It brings us closer to ourselves and others.

In other words, all the things we need to increase our resilience!

According to long-term travelers:

Konrad Waliszewski asked long-term travelers why they travel. He received responses like:

"It has deepened my life!"

"My perspective has shifted."

"It opens up your possibilities and your horizons and the kinds of conversations you can have, the kinds of experiences you can have."

"It changes how I see and interact with nearly every aspect of the world around me."

"I travel to learn."

"It provides context apart from me."

Our brain:

Our brain filters constantly all the information around us. It decides how we experience and interpret the world. What we see, hear and feel depends not only on our senses. It also strongly build upon what we believe, value, know and on our ability to imagine alternatives. On top of all that our brain is developed for challenges; we need them to feel good.

By submerging ourselves in new cultures, environments, culinary traditions,... we enrich ourselves with new frameworks for comparison and give our world room to grow.

That what makes people different, we find intriguing.

Things we don't understand, we want to figure out.

Places unknown to us, we will explore.

Travel graces us with unique opportunities to (re)discover our dreams and talents, and to share these with others.

"The meaning of life is to find your gift. The purpose of life is to give it away."

——Pablo Picasso

What are you waiting for? Go out there and explore!

Happy travels!

（来源：https://www.terratrotter.eu/why-travel-purpose/）

3.3 Critical thinking 环节

英语文章：Understanding Cultural Differences: A Guide for Travel Professionals

当人们身处他乡，必然会领略到不同的文化魅力，甚至会经历一些文化冲击。因此，旅行时对多元文化抱有开阔的胸怀和积极的理解是十分必要的。文化的多样性令我们的世界精彩纷呈，作为旅行者，兼容并包和谦和之心能让你一直"学在路上"，不经意间就能偶有所得。教师可以在课前布置学生阅读本文，在课上进行讨论和交流：你在旅行中遇到过哪些令人印象深刻的异乡文化？

The United Nations celebrates World Day for Cultural Diversity for Dialogue and Development on 21 May. Recognizing the importance of bridging the gap between cultures and deepening our understanding of the values of cultural diversity — especially in the context of travel and tourism — we're excited to share this article about recognizing and appreciating cultural differences.

On my first reconnaissance trip to Peru, I hiked the Inca Trail with a well-respected local operator that prided itself in its social and sustainability practices. Our group of 14 hailed from the United States and Europe and bonded quickly over coca tea and snacks after strenuous days of trekking. Our local porters and guide would join us, practicing their English and teaching us words in Quechua. It was as if we were family after only a few short days.

The very last night before the long-anticipated sunrise hike to Machu Picchu, it was time to bid our porters a proper farewell. After dinner, our guide, José, led all of us guests into the meal tent where he told us a flat tip amount that the guides would expect and divide between themselves. Then he left for us to work it out.

An uncomfortable silence ensued. "I want to tip, but I don't want to be told how much," one guy commented. "Can we do it privately?" another asked. "This is awkward," a girl said.

What happened? It's not that the group didn't want to tip, but the discomfort was palpable.

As travel industry professionals, we all have experience in international settings with partners from around the world. However, despite our many commonalities, we also have deeply ingrained cultural differences that — if ignored or not recognized — can create misunderstandings, miscommunication, and otherwise uncomfortable situations.

The story above is a classic example of two cultures colliding. In cultural theory, we often reference the iceberg: You see just the tip on the surface, but the mass lies underneath. We see behaviors and tendencies that are driven by societal norms, philosophy, and belief systems that run profoundly deep. One of the pioneers of cultural research is Geert Hofstede, whose work is internationally respected in academia, social science, and business. Hofstede's cultural dimension models are based on data gathered worldwide to understand culture through the lens of economics, communication, and cooperation.

For this article, we'll focus on four such dimensions often encountered in the adventure travel industry. Before we begin, it's important to remember not to just talk about other cultures but stress the need to reflect on our own cultural orientation. We must consider our geography, upbringing, and beliefs so we can be dynamic and responsive to the many various cultures we will encounter in an ever increasingly globalized world.

Individualism vs Collectivism

What is it? In the example from Peru, we see individualism at work. On Hofstede's scale, Peru and the United States are about as wide apart as they come. Like much of Latin America, Peru is highly collectivist, meaning society is interdependent and defines itself in terms of "we" rather than "me". Individualist societies, on the other hand, are largely self-reliant. When it comes to money, in a collectivist culture, one person's salary may support much more than just the immediate family, whereas someone from a more individualistic society might see money as extremely private. What I experienced in Peru was the group-oriented perspective of the guides and porters clashing with the more private, individual orientation of the guests.

Where might you encounter it? Generally speaking, Latin America, Africa, and Asia are primarily collectivist regions while much of Europe, North America, and Western-oriented countries are more individualist. On a ground level, your guides, vendor partners, suppliers, and guests are where this cultural dimension is likely to come into play.

How to address it? For those coming from an individualist background, it's important to recognize group thought and understand that decision-making is not autonomous. For those coming from a collectivist background, recognizing values such as independent thought and privacy is paramount.

In our small-group trips, I address individualism versus collectivism during one of our dinners. I invite the local guide to talk about related cultural values, such as the importance of family. Engaging conversations ensue and often lead to introspection and new perspectives. Regarding tipping, I supply an envelope for tips to be added at will. I then count the total at the end to make sure there's enough before giving to the guide to distribute equally to the local team. This satisfies the needs of both cultures while preventing discomfort.

Direct vs Indirect Communication

What is it? American anthropologist Edward Hall as well as Dutch culturalist Fons Trompenaars explored the concept of high-context and low-context communication, or indirect versus direct communication. A U.S. American might take a "yes" at face value while missing high-context clues such as evasiveness that actually indicate "no". Saving face, or not embarrassing oneself in front of a group, is another very common cultural value related to this dimension that is often encountered in intercultural situations.

Where might you encounter it? Germany is a classic example of low-context, direct communication where the emphasis is on words and clear speech to convey meaning. On the opposite end, Japan, China, or Brazil clue us in to the nuances of indirect communication through body language, eye contact (or not), and flowery speech where the delivery and contextual clues matter just as much or more than the words themselves.

How to address it? Like with every cultural dimension, first evaluate where you stand relative to the other party. Are you having a hard time getting a firm or quick answer from a vendor? It may be that he's trying to say no without directly telling you so. Instead of asking, "Can you have the revised itinerary to me by Friday?" ask open-ended questions that will draw a more holistic response: "What do you need from me in order to finish this itinerary by the end of the week? Can you tell me the steps it will take to complete this task?"

Power Distance

What is it? Power distance is an important cultural dimension that comes into play in instances involving hierarchy, how authority is distributed, and the degree to which inequity is accepted in a given culture. In a high-power distance society, hierarchy is a given aspect of social structure where one's place in society is accepted and further justification might not be needed. A subordinate is unlikely to challenge or even gain access to a higher-up whereas in a low-power distance context, decision-making and rank is much more egalitarian.

Where might you encounter it? Power distance can be found in a range of cultures and is often the highest in countries with a large gap between rich and poor. Formality, material possessions, and rank are all indicative of power distance. Do your business partners dress sharply and use formal titles? Are dinners hosted at a restaurant in a five-star hotel? Is there an emphasis on how old or established your partner's company is? These are all indicative of a society with higher power distance.

How to address it. Power distance can be a tricky cultural conflict in adventure tourism particularly in developing and/or conservative regions. Many of us from progressive backgrounds look at fairness and equality as an ultimate truth, especially when it comes to women, gender, and society.

In Morocco, for example, there's a power distance aspect between myself as a 30-something female and the often older males involved in the tourism industry. I have found the best way to quickly establish status in a way that results in respect is to have a Moroccan colleague introduce me. Rather than be offended and peg it all on gender inequality, I recognize the role that power distance has in this society and the value of referral to build cultural trust and break down barriers.

It can be easy for us to quickly judge a place or circumstance based on perceived inequity. With women in rural communities, for example, family may be a significant cultural value attached to identity as well as a source of pride, even if, from our perspective, having 10 kids is a financial and social disadvantage. The strategy here is to listen rather than judge, encourage rather than force, and know when to check your own perspectives. Also recognize that change, especially around conservative traditions and gender roles, does not happen overnight but rather over generations.

Rules vs Relationship Orientation

What is it? In rule-based societies, such as the United States, emphasis is placed on external rules that theoretically apply universally, such as fixed prices at the store or legal business contracts. Relationship-based societies rely much more on fluidity and context. Prices or contracts are determined based on the relationship, not some arbitrary external force. Rule-based societies often gravitate toward direct communication and relationship-based cultures are often more indirect.

Where might you encounter it? Relationship-oriented cultures often go hand-in-hand with places that have historic distrust of government through dictatorships, oppressive regimes, or general disorganization. If you can't depend on the law to enforce business agreements, you have to trust your partners. Latin America, China, and much of the Middle East are great examples of relationship-oriented cultures where establishing a network and getting to know your counterparts is key to success.

Have you ever been lost in the dizzying medina of Fes, Morocco, and needed a local to guide you out of the labyrinth? This is relationship-based orientation in action and can be bewildering for a rule-based person accustomed to streets that can be navigated alone by clear signage and grid patterns.

How to address it? For contractually minded individuals that are more accustomed to binding agreements on paper, invest time in getting to know your partners. This may mean many cups of tea in Jordan, drawn out lunches chatting about football in Mexico, or Karaoke outings in South Korea. Recognize that trust may take a long time but once your relationship with your partner is established, it is taken seriously and you will be well cared for. For a relationship-oriented culture dealing with a more rule-based partner, recognize that paperwork and contracts are important to their business process and be willing to look them over, ask questions, and have a dialogue about them.

Putting Cultural Competency to Work

Cultural psychology is a vast field of its own with a host of incredibly valuable resources. Hofstede's Cultural Compass tool is a quick and easy way for travel professionals to compare countries across their different dimensions. These dimensions along with key cultural tips are easily referenced in the CultureMee app, a fantastic platform to help navigate cultures while on the road (and a great one to share with clients).

Travel is the perfect opportunity for cultural education to bridge the gap of understanding among both internal teams and external partners. Host and guest, vendor and supplier, community and visitor all play a role in the dance of cultures.

As Henry Miller wisely said, "The destination is never a place, but a new way of seeing things."

（来源：https://www.adventuretravelnews.com/understanding-cultural-differences-a-guide-for-travel-professionals）

3.4 主题拓展资源

英语文章：Safety in Mexico: You Have to See It for Yourself

安全是旅行中至关重要的一环。作为旅行者，我们首先就要确保自己在旅行中的安全。你有否经历过与旅行安全相关的故事呢？教师可在课后分享这篇拓展阅读材料，并引导学生去思考如何在旅行中保护好自己。

Listen to all the tales others will tell you, but you will never know what a place is like until you experience it for yourself. We spent six months traversing Mexico and now I can say with certainty: I did not feel unsafe.

You can listen for forever to someone telling you what a place is like. The list of things that other people know is unending, a collection of rumors that others have heard that must somehow add up to wisdom. Travel defies these hand-me-downs, and gives you a chance to sift through what others tell you and see for yourself what a place is like. You get your own story, your own personal experience.

You will never know what a place is really like until you have experienced it. Gone there, tried it, collected experiences that help you form an educated opinion. Nearly everyone we met before we crossed the border into Mexico told us something along the lines of "Mexico is dangerous" "Be careful in Mexico," or "I heard about this one guy down in Mexico..." (followed by something negative that happened to that guy). All this time, I tried not to let stories like these make me nervous and focused on what I believed in: I didn't know if Mexico was dangerous, but the only way to find out was to go there and see it for myself.

Of course, your experience will not mirror mine; factors like when you go or who you meet — or even just who you are — will make your experience uniquely your own. I can only speak here for myself.

Spoiler alert: we did not experience Mexico as dangerous. In fact, we barely met an unfriendly person during the six months we spent traversing the country.

How dangerous is dangerous?

Back on Baja California, we were couch-surfing in La Paz. I asked our host, in my very bad Spanish, why all the houses had bars on the windows. I had been to Latin America before and knew it was a common sight, but I had never actually asked anyone about it. "Everybody has them," she told me. I nodded and asked, "But do you need them? Or does everybody just think they need them? Are they actually necessary?" She thought for a moment. "No, you need them, you'll get robbed if you don't have them."

But my question was unfair. Where do people even draw the line between needing something and the perception of necessity? How are you supposed to tell the difference between the two? When does one turn into the other, and does it ever turn back? I guess you never know, unless yours is the house that didn't have bars on the windows, you got robbed, and the burglar left a note saying, "I only came here because you didn't bar your windows." You will never know, actually, if you need a safety feature like barred windows until you find out that you do. That is why, after our bus got broken into in Guadalajara, we added a number of extra locks to our cabinets and to the windows that the robbers used to climb inside. The ironic thing is, though, that I will never know if those new locks worked to deter a thief — I will only ever know if they did not.

Our route through Mexico: states and tolls

After crossing over from Baja, we traveled through the Mexican countryside, from Sinaloa to Nayarit, on to Guadalajara in Jalisco, and down towards Puebla. We entered Oaxaca from the northwest and continued south down to the coast.

After staying for over a month in Puerto Escondido, we headed back up towards San Cristóbal de las Casas in the mountains of Chiapas. From there, we drove towards the Yucatán Peninsula through Quintana Roo and the Riviera Maya before spending two weeks on the northern Yucatán coast with Sven's family. We returned to Quintana Roo and left Mexico from there, driving south into Belize.

We had heard that it was safer to take toll roads (cuota). There are not very many exits along tolls, which makes it harder for roadblocks or carjacks to happen there. There are almost no toll roads on Baja, but we tried one out when we got to Jalisco. Not actually because of safety concerns; Sven just wasn't feeling good, and we wanted to get where we were going a little faster (toll roads also let you skip hundreds of irritating speed-bumps, or topes).

After two hours of driving cost us almost $20 USD (an absurd amount of our Mexico-budget), we decided we hated Mexican quotas. Apart from a similar stint on the Yucatán, we never took a toll road again. By Mexican law, there always has to be a free alternative to a toll road. We crossed nearly all of Mexico on free, unpaid roads that took us through villages and around towns. We never had any problems. Not a one. In our experience, you do not need to take toll roads to stay safe in Mexico; you might only want to use them to save some time. In many places, there are no toll roads; the free option is all you've got.

Caution is a important, wherever you are

However, I need to add to that: we are careful travelers, and do not tend to go to places we consider high-risk. Over and over again, we had heard that the Mexican states of Michoacán and Guerrero were not the safest places to be. Along with some of the northern states, they have the roughest problems with drug and gang violence and police clashes.

The US Travel Advisory currently completely prohibits travel to Guerrero for US government personnel (but, in my opinion, they are not always the best source of information for safe travel. If you lose yourself on their site, you will realize the whole world is dangerous). We were also told that the state of Veracruz is somewhat dangerous in certain areas. We decided to avoid these states; partly because there was not a lot we really wanted to see there, and partly because we could go a different way. We don't believe in playing with fire.

That being said, I do realize it contradicts what I said above: you never know until you see it for yourself. I have just blatantly assumed that states like Guerrero or Veracruz are dangerous without first-hand knowledge of having been there.

Tourism attracts people to certain areas; be it due to actual attractions, beautiful locations, a well-maintained tourist infrastructure, off-the-beaten-track appeal, or whatever else people like. Tourists tend to hang around the places that are attractive to them; if it is not attractive, they do not stay (or stop in the first place). Just like any place, anywhere in the world, I would avoid the bad part of town, tourist or not.

I tend to stay in the places where I feel safe, and where I can find comforts and resources that I need. Part of this is about the natural flow of travel, but a part is also about common sense. Don't put yourself in risky situations is something that applies to anybody, wherever you may live. It applies to travelers just the same, and I do not feel the need to go to Guerrero at the moment in light of this fact.

However, we personally know many travelers who did go through these parts of Mexico. The coastal highway — which goes through both Michoacán and Guerrero — is the road for surfers, and all travelers who do the Panamericana for the best surf spots do not skip these parts of Mexico. Everyone we have heard of traveling there has been fine. On the other hand, we also met one woman in Quintana Roo from Acapulco (in Guerrero), who told us we should stay away from there. "The Yucatán is much better," she told us, "you don't have to worry here."

Safety is only a matter of perspective

Our months of experience gave us a feeling of relative safety traveling through Mexico. Eventually, we began to be less wary of the country we had heard so many horror stories about. The bad thing about safety, however, is that it is not a fixed state. As safe as you may feel, it may be just an illusion, a mirage to fool you.

Just as we felt we had figured out the topic of "Safety in Mexico", our roommate in Puerto Escondido — a fellow overlander — came over to the breakfast table with some daunting news. A traveler she had met a few months earlier had just been carjacked in Veracruz. Everything he had was gone and the carjackers had shot him in the leg in the process. He was okay, but was flown back to his home country of Israel to recover.

Around the breakfast table we looked at each other in disbelief, and immediately our walls were back up, we were thinking about which roads we should drive, what precautions we needed to take, if we needed to hide our laptops while we drive, if our Canadian bear spray was in reach of the driver's seat.

Within the blink of an eye, all of us were cautious again. Were we kidding ourselves? We thought. Was Mexico really as dangerous as everyone believed? Had we just been lucky up until now? We felt the need to reassess our opinion of Safety in Mexico sitting around that table.

This was — and continued to be — the only story of someone that we, through our friends, actually know who had encountered serious problems in Mexico as a traveler.

Bringing these uncertainties back to the forefront highlights one of the things that characterized our travels through Mexico: we felt like we had to be aware of safety concerns. Because of all the things you hear, of everybody's concerns regarding the possibilities of danger, you keep that in your head. These thoughts dictate where you make camp, what roads you want to take, how many locks you put on your car and how often you actually lock them. These were not things that would play in the back of our heads on a typical day traveling through the US, Canada, or Belize. More than anything actually happening to us, it was these thoughts that plagued us while we traveled through Mexico.

Police corruption, military checkpoints, and civil blockades

Another topic comes up when travelers think of safety in Mexico: police corruption. We, like many other good overlanders, made laminated copies of our IDs, hid our passports deep in the corners of our car, and tried to never leave extra cash or electronics lying around. Many travelers are afraid of getting stopped by the police. Not because they are usually doing anything wrong, but because they are scared of crooked cops looking for bribes from gullible tourists. One of the common fears is handing over original documents like driver's licenses or passports, and only getting them back for a donation. Another is being accused of a bullshit charge, which can also be solved via a donation to the accuser.

We never encountered anything of the sort. We experienced the most military checkpoints on Baja, and the most police checkpoints on the Yucatán Peninsula. We crossed numerous state borders, went through many police and military checkpoints, and got stopped by a cop once. The cop seemed to be doing a routine check; although we were definitely nervous, he took a look at all our paperwork and let us go on our way. He was both professional and friendly. At checkpoints, our car never got searched more than opening a door or officers looking in through the windows. One cop even said, "Oh you're from Germany? I love Germany!" and waved us on with nothing more than that.

Civilian blockades were also an issue, almost exclusively in the state of Chiapas. Once or twice, it was someone blocking the road with a rope or chain and asking for money. Once it was a little boy. We gave him coins and gummy bears and went on our way. Once it was a group of village men with a board decorated with nails that they strung across the highway. The event pissed me off, but for about $1 USD, the problem is easily solved. I might not like it, but I imagine they can genuinely use the money.

Experiences are individual — communication is key

In Tulum, we met a few other overlanders. After a day excursion, their group came back exhausted. They had been stopped by the cops, who had attempted to plant a bag of seeds in their car while searching it, claiming it was marijuana. According to the travelers, the cops then refused to give them their IDs back and wanted to take them to the station, which the travelers adamantly refused. Then, along came two others — both Mexicans, also staying at our campground — who proceeded to talk to the cops and eventually everyone went on their way with no further problems.

According to the the travelers, their Mexican friends saved the day. According to the Mexicans (whom Sven can speak with in Spanish), the whole issue was simply a misunderstanding about IDs because the travelers didn't speak much Spanish. It makes you wonder if many of the fears that travelers have regarding crooked cops stem from simple miscommunications.

We felt safe in Mexico

Safety is always a matter of perspective, and a matter of experience. It is neither an illusion, nor is it a guarantee.

From the perspective of white, Western travelers in an obvious overlanding rig, we felt safe in Mexico. We were cautious, and tried our best to use that skill that people call common sense. We also spoke in Spanish and thought about how and where would travel. We payed for camping a lot more often than before; in the States, we barely ever did, while in Mexico it became the norm.

Despite the precautions we took, the conclusion is a satisfying one: we did not experience a dangerous Mexico. That is not to say that others will not, but we are among the majority of travelers who had a hell of a time. The best advice we can give others is to make sure all your windows have locks. And learn Spanish.

Every country is dangerous; every country is safe. The exception to this rule – as I see it – are countries that are in the midst of civil unrest or war, but those are probably not countries you will be eager to travel to in the first place. The nearest big city to where I come from is Chicago. There are places in Chicago that I would avoid, whether I am a tourist or not.

Our experience of Mexico was no different. But at least I can now say it for myself.

（来源：https://gobigemma.com/2017/11/30/you-have-to-see-it-for-yourself-six-months-of-experience-on-safety-in-mexico/）

Passage B

3.5 Warm-up 环节

双语视频：What's the Point of Travel?

教师可在网上找到本视频，在 Warm-up 环节让学生观看，之后在课上一起讨论：何为内在的成长？外在的旅行能否协助我们实现自我提升的内在之旅？

What's the point of travel? It's to help make us into better people; it's a sort of therapy. Without anything mystical being meant by this, all of us are, in one way or another, on what could be termed "an inner journey". That is, we are trying to develop in particular ways. In a nutshell, the point of travel is to go to places that can help us in our inner evolution; the outer journey should assist us with the inner one.

Every location in the world, contains qualities that can support some kind of beneficial changes inside a person. Take those 200 million year-old stone in America's Utah Desert, it's a place, but looked at psychologically, it's also an inner destination, a place with perspective, free of preoccupation with the petty and the small-minded, somewhere imbued with calm and resilience.

Religions used to take travel much more seriously than we do now. For them, it was a therapeutic activity. In the Middle ages, when there was something wrong with you, you were meant to head out for a pilgrimage to commune with relics of a saint or a member of the holy family.

If you had toothache, you'd go to Rome, to the Basilica of San Lorenzo and touch the arm bones of Saint Appolonia, the patron saint of teeth. If you were unhappily married, you might go to Umbria to touch the shrine of Saint Rita of

Cascia, patron saint of marital problems. Or if you were worried about lightning, you were sent to Bad Munstereifel in Germany to touch the skull of Saint Donatus, believed to offer help against fires and explosions.

We no longer believe in the divine power of journeys, but certain parts of the world still have a power to change and mend the wounded parts of us. In an ideal world, travel agencies would be manned by a new kind of psychotherapist. They'd take care not just flights and hotels, they'd start by finding out what's wrong with us and how we might want to change. The anxious might be sent to see the majestic, immemorial waves crashing into the cliffs on the west coast of Ireland; People a bit too concerned with being admired and famous might be sent to contemplate the ruins of Detroit; Someone out of touch with their body might be recommended a trip to Porto Seguro in Bahia in Brazil.

Nowadays, too often, we head off without fully knowing what's wrong with us and precisely understanding how are chosen destinations meant to help us. We should become more conscious travelers on a well-articulated search for qualities that places possess, like calm or perspective, sensuality of rigor. We should follow old-fashioned pilgrims in striving to evolve our characters according to the suggestions offered up by the places we've been to. We need to relearn how to be ambitious about travel, seeing it as a way of helping us to grow into better versions of ourselves.

（来源：https://www.bilibili.com/video/BV18J411H7mp/?spm_id_from=333.788.recommend_more_video.3）

旅行的意义是什么？是帮助我们成为更好的人，是一种治疗而没有任何更神秘的含义，每一个人都在以某种方式进行着内在之旅，也就是说，我们都在以某种方式试图成长。简而言之，旅行的意义是去一个能帮助我们内在成长的地方，而外在的旅行应该协助我们的内在之旅。

世界上的每个地方都存在一些能帮助我们的特质，有利于个人内在的转变。例如，美国犹他州荒漠上有21年历史的大石头，这是一个地方，但就心理的角度而言，这也是一个内在目的地，一个有观点的地方，不再有琐碎狭隘的偏见，而是充满平静、韧性。

宗教曾经比我们现在更认真严肃地看待旅行。对宗教而言，旅行是一种治疗活动。在中世纪时如果你有什么问题或烦恼，你必须开始一趟朝圣之旅，去接触圣物。如果你牙痛，你应该去罗马参观圣罗伦佐教堂，去抚摸圣阿波罗尼亚的手臂——她是牙齿守护神；如果你婚姻不美满，你应该去意大利的翁布里亚，去抚摸卡夏圣利塔的圣灵——他是婚姻的守护神；如果你害怕闪电，应该去德国的巴特明斯特埃弗尔，去抚摸圣图斯的头颅——人们相信他能保护世间免于火灾和爆炸。

如今，我们已经不再相信旅行的神圣力量，但是这世界仍然有些力量足以改变并修复我们的伤痕。在理想的情况下，旅行社的员工应该是新一代的心理治疗师，他们应该不光负责机票和住宿，而该先找出我们的烦恼，建议去看壮丽的风景，看亘古不变的海浪、看拍打爱尔兰西岸的断崖；对于那些太在意别人的眼光和名声的人，应该建议他们去底特律的废墟前沉思；不注重自己身心的人，应该建议来一趟巴西之旅。

如今大多时候，我们在不清楚自己的烦恼和缺陷的情况下就出发了，也并不清楚我们选择的目的地能如何帮助我们。我们应该成为更自觉的旅行者，能够准确说出某个地方拥有什么特质，比如平静或有观点，感性或严谨。我们应该仿照老派的朝圣，以努力改进个人特质为目标，从我们去过的地方中学习改进。我们需要重新学习如何对旅行更富有野心，把旅行视为一种能把我们变成更好的自己的途径。

3.6 Discussion 环节

英文文章：How to Know When to Travel Solo or with a Companion?

对下一段新旅程满心期待、跃跃欲试的同学们会更喜欢独自旅行还是结伴旅行呢？对于选择是否结伴出行这个问题，每个人都有自己不同的见解。教师可以引导学生在阅读此篇文章前，就这个话题进行短暂讨论。阅读过后，再请学生来说说，是否有了不同的想法和选择？独自旅行和结伴旅行的利弊分别是什么？

Has it happened to you that you want to travel somewhere but you haven't been able to persuade any of your friends to travel with you? And just because of that you decide not to travel since you don't want to go by yourself? Well, this is something that happens very often.

A lot of people are afraid of traveling alone, especially if it is to a foreign country with a completely different culture. But this shouldn't be your reason not to travel. You should know that you could still have an amazing trip while traveling solo.

I have traveled by myself to many countries as well as with groups of 6 to 30+ friends. Obviously, traveling with friends and traveling by yourself have a different effect on how you spend and enjoy your trip.

So, I'll describe briefly these two travel styles according to my experience.

Traveling solo

If you are brave enough to consider traveling by yourself, you should know beforehand some of the pros and cons of this traveling style.

You manage your trip as you wish. You do what you want, when you want, how you want.

Your itinerary can be changed at any time according to your priorities.

Meeting other people is really easy since you are open to interacting with other travelers. (one of the best pros)

You learn, develop, and personalize travel techniques.

You learn to be completely independent.

Cons:

It forces you to overcome your shyness. (it really does)

Traveling alone can be intimidating.

Sometimes you don't have someone to share your stories and memories.

Everything is dependent on you and you have to be able to make decisions by yourself.

You are dependent on other people to take your pictures.

Just so you know, I am generally considered a shy person, but when traveling by myself I tend to be really open, outspoken, and sociable. I have made a lot of friends when traveling by myself, and some of them have become lifelong friends.

Traveling with a Companion

If you are not up for the challenge of traveling solo and like to roam with company, you should take into consideration some of its pros and cons and know how they can influence your trip.

Pros:

You can share some of the costs with your companions. (big pro)

There is always someone who can take your pictures or take your pictures with.

You can talk, share your stories and memories with someone.

Traveling with someone can develop a long-lasting friendship.

You don't feel the pressure of making every decision.

Cons:

Companions are not always trusted persons. This can turn a trip into an uncomfortable situation.

Traveling in a group can make meeting other travelers a difficult task. Groups tend to portray "exclusivity" and shun other travelers away.

Not everyone is compatible. Spending every single minute of the trip with the same person can be annoying. Friendships can be lost over this.

A good trip can turn into a nightmare when trying to reach a decision on something between you and your companions. This can bring a lot of arguments (believe me, I have seen it happen).

Before you start planning your next trip, consider first if you want it to be a companion experience (and more importantly, with whom), or if you want it to be an open solo trip. Both options are good ways to travel; it just depends on your preferences and pairing.

（来源：https://www.globotreks.com/planning-tips/travel-solo/）

3.7 Critical thinking 环节

英文文章：How to Plan a Travel Itinerary?

如果让同学们来策划一场舒适惬意的旅行，会如何规划自己的行程呢？教师可以引导学生在阅读本文之后进行思考、讨论和小组设计，规划出自己的旅行目的地和行程。

Before you travel, creating a document that outlines where you'll go, when you'll arrive and how you'll get there — an itinerary — is a common way to ensure that your travels go smoothly after you embark. Itineraries don't have to be binding, but they allow you to represent the proposed trajectory of your trip tangibly, which makes it easier to make last-minute changes that don't affect the overall course of your travels. Planning a basic itinerary is simple to do but requires some time and concentration.

STEP 1

Make an ideal outline of all the places you'd like to visit and arrange them in a sequence that makes sense with the local or regional geography. If you're traveling to India, for example, and want to visit the southeastern city of Kolkata, the southwestern city of Mumbai, the northeastern city of Agra, the northern city of Delhi and the northwest city of Jaipur, plan to travel between adjacent cities — Mumbai to Kolkata or Delhi to Jaipur, for example — rather than making long hops across the country, which will not only cause you to "backtrack" in your travels, but also cost more.

STEP 2

Notate ideal travel and accommodation options on your itinerary, even if you don't end up using them. If you're traveling in Europe, download a European rail timetable and make note of two to three trains that run between cities as options to take between them. Make a list of possible hotel options in a given city, either from a travel guide like *Lonely Planet* or *Rough Guides* or from online resources like Trip Advisor or Orbitz.

STEP 3

Book transport and accommodation in advance whenever your plans are set. If you're traveling internationally, for example, book a round-trip ticket to and from the foreign country before you depart. If, on the other hand, you're traveling to Thailand and know your visa runs out after 30 days, book a train to a neighboring county in advance to avoid paying a penalty.

STEP 4

Plan for activities within cities and regions whenever possible, again keeping in mind that these may be subject to change — plan alternates accordingly. Plan activities with the arrangement of your city and region in mind, as well as the time you'll need for an activity. The Palace of Versailles in France, for example, is about 17 miles from the center of Paris and requires not only time to get there and away, but to explore the massive extent of the palace. Plan to visit attractions within the city, such as the Eiffel Tower and Jardin de Luxembourg, on a different day.

STEP 5

Remember that itineraries are often tentative and understand that your plans can change — and they probably will. Use your itinerary not as a fixed representation of where you'll be or what you've been doing at any given time — and how you'll get there — but as a means of helping you make abstract travel plans concrete.

（来源：https://traveltips.usatoday.com/plan-travel-itinerary-27657.html）

参考文献

[1] 陈希. 将创新创业教育贯穿于高校人才培养全过程 [J]. 中国高等教育, 2010(12):4-6.

[2] 董毓. 批判性思维原理和方法——走向新的认知和实践 [M]. 北京:高等教育出版社, 2010: 5-14.

[3] 董毓. 我们应该教什么样的批判性思维课程 [J]. 工业和信息化教育, 2014(3):36-42.

[4] 谷振诣. 批判性思维教学:理论与实践 [J]. 工业和信息化教育, 2014(3):43-53.

[5] 侯莲梅. 新时代大学生理想信念教育状况及对策研究 [J]. 岭南师范学院学报, 2020(12):18-25.

[6] 联合国教科文组织国际教育发展委员会. 学会生存 [M]. 北京:教育科学出版社, 1996:223.

[7] 林崇德. 中国学生核心素养研究 [J]. 心理与行为研究, 2017, 15(2):145-154.

[8] 林银, 谢志远. 大学生创业教育中的价值观引导 [J]. 创新与创业教育, 2012(4):38-40.

[9] 刘辉, 等. "双一流"建设下拔尖博士研究生自我驱动能力培养研究 [J]. 教育教学论坛, 2020(19).

[10] 屈丽娜. 自律性对学生学习的影响分析 [J]. 华东理工大学学报(社会科学版), 2017(2).

[11] 孙云龙, 刘万兆. 大学生创业教育模式探索——基于企业家精神培养视角 [J]. 思想教育研究, 2013(11):87-89.

[12] 谭建光. 论青年志愿服务的"双功能":助人与育人 [J]. 中国青年社会科学, 2020(2):84-85.

[13] 王利国. 不忘初心使命 加强新时代大学生理想信念教育 [J]. 税务与经济, 2022(1):3-4.

[14] 王卫杰, 等. 基于自律学习者培养的PBL教学探索 [J]. 黑龙江高教研究, 2020(1).

[15] 习近平. 习近平致中国志愿服务联合会第二届会员代表大会的贺信. 2019-07-24, http://www.xinhuanet.com//politics/2019-07/24/c_1124792815.htm.

[16] 习近平. 在纪念五四运动100周年大会上的讲话[N]. 人民日报, 2019-05-01(2).

[17] 谢小庆. 应将思维品质的考核列为高考重要目标[J]. 湖北招生考试, 2019(25):1.

[18] 徐媛媛. 中国海外志愿服务参与对外传播的分析与思考[J]. 对外传播, 2021:44-46.

[19] 衣凤先. 加强高校大学生理想信念教育的有效路径探析[J]. 现代交际, 2021(1):156-158.

[20] 尹申. 成功有学问[M]. 北京：中国戏剧出版社, 2002.

[21] 张映婷. 英语教学中跨文化教育与创新创业教育双融合的路径探究[J]. 沈阳工程学院学报（社会科学版）, 2021(4):116-119

[22] 中共中央关于坚持和完善中国特色社会主义制度 推进国家治理体系和治理能力现代化若干重大问题的决定[N]. 人民日报, 2019-11-06.

[23] 周济. 注重培养创新人才，增强高水平大学创新能力[J]. 中国高等教育, 2006(15):4.

[24] 朱艳红, 张立. 高校大学生理想信念教育的时代价值与模式构建[J]. 教书育人, 2021(11):54-56.

[25] 朱勇. 海外志愿者跨文化交际影响因素与对策[C]. 中华文化海外传播研究. 2018(1), 107-109.

[26] Teo, Peter. Teaching for the 21st Century: A Case for Dialogic Pedagogy [J]. Learning, Culture and Social Interaction, 2019 (21):170-178.